JEWISH MYSTICISM

The most beautiful experience we can have is the mysterious.
It is the fundamental emotion which stands at the cradle of true art and true science . . .
It was the experience of mystery—even if mixed with fear—that engendered religion.
A knowledge of the existence of something we cannot penetrate, our perceptions of the
profoundest reason and the most radiant beauty, which only in their
most primitive forms are accessible to our minds—it is this knowledge and
this emotion that constitute true religiosity. In this sense,
and in this sense alone, I am a deeply religious man

ALBERT EINSTEIN, 1931

T0341381

THE LITTMAN LIBRARY OF
JEWISH CIVILIZATION

*The Littman Library of Jewish Civilization is a registered UK charity
Registered charity no.* 1000784

JEWISH MYSTICISM

◆

The Infinite Expression of Freedom

◆

RACHEL ELIOR

Translated by
YUDITH NAVE
and
ARTHUR B. MILLMAN

London
The Littman Library of Jewish Civilization
in association with Liverpool University Press

The Littman Library of Jewish Civilization
Registered office: 4th floor, 7–10 Chandos Street, London, W1G 9DQ

in association with Liverpool University Press
4 Cambridge Street, Liverpool L69 7ZU, UK
www.liverpooluniversitypress.co.uk/littman

Managing Editor: Connie Webber

Distributed in North America by
Oxford University Press Inc., 198 Madison Avenue
New York, NY 10016, USA

First published in Hebrew 1997
First published in hardback 2007
First published in paperback 2010

Catalogue records for this book are available from
the British Library and the Library of Congress
ISBN 978-1-906764-04-3

Publishing Co-ordinator: Janet Moth
Copy-editing: Bonnie Blackburn
Proof-reading: Philippa Claiden
Index: Sarah Ereira
Design by Pete Russell, Faringdon, Oxon.
Typeset by Hope Services (Abingdon) Ltd

Printed and bound by CPI Group (UK) Ltd., Croydon, CR0 4YY

To my beloved family,
with whom I share great happiness in the present, and
everlasting curiosity about life

MICHAEL

ABIGAIL, SHAHAR, and MIKA

ARIEL and NILI

DANIEL and FRANCES

And to my dear friends,
with whom I share enthusiasm about the hidden past
revealed in books and conversation

SANDY and MELANIE MARGOLIES

SHIMON and AMI BRAND

ADA RAPOPORT-ALBERT, ASI FARBER-GINAT

ESTER JUHASZ, YUDITH NAVE, ARTHUR MILLMAN

ENID SOIFER and LEONA Z. ROSENBERG

PUBLISHER'S NOTE

*

The author and publisher wish to thank

MR FELIX POSEN

and

THE FACULTY OF HUMANITIES OF THE
HEBREW UNIVERSITY

*for their generosity in contributing towards the cost of
translating and publishing this book*

Translators' Preface

THIS translation is the collaborative work of the Hebrew Institute of Boston, a non-profit organization whose mission is to translate Hebrew scholarly works into English. We believe that translation benefits from such collaborative effort because the process of discussion and mutual criticism that accompanies the pooling of linguistic resources allows for a more nuanced understanding of complicated texts and better interpretation of philosophical ideas. Teamwork taps into deeper wells of cultural allusions, and thus generates better solutions to the complex problems of translation.

We were particularly interested in translating this book because of the extraordinary challenges it presented and because of the importance of its inclusive cultural message. As we worked we found ourselves drawn deeper and deeper into the subject matter and the translation became a labour of love.

In building her thesis, Rachel Elior draws extensively on the source texts of Jewish mysticism, from antiquity to the modern era. Most of these texts are very obscure, even for the native speaker of Hebrew. The ordinary reader trying to grapple with an obscure text can generally make some sense of it without necessarily accounting for all its details. Translators, however, are accountable for every aspect: we have therefore tried to convey the meaning as clearly as possible while also capturing the style and content, in the hope of facilitating the reader's understanding of the use Elior makes of these quotations to advance her argument.

A couple of examples may help convey some of our considerations and choices. A quotation from *Synopse zur Hekhalot-Literatur*, §19 (see pp. 78–9) is used to illustrate the transformation of a human being (Enoch; Gen. 5: 21–4) into a divine creature (Metatron). In the Hebrew text Metatron says that he was taken by God בשמשות (*beshemashot*) to serve לשמש (*leshamesh*) the Throne. The noun שמשות (*shemashot*) can mean 'dusk', as in *bein hashemashot*, or 'suns'; the prefix –ב (*be-*) can mean 'at' or 'by'; so *beshemashot* may mean 'at dusk' or 'by suns'. In addition, because Hebrew is written without vowels, the word שמשות might equally be read *shamashut*, which means 'service'. This possibility needs to be considered since the context indicates that Metatron was taken for service. However, the combination *beshamashut leshamesh* is strange. Philip Alexander's translation of this verse reads: 'When the Holy One blessed be He, took me to serve the throne of Glory . . .' (*Old Testament Pseudepigrapha*, ed. Charlesworth, i. 267). Alexander solves the problem by omitting any reference to בשמשות. Elior's main point is that this transformation takes place by means of fire. This led us to choose the English word 'fire', assuming that שמשות means 'suns' (*shemashot*), which fits the dominant imagery of fire in the entire passage and best illustrates Elior's argument. Our translation then is: 'Because the Holy One, blessed be He, took me by fire to serve the Throne . . .'.

The translation of a passage quoted from *Shirot olat hashabat* 4Q405 20 ii, 21–2 (see below, p. 125) can illustrate the problems that arise from an unpunctuated source text. When we compared the translations by Carol Newsom and Geza Vermes we realized that their reconstructions of the fragmentary scrolls do not agree; there are significant differences in word choice and punctuation. Newsom's translation, ll. 6–8, reads:

[Praise the God of wo]ndrous [years] and exalt Him according to the Glory. In the tabern[acle of the God of] knowledge the [*cheru*]*bim* fall before Him; and they bl[es]s as they lift themselves up. A sound of divine stillness is [heard;] and there is a tumult of jubilation at the lifting up of their wings . . .

Vermes's translation reads:

[Praise the God of . . . w]onder, and exalt him . . . of glory in the te[nt of the God of] knowledge. The [cheru]bim prostrate themselves before Him and bless. As they rise, a whispered divine voice [is heard], and there is a roar of praise. When they drop their wings . . .

Elior quotes a reconstructed Hebrew text. Nevertheless, because of its obscurity we decided to consult other translations based on variant reconstructions. In the end we had to take responsibility for our own choices. Our translation reads:

> Praise the God of cycles of wonder and exalt Him.
> Glory is in the tabernacle of the God of knowledge.
> The cherubim fall before Him and bless Him.
> As they rise the sound of divine stillness [is heard].
> There is a tumult of jubilation;
> as their wings lift up, the sound of divine stillness [is heard].

The first line of the text in Elior's book included the phrase 'years of wonder' following the Newsom English text. We, however, preferred 'cycles of wonder' because of the basic premiss of the Qumran literature that emphasizes sacred cycles. Since the syntax of the passage is indeterminate, our choice of syntax aimed at capturing the poetic imagery and rhythm of the text. The text conveys a vision all of whose details occur simultaneously. Thus we chose a sentence and line structure making use of enjambement with an eye to conveying this.

We consulted standard translations when they were available and incorporated them in our work in varying degrees. Our final versions are the result of considering word choice, syntax, and aesthetics while maintaining the highest level of accuracy we could. In each case we attempted to highlight the inferences the author invites. We would like to acknowledge the translations we consulted: for the Hebrew Bible, the new Jewish Publication Society translation of the Tanakh and the New King James Version; for the Talmud, the Soncino translation; for the

Songs of the Sabbath Sacrifice, Carol Newsom's critical edition of the *Songs of the Sabbath Sacrifice* and Geza Vermes's translation in *The Complete Dead Sea Scrolls*; for *Synopse zur Hekhalot-Literatur*, §19, Philip Alexander's translation; Aryeh Kaplan's translation of *Sefer yetsirah*; Louis Jacobs for *The Holy Epistle*; Jacob Immanuel Schochet's translation of *Tsava'at harivash*; Arthur Green's translation of 'The Sign' by S. Y. Agnon; and Ruth Nevo's translation of *Hetsits vamet* by H. N. Bialik.

The undersigned translated and revised the entire manuscript, with the exception of the Appendix and Bibliography, which were done by the author. We thank the following for their help with parts of the translation: Samuel Tarlin, Paul Solyn, Michael Isaacs, and Leonard Gould. We would also like to express our gratitude to the Hebrew University of Jerusalem and the Posen Foundation for financial support. Finally, we thank Professor Elior for entrusting us with this work. It was a great pleasure to work with her throughout the project. We enjoyed her good advice, encouragement, appreciation, and the freedom to adjust her Hebrew text to make it more accessible to the wide range of readers interested in Jewish civilization.

Boston, June 2006   YUDITH NAVE
                                                          ARTHUR B. MILLMAN

Contents

Note on Transliteration   xii

1. The Jewish Mystical Library and New Visions of Reality   1

2. The Infinity of Meaning Embedded in the Sacred Text   33

3. The Mystic: Life without Limits   57

4. Mystical Language and Magical Language
   'Though I speak with the tongues of men and of angels . . . and
   though I have the gift of prophecy and understand all mysteries . . .'   104

Appendix: Historical and Literary Figures, Kabbalists, and Mystics
Mentioned in Jewish Mystical Literature   135

Bibliography   159

Index   191

Note on Transliteration

THE transliteration of Hebrew in this book reflects consideration of the type of book it is, in terms of its content, purpose, and readership. The system adopted therefore reflects a broad approach to transcription, rather than the narrower approaches found in the *Encyclopaedia Judaica* or other systems developed for text-based or linguistic studies. The aim has been to reflect the pronunciation prescribed for modern Hebrew, rather than the spelling or Hebrew word structure, and to do so using conventions that are generally familiar to the English-speaking Jewish reader.

In accordance with this approach, no attempt is made to indicate the distinctions between *alef* and *ayin*, *tet* and *taf*, *kaf* and *kuf*, *sin* and *samekh*, since these are not relevant to pronunciation; likewise, the *dagesh* is not indicated except where it affects pronunciation. Following the principle of using conventions familiar to the majority of readers, however, transcriptions that are well established have been retained even when they are not fully consistent with the transliteration system adopted. On similar grounds, the *tsadi* is rendered by 'tz' in such familiar words as barmitzvah. Likewise, the distinction between *ḥet* and *khaf* has been retained, using *ḥ* for the former and *kh* for the latter; the associated forms are generally familiar to readers, even if the distinction is not actually borne out in pronunciation, and for the same reason the final *heh* is indicated too. As in Hebrew, no capital letters are used, except that an initial capital has been retained in transliterating titles of published works (for example, *Shulḥan arukh*).

Since no distinction is made between *alef* and *ayin*, they are indicated by an apostrophe only in intervocalic positions where a failure to do so could lead an English-speaking reader to pronounce the vowel-cluster as a diphthong—as, for example, in *ha'ir*—or otherwise mispronounce the word.

The *sheva na* is indicated by an *e*—*perikat ol*, *reshut*—except, again, when established convention dictates otherwise.

The *yod* is represented by *i* when it occurs as a vowel (*bereshit*), by *y* when it occurs as a consonant (*yesodot*), and by *yi* when it occurs as both (*yisra'el*).

Names have generally been left in their familiar forms, even when this is inconsistent with the overall system.

ONE

The Jewish Mystical Library and New Visions of Reality

The really important things are those that are concealed from the eye.

ANTOINE DE SAINT-EXUPÉRY, *The Little Prince*

MYSTICISM has not been well received in the modern world. Its popular expressions, as well as political applications that have frequently involved manipulative and cynical distortions, have led contemporary writers to label as 'mystical' any dubious phenomenon lying outside accepted canons of rationality. The term 'mystical' is frequently applied in a derogatory way to anything that does not accord with common sense or is not respected for cultural, social, religious, or other reasons. When dealing with complex cultural issues, however, it is prudent to refrain from hasty judgements and avoid presenting the rich diversity of the past in the light of the disputes of the present. The corpus of mystical writings in the traditional Jewish world developed over the course of thousands of years. With all its cultural and historical manifestations, mysticism embraces a rich world of thought, creativity, imagination, and inspiration, transcending existential experience. Currently disputed manifestations of mysticism should not be used as a basis for evaluating the entire mystical corpus, the religious and spiritual experiences that served as its foundation, or its manifold historical expressions.

The creators of mystical thought and those who gave expression to mystical experiences tried to decode the mystery of divine existence by penetrating to the depths of consciousness, language, memory, myth, and symbolism. They strove to rescue reality from its concrete, univocal meaning by delving deep into the psyche. They set out to discover concealed worlds and to create alternatives that would shed new light on reality as it is. Mysticism belongs to the history of human imagination, creativity, and language, and to the attempt to decode and transcend literal meaning. It is part of a sceptical and subversive outlook that defies the constraints of existence and opposes a single interpretation of reality. Mysticism draws from domains in which distinctions fade, norms are indefinite, paradoxes abound, and a unity of opposites is allowed—that is, from dream, myth, legend, imagination, vision, and madness. It uses paradoxical thinking, which is 'beyond reason and knowledge', and creative interpretation, which reveals concealed layers in the psyche and suppressed strata in language. In addition, it draws on mythical archetypes and ancient symbols, which both conceal and suggest. It descends to the depths of the soul through moments of semiconsciousness, visions, hallucinations, dreams, and inspired wakefulness. Mysticism takes off on wings of imagination to higher worlds, to mixtures of legend and myth, and through poetic inspiration it seeks to penetrate the mysteries of language and symbol. Its creators blur the distinctions between the visionary and the real, the concrete and the abstract, inner meaning and outer expression, the symbolic and the ritual. Even norms and the boundaries between prohibited and permissible acts, in both the private and public domains, are sometimes blurred in the minds of its creators.

Mysticism, which transcends the boundaries of time and space and refers to a reality not grasped by means of ordinary human cognition, is one of the central sources of inspiration of religious thought. It is one of the phenomena that generate meaningful cultural changes in the course of history, not despite but because of the obscurity of the sources of its inspiration and their complexity. In the traditional world mystical creativity served as a primary channel for introspection and reflection, attributing primary meaning to subjective experience free of conventional limitations. The manifestation of a dynamic inner life and of individual expression need not conform to a specific time and place. Mysticism was the obvious route for breaking down concrete and abstract structures, developing an alternative perspective on reality, crystallizing new forms of authority and leadership, and expressing yearnings for freedom and change. A number of these causal factors, both known and unknown and springing from the domains of spirit and creativity, played a decisive role in moulding the religious and social history of the traditional world. For these and other reasons, there is no doubt that the mystical corpus deserves study and discussion in the framework of cultural criticism and research on the diversity of spiritual creativity.

*

Mysticism has many definitions.[1] These depend not only on the traditional religious context in which it functions and the cultural, social, and historical circumstances in relation to which it is examined, but also on the standpoint of those who try to analyse it: the essence of mysticism as seen from the viewpoint of the mystic differs from that of outside observers. Despite diverse starting points, it is

---

[1] On different definitions of mysticism in various religious traditions see Inge, *Christian Mysticism*; Otto, *Mysticism East and West*; Zaehner, *Mysticism Sacred and Profane*; Underhill, *Mysticism*; Louth, *Eros and Mysticism*; Woods, *Understanding Mysticism*; McGinn, *Foundations of Mysticism*; Scholem, *Major Trends*; Scholem, *On the Kabbalah*; Dan, *Jewish Mysticism*; Dan, *On Holiness*; Scharfstein, *Mystic Experience*; Otto, *Idea of the Holy*; Ben-Shelomoh, 'On the Problem of the Uniqueness of Religion'; James, *Varieties of Religious Experience*.

possible to find a common denominator for the different definitions. Mysticism presupposes that there is a hidden world beyond the revealed world and that there is a way for a human being to attain this hidden world spiritually through imagination and contemplation and to have a deep inner experience of uniting with the higher reality. Such a conviction can be validated by religious faith or cultural tradition. It can also take shape in the human spirit through direct experience linked to dreams, visions, and revelations, or the projection of inner spiritual experiences onto the unseen realm. Certainty of the existence of a hidden world might also develop in other ways: as a result of a new illumination of a sacred ritual tradition, by means of a deep mental transformation that brings about a new outlook on everyday reality, or through the inspiration of a new hermeneutics, unknown in the written tradition, that adds an original vantage point to a plain meaning.

Mysticism deals mainly with another reality that exists beyond the perceptible world, a reality that is revealed to visionaries when the veils obscuring everyday consciousness are lifted.[2] Mystics argue that visions of the imagination as well as entities perceived to transcend the natural order of things are real. From time to time mystics have direct spiritual contact with those entities, since the essential goal of mysticism may be conceived of as a particular kind of heightened encounter between God and the human, between the Infinite spirit and the finite human spirit, or between the hidden and the revealed. This 'other reality', which bestows sense and meaning on different dimensions of human experience, is not fixed and one-dimensional. Rather, it reshapes itself in the mystical imagination, influenced by external and internal, historical and spiritual changes. This other reality is perceived by means that lie between the concrete and the verbal, characterizing the physical world, and the abstract and imaginative, which go beyond it. The hidden reality—whether revealed in a dream or a vision, in the imagination or the psyche, in symbol or metaphor, or in the depths of language and the insights of poetry—has different visual realizations in different historical periods. In Jewish mysticism it relates to secret theological and cosmological systems that add hidden structure, inner sense, depth, flexibility, and secret meaning to revealed reality, a reality assumed not to be subject to any change.[3]

---

[2] On the 'other reality' see Otto, *Idea of the Holy*; Elior, 'Mysticism, Magic and Angelology'; Elior, 'From Earthly Temple to Heavenly Shrines'.

[3] For different opinions on Jewish mysticism from historical and phenomenological points of view see Scholem, *Major Trends*; Scholem, *Origins of the Kabbalah*; Scholem, *On the Kabbalah*; Scholem, *Jewish Gnosticism*; Tishby, *Kabbalah Research and its Ramifications*; Tishby, *Commentary on Aggadot*; Tishby, *Doctrine of Evil*; Tishby (ed.), *Wisdom of the Zohar*; Tishby, *Paths of Faith and Heresy*; Tishby, 'Revolution in Kabbalah Research'; Dan, *Jewish Mysticism*; Dan, *Ancient Jewish Mysticism*; Dan, *On Holiness*; Idel, *Kabbalah: New Perspectives*; Idel, 'The New is Forbidden by the Torah'; Idel, *Studies in Ecstatic Kabbalah*; Liebes, 'How the Zohar was Written'; Liebes, 'New Directions in Kabbalah Studies'; Wolfson, *Through a Speculum*; Hallamish, *An Introduction to the Kabbalah*; Urbach, 'Traditions about Merkabah Mysticism'; Hellner-Eshed, *A River Issues Forth*.

The 'other reality' in the ancient Jewish tradition relates to the 'mysteries of creation' (*razei olam*), the 'seven firmaments' (*shivah reki'im*), the 'seven wondrous sanctuaries' (*shivah devirei pele*), the 'seven throne chariots' (*sheva merkavot*), the 'divine inner sanctum' (*pardes*), the 'seven supernal sanctuaries' (*shivah heikhalot elyonim*), 'fiery flames scattered and reassembled' (*shalhavot shel esh mitpazerot umitkabetsot*), the 'Divine throne chariot' (*merkavah*), cherubs, angels, heavenly living creatures (*hayot hakodesh*), and the 'stature of God' (*shiur komah*).[4] These terms are related to a visionary metamorphosis of the destroyed Temple and the divine service that had been abolished. This metamorphosis took place in the midst of a reality of destruction and loss. Defiance of the arbitrariness of a reality in which the Temple was destroyed and the service abolished resulted in their eternalization in heaven in the form of temples, chariot, and cherubs, organized in eternal septuples in a sacred time, sacred space, and sacred ritual.

Visionaries sometimes describe the hidden world in prophetic language as the 'translucent whiteness of sapphire' (*livnat hasapir*), or 'holy living creatures running to and fro' (*hayot hakodesh ratso vashov*), and sometimes they connect it to unknown conceptual worlds such as the 'thirty-two wondrous paths of wisdom' (*lamed bet netivot peliot hokhmah*), 'a fiery flame held in the coal' (*shalhevet ahuzah begahelet*), and the 'ten *sefirot* of infinite nothingness' (*eser sefirot belimah*), which are all mentioned in *Sefer yetsirah* (The Book of Creation), written in Hebrew in the first century CE.[5] These concepts connected the secrets of creation to their visionary/mystical manifestation without reference to historical reality. But it seems that the visionary and numerical patterns that undergird the hidden world constitute a fixed cosmic foundation and a predetermined divine pattern fraught with meaning, standing in opposition to the unexplained arbitrariness of concrete reality and the chaos of existence.

In the Middle Ages this hidden reality was described in the twelfth-century *Sefer habahir* (The Book of Elucidation) and the thirteenth-century Zohar (The Book of Splendour) as 'the tree of the spirits' (*ilan haneshamot*) or 'the tree of the spheres' (*ilan hasefirot*). It was connected to the 'world of speech' (*olam hadibur*),

---

[4] On the mystical concepts of late antiquity and the first five centuries of the first millennium, *pardes* (paradise), *merkavah* (divine chariot), *heikhalot* (heavenly shrines), *shiur komah* (the mystical divine stature), *razim* (mysteries), *malakhim* (angels), *shemot* (holy names), see Scholem, *Jewish Gnosticism*; Scholem, *Major Trends*, ch. 2; Gruenwald, *Apocalyptic and Merkavah Mysticism*; Gruenwald, *From Apocalypticism to Gnosticism*; Dan, *Ancient Jewish Mysticism*; Dan, *Jewish Mysticism*, i: *Late Antiquity*; *Heikhalot zutarti*, ed. Elior; Elior, *Three Temples*; Elior, 'Mysticism, Magic and Angelology'; Elior, 'From Earthly Temple to Heavenly Shrines'; Elior, 'Concept of God in Hekhalot Literature'; *Synopse zur Hekhalot-Literatur*, ed. Schäfer et al.; Schäfer, *Hidden and Manifest God*; Schäfer, *Hekhalot-Studien*; Himmelfarb, *Ascent to Heaven*; Halperin, *Faces of the Chariot*; Green, *Keter: Crown of God*; Cohen, *Shi'ur Qomah*; Farber-Ginat, 'Studies in Shi'ur Komah'; Arbel, *Beholders of Divine Secrets*; Lesses, *Ritual Practices*; Kuyt, *Descent*.

[5] On *Sefer yetsirah* see Liebes, *The Creation Doctrine*, and Dan, 'The Religious Significance of *Sefer Yetsirah*'.

also known as 'the Divine Presence or Shekhinah', to 'the unique cherub' (*hakeruv hameyuḥad*), to 'the darkening light' (*or haneḥshakh*), to 'the Infinite' (*ein sof*), and to 'the crown' (*keter*).[6] All these concepts connect the inner life of human beings and the realm of divinity, both of which are conceived of as deeply interrelated infinite dynamic processes. This hidden reality is sometimes described in kabbalistic literature as 'sevenfold cosmic cycles' (*shemitot*), 'splendorous lights' (*tsaḥtsaḥot*), or 'primordial man' (*adam kadmon mikol kedumim*), and sometimes as 'the unique cherub' and 'splendorous, brilliant light' (*or tsaḥ umetsuḥtsah*), expressions originating with the twelfth- and thirteenth-century German pietists and the thirteenth-century circle of contemplation (*ḥug ha'iyun*).[7] Almost always, however, these expressions combine concrete representations of visions with intellectual abstractions derived from them. Such a combination sometimes creates new linguistic strata, which include concepts overwhelming in their inexplicable beauty, concepts that gain mystical meaning and turn into objects of contemplation. For example, we find in the thirteenth-century *Book of Contemplation* the following description:

therefore, the Holy One, blessed be He, is called 'God of Truth' (Deut. 32: 4). His truth, may He be blessed, which we are able to imagine, is that of the pure light of life. It is pure gold, written and sealed (cf. Exod. 39: 30) in the radiance of His beauteous canopy. It consists of a brightly shining radiance, like the image of the spirit and the form of the soul [cf. *Heikhalot zutarti*, ed. Elior, 26] that no living creature is able to perceive.[8]

Other times it brings about a visionary reality that becomes the object of new mystical experiences.

In the kabbalistic circles that developed in Safed in the early modern era, i.e. during the sixteenth century, this hidden reality, which emerged within the constraints of exile and tragic experience, was described using abstract and mythological terms, such as 'transmigration of the souls' (*gilgul neshamah*), 'divine speech' (*dibur shekhinah*), 'restitution of the world (*tikun olam*), 'circles and straightness' (*igulim veyosher*), 'contraction' (*tsimtsum*), 'the death of kings' (*mitat hamelakhim*), 'countenances' (*partsufim*), and 'the breaking of the vessels'

---

[6] On the medieval mystical vocabulary pertaining to the structure of the hidden heavenly world, such as *sefirot, shemitot, tsaḥtsaḥot*, see Scholem, *Origins of the Kabbalah*; Scholem, *Kabbalah of* Sefer hatemunah; Gottlieb, *Studies in Kabbalah Literature*; Gikatilla, *Sha'arei orah*, ed. Ben-Shelomoh (English trans. by Weinstein as *Gates of Light*); Verman, *Books of Contemplation*; Tishby, *Commentary on Aggadot*; Isaac of Acre, *Me'irat einayim*, ed. Goldreich; Wolfson, *Through a Speculum*.

[7] On the circle of contemplation see Verman, *Books of Contemplation*, 1. In western Europe around the year 1230 an obscure Jewish luminary writing under the nom de plume Rabbi Hammai (the Aramaic name connotes seer or visionary, derived from seeing or observing) composed a short yet profound theosophical treatise known as the *Book of Contemplation*, probing the recondite nature of the divine realm. It circulated throughout Spain and Provence and influenced other Jewish mystics. Within a few decades dozens of texts were composed reflecting the language of the *Book of Contemplation*. See Verman, *Books of Contemplation*.   [8] Ibid. 42.

(*shevirat kelim*).[9] These terms stem from the teachings of Joseph Karo and Solomon Alkabets in the first half of the sixteenth century and from Lurianic kabbalah, and refer to the human soul transcending existential limits and to the divine autogenesis, or the divinity that creates itself within the framework of cosmic processes described according to the patterns of human experience. These terms, which include expressions like 'father' (*aba*) and 'mother' (*ima*), 'conception' (*ibur*) and 'suckling' (*yenikah*), begetting and death, belong to the divine world. They express unexpected combinations of (i) phenomena and facts that are seemingly unrelated to a religious reality with (ii) visionary components that represent abstractions and projections of human experiences onto the divine realm. These combinations are the result of the unique point of view of those who possess a mystical temperament blending the concrete and the abstract, the human and the divine. Some of the new anthropomorphic concepts in the divine realm had to do with the tragic consequences of the exile from Spain, which caused great loss of life. The new perception of the divinity in relation to procreation and family life reflects deep human despair and is the focus of human hope. The revival of the doctrine of transmigration of the soul responded to the same agony.

In seventeenth-century Shabatean literature, the hidden world was conceived in relation to new formulations such as 'light that includes thought' (*or sheyesh bo maḥashavah*) and 'light that does not include thought' (*or she'ein bo maḥashavah*)[10] and to previous concepts such as 'the other side' (*sitra aḥra*), 'the holy side' (*sitra dikedushah*), 'shell' (*kelipah*), 'the depth of the abyss' (*nikbat tehom rabah*), 'the redemption of the sparks' (*ge'ulat nitsotsot*), 'messiah', and 'the redemption of the exiled Shekhinah' (*ha'ala'at hashekhinah*).[11] These masculine and feminine concepts, which attribute a polarized dualistic character to the divine realm, and many additional concepts that express relationships between the forces of good and evil, exist simultaneously on the cosmic and mental and on the ritual and textual levels. These concepts gain life in the mystical imagination, become concretized in sacred texts and in ritual tradition, and illuminate and conceal the manifold being of the divine world revealed in its permutations in the human psyche.

This visionary reality is sometimes connected to an immediate experience of

[9] On the mystical vocabulary of the early modern period see Scholem, *Major Trends*, 244–86; Tishby, *Doctrine of Evil*; Werblowsky, *Joseph Karo*, 38–83; Zak, *In the Gates of Rabbi Moses Cordovero's Kabbalah*; Fine, *Physician of the Soul*; Elior, 'R. Joseph Karo and R. Israel Ba'al Shem Tov'; *Galya raza*, ed. Elior.

[10] On Shabatean concepts see Scholem, *Sabbatai Sevi*, index; Scholem, *Major Trends*, 287–324; and Goldish, *Sabbatean Prophets*.

[11] On 'the other side' and 'the holy side', the 'shell', the 'depth of the abyss', and the redemption of the Shekhinah, see Tishby (ed.), *Wisdom of the Zohar*. On *devekut* (mystical unity), Shekhinah, and 'raising of the sparks' see Scholem, '*Devekut* or Communion with God'; Scholem, 'Shekhinah: Feminine Element in Divinity'; Wolfson, *Through a Speculum*, index under 'Shekhinah'; Schatz-Uffenheimer, *Hasidism as Mysticism*; Weiss, 'Mystical Hasidism and Hasidism of Faith'.

the divine presence or engagement with sublime holiness.[12] Numerous examples of the encounter with the angelic world and the divine presence are found in the descriptions of ascending to the chariot in Heikhalot literature. For example:

R. Akiva said: When I ascended and saw a vision of the heavenly realm and a glimpse of the Mighty One I observed all the living creatures which are in all the pathways of heaven, and their upward length and their downward width and their upward width and their downward length.

R. Ishmail said: How do the angels of service stand upon the pathways of heaven? He said to me: 'Like this bridge that rests over a river and the whole world passes over it. Thus rests the bridge from the start until the end of the passage and angels of service circle on it and sing a song before Adonai, God of Israel, and thousands of thousands of thousands and myriads of myriads of myriads extol praise before the throne of Adonai God of Israel.'[13]

At other times visionary reality is a reflection of a deep spiritual experience that obscures the demarcation between reality and imagination. It may also be connected to a poetic realization of symbols and metaphors that reveal new worlds:

I looked above the Seraphim who stand above the head of Adonai God of Israel and said a prayer: Blessed are you Adonai . . . creator of his world in his name . . . in the heights of the heavens you founded your throne and your dwelling place you placed in the elevations of the heights. Your chariot you placed in the upper firmaments on high, your residence you established near the *ophanim* of majesty. Companies of fire adorn praise for your remembrance, Seraphim of fire praise you . . . in awe they stride, in fear they wrap themselves, laden with pride to adorn the creator of all. Covered with eyes on their backs, their appearances are like the appearance of lightning. Their splendour is marvellous, wise, sweet . . . they exalt and bring forth pure creatures: Holy, Holy, Holy. Angels of service utter praise before you. A globe of sun is in their mouth. Their splendour glistens like the brilliance of the firmament.[14]

This visionary reality may express yearnings for an alternative reality with different laws and different rules of time and space. It may reflect a longing for a mythological past or a utopian future. This 'other reality' creates the hidden divine world, inspired by human vision and the depths of existential experience. It is revealed in a vision, dream, or spiritual experience, creating new combinations among the imagination, the concrete and the abstract, the conscious and the unconscious, and also between a yearning for a different reality and a defiance of the rules of the actual reality, which cannot be changed. This 'other reality' is based on a decoding of the different layers of language suggested in the religious corpus throughout history, and on new combinations of images, in language and

---

[12] On the experience of the divine presence see James, *Varieties of Religious Experience*; Otto, *Idea of the Holy*; Ben-Shelomoh, 'Problem of Pantheism'. On the visionary nature of the experience see Wolfson, *Through a Speculum*.

[13] *Synopse zur Hekhalot-Literatur*, ed. Schäfer et al., §§545–6.   [14] Ibid. §§595–6.

imagination, in vision and attentive listening. This visionary reality is created in the imagination of the mystic, who fathoms the depths of the sacred text, throwing new light on it and inducing new life in it. The mystic penetrates to the depths of the language, to its images and symbols, and reaches the ancient mythic layers of the written tradition. This reality can be conveyed in oral testimony based on revelation and the immediate experience of contact with the upper worlds, or it can be transmitted as a written tradition, which derives from a vision in which the world becomes transparent to the mystic. Mysticism deals with the essence of the concealed world, revealed in prophecy and vision, the world woven between the human spirit and the divine spirit. This concealed world is suggested in sacred texts and decoded in the imagination of the visionary and expressed in his idiosyncratic language. Mysticism is concerned with defining the concealed world and the stages of its development. It describes its appearance, its attributes, and its relation to the human world, and tries to explain its essence and laws from creation to redemption. This hidden essence expresses the transformations that occur in the depths of the human spirit and their reflections on different levels of existence and on other worlds. Mystical literature analyses the interrelations between the hidden world and the revealed world, metahistory and history, the eternal and the temporal, the depth of human experience and the secrets of divine sublimity, and explores the implications of these insights for human experience.

As the understanding of the hidden world changes, so may that of the real world. Such a change results when a person is called or might be called to explain the revealed religious system in the light of the hidden mystical system and to study the interrelations between the man who was created in the image of God and God, who is referred to as 'ancient primordial man' (*adam kadmon lekhol kedumim*).[15] The mystic sees in that which is apparent to the eye testimony to that which is hidden and tries to penetrate to the inner spiritual being of the revealed world and to experience directly the presence of God embedded in it. A mystic is one who 'enters the *pardes*' or 'ascends to the *merkavah*', one who tries to express his consciousness of complex interrelations between the revealed and the hidden either in a symbolic, poetic, and visionary way or in a scholarly, contemplative, and interpretative way.

In the mystical corpus a person speaks to himself in different languages. Sometimes he speaks in an ancient symbolic language that arises from deep layers of his subconscious, a different language from that of clear logical conceptual thought. Sometimes he speaks in the language of myth, legend, vision, and dream, all of which are linked to his historical and cultural heritage. Each mystical language, in its own way, deconstructs the boundaries of the world in which we live, bursts through the limitations of time and space, and creates new constructs

[15] See Elior, 'The Metaphorical Relationship between God and Man'.

beyond the domains of empirical plausibility and common sense. These languages are revealed in 'ascending' (*aliyah*) and 'descending' (*yeridah*), in 'entering' (*kenisah*) and 'exiting' (*yetsiah*), in 'watching' (*tsefiyah*) and 'listening' (*shemiah*), all of which take place in the depths of one's soul, in one's spirit and imagination, while one strives to experience the presence of God and attempts to express direct consciousness of the divine presence and the heavenly sanctuary, in that atemporal place in which the demarcation between the earthly and the heavenly fades. Sometimes the mystic 'ascends to the *merkavah*' or 'enters the *pardes*' or stands at the 'entrance of the sixth temple and it seems as if it contains thousands of myriads of sea waves without even one drop of water, but rather splendorous air, crystal-clear stones of pure marble as the temple whose splendorous image resembles water'.[16] Sometimes he gets a glimpse 'of the splendour of the marble stones and an appearance which is water . . . and he loses his mind'.[17] Sometimes he gazes at 'the darkening light'[18] or observes 'the ten *sefirot* of infinite nothingness'.[19] He has a vision of 'primordial man'[20] or sets the 'unique cherub' before his eyes.[21] He hears the 'voice of my beloved knocking, a harp playing by itself'.[22] He listens to the voice of 'the responding angel' (*hamalakh hameshiv*)[23] or talks with the messiah, who promises him that 'your teachings will be proclaimed'.[24] From time to time he hears the words of the Shekhinah promising him 'I will make you worthy of being burned for the sake of sanctifying God's Name',[25] and sometimes he hears heavenly voices that are such that 'anybody who listens to them becomes mad and loses his mind'.[26] The mystic watches the 'splendorous light',[27] or he listens to the words of 'Metatron the angel of the countenance',[28] or 'he sees the voices', or 'the angel Gabriel is revealed to him',[29] or he hears the 'angel who reveals wonderful secrets to him'.[30] These and similar constructs refer to the mystical experience of the creators of Jewish esotericism, from Rabbi Akiva

---

[16] *Heikhalot zutarti*, ed. Elior, 30. [17] Ibid. 23.

[18] 'The light that is darkened from illuminating' and 'the hidden light that is darkened from illuminating': see Verman, *Books of Contemplation*, 159.

[19] *Sefer yetsirah*, 1, §1. [20] Hayim Vital, *Ets ḥayim*, 21–67.

[21] Manuscripts of the Hasidei ashkenaz; see Dan (ed.), *Heart and the Fountain*, 96–100, and Dan, *Unique Cherub Circle*.

[22] Joseph Karo, *Magid meisharim*, 8. See BT *Ber.* 90b. Cf. Werblowsky, *Joseph Karo*, 9–23; Elior, 'R. Joseph Karo', 148–53.

[23] *Sefer hamalakh hameshiv*, 69–112. See Idel, 'Inquiries into the Doctrine'.

[24] Israel Ba'al Shem Tov, *Igeret hakodesh*; *Ben porat yosef*, 245–56 at 255. See Jacobs, *Jewish Mystical Testimonies*, 148–53. Cf. Scholem, *Messianic Idea*, 182–3.

[25] Joseph Karo, *Magid meisharim*, 166. See Werblowsky, *Joseph Karo*; Elior, 'R. Joseph Karo'.

[26] *Heikhalot rabati*, §104 (pp. 50–1). See Scholem, *Jewish Gnosticism*.

[27] *Sefer ha'iyun*. See Verman, *Books of Contemplation*, introduction and p. 59.

[28] 3 Enoch (*Sefer heikhalot*). In the Alexander translation (*Old Testament Pseudepigrapha*, ed. Charlesworth, 256) it is given as 'Metatron, Prince of the Divine Presence'.

[29] *Galya raza*, 16; cf. 9, 12, 39. See Elior, 'Doctrine of Transmigration'.

[30] Luzzatto, *Igerot ramḥal*, 19–21, 39. See Tishby, *Kabbalah Research*, iii. 658, and index under 'angel' and 'maggid'.

and the author of *Sefer yetsirah*, through Isaac Sagi Nahor (the Blind) and the author of the Zohar, and concluding with Joseph Karo, Isaac Luria, Moses Hayim Luzzatto, and the Ba'al Shem Tov, all of whom draw from the deep layers of consciousness revealed to perceptive readers of sacred scriptures who were infatuated with the mysterious. In the past these layers were called *avanta deliba*, or the understanding of the heart, and those endowed with mystical inspiration were designated 'descenders of the chariot'.[31] These people burst through the straits of the 'self' by virtue of exultation and inspiration. They transcend the demarcations between the prohibited and the permitted, the revealed and the hidden, the human and the divine, by virtue of creative imagination focused on the mysterious realm. They permit paradoxes, contradictions, and ambiguities, and different flights of the spirit of man. All these are expressed in a visionary language, in descriptions that defy limits, in testimonies from higher worlds, in symbols, in oxymorons, in synaesthesias, and in metaphors that unify opposites.[32]

The mystic blurs the borderlines between empirical experience and imaginative voyage. He bursts the accepted limits of his period and place, which separate the terrestrial from the heavenly. He looks into the domain of the forbidden and knowingly breaks explicit prohibitions that ban the observation of 'what is beyond reason and knowledge' and forbid the study of the mysteries of the divine being.[33] In antiquity the Jewish tradition powerfully expressed this demarcation and the severity of the prohibition against the study of the hidden: 'Whoever looks into [these] four things would have been better off not having been born: what is above, what is below, what is before, and what is after';[34] 'What is superior to you do not seek and what is concealed from you do not study; observe what you were permitted; you have no business with the hidden';[35] 'Don't understand what is behind you and don't study the utterances of your lips';[36] 'One should not expound the *merkavah*';[37] 'ten *sefirot* of infinite nothingness'; 'keep your mouth from speaking and your heart from thinking'.[38]

These explicit prohibitions against observation of the superior and the hidden did not stop 'the seekers of the hidden', 'the *merkavah* voyagers', 'the masters of the heavenly mysteries', or those who enter the 'heavenly sphere' (*pardes*). And it did not stop kabbalists, hermits, and visionaries from glimpsing 'beyond the curtain' and in their imagination or mystical enthusiasm and curiosity seeing 'the unique cherub', 'the King in his beauty', the luminous spheres, the 'prince of the countenance', or the world of the chariot, because, as Plotinus perceptively

---

[31] BT *Meg.* 24a. Cf. *Heikhalot zutarti*, ed. Elior, 22–5; R. Hai Gaon, *Otsar hage'onim*, 14.

[32] On the dialectical connection between opposites in mystical thought see Stace, *Mysticism and Philosophy*, 251–70; Elior, *Paradoxical Ascent*, 25–36, 97–102; McGinn, *Foundations of Mysticism*, 32–3, 49–52.

[33] On the prohibition of dealing with mysteries see *Heikhalot zutarti*, ed. Elior, 59–60; Mishnah *Ḥag.* 2: 1; Urbach, 'Traditions about Merkabah Mysticism'.

[34] Mishnah *Ḥag.* 2: 1.   [35] Ben Sira 3: 19.   [36] *Heikhalot zutarti*, 22.

[37] BT *Ḥag.* 13a.   [38] *Sefer yetsirah*, ch. 1, mishnah 8.

observed in the third century, 'contemplation and vision have no limits'.[39] But there is no doubt that these prohibitions and restrictions influenced the extent to which mystical experience was disclosed in the traditional world and the manner in which it was expressed in the consciousness of those who regarded themselves as entering the forbidden domain. The tradition defined the status of this domain by words ascribed to Yohanan ben Zakai: 'A great thing and a small thing—a great thing is the *merkavah* work, a small thing is the affairs of Abaye and Raba',[40] and also added a restriction that only 'the wise one who understands by himself' is allowed to study 'the work of the *merkavah*'.[41] Because only the very few with special qualifications were allowed to concern themselves with the *merkavah*, it became the desired end in spite of restrictions and prohibitions, and perhaps because of them.

In order to overcome the prohibition of concern with mysteries and fulfil the desire to express what was revealed to them in this domain, the mystics often gave their hidden world a suggestive, enigmatic, and poetic expression. Sometimes they expressed it in a visionary symbolic way that reveals no more than the slightest hint, and sometimes in a contemplative observational way and other times in a conceptual systematic way, as we learn from mystical literature throughout history. This literature reflects repeated efforts to give verbal expression to the hidden and to transfer spiritual experience with a mystical character from the individual domain to the public domain. These efforts were made by those who were called during different historical periods 'angelic priests of the inner sanctum' (*kohanei korev*), '*merkavah* voyagers' (*yoredei merkavah*), 'preachers of tabulations' (*doreshei reshumot*), or charismatic experts in magical practice who were wise in healing (*ḥakhmei ḥarashim unevonei laḥash*), kabbalists, masters of secrets, visionaries, true seers, false prophets, pietists, and hermits, all of whom were mediating between the hidden heavenly realm and the human desire for vision, poetry, mystery, dream, and knowledge.

Mystical creativity, ever striving to reach 'the limits without limits', 'the place in which opposites unify', or 'a time in a place where there is no time and no place',[42] is reflected in Hayim Nahman Bialik's poem 'Hetsits vamet' ('He glanced and died'), about one of the four who entered paradise, in which his language sensitively recognizes the complex relation between opposites. Thus it allows for a variety of possibilities with regard to the relations among the revealed and the hidden, the finite and the infinite, the human and the divine. It opens many doors to atemporal interrelations between the overt and the secret, the real and the imaginary, the external and the internal—though it does not endorse any of these qualities exclusively. This openness stems from the fact that mystical perception is based on the recognition of interrelations between the infinity of the divine

[39] *Enn.* 3. 8. 5.   [40] BT *Suk.* 28a.   [41] BT *Ḥag.* 13a.
[42] See Bialik, 'Language Closing and Disclosing'.

essence and its creative power, on the one hand, and the infinity of human language and its manifestations in written tradition, creative thought, and imagination, on the other hand. By its mere existence, mystical perception attempts to eliminate the partition between being and nothingness, or to break through the boundaries that separate the concrete from the abstract, the human from the divine, the manifest from the hidden, the temporal from the eternal. It also seeks to blur the conventional distinctions between the forbidden thing that is incomprehensible and the permitted thing that is in plain sight. The creators of mystical thought express the yearning to study the concealed and superior reality, which sometimes is inexpressible and other times is experienced through verbal richness and in a multisensory manner, described as illumination or lightning. Plato's words in the Seventh Letter describe mystical perception or the knowledge of the hidden realm: 'It does not at all admit of verbal expression like other studies, but . . . it is brought to birth in the soul on a sudden, as light that is kindled by a leaping spark' (341 CD).[43]

A complex and varied mystical corpus has been created in Eastern and Western religions, in most of the cultures known to us in the course of recorded history. As has been mentioned before, mysticism in the traditional world is a major expressive channel for individual consciousness, religious inspiration, experience of the mysterious, poetical insight, and creative imagination. In spite of the conceptual closeness—or the phenomenological resemblance in a few of the essential characteristics—of the mystical phenomenon in different religions and cultures (and sometimes it is even possible to establish the cultural relationship through its archetypal imagery), the study and profound exploration of the meaning of the phenomenon require that it be interpreted within the cultural context in which it has been created and in which alone it may have meaning.[44] Mysticism is connected to language, culture, religion, Scripture, underlying experiences, mythological memories, and stories relating to the beginning and end of things. It is anchored in a literary and ritual tradition, in sacred and profane concepts, in a web of spiritual, symbolic, mythic, poetic, imaginative, psychic, and linguistic associations. This conceptual totality is connected by its very essence to distinct historical circumstances of a certain culture and religion that share a common past, a common existential meaning derived from a unifying life experience, and hopes for a common future. It is connected to a language and the totality of its creation, which express the life experience, memories, and yearnings of a certain

---

[43] Plato, *Epistles*, trans. R. G. Bury (Loeb Classical Library; Cambridge, Mass., 1966), 531.

[44] On the theory of universal transcendental truth, which divests mystical experience of its particular historical characteristics such as language, tradition, and particular symbolism, see Underhill, *Mysticism*, and *Practical Mysticism*. For the opposing position, which argues that mystical truth is achieved only through a particular religious tradition and a unique system of symbols founded on a particular history, culture, and language, see S. Katz, *Mysticism and Religious Traditions*, and 'Language, Epistemology, and Mysticism'.

community and have meaning only in unique social, cultural, and historical contexts.[45]

Jewish mysticism would not exist had it not been for the Temple and the priesthood, the destruction, the exile, and the hopes for redemption, the *pardes* and the *merkavah*, the mysteries of *shiur komah*, and the enigmatic figures of Moses, Enoch, Ishmael, and Akiva, the ascent to the heights and *kidush hashem* (sanctification of the divine name), the Torah and the Mishnah, the dream of Jacob and the ladder on which 'angels are descending and ascending', and the vision of Ezekiel in which 'divine visions' are revealed to the prophet—and had it not been for Shimon bar Yohai in the Zohar, the messiah and the Shekhinah, halakhah and aggadah.[46] When a mystical corpus develops in another religion, it draws from the underlying concepts, archetypal figures, local legends, sacred text, and cherished memories that are formulated in a certain language of a certain culture of a certain people. This means that a resemblance in words is not necessarily a resemblance in meaning, and does not necessarily reflect an identity or a similarity in the mystical experiences themselves. Such superficial pseudo-resemblances between phenomena are negligible in comparison with the essential differences in context and meaning.

Scholars investigating mystical phenomena do not always agree on the appropriate modes of study. There is also a difference of opinion as to the degree of benefit to be found in ahistorical, cross-religious, and cross-cultural comparisons that attempt to clarify issues that relate to a certain culture and always take place in specific historical circumstances. Yet there is agreement that it is possible to benefit greatly from a comparative investigation of different cultural insights in order to evaluate unique spiritual phenomena in a balanced way. It is also possible to refine and sharpen the acceptable methods of analysis by comparing them with those used in other theoretical conceptual systems. One should not, however, confuse similarity in the tools of investigation and methodological categories with similarity in content and identity in meaning. An accidental similarity is not a meaningful relationship. The bibliographical notes detail various approaches to studying the phenomenon of mysticism. The following chapters, however, are based on an approach that focuses on the investigation of Jewish mystical phenomena within the context of the religion, culture, language, and changing spiritual and historical circumstances in which the destiny of the Jewish people evolved.[47]

*

[45] On the comparative study of mysticism in the religions of the East and the West and on the principal question of comparing mystical phenomena see Otto, *Mysticism East and West*; S. Katz, 'Language, Epistemology, and Mysticism'; S. Katz, *Mysticism and Religious Traditions*; Zaehner, *Mysticism Sacred and Profane*.

[46] Aggadah is the general name for the homiletic passages in rabbinic literature which include mythical and mystical sections.

[47] On the historical development of Jewish mysticism see Scholem, *Kabbalah*, 1974; Scholem, *Major Trends*; Scholem, *Origins of the Kabbalah*; Scholem, *Sabbatai Sevi*; Gottlieb, *Studies in*

In the following, several definitions of Jewish mystical thought will be suggested that will determine the boundaries of our analysis in the realms of the concrete and the abstract.

In the field of the concrete, the analysis will deal with mysticism that has direct or indirect written documentation to which we can apply tools of textual analysis. That is to say, the discussion will relate to the mystical library, which includes hundreds of volumes of mystical thought, handwritten and printed, and thousands of pages of multifaceted literature that include mystical testimonies from all the world cultures in which Jews lived and acted throughout thousands of years.[48] Here I focus on parts of the Jewish mystical library that were written at various times and places from late antiquity to the beginning of the twentieth century. Briefly, the essence of this library can be regarded as an ancient mosaic revealed in archaeological excavations: some of it is clear to the examining eye with its pattern defined with precision, while other parts are fragmented, faded, hinted at, or missing altogether. The meaning of this metaphor is that the library at our disposal is not complete and does not necessarily represent the total mystical corpus or its full historical development. Rather, it reflects the arbitrary collection of what has survived over time and has been randomly protected in manuscripts and books.[49]

The fragmented and arbitrary character of the mystical corpus and its wide geographical and historical distribution make it impossible accurately to trace all the sources that influenced its creation as well as the individual parts of the spiritual mosaic from which individual creators drew. There are, of course, works that acquired central and sacred status, giving them cultural advantages and influence. Furthermore, there are specific historical facts that are easily discerned. However, next to the known facts and sources of influence that we can uncover there exists a wide range of concepts that we cannot possibly encompass or exhaust. These are written, oral, visual, conscious, and unconscious, and are present in stories, legends, myth, art, poetry, ritual, folklore, customs, and cultural prejudice. Besides these factors, which directly and indirectly influence the creative mind, there are also the influences of languages and cultures in proximity to both the 'elite' culture and the popular religious culture that surrounded it. In addition, there are individual, social, and historical circumstances that are not always suffi-

Kabbalah Literature; Dan (ed.), *Early Kabbalah*; Dan, *Ancient Jewish Mysticism*; Idel, *Kabbalah: New Perspectives*; Liebes, 'How the Zohar was Written'; Tishby, *Paths of Faith and Heresy*; Tishby (ed.), *Wisdom of the Zohar*, introduction.

[48] On the Jewish mystical library see Scholem, *Bibliographia Kabbalistica*; Dan and Liebes (eds.), *Library of Gershom Scholem*.

[49] In the National and University Library in Jerusalem the printed books of the Jewish mystical library are in the Gershom Scholem Collection and the numerous manuscripts of all periods of Jewish mysticism are collected in microfilm in the Institute of Microfilmed Manuscripts housed in the Library.

ciently known to us and, in most cases, are impossible to trace. All this indicates that it is impossible to give absolute answers, with clear, chronological sequences of development, to the following questions. What were the sources that influenced the mystical corpus? How were the visionary, symbolic concepts created? By contrast, the literary expressions that we possess often enable us to explore the characteristics of the author, his unique voice, ideas, and message, as well as to examine certain interactions between the sources that inspired him and to appreciate the distinctiveness of the creative metamorphosis. All these are visible in the conscious selective processes and the singular choices that establish novelty in the written text and define the thematic boundaries as well as the new meaning relating to the writer's time and place.

This archaeological metaphor has an additional aspect: as the archaeologist uncovers the mosaic and reconstructs it within its historical and geographical context, he or she finds its meaning and explains it within a certain cultural context, without being committed to a priori assumptions and value judgements. In the same way, my analysis is not committed to metaphysical assumptions, value judgements (positive or negative), identification, or criticism. My purpose is to present, as accurately as possible, the meaning of mystical works as perceived by their creators and readers during different historical periods. I also wish to present them within a wide cultural context, analysed from the critical point of view of our contemporaries who in some way identify with their historical and spiritual past or take a profound interest in its creative diversity.

With respect to the abstract boundaries mentioned earlier, we are dealing with a consciousness that develops from some elementary ideas of an esoteric discipline. These ideas draw on a religious tradition and ultimately transcend its boundaries. The basic assumption of mysticism is that sensory reality is part of a wider, enigmatic, and complex reality, suggestive of secret elements and intimated in various symbolic dimensions of human experience. These dimensions are expressed in complex concepts drawing from many domains: dream and revelation;[50] psyche and memory; ritual and religion; and literature, music, and other aspects of tradition. These concepts exist in different modes—concrete and abstract, mythical and transcendent—which are revealed in different layers of language. They may be either parts of a complete vision or parts of an encapsulating system in which there is importance in the sequence of levels connecting the divine being and human consciousness. They may also be fragments of a vision or flickering moments of consciousness that, when combined, form a meaningful sequence or a

---

[50] On the importance of dreams in mystical thought see Scholem, *Dreams of R. Mordekhai Ashkenazi*; Hayim Vital, *Sefer haḥezyonot* (Book of Visions), ed. Aescoly and Ben-Menahem, and in *Jewish Mystical Autobiographies*, trans. Faierstein; Kopfer, 'Visions of Asher ben Me'ir of Lemlein'; Tamar, 'Messianic Dreams and Visions of Rabbi Hayim Vital'; Elior, 'Reality in the Test of Fiction'; Oron, 'Dream, Vision, and Reality'; Jacobs, *Jewish Mystical Testimonies*; *Jewish Mystical Autobiographies*, trans. Faierstein. On dreams in a mystical context in antiquity, see *Old Testament Pseudepigrapha*, ed. Charlesworth, i. 13–100.

fundamental principle. However, whether they combine into a meaningful sequence or remain fragments of revelation, they are always connected with verbal images and compound concepts that through language link the different layers of existence.

Some of the participants in mystical consciousness try to decipher multilayered reality, in all of its expressions, and penetrate, through their consciousness, beyond its concrete boundaries. Sometimes they experience its spiritual power as a living reality—symbolically, imaginatively, and visually. Sometimes they describe their experience of passing from the concrete to the hidden as a frightening meeting with heavenly powers. Writing in the first centuries of the Common Era, one of the anonymous authors of the Heikhalot literature testifies to the magnitude of the experience: 'When I saw him my hands burned and I was standing without hands or feet.'[51] This experience is sometimes described as requiring one to give up an external, discursive, rational understanding in order to acquire an inner, contemplative, mystical consciousness: 'If you want to become unique in this world, to have the secrets of the world revealed to you and the secrets of the *merkavah*, you should learn this *mishnah*: "Don't seek to understand what is beyond you and don't enquire into what your lips utter, understand what is in your heart and be silent so you will be worthy of seeing the beauty of the *merkavah*".'[52] This moment of mystical transition has been artfully described:

The doors of the holy ark opened and I saw a figure that looked like a human being standing there and his head was resting between the scrolls of the Torah and I heard a voice coming out of the ark emanating from among the branches of the trees of life. He did not speak to me face to face. Thought on thought was engraved, his holy thought within my thought. And all the communicated words were etched in letters, and the letters joined into words, and the words formed what he had to say . . . My flesh crawled and my heart melted and I was annihilated from being and I was as if I were not.[53]

In the history of Jewish mysticism, the mystical crossing of boundaries is often related to chaotic events: destruction, catastrophe, exile, expulsion, persecution, devastation, situations of distress, or moments of crisis. The breakdown of concrete reality has allowed the 'ascent to heaven' ever since the days of Ezekiel, who saw the divine chariot when he was exiled from Jerusalem in the decade of the destruction of the Temple (Ezek. 1: 1–25) and the days of Ishmael the high priest, who ascended to heaven when Jerusalem was destroyed by the Romans in the second century. This breakdown catalyses the mystical revelation in which there is a metamorphosis from death and annihilation to eternity and consolation; or perhaps it allows one to escape from destruction and the unbearable pain of the concrete world to the divine reality, which abides eternally in

---

[51] *Heikhalot zutarti*, 36.   [52] Ibid. 22.
[53] Agnon, 'Hasiman', 308–12; translated by Arthur Green, 'The Sign'.

heaven.[54] Timeless memory stored in language describes heavenly visions of a concrete reality that no longer exists or of a divine being who explains it. Language, then, is the bridge between the lost reality and heavenly eternity.[55] In mystical language, Temple, chariot, altar, priesthood, the people of Israel (*keneset yisra'el*), and the Shekhinah are restored. The dead are brought back to life through reincarnation. The martyrs who live in assemblies on high, the angels and the messiah, the holy creatures of Ezekiel's vision, the heavenly temples and other heavenly beings, and immortal figures are all a means of connecting past and future through vision, text, and ritual, and thus they are reborn beyond the limits of space and time.

In different historical periods the mystics of the Jewish tradition strive to escape from the limits of the concrete world and its earthly predicaments in order to attain the hidden heavenly timeless world. In antiquity, they hope 'to enter the *pardes*', 'to descend in the divine chariot', 'to ascend to the heavenly temples', 'to gaze on the *merkavah*', to contemplate 'the stature of God', 'to enter the inner sanctum' (Holy of Holies), 'to know heavenly mysteries', or 'to see the King in his beauty'.[56] In the Middle Ages, they yearn to 'unify' the 'realm of the *sefirot*', to gaze on the luminous spheres (*tsaḥtsaḥot*), to contemplate the mystery of the cosmic cycles and divine visions, 'to ascend to the *heikhal ken tsipor*' (the place where the messiah dwells in paradise), or 'to descend to the evil side' (*sitra aḥra*).[57] At the beginning of the modern era they seek to hear 'angelic mentors', 'to cleave' to the heavenly spheres, to redeem the Shekhinah, 'to raise the sparks' (*nitsotsot*), to decipher the 'mysteries of redemption', and to be 'members of the Temple of Yearning'.[58] These mystics—living in the depth of the textual reality that is revived within their souls and is decoded and restructured beyond the limitations of time and space—yearn to explain the unexplainable and observe the hidden. By way of their consciousness they seek to break through the boundaries of language and perception to approach a higher, deeper, and more concealed spiritual level. They capture in various enigmatic concepts their yearning to know, see, and conceive the hidden, obscure, multifaceted, indefinable, timeless truth that lives in the highest realms. Perhaps revealed for the first time, this truth is perceived by the mystic in a vision or dream, in an epiphany or in 'lightning'. It is 'engraved' in

[54] The quotation above was written by S. Y. Agnon in 1944, reflecting a mystical experience he had as a response to the unbearable pain he had experienced on the eve of the holiday of Shavuot when he heard the terrible news of the murder by the Germans of all the Jews in his home town, Buczacz. The cognitive dissonance between the holiday that prohibits mourning and his profound sense of tragedy caused a loss of consciousness and a mystical experience that gave meaning to the chaotic experience and integrated it into Jewish memory beyond the boundaries of time and space.

[55] On the mystical language see Scholem, 'Meaning of the Torah'; Scholem, 'Name of God'; S. Katz, 'Language, Epistemology, and Mysticism'; Dan, *On Holiness*.

[56] See Elior, *Three Temples*; Halperin, *Faces of the Chariot*; Schäfer, *Hidden and Manifest God*; Scholem, *Jewish Gnosticism*; Cohen, *Shi'ur Qomah*.

[57] On the medieval concepts see Tishby (ed.), *Wisdom of the Zohar*; Dan, *Unique Cherub*; Verman, *Books of Contemplation*; Wolfson, *Through a Speculum*; and above, n. 6.   [58] See above, n. 9.

the mind or kindles 'sparks' in the soul. The mystic may create this truth in his imagination while decoding the secrets of hidden traditions that are delivered by hints in a sacred text, or it may be that a sacred truth is being drawn in the imagination of one visionary and delivered by the tradition to be re-experienced in the imagination of another visionary, thereby becoming the possession of many others by oral or written means.[59]

From a different angle, it is possible to present the mystic's world-view as an attempt to reveal hidden realities, connected to our world in a complex fashion, and to create through language something that never before existed. This desire brings about a reality conceived of as founded on combinations and interrelations among categories and different layers of hidden dimensions. Reality is re-examined in the light of different relations between the revealed and the hidden— between the world of the *merkavah* and the temple, 'the spirit of light' and 'the spirit of darkness',[60] the world of angels referred to as 'angelic priests of the inner sanctum' (*kohanei korev*), and the world of priests, conceived of as angels, following the verse 'For the lips of a priest guard knowledge . . . For he is an angel of the Lord of hosts.'[61] The interrelations among different concepts, such as the 'bright light' and the 'dark light'; the 'doctrine of the tree of life' and the 'doctrine of the tree of knowledge'; the 'doctrine of creation' and the 'doctrine of emanation'; 'God, Israel, and the Torah'; God, the Torah, and the world; letters, the spheres (*sefirot*), and the world of emanation and the worlds of 'creation, formation, and actualization'; the 'destruction of the harmony of the divine world [the breaking of the vessels]' and the 'restoration of harmony'; the 'divine abundance that sustains the world' and the 'divine withdrawal'; the 'substance' of the divine, or the 'vessels', the 'sparks', and the 'shells', holiness and impurity, being and nothingness, exile and redemption, the 'essence' and the 'garment'[62]—these interrelations establish a dialectical commentary on being and, at the same time, juxtapose the revealed world with the hidden world, arguing that the meaning of human history should be sought beyond it, in the hidden spheres revealed in mystical experience. The conceptual systems are dialectical patterns that focus on and attempt to decipher the fundamental structures existing beyond time and space that establish the world. These patterns remould the inner relations between revealed and concealed realities and have a major influence on the concept of God and of divine worship, interpreting perceptible reality in the light of hidden reality.

[59] See the biographies of Joseph Karo and Moses Hayim Luzzatto for examples of the mystics.

[60] On 'spirit of light' and 'spirit of darkness' see *Megilat haserakhim*, ed. Licht; *Megilat hahodayot*, ed. Licht; *Megilat milḥemet*, ed. Yadin.

[61] Mal. 2: 7. On angelic priests and priestly angels see *Megilat hahodayot*, ed. Licht, 29, 84, 162–3, 113, and English translation; *Songs of the Sabbath Sacrifice*, ed. Newsom, 23–58; Elior, *Three Temples*, 165–200; Yadin, *Temple Scroll*, ch. 8.

[62] On these concepts see Scholem, *On the Kabbalah and its Symbolism*, index; Scholem, *Major Trends*, index; Tishby, *Doctrine of Evil*, index; Hallamish, *Introduction to the Kabbalah*, index.

The basic assumption necessary to understand Jewish mystical thought is that the divine and the mundane are interrelated. Everything exists within every other thing, as a reflection of a greater pattern, and every examination reveals the infinite number of reflections and interrelations. The hidden upper world and the concrete lower world are connected; they reflect one another and they create and influence each other. This relation stems from the divine duality revealed through language, but concealed within its meaning. Language, according to the mystical point of view, emanates from the divine and is an eternal, ever creative, multifaceted entity shared by God and human beings. Divine language is the revelation of the creative power of God in perceptible concepts, its dynamic realization in abstract and concrete expressions understandable to a human being, and the unfolding of His infinitude within both the Creation and the limits of time, space, language, and consciousness. Mystical thought seeks to investigate, in its earthly and heavenly revelations, this dialectical infinitude of revealing and concealing. According to this view, those human actions, thoughts, and utterances that are derived from language are not independent. Rather, they relate to a cosmic reality, which they either describe, modify, or wish to bring about. Knowledge of the many manifestations of being and the intricate inner relation between its concealed and revealed aspects gives rise to the yearning to reveal the hidden essence of the revealed being and the impulse to decode the concealed relation among the different aspects of being. This yearning focuses either on the investigation of the mutable interrelations between the revealed and concealed markers or on those between the language, including all its components, and reality, in all its layers.

In mystical thought, which detects the hidden pulse of being and the living connection between the Creator and the creation, there are usually no isolated phenomena. Everything is interconnected within a complete world conception—connected through a system of mystical laws, basic patterns that decode the revealed world in comparison with a hidden world, an expected time order, from the beginning to the end, or different determinate attributes that combine the separated, deconstructed components of being into a hidden unity. These attributes usually are suggested in the sacred texts of the past and are related to the concept that is being developed anew each time. This new concept interprets in the present or future the hidden connections that meld the human and divine into a single totality.

Mysticism offers a complete explanation of the totality of being. It defines a major metaphysical principle that establishes the nature of reality. It may uncover a metahistoric process that spreads from the creation until the end of time or it may establish a hidden purpose towards which everything develops. It discusses other realities, which exist parallel to the earthly world, beyond the limits of time and space, or describes an alternative reality in the past or future. Mysticism focuses on certain aspects of the heavenly world or establishes a complex system that provides meaning for the parts of the complete reality. It discusses the origins of good and evil and the hidden relation between exile and redemption. It draws connecting lines between existing reality and the desired world. It outlines an 'ascending ladder' which connects the different attributes, or it describes in detail 'a spit linking heaven and earth with the world skewered upon it'[63] through which one attains higher worlds.

The complex relation between material and spiritual realities is acknowledged; awareness of the complexity of language is crystallized; and the limitations of the senses and logical thought are established. In addition, there is an acknowledgement of the existence of other modes of conception that are outside the realms of the perceptible and rational and exist within the unlimited realm of language. In the same context, a principal assumption is formulated that states that there is an analogy between the revealed psychic structure of the human being and the deeper psychic layers that do not have an external common expression, which is parallel to the relation between the common spoken language and the hidden mystical language. In addition to these assumptions, which by nature free fixed patterns, disagree with popular norms, and influence the conception of the relation of human beings to the intricate reality in which they live, a dialectical cognition is crystallized that acknowledges the contradictions and opposites that compose the revealed and hidden reality. This cognition, which points out the duality of being, assumes that under certain conditions it is possible to realize the potential, opposing, spiritual powers that are hidden within the human being's psyche and through this process rise to higher spiritual levels hidden behind the revealed world. In the mystical tradition, the possibility of realizing these hidden powers is contingent upon three conditions:

1. The assumption of a multilayered, eternal, sacred, textual entity, which includes metaphysical truths that by nature cannot be comprehended in any way other than revelation.[64] This sacred entity establishes a frame of reference and a theoretical point of departure for deconstructing the infinite divine language and reconstructing it anew.

2. Activity within a cultural reality that acknowledges the existence of a cosmological and linguistic conception bridging the revealed and concealed worlds and serving as a point of departure for a conscious internalization of opposites: 'His glorious chariots . . . holy cherubim, luminous *ofanim* in the *devir*

---

[63] *Heikhalot rabati*, in *Synopse zur Hekhalot-Literatur*, ed. Schäfer et al., §201.

[64] Cf. the description of the sacred text and its revelation on Mount Sinai in the Dead Sea Scrolls: 'And He spoke with the assembly of Israel face to face, as a man speaks with his friend. And He showed us in a fire burning above from heaven . . . He stood on the mountain to make known that there is no God beside Him and there is no rock like Him. And the assembly they answered; trembling seized them before the glory of God and because of the wondrous sounds [. . .] and they stood at a distance. And Moses, the man of God, was with God in the cloud. And the cloud covered him . . . and like an angel he would speak from his mouth.' 4 Q 377 frag. 2 ii, 1–2, in *Wadi Daliyeh II*, ed. Gropp, 213–14.

and the splendor of the luminous firmaments do they sing beneath His glorious seat.'[65]

3. The existence of a sacred tradition that sketches a mystical, ascending ladder, or the existence of a linguistic system, whether mystical or magical, bridging the revealed and concealed in theory and practice. An example is the sacred tradition pertaining to the Holy of Holies where the Ark made from an acacia tree stood:

> Sing, oh sing, acacia tree,
> Ascend in all thy gracefulness.
> With golden weave they cover thee,
> The *Devir* palace hears thy eulogy,
> With diverse jewels art thou adorned.[66]

These conditions are created and usually exist either in a historical reality that sharpens the perception of the gap between the available and the desirable, a cultural reality that cultivates mystical, magical, and occultist values bridging different realities, or a social environment that ascribes to them a value and recognizes their importance. These values, giving rise to a new language, are created and developed by renewed exegetical study of an ancient tradition and by inspiration, contemplation, or vision. They might be created by imitating rituals that support the development of a changing consciousness, or by contemplative concentration on the nature of the hidden realm. Inspired by a charismatic leader, the sacred tradition is renewed through his spirit, and a new conceptual world formulated in an unfamiliar language may be bestowed upon the members of his circle.

These innovative conceptions and insights pertaining to the divine realm, gained as a result of the previous assumptions, influence the language and give rise to unfamiliar entities from an inner reality, extending the boundaries of existence.[67] The portrayal of historical reality, developed next to a living and hidden existence, is diversified and enriched in new perspectives by their influence. These conceptions, which are crystallized in the mystical tradition, influence the patterns of the mythopoetic work occupied with the creation of mythical entities and the structuring of the unknown. They form a mystical reality that serves as a

---

[65] *Songs of the Sabbath Sacrifice*, ed. Newsom, 306. The term *ofanim* refers to the 'wheels' from Ezekiel's vision of God (Ezek. 1), which were promoted to independent mystical creatures in rabbinic thought following the mystical chariot tradition in the Dead Sea Scrolls angelic liturgy and in the Heikhalot hymns and the *piyutim* (liturgy).   [66] BT *AZ* 24*b*: *Bereshit rabah* 54.

[67] Examples from Heikhalot literature, the *Book of Creation*, and the *Book of Contemplation* of such conceptions are 'the divine chariot of the cherubs'; 'the tree of souls'; 'the supreme crown'; 'the wondrousness of His Unity'; 'the account of the chariot'; 'the celestial orchard'; 'the ten hidden powers that emanated from the supreme Realm that is exceedingly hidden and not revealed'; 'the shining lights of the splendour'; 'ten *sefirot* without substance which emanated from the power of the Marvellous Light'; 'ten *sefirot* derived from *mispar* (number) and from *sapir* (sapphire)'; 'the spirit of the Living God'.

background to the decoding of all of being. All this directly or indirectly influences the perspective of the surrounding reality, the changes in the concept of God and human beings, the creation of new linguistic layers, and the recognition of the existence of different patterns of consciousness as well as of a new conceptual system.

The mystical corpus is sustained by uncovering mystical truth, casting light on the concrete word through new commentary, analysing the depths of language, directly experiencing the hidden and describing it. It combines a creative impulse that strives to reach hidden worlds with a deep need to give expression to idiosyncratic experiences, to break the boundaries of time and space, and to decipher the mysteries of language. The creators of mysticism are frequently characterized by their alertness and attentiveness to inner voices, vague feelings, dreams, and visions that conceal secrets. They ascribe deep meaning to inner experience that is exempt from the limitations of common sense and to consciousness of the infinitude of the hidden reality existing beyond the concrete world. The mystical corpus blends inspiration and freedom and the breaking of boundaries by those who seek to reach hidden worlds and to verbalize their experience with the freedom to re-evaluate the limits of reality through reference to a divine authority acquired through inspiration, illumination, dream, or vision.

Mystical thought, which takes form within the individual and draws from inner reality, imagination, and inspiration, is revealed through language. This language—which originally might have been a language of visions or dreams, an inner language of the psyche, or a unique expressive language of one kind or another—turns into a communicative language that lives in the public domain from the moment that it is delivered to someone else, discussed in public, sung, proclaimed, or written down. The contemplation of the boundaries of reality, which is done through decoding the connotations of the language, reveals unknown dimensions of inner psychic reality and hidden divine reality. This contemplative process brings forth poetic, imaginative, and visionary expressions that deal with the relation between the hidden and the revealed, combining the divine and the human and broadening the boundaries of existence:

All the letters of the Torah in their forms, in their combinations, and individually, are forms of God, may He be blessed.[68]

You will know the exaltedness of the letters . . . For each letter corresponds to the supernal powers and the vowels correspond to the lower powers. When you know the significance of each letter, then you will be heard and inscribed before Him.[69]

One angel among the living beings of the chariot, his name is Sandalfon; he is tying diadems on the Glorified One. He is adjuring the crown in the tetragrammaton and the crown is ascending to the head of the Master.[70]

---

[68] *Sefer hatemunah*, 1.   [69] Verman, *Books of Contemplation*, 208.
[70] *Synopse zur Hekhalot-Literatur*, ed. Schäfer et al., §655.

There are mysterious chambers beyond enigmatic depth in each letter among the letters of the Torah.[71]

These are the ten *sefirot* of infinite nothingness that the world stands on.

The ten *sefirot* of infinite nothingness are the Creator Himself and His image.

The Blessed be He has seven sacred forms and all of them can be found in man, as it says, 'In the image of God He created man'.[72]

The mysteries of the Torah are composed of all the lower and upper forms.

For man is compounded of all the spiritual elements because he was created in the image and form [of God].

You should know that the letters of the Torah are living and moving and flying in the air unto the upper chariot.

They [the descenders of the chariot] are not really ascending on high, but they observe in the depth of their heart, and they gaze as a person who sees clearly and they hear and speak like the one who gazes on the holy spirit.[73]

Expressions like these are composed and deciphered in the depths of the spirit of the special few who are infatuated with the radiant beauty of the mysterious and in the language of the inspired ones who seek the secret of the world and combine the revealed with the hidden. However, only when this language is transferred from the private experience of the individual to the public realm does it acquire influence and become an object of observation, study, analysis, and research.

The individuality, freedom, and flexibility of mystical thought give rise to the question of the relation between mysticism and the rigid normative religious tradition.[74] Generally speaking, one can say that religion represents the fixed system that establishes norms, which draw their validity from sacred values inherited from the past. These values derive their authority from a single heavenly revelation that was publicly witnessed in a mythical past or in historical time, has been documented, and has been accepted as a sacred text underlying myth, law, basic concepts, institutions, leadership, and custom. These norms are expressed in the principles of halakhah and are anchored in tradition. The religious system does whatever it can to give them a permanent and sacred validity. These norms, which cannot be changed because of their divine origin, are subject to interpretation and adjustment by the authorized leaders and interpreters of the tradition. The sacred norms are embedded in the Torah, divine commandments, halakhah, customs, religious interpretations, legal discussions, ritual language, and modes of conduct, and are asserted in the institutions, values, ideals, and sanctions of society. All these are unified in a sacred tradition transmitted from the past in the holy language that reflects it and in the collective memory that asserts it.

[71] Gikatilla, *Sha'arei orah*, ed. Ben-Shelomoh, 211.   [72] *Sefer habahir*, 74, §172.

[73] R. Hai Gaon, *Otsar hage'onim*, 14.

[74] On the relations between tradition and mysticism see Scholem, 'Religious Authority and Mysticism'; J. Katz, *Halakhah and Kabbalah*, 9–127; Scholem, *On the Kabbalah and its Symbolism*.

Mysticism, on the other hand, presents a new vision of all this and often does not accept the traditional conventions, but rather illuminates them through on-going discovery.[75] Mystical thought, which sees itself as the deepest layer of the Torah, filled with metaphysical truths regarding the essence of God, the meaning of the Torah, and the secret of the world, derives its authority from the higher revelation that is vouchsafed to individuals, and from the public transmission, orally or in writing, of concepts that shatter the limits of comprehension. Influenced by such a new revelation—conceived of by the mystics as a divine illumination, vision, mission, dream, angelic revelation or prophecy, emanating from a higher source—various traditional concepts are re-examined and new ways of interpretation and conduct are suggested.[76] Layers of original meaning in the sacred texts are uncovered through mystical inspiration, establishing new modes of relationship between the hidden and the revealed. Original norms, newly derived through on-going revelation and recorded by the mystics, join accepted norms based on the written tradition. New rituals are created to express significant mystical values, and previously unknown customs expressing new modes of being deciphered in the mystical vision join those that already exist. Naturally, these innovations, which took place in the individual and public realms, did not always accord with the values of the traditional world. They often involved a struggle over authority, a debate on the right of interpretation, and created social and religious tension over new meanings that were attributed to the concept of divinity and to the divine worship.[77]

In general, the normative Jewish tradition is based on the assumption that divine revelation in public ceased to exist at a certain moment in Second Temple history.[78] In addition, the Torah, which manifests the divine revelation through the holy spirit, was canonized, and nothing could be added to it or removed from it. Everything one should know about the divine dictum exists in the Torah, though it is open to human explanation and to creative interpretation, while preserving the sacred text. Such interpretation, based entirely on the human wisdom

---

[75] On the ground-breaking nature of the mystical tradition see Weber, *On Charisma and Institution Building*; Scholem, 'Redemption through Sin'; Elior and Liebes (eds.), *Lurianic Kabbalah*; Elior, 'Jacob Frank's *Divrei ha'adon*'; Faierstein, *All is in the Hands of Heaven*.

[76] On mystical revelations see Aescoly, *Messianic Movements*; Scholem, *Dreams of R. Mordekhai Ashkenazi*; Vital, *Sefer haḥezyonot*, ed. Aescoly and Ben-Menahem, trans. in *Jewish Mystical Autobiographies*, trans. Faierstein; Kopfer, 'Visions of Asher ben Me'ir of Lemlein'; Tamar, 'Messianic Dreams'; Elior, 'Reality in the Test of Fiction'; Scholem, *Sabbatai Sevi*; Liebes, *Secret of Shabatean Faith*; Scholem, *On the Kabbalah and its Symbolism*; Werblowsky, *Joseph Karo*; Scholem, '"Divine Mentor" of Rabbi Yosef Taitazak'; Idel, 'Inquiries into the Doctrine of *Sefer hameshiv*'; Idel, '*Hitbodedut* as Concentration'; Elior, 'R. Joseph Karo and R. Israel Ba'al Shem Tov'; Jacobs, *Jewish Mystical Testimonies*; *Jewish Mystical Autobiographies*, trans. Faierstein; Fine, *Physician of the Soul*; Wolfson, *Through a Speculum*; Goldish, *Sabbatean Prophets*; Chajes, *Spirit Possession*; Goldish (ed.), *Spirit Possession*.

[77] On mysticism and religious authority see Scholem, 'Religious Authority and Mysticism'; J. Katz, *Tradition and Crisis*, chs. 20–2; S. Katz (ed.), *Mysticism and Religious Traditions*.

[78] See BT *Sot.* 48*b*; BT *Yoma* 9*b*.

of the sages, on the authority of tradition, and on human intellect, is offered and analysed in public and does not rely on personal heavenly revelation, as the well-known story about Akhnai's oven clearly demonstrates.[79] In the normative tradition, the religious corpus is based on several modes of relating to the apparently fixed canonical text—the explanatory mode, the hermeneutic mode, the legal mode, and the pluralistic analytical mode—and on the acceptance of the absolute dicta that arise from the literal written text.

The mystical tradition is based on the opposite assumption, that divine revelation never ceased: it continues throughout history and is disclosed to people who possess unique qualities. In some circles or periods of the mystical tradition it seems as if the biblical text was not canonized, and that it was possible to add to it works that were composed in accordance with the holy spirit or were heard from the mouth of a *bat kol* (a secondary divine voice), or that were revealed from the mouth of God, who speaks directly to the initiates, or that were heard from the mouths of angels or were discovered through the inspiration of 'the revelation of the Shekhinah', 'the revelation of a *magid*', or 'the revelation of Elijah'.[80] In the mystical tradition, the sacred text is illuminated through commentary and interpretation, based on renewed revelation of the divine spirit. This revelation can be defined as intensive listening to a heavenly voice that arises from the text and is absorbed into the soul of the listener, or as the 'voice coming out of the ark emanating from among the branches of the trees of life. Thoughts being engraved in my prayer book . . . Thought on thought was engraved, his holy thought within my thought',[81] or as a deep analysis of what is revealed and concealed in the language, creating new textual layers or an audio-visual metamorphosis of the text, exposing its secret layers. In the halakhic normative tradition hardly any independent literature was created that was unrelated to the creative, commentary mode and not directly connected to the canonical text and to its literal meaning. In the mystical tradition, on the other hand, a vast independent library was created. This mystical library was not based on a fixed mode of relating to the sacred text, but rather on a flexible mode relating to its hidden meaning and creative potential, one revealed to the inner eye of the beholder and resonating in his soul.

Anonymous mystical works from late antiquity are independent of the biblical text and are not direct interpretations of it, but they shape new concepts that relate to the hidden meaning of the text. These works include:

1 Enoch, describing the heavenly journey of Enoch son of Jared (Gen. 5), written in the second century BCE, included in the pseudepigrapha and among the Dead Sea scrolls

[79] BT *BM* 79*a–b*.

[80] On these concepts see Werblowsky, *Joseph Karo*, index under Elijah the Prophet, Maggid, Shekhinah, and Angels; and *Jewish Mystical Autobiographies*, trans. Faierstein, same index entries.

[81] See above, n. 53.

Shirot olat hashabat (Songs of the Sabbath Sacrifice), describing the angelic liturgy in the celestial temple, from Qumran from the second and first centuries BCE

2 Enoch, describing the heavenly ascent of Enoch in a conceptually new way, written in the first century BCE or first century CE

Heikhalot zutarti (The Small Treatise of the Heavenly Sanctuaries), and *Shiur komah* (The Stature of God), written in the first centuries CE, both ascribed to R. Akiva, the mystical hero of the rabbinic tradition

Shivḥei metatron (In Praise of Metatron), from the pseudepigraphic Heikhalot literature, ascribed to Akiva and Ishmael and composed in the first centuries CE.

Some unique mystical works reflect neither the direct meaning of the text nor an interpretative relationship to it, but express the creation of conceptual worlds that are influenced by a new vision of the hidden meaning of the biblical text. This is the case with:

Sefer yetsirah (The Book of Creation), ascribed to the patriarch Abraham but composed in the middle of the first millennium according to some scholars, or in the first century according to others

Sefer harazim (The Book of Mysteries), written in the middle of the first millennium

Sefer habahir (The Book of Elucidation), ascribed to Nehuniah ben Hakanah but composed in the twelfth century

Other works ascribed to later authors develop a new conceptual world:

Sha'arei orah (Gates of Light) by Joseph Gikatilla, composed in Spain in the thirteenth century

Sefer hazohar (The Book of Splendour), written anonymously at the end of the thirteenth century, but ascribed to Shimon bar Yohai, who lived a millennium earlier

Sefer berit menuḥah (The Book of the Covenant of Rest) by Abraham ben Isaac of Granada

Sefer hatemunah (The Book of the Image) and *Sefer hakaneh vehapeli'ah* (The Book of Reed and Wonder), composed anonymously and pseudepigraphically in the fourteenth and fifteenth centuries

Sefer hapeliah or *Sefer hakaneh* (The Book of Wonder), written in the fourteenth and fifteenth centuries and ascribed to Avigdor Kara of Prague

Sefer hamalakh hameshiv (The Answering Angel), a visionary autobiography by an unknown author, probably written in the fifteenth or early sixteenth century

Hayat hakaneh (The Creature of the Reeds) by Solomon Molcho, written in the third decade of the sixteenth century

Magid meisharim (Upright Sayings) by Joseph Karo, written between 1533 and 1575, the first printed mystical autobiography based on the sayings of the Angelic Mentor

Galya raza (Revealed Secrets), mid-sixteenth century, anonymous

Ketem paz (Pure Gold) by Simeon Lavi, written in north Africa in the sixteenth century

Sefer hahezyonot (The Book of Visions), a mystical autobiography, and *Ets hayim*, a mystical theological volume, by Hayim Vital, written at the end of the sixteenth century and early seventeenth century in Safed and Damascus

Sefer gerushin (The Book of Banishments) by Moses Cordovero, a mystical diary of a group of mystics written in Safed in the sixteenth century

Raza demeheimanuta (The Secret of Faith), written in the seventeenth century by Abraham Michael Cardozo, who ascribed it to Shabetai Tsevi

Hemdat yamim (Beloved of Days), written anonymously in Turkey in the first third of the eighteenth century

Adir bamarom (Mighty in Heaven) by Moses Hayim Luzzatto, written in the first half of the eighteenth century in Italy under the inspiration of angelic visitation

Divrei ha'adon (The Words of the Lord) by Jacob Frank, and *Megilat setarim* (Scroll of Secrets) by Isaac Safrin of Komarno, which were composed in the eighteenth and nineteenth centuries

Arpilei tohar (Clouds of Purity), a mystical tract by Abraham Isaac Hakohen Kook, written in the twentieth century

Some of these works draw on direct visionary experience and mystical interpretative illumination, and some were written as translations, commentary, and reworkings of this experience into new studies.[82]

The mystic does not necessarily strive to change accepted norms or to contradict conventional concepts of time and space. His intention, rather, is to ascribe new meanings to them and put them in unfamiliar contexts through new linguistic

[82] On anonymous mystical writings and on the diversity of books on kabbalah see the Appendix under anonymous and pseudepigraphic writings.

layers that create or reveal unknown worlds. *Sefer harazim* (The Book of Mysteries), an anonymous mystical and magical text associated with the Heikhalot literature written in the middle of the first millennium, offers an example of the revelation of an unknown world:

The seventh firmament, all of it is sevenfold light, and from its light all the heavens shine . . . There is no calculation or limit to the great light within it, and the fullness of the light illumines all the earth. The angels are fixed in pillars of light, and their light is as the light of the brilliant star and cannot be extinguished, for their eyes are like flashes of lightning, and they stay upon the margins of [the Divine light] and glorify in fear the One who sits upon the throne of glory.[83]

At times the mystical literature conceives unexpected perspectives connecting the past and the future and establishes new dimensions that combine the revealed and the hidden in an original way, sometimes clashing with existing norms. Expanding the limits of reality and establishing new perspectives might engender profound changes and give rise to a completely different religious mentality, diverging from the commonly accepted norm. This can occur because, in mystical thought, human perfection is not dependent on the sacred traditional values that are manifested in public, but on the complex relationship to the hidden meaning of Being that is revealed to a few. This meaning is embedded in a language that is decoded anew, idiosyncratically, and in an original vision of the relationship between the higher and lower worlds that is revealed in the sacred text and its mystical manifestations.

To demonstrate briefly one of the critical differences between the normative tradition and the mystical tradition, I shall compare the beginning of the foundational text of the Jewish religious tradition, the book of Genesis, with the opening of *Sefer yetsirah*, one of the principal works of the mystical tradition, whose time of composition is disputed, but which is generally accepted to be from late antiquity.[84]

In the beginning God created the heavens and the earth. The earth was without form and void, and darkness was on the face of the deep. And the spirit of God was hovering over the face of the water. (Genesis 1: 1)

In thirty-two wondrous paths of wisdom engraved YH the Lord of Hosts, God of Israel, the Living God, El Shadai, high and exalted, dwelling all the way to the heights, whose name is holy, and He created His world through three books (*sefarim*) through *sefer* (book) and *sefar/sefor* (number) and *sipur* (story).[85] Ten *sefirot* of infinite nothing-

---

[83] *Sefer harazim*, trans. Morgan, 91.

[84] On the *Sefer yetsirah* see Liebes, *Creation Doctrine*; Gruenwald, 'A Preliminary Critical Edition of Sefer Yezira'; Dan, 'Religious Significance of *Sefer Yetsirah*'; Dan, *On Holiness*. See Bialik, 'Language Closing and Disclosing', which is inspired by the *Sefer yetsirah*.

[85] The Hebrew root *s.p.r* or *s.f.r* is found in many words associated with the sacred tradition in general and the mystical tradition in particular. It is the core of the Hebrew words rendering books,

ness and twenty-two principal letters . . . ten *sefirot* of infinite nothingness, ten and not nine, ten and not eleven. Understand in wisdom and search with understanding. Analyse with them and search from them. Know and contemplate and create and establish things on its entirety [truth] and restore the Creator to His place. Because He creates and crafts by Himself and there is no one else. And its measures are ten and they have no end. Ten *sefirot* of nothingness. Stop your heart from contemplating and stop your mouth from talking, and if your heart runs, return to the place, about which it was said, 'And the living creatures ran back and forth.' And because of this, the covenant was enacted: ten *sefirot* of infinite nothingness. Its end is connected to its beginning and its beginning to its end as the fire is connected to the burning coal. Know and think and create: the Master is one, and the Creator is one, and no one else is comparable with Him, and in front of the One what are you counting? Ten *sefirot* of infinite nothingness. Their measure is ten, and they have no end. Depth of a beginning and depth of an end; depth of good and depth of evil; depth of the top and depth of the bottom; the depth of east and the depth of west; the depth of north and the depth of south. And only one Master, Lord faithful King, ruling over all from His sacred dwelling-place for all eternity. (*Sefer yetsirah*, 1–6)

In contrast to the Book of Genesis, which ascribes the creation to God alone and briefly describes in precise, simple language an active aspect of the creation from an earthly point of view, the mystical text of *Sefer yetsirah* describes in an unprecedently elevated language a new conceptual world that includes unknown aspects of the hidden being. In spite of its strangeness, multiple layers, and lack of clarity, the book establishes new orders of being next to unknown categories of time and space, and incorporates the human being into the creation to a much greater extent. The anonymous writer addresses the reader in the second person, decodes the elements of the divine, ongoing creation for him, instructs him in basic abstract concepts shared by God and man—letters, numbers, spheres, wisdom, books, depths—that have a creative power and mediate between the creator and the creation, and points out enigmatic concepts such as 'wondrous paths of wisdom' or 'infinite nothingness', 'depth of beginning', 'fire connected to the burning coal', 'ten *sefirot* of infinite nothingness', 'sacred dwelling place for all eternity' that stimulate the imagination and establish an unknown reality. The human being does not merely listen obediently to the story of creation, which took place somewhere in mythological time beyond the limits of his understanding. Rather, he is called upon simultaneously to analyse, imagine, consider, know, create, and think in the presence of the depth of the infinite, to be acquainted with the limits of human knowledge in the presence of the divine creation, and to stop his heart from thinking in the presence of a new perspective of the infinite Being.

Mysticism is twofold. On the one hand, it refuses to be contented with the immutable revealed world and it negates the exclusiveness of a single interpretation.

author, spheres, numbers, sapphire, counting, recounting, narrative, and other words associated with the world of the *sefirot*.

On the other hand, it recognizes this place (*olam*), time (*shanah*), spirit (*nefesh*), using the language of *Sefer yetsirah*, and the infinity of the Being that is experienced and that exists beyond the limits of time and space and is reflected in the depth of spirit and language. This refusal and negation stem from the conviction that a hidden reality exists beyond the one that is revealed. The recognition of this hidden reality relates to the secret that lies beyond common sense, and stems from consciousness of the infinitude of the divine being, the human mind and imagination, and the creativity of language, all of which transcend time and space. This infinitude, ascribed to God and human beings alike, opens up the possibility of a creation that renews itself and of a freedom of thought and imagination beyond the limits of ordinary human experience.[86] It also opens up the possibility of a contingent and changing vision of supposedly immutable aspects of the traditional world, with its stable constraints and fixed borders.

The mystical path leads to an experience that cannot always be expressed in words because it happens beyond the limits of language, in a place where a human being seeks to experience the presence of God directly. The domain in which the experience takes place in 'the other reality' is often described in negative terms as an unachievable depth, as null and void, as nothingness and infinity, or 'as something the mouth cannot utter and the ear cannot hear'.[87] This domain is also described as the domain of 'turning the self into nothingness', as the domain of 'nullification of being': 'My flesh crawled and my heart melted and I was annihilated from being and I was as if I were not . . . because my soul left me because of the power of the song.'[88] This domain is described as a reality that is 'beyond reason and knowledge', beyond the abyss of nothingness, or as a being that represents the unity of paradoxical opposites, which is beyond the means of expression. In spite of all this, mysticism is in no way only an experience beyond expression or an experience based on the denial of reality; it is also a variegated system of symbolic and metaphoric abstract thought patterns, fundamental poetic images, complex doctrines, systematic conceptions, personal descriptions, penetrating insights, practical guidance, instructive concepts juxtaposed with obscure expressions, imaginary pictures, and allusive sketches—all of which are related to the hidden domain of the 'other reality'. These expressions are based on decoding and encoding in relation to common sense and on deepening and renewing tradi-

[86] An example of such transcendence of borders can be found in the mystical tradition concerning Enoch son of Jared, of whom Genesis says 'and he was no more, for God had taken him' (Gen. 5: 24). This verse was expounded many times in the mystical literature because it pertains to a human being who passed from the earthly realm to the heavenly domain. In the 16th c. Rabbi Joseph Karo, who yearned for such a transformation, wrote in his diary: 'The Holy One Blessed be He, elevated him from this world . . . and he became a fire amidst the torches of fire. Hence Metatron [= Enoch] was transformed from flesh into fire, which is the meaning of "and he was no more, for God had taken him".' Joseph Karo, *Magid meisharim* (1960), 42.

[87] See Israel Ba'al Shem Tov, *Igeret hakodesh* (The Holy Epistle) (1781), 255.

[88] Agnon, 'Hasiman', 312.

tional religious thought, and they are carried out, whether consciously or unconsciously, by mystical metamorphoses, visions and illuminations, creative commentary, and deep study which deciphers hidden meaning in the sacred texts. This system tries to connect divine and human wisdom, thought, and knowledge (Exod. 31: 3)—Hokhmah, Binah, and Da'at[89]—with whatever exists 'beyond reason and knowledge', and strives to give complex linguistic and experiential expression to the hidden and revealed aspects of the relations among divinity, man, and the world.

The inner experiential dimension, which refers to the intensive experience of the supreme religious reality beyond the usual realm of expression, caused mysticism to be identified with the irrational basis of religion.[90] Indeed, many mystics tried to penetrate to the heart of spirituality, which is 'beyond reason and knowledge' and beyond the limits of perceptible reality. At the same time, once the mystic's experience, whether his spirit, his dream, his vision, or his study, was written or delivered orally, it moved from the individual to the community. The mere fact of putting a spiritual experience into words required a change of context and meaning, divesting the experience of its irrational and wordless traits. Indeed, large segments of the mystical corpus are literary creations in a variety of styles. They may be mythopoetic, metaphoric, and symbolic, or systematic, in the style of the reasons for the commandments. Some are in an autobiographical visionary mode or in a midrashic exegetical mode. In some the language of narrative unfolds at length or as a fragmented vision, in others as a mystical unintelligible language of magic or the suggestive language of mystical revelation, or as poetical inspiration expressed in a language that conveys a variegated system of inner experiences of a superior reality and the relations between it and physical reality. This spiritual reality moves from the hidden to the revealed when formulated in words through the mystic's spirit and imagination and becomes a sacred source of inspiration for his listeners and readers.

When evaluating the meaning and place of mysticism in the religious corpus, one should consider that each culture is linked to at least two worlds: (i) the 'real' external world of the public domain, fixed within clear limits of rules and norms, laws, and customs, and (ii) the imaginary inner world of the private domain, formulated in the unclear realm of thought, dream, memory, imagination, hallucination, poetry, mystery, and vision. We learn about the real world by means of sensory perception, a value system that is conveyed by society, patterns of authority accepted in the public domain, long-standing tradition, the common language,

---

[89] These concepts refer to the names of the divine spheres, which are human properties or virtues and divine attributes at the same time. The literal translation of these concepts is wisdom, thought, and knowledge, but in the Scriptures they describe the virtues of God and man alike and in mysticism they are the names of three of the ten spheres, *sefirot*.

[90] On the irrational element in religious thought see Dodds, *Greeks and the Irrational*; on the hasidic mystical irrational tradition defined as 'beyond mind and reason' see Elior, *Paradoxical Ascent*, and Mark, *Mysticism and Madness*.

and social conventions and cultural norms that bridge past and present and shape the dominant world-view and its expectations within set limits. In the world of the imagination, where there are no limits, one learns from the depths of the soul, dream and hallucination, the mysteries of the language, the symbols of the tradition and their implications, as well as from the realm of contemplation and vision and from the haziness of legend, literature, art, and ritual. In addition, the spiritual breakthroughs that occur in moments of crisis and distress are sources of inspiration as well as insights that are revealed in one's spirit in the presence of the great beauty of the radiance of the mysterious hidden world. These two worlds are not frozen in place, but are constantly renewed and changed as a result of the passage of time and the progress of history. The real world changes by virtue of social and political events, legal and economic developments, and changes in science, technology, art, and culture, which take place in the public domain, influence the world of practical affairs, and reshape the norms that define reality. But the imaginary world is recreated by virtue of the vision that takes place in the private domain through observation of the depths of the psyche, the influence of symbols, myths, rituals, mystical illuminations, legends, and poems, and new ideas, mental images, prognostications, unexpected experiences, meditations and dreams, pain and madness, intellectual breakdown, spiritual exaltation, criticism and conspiracy, hopes and yearnings—all of which influence the world of thought and its patterns of meaning. This system of thought, anchored in tradition and myth, religion and music, language and literature, and unique human experience of the immediate presence of the divine and the beauty and mystery of nature, is reinvented and revitalized in the creative imagination, engraved in the thought of different historical periods, and nurtures inspiration and creativity. It also, consciously or unconsciously, upsets existing norms and undermines the foundations of reality.

TWO

The Infinity of Meaning Embedded in the Sacred Text

Open my eyes, that I may perceive the wonders of your teaching.

PSALM 119: 18

JEWISH MYSTICISM developed within a traditional religious world that placed its collected holy scriptures at the focal point.[1] The Torah was seen as evidence of the direct bond that existed at one time between God and the people of Israel. It was understood also as the written expression of the divine word, with unshakable authority and timeless validity. The creators of mystical literature that emerged in a culture that put a sacred text at its centre illuminated the Torah with a timeless mystical-mythical light.[2] They experienced the power of the permanent presence of God in Scripture and searched for the infinitude of the divine word in the written text. The words of Moses ben Nahman (Nahmanides/ Ramban), in the preface to his thirteenth-century commentary on the Torah, cogently illustrate this mystical-mythical position, which releases the Torah from concrete reality and anchors it beyond the limits of time and space:

Moses our teacher transcribed this book together with the whole Torah from the mouth of the Holy One, blessed be He . . . and the reason to write the Torah in this language was that it preceded the creation of the world and, it goes without saying, the birth of Moses our teacher, as has been passed down to us that it was written in black fire on white fire.[3]

His comment was based on the legend that describes the heavenly origin of the Torah and its concealed essence:

The Torah that the Holy One, blessed be He, gave Moses was given to him in the form of white fire engraved within black fire, which is fire mixed within fire, quarried from fire and given by fire, as it is written, *the fire of law is on his right.*[4]

---

[1] On the consolidation of the sacred biblical canon see Haran, *Biblical Collection.*

[2] On the mystical and mythical nature of the Torah see Scholem, 'Meaning of the Torah'; Heschel, *Theology of Ancient Judaism.*

[3] Nahmanides, *Perush al hatorah,* Introduction.　　　　　　　　　　　　　[4] JT *Shek.* 6: 1.

He expressed the enigmatic dimension of the text by another identification of God with the Torah: 'We have received a true kabbalah [tradition] that the entire Torah consists of Names of the Holy One, blessed be He—for the words can be divided into various Names.'[5]

A different mystical perception of the origin of the divine word and its framework in regard to the sacred divisions of time is introduced at the beginning of the Book of Jubilees, written in the middle of the second century BCE:

This is the account of the Division of Days of the Law and the Testimony for annual Observance according to their weeks (of years) and their Jubilees throughout all the years of the world just as the Lord told it to Moses on Mount Sinai when he went up to receive the tablets of the Law and the Commandment by the word of the Lord, as he said to him 'Come up to the top of the mountain' (Exod. 24: 12). . . . And Moses went up to the mountain of the Lord. And the glory of the Lord dwelt upon Mount Sinai, and a cloud overshadowed it for six days. And he called to Moses on the seventh day from the midst of the cloud. And the appearance of the glory of the Lord was like fire burning on top of the mountain. And Moses was on the mountain forty days and forty nights.[6]

The sacred relationship between the hidden divine source and the revealed text set the mystical tradition's point of departure and consisted of three elements: (i) a perpetual search for the hidden essence of the revealed text; (ii) an intense attentiveness to the divine word embedded in the sanctified version and suggested in its different layers; and (iii) the deciphering of the divine meaning of the literal text transmitted in the holy language and connected to higher worlds. The perpetual search for the hidden meaning takes place within the soul of the mystic, who reads the revealed and hidden versions at the same time, endorsing the contention of the Zohar (Book of Splendour): 'And the Torah is the Holy One, blessed be He' (Zohar I. 24*a*).

One way to analyse the mystical tradition is to focus on the dialectic between the rigid framework of the canonical text and the flexible contents and ever-changing meanings discovered by readers of different periods in a text that has eternal validity and embodies infinite meanings. In most of its historical manifestations, Jewish mysticism develops by means of a complex link to both the canonical text and its open, flexible reading. This link is based on six first principles of the mystical tradition's conception of the essence of the Torah:

1. 'The Torah was given from heaven.' The Torah is eternal and infinite because it embodies the divine word, comprising its creative power and its unchangeable validity, which transcends time and space. In the minds of the creators of mystical thought, the Torah, by its nature as the written crystallization of divine revelation, transcends the limitations and constraints that characterize human creation, and serves as an eternal bridge between heaven and earth. Moses Cordovero

---

[5] Nahmanides, *Perush al hatorah*, Introduction. See also *Kitvei rabenu mosheh ben naḥman*, i. 167.

[6] Trans. O. S. Wintermute, in *Old Testament Pseudepigrapha*, ed. Charlesworth, 52.

expressed this idea in the sixteenth century: 'The Torah and the souls and the *sefirot* are all one thing.'[7]

2. 'The Torah has seventy faces.' The Torah, as the word of the Eternal God, contains infinite layers of meaning and is open to countless interpretations. Thus the Torah is not limited to one interpretation in the domain of creative thought or in the domains of belief and opinion.[8] The different facets of the Torah and its hidden meanings are exposed over the generations by a multitude of readings, deepening the meaning of the *midrash* that says 'as a hammer explodes a rock into many fragments, every word of God, blessed be He, is divided into seventy languages'.[9]

3. 'Your word, O God, stands eternally in heaven.' The Torah exists simultaneously in heaven and on earth, and constitutes the two-way bridge between the heavenly word of God and its earthly manifestation. In the same way that the Torah contracts the infinite into the finite (the message of God contracts into words), it allows the expansion from the finite to the infinite—from the concrete word to the abstract conception, from human speech in its earthly manifestations to divine, infinite speech in its concealed manifestations. The mystical tradition ascribes to the Torah a cosmic and eternal character. Just as the timeless laws of nature are suggested to us through the partial manifestation that we perceive, the holy text is only a partial expression of the infinite power continually revealed to human consciousness. The Torah, existing in heaven and on earth, is anchored in the divine word that is revealed and concealed in many layers of being. The Torah's Janus-faced existence, as revealed and concealed, allows the deciphering of its meaning and the use of its letters to form a magical and mystical bridge between earthly reality and its heavenly source.

4. 'The holy language'. The Hebrew language, in which the Torah is written, embodies the word of God and his creative power and is regarded as a sacred language.[10] It transcends syntax and human communicative purposes and has been intended from the beginning as a continuous link between heaven and earth. The mystical trend within Judaism is unique in its attitude to the Hebrew language—to its letters and their combinations, its vowel system and tropes, the shapes of its letters and their sounds. The reason is that the language is regarded as the key to decoding the secrets of the Creator and the creation, and, further, as the means to influence higher worlds. The creative power of the language serves as a

---

[7] Cordovero, *Or yakar* (Glorious Light), on *Zohar ḥadash* Song of Songs, 17 (Jerusalem, 1989), quoted in Zak, *In the Gates*, 103.

[8] On the issue of a fixed permanent version vs. a constantly changing meaning expressed as 'seventy dimensions of the literal version of the Torah' see Scholem, 'Meaning of the Torah'; Bialik, 'Language Closing and Disclosing'; 'Halakhah ve'agadah' in Bialik, *Collected Works*; Dan, *On Holiness*; Idel, *Absorbing Perfections*.   [9] BT *Shab.* 88*b*.

[10] On the divine speech see R. Shneur Zalman of Lyady, *Tanya* and *Sha'ar hayiḥud veha'emunah*.

fundamental assumption in different branches of the esoteric tradition.[11] This creative power is derived from the description of creation in Genesis, the midrashic tradition contending that the world was created in ten utterances, and the mystical tradition maintaining that the world was created by letters and numbers. In this literature we can find comprehensive discussions of the creative power of language, its capacity to be transformed in different worlds, and the complex meanings of names and letters in their hidden and perceptible manifestations. This power is not conceived of as the possession only of God, who creates His world with utterances and combinations of letters, but is ascribed also to the human being, who combines letters, builds worlds through language, and reveals within his mind new combinations of words and letters and new meanings.

5. 'Torah—because it shows the image of God'. The Torah is grasped in the mystical tradition through anthropomorphic images of the divinity and the system of commandments. Kabbalistic literature draws a three-way analogy among the body of God, pictured in the form of 613 parts of the upper *merkavah* (the chariot); the body of man, divided into 613 organs; and the body of the Torah, divided into 613 commandments in the upper and lower worlds.[12] This perspective provides a basis for mystical, magical, and theurgic conceptions, which serve as a bridge between the revealed and the hidden realities. In the middle of the sixteenth century Moses Cordovero concisely expressed the conclusion that follows from this analogy: 'Whoever fulfils the commandments of the Torah is like one who holds the ends of flaming threads of the uppermost Torah and by doing so moves the *sefirot*.'[13]

6. 'Arousal from below [human awakening]'. The Torah, entrusted to man, is part of God's essence and is identified with his attributes, thus bridging the gap between the human world and the divine world, for each one of its words refers simultaneously to an earthly and a heavenly attribute. In mystical thought divinity is conceived of as a multi-directional process that is in a reciprocal relationship with the Torah, the world, and man. Therefore, because religious activity is connected to the study of Torah and to the practice of commandments, it receives a new metaphysical meaning. The observance of the commandments of the Torah by man affects the system of divinity and is called 'arousal from below', that is to say, the awakening of the lower worlds causes a change in the upper worlds. A man who observes the commandments of the Torah in thought and action supports God in initiating the various processes in the divine world and establishes new reciprocal relationships between the human and the divine. This

---

[11] On the creative power of the holy language see *Sefer yetsirah* 1; Bialik, 'Language Closing and Disclosing'.

[12] On the threefold division of the 613 commandments see Tishby (ed.), *Wisdom of the Zohar*; Gottlieb, *Studies in Kabbalah Literature*; Cordovero, *Palm Tree of Deborah*, trans. Jacobs.

[13] *Pardes rimonim*, 12: 2.

starting point is called theurgy and concerns the influence of human actions on higher worlds.[14]

The mystical tradition is based on the assumption that the divine infinitude in space, time, thought, speech, and action is suggested in the Torah and is embodied and unfolded in language. A human being who studies the totality of revealed and hidden layers in the Torah, who interprets its duality and fulfils its explicit and implicit commandments, has various tools to reveal this dynamic infinity and to delve into many dimensions within his own consciousness. The blurring of the boundaries between the divine source of the Torah and its revealed existence is derived from the saying quoted by Rabbi Moses Hayim Luzzatto (1707–47), known as Ramhal: 'For the Holy One, blessed be He, and the Torah and Israel are one.'[15] This blurring of the abstract essence and the perceptible expression of the Torah transforms the finite text into an encoded revelation of the infinite divine will, which rules over all realms without limits. The relationship between the divine being and the holy text is not subject to the laws of nature, to human limitations, or to rational considerations, but is similar to the relationship between God and world, hidden and revealed, and implicit secrets and literal meanings. The fact that the revealed essence of the Torah is composed of letters and words that have meaning in the language of humans and are decipherable by the human mind, despite their divine source, transfigures the holy text into the pivotal meeting point of the finite and the infinite, or, in the language of the kabbalists, into 'a ladder placed on earth whose top reaches heaven'.

The kabbalistic tradition regards the holy text as an open semantic unit that does not attest to a fixed subject matter dictating a single truth. The understanding of the written formulation as possessing a literal meaning that is binding in the world of action but open to countless interpretations in the world of thought was formulated by Yokheved Bat-Miriam as follows: 'Beyond the distance—there is a second distance and a horizon in the innermost horizons.'[16] This idea is unique to Jewish mysticism and epitomizes the freedom embodied in the infinite meanings of the divine word. The concealed divine intention in the holy text is open to a variety of interpretations, without challenging its basic truth and its sanctified formulation.

Several features are inherent in the legitimacy of freedom of thought and the infinity of interpretation: the certainty of the infinite word of the sacred text, the acceptance of its cosmic and transcendent character that goes beyond a single meaning, and the resulting awareness that the mystics, who unveil new meanings, occupy themselves with uncovering an ancient metahistoric truth and with exposing meanings that were contained in this text from ancient days, yet not fully revealed and exhausted.

---

[14] On theurgy see Dodds, *Greeks and the Irrational*, 291–5.   [15] *Adir bamarom*, 61.
[16] See Bat-Miriam, *From Afar: Songs*, 187; 'the innermost' refers to the talmudic expression pertaining to the holy of holies (BT *Yoma* 61a).

The Jewish mystical tradition is unique in its conception of infinity. The infinitude of meaning embedded in the sacred text stems from its divine source. The infinitude of the divine being transcends the boundaries of time, place, and language simply because the essence of God is infinite. The infinitude of human thought and its creative power is reflected in the infinitude of language. The infinite possibilities of reading, interpreting, and rewriting latent in the Torah—through creative commentary, dreams and visions, angelic revelations, inspired hermeneutics, dismantling and reconstructing, metamorphosis, and the idiosyncratic reading of the hidden meanings embedded in the plain meaning of the text, including all its layers—are responsible for the varied manifestations of Jewish mysticism.

An example of a new reading of the sacred text under mystical inspiration is found in the correspondence describing the angelic revelations that were bestowed upon Rabbi Moses Hayim Luzzatto in his early years at the beginning of the eighteenth century in Padua:

There is here a young man, tender in years, no older than the age of twenty-three. He is a holy man, my master and teacher, the holy lamp, the man of God, his honor Rabbi Moses Hayim Luzzatto. For these past two and a half years a MAGID has been revealed to him, a holy and tremendous angel who reveals wondrous mysteries to him . . . He is a spark of Akiva ben Joseph. Eight months have passed since the time that the holy and tremendous angel was first revealed to him. He delivered to him numerous mysteries and imparted the methods by which he could summon to him the members of the heavenly Academy. With the approval of the Holy One, blessed be He, and His Shekhinah, he ordered him to compose a Book of the Zohar, called in heaven the second Zohar, in order that a great *tikkun* known to us should be carried out. This is what happens. The angel speaks out of his mouth but we, his disciples, hear nothing. The angel begins to reveal to him great mysteries. Then my master orders Elijah to come to him and he comes to impart mysteries of his own. Sometimes, Metatron, the great prince, also comes to him as well as the Faithful Shepherd, the patriarch Abraham . . . and sometimes king Messiah and Adam. He has already composed a marvelous and tremendous work on the book of Ecclesiastes. Now he has been ordered to compose seventy *tikkunim* on the last verse of the Torah . . . He has also composed three works on the Torah, all three . . . in accordance with the great mystery and in the language of the Zohar.

The writer of the letter, Jakuthiel Gordon, son of Rabbi Leib of Vilna, a student of medicine at the University of Padua, reported Luzzatto's claim to be a recipient of a *magid* from heaven to Rabbi Mordecai Joffe of Vienna. All the books mentioned in the letter are known to us today and have been published.[17]

The dialectical relation between the infinitude of hidden meaning in writing and the finite revelation reflected in the literal version is contained in the kabbalis-

---

[17] On the letter and its consequences see Jacobs, *Jewish Mystical Testimonies*, 136–8. Cf. Tishby (ed.), *Wisdom of the Zohar*, iii, and Ginzburg, *R. Moses Hayim Luzzatto*.

tic concepts of *ayin* and *yesh*. The principle of material finitude, which relates to the contracting and revealing element, called in the kabbalistic language garment, letters, or *yesh*, stands in contrast to the principle of divine infinitude, which relates to the emanating, expanding, and concealing element called essence, thought, or *ayin*. All defined being must clothe itself in a garment. This garment is defined by and derived from the plane of reality in which it exists or to which it passes. The divine infinitude, in which there is a dimension of chaos, infinite abundance, absolute control, expansion without boundary or contraction, limitless spirit, *tohu* (which reflects the void of the cosmos prior to creation), and abyss (the bottomless dimension of creation), clothes itself in the same world that enwraps or 'conceals' it. The kabbalists, who interpret *olam* (world) to come from the same root as *he'elem* (concealment), say: 'The concealment is the cause of the revelation and the revelation is within the cause of the concealment.'[18] The infinite expansion of the divine spirit clothes itself in matter, which determines its shape, limits the infinite depths of the *tohu*, and confines the emanating and expanding chaos. As the kabbalists have written: 'All creation is a harsh limitation [i.e. judgement].'[19] That is to say, divinity is understood as a process in which the infinite divine essence constantly transforms the limitless into the limited, *tohu* into creation, hidden revelation into revealed concealment, thought into speech, and abstract spirit into material substance.[20]

This two-way process takes place continuously from the *ayin* to the *yesh* and from the *yesh* to the *ayin*: every limited element strives to expand, to divest itself of corporeality, and to return to its abstract source, and every abstract element strives to contract, to clothe itself, and to be revealed in its limited expression. Borrowing from Ezekiel's vision, this two-way movement is referred to as 'the living creatures running back and forth'. The kabbalists, however, revocalized and reinterpreted the word *ḥayot* (living creatures) as *ḥayut*, 'divine vitality'. As human thought clothes itself in the speech that reveals it, so the infinite divine thought clothes itself in the divine word of the Torah. The divine speech is reflected in the concealed Torah, which clothes itself in the revealed Torah, in the literal written meaning, in letters and words. In the same manner that the abstract clothes itself in the perceptible, so also measureless eternity clothes itself in a fixed time, and eternal, indivisible, infinite essences clothe themselves in defined, finite, and divisible units—the *ayin* clothes itself in the *yesh*.[21]

In the other direction the garments and the concealments are removed; the *yesh* returns to the *ayin* and the finite returns to the infinite. In the mystical tradition

[18] Cordovero, *Pardes rimonim* (1592), F. 30 A.

[19] See Ben-Shelomoh, *Theology of Moses Cordovero*, 231; Zak, *In the Gates*.

[20] On concealment as the precondition of revelation, see Ben-Shelomoh, *Theology of Moses Cordovero*, 95; Zak, *In the Gates*, index under *he'elem vekisui*.

[21] On 'being' (*yesh*) and 'nothingness' (*ayin*) see Elior, 'Paradigms of *Yesh* and *Ayin* in Hasidic Thought'; Elior, *Paradoxical Ascent*; Green, *Tormented Master*; Matt, 'Ayin: The Concept of Nothingness in Jewish Mysticism'.

the reciprocal relations between the concealing infinitude and the revealing finitude, between the veiled essence that emanates without cessation and the revealed garment that limits and demarcates domains, are dialectical, conditioned relations.[22] The essence and vitality of the *yesh* are contingent on the *ayin*, while the determinate revelation of the *ayin* is contingent on the *yesh*.

The multifaceted sacred text is understood as a perceptible garment for the abstract divine essence. The written revelation is considered to embody a mysterious divine dimension; the letters are perceived as the material aspect of the spiritual power that is beyond perception or as delimited vessels or containers, holding the infinite divine light. The essence of the text is like a hologram that reflects the 'vitality running back and forth' or the two directions of concealing and revealing, in which each part contains in miniature the complete whole including its processes and opposites. This has been described poetically by Israel Ba'al Shem Tov (the Besht) in *Igeret hakodesh*: 'In each and every letter there are worlds and souls and divinity, and they ascend and unite and unify one with the other. Afterwards the letters join and unify and become a word.'[23] The words or the arks—in Hebrew *tevah* means both 'word' and 'ark'—are understood as dual entities that conceal behind their revealed being a hidden essence suggested by 'lower, second, and third [decks]'. The mystical tradition stipulates that one should decipher the apparent physical meaning of the words and expose their real divine essence to open a window to their hidden existence, or illuminate their essence, which is hiding behind the words in the sense of 'An opening for light shalt thou make for the ark':

Rabbi Israel Ba'al Shem Tov said: 'An opening for light shalt thou make for the ark [word]' . . . teaches that in each and every letter there are worlds and souls and divinity, and they ascend and unite and unify one with the other and with divinity. Then they unify and join together and the letters become a word and they unite completely with the divinity. And one should unite one's soul with every aforementioned attribute, to make all the worlds unify, ascend, and transform into a great happiness and felicity. That is what the lower, second, and third storeys mean—worlds, souls, and divinity.[24]

In the words of the Besht, the opening of Noah's Ark becomes a beacon, or portal, of light that brightens, or adds lustre, and illuminates the verbal ark (word), revealing through its finite written representation its infinite meanings such as 'worlds, souls, and divinity'.

The connections between the literal biblical text existing in the revealed domain and its infinite essence and flexible meaning existing in the hidden realm, i.e. 'the ark' (the physical word in its final form) and 'the opening' (the divine

---

[22] On the divine infinity as the enlivening force of the finite, and on the finite as the condition of the revelation of the infinite, see Elior, *Paradoxical Ascent*.

[23] On the 'Holy Epistle' see *Shivḥei habesht*, facs., ed. Mondshine, 229–42; translation and discussion in Jacobs, *Jewish Mystical Testimonies*, 148–53. See also Rosman, *Founder of Hasidism*, 99–113.

[24] *Tsava'at harivash*, §75, p. 12; trans. Schochet.

reflection), are expressed in various ways. There are kabbalists who see in each letter an opening to higher worlds; there are those who see in each word a hint or suggestion of the world of the *sefirot*; and there are those who take further liberties in decoding and exposing the hidden meaning of the revealed text. The treatment of the plain meaning of the text is transformative, trying to free the literal meaning of its literality, the singular meaning of its singularity, and to reconstruct it in new combinations that reveal its multiple meanings. The essence of the freedom of deconstruction and reconstruction is expressed in the words of a hasidic kabbalist of the eighteenth century, Ze'ev Wolf of Zhitomir, author of *Or hame'ir* (Shining Light):

Because in truth the Torah in its entirety is only letters and every member of Israel, according to his understanding and merit, makes combinations out of the individual letters, and these combinations that were done now anew by the merit of his actions and the depth of his understanding were also potentially in the letters from the beginning. . . . The enlightened one needs to strip them [the letters] of their physical traits and to clothe them in spirituality, which is the same as making holy combinations . . . because in truth this is the essence of His pleasure, blessed be He, when they also raise letters of the Torah from the lower levels to be stripped of their physical form and clothed in a spiritual form . . . And everywhere that one sees and hears even one utterance from one person to another about issues of physicality and takes from there a hint of the wisdom and strips it of its physical form and makes holy combinations to connect his soul with the heights of His divinity, blessed be He, and transforms the combination of the physical to make out of these letters combinations of love or fear of God . . . this [transformative effort] needs the help of God to establish his thoughts, to know how to strip off the physical shape and to clothe it with spiritual form in holy combinations.[25]

According to the mystical conception nothing has a singular precise meaning, a simple appearance, or a fixed content. Instead, every element in the text, in the language, or in reality is constructed from materials that can be deconstructed, as well as from combinations containing many secrets that are suggested in the plain meaning of the text (*peshat*) and are decoded within the spirit of the reader. The human being, who strips the simple meaning of its univocality and clothes it in new combinations, participates in the divine dialectic process of wrapping and unwrapping, becoming and erasing, creating and annihilating, constructing, forming, and decoding, revealing and concealing: 'And the righteous one, by virtue of his understanding, strips it [the Torah] from its wrapping in fables and dresses it in a form of spirituality, of heavenly lights and supreme secrets made from the holy names that are suggested in these stories.'[26]

The dynamic treatment of the sacred text stems from the assumption that beyond the explicit meaning an implicit secret is hidden, and beyond the narrative layer (the enwrapping in fables) a divine layer is concealed (holy names). Exposure

---

[25] *Or hame'ir*, 'Vayeḥi', p. 38*b*; 'Vayishlaḥ', p. 25*a*; 'Mikets', p. 34*b*.   [26] 'Mikets', ibid.

of the divine meaning takes place within the human mind. The reader divests the tangible and enwraps the abstract with vestments, taking apart the known text and reconstructing it within his spirit in a 'form of spirituality, of heavenly lights and supreme mysteries'. No mystic or kabbalist is content with the literal meaning of the text or with its legal content. Some decipher in their dreams the secret, divine entities that are suggested beyond the plain text, as Luzzatto testified in his letter to the master of his teacher, R. Binyamin Hakohen, the elder of the Italian kabbalists:

When I awoke, I heard a voice saying: 'I have descended in order to reveal the hidden secrets of the Holy King'. For a while I stood there trembling but then I took hold of myself. The voice did not cease from speaking and imparted a particular secret to me . . . one day he revealed to me that he was a *magid* sent from heaven.[27]

Some turn the text into a mystical, ascending ladder leading from the revealed to the concealed, as the questions of Jacob of Marvège (12th–13th century) addressed to heavenly mentors and collected in his book *She'elot uteshuvot min hashamayim* (Responsa from Heaven) indicate. He wrote down the answers that were revealed to him in dreams:

I asked another question: is it permitted to make theurgic use of the holy name of forty-two letters (see BT *Kid.* 71a), to conjure the holy angels appointed over the Torah, to make a man wise in all that he studies and never forget his learning? And is it permitted to conjure by means of the names of the angels appointed over wealth and victory over enemies . . . or is it forbidden to make theurgic use of the name for any of these purposes? They replied: 'Holy, holy, holy is the name of the Lord of Hosts. He alone will satisfy all your needs.'[28]

Some use the text as a mystical, magical language that decodes the secret of the unified divine vitality embedded in the separate facets of revealed reality, and some deconstruct and reconstruct the literal revealed text. The essential duality of being, which establishes the mystical starting point, is reflected in the relationship between the hidden and the revealed, the plain meaning and the secret. The words of the fourteenth-century Italian kabbalist Menahem of Recanati well attest to this:

All the lower things depend on the higher things . . . [A]nd from the lower world we understand the secret of the order of the higher world and everything that exists in all creatures is like the pattern of the ten *sefirot* of nothingness . . . [A]nd these ten *sefirot* are called attributes of the Holy One, blessed be He, as a flame is connected to the embers from which it emanates, and through them the world was created . . . [A]s it is known to the sages of the kabbalah.[29]

Among the esotericists who decode the hidden within the revealed two approaches are found: moderate and radical. In the moderate outlook the lower

---

[27] Jacobs, *Jewish Mystical Testimonies*, 143.   [28] Ibid. 77.
[29] *Ta'amei hamitsvot*, Introduction.

world reflects the higher world in a complex way and the biblical text in general is understood as a reflection of the relations between the revealed and the concealed, which are compared to the relation between body and soul or husk and fruit.[30] Another version compares the sacred text to a nut whose shell is apparent on the outside and whose essence is hidden: 'As a nut has a shell on the outside and marrow within, so also words of Torah have action, commentary, legend, and secret and all is one within another.'[31] The biblical story embodied in the written plain meaning is only one reading out of the totality of possible readings that refer to the upper worlds. This idea is beautifully expressed by the image of the Torah as black fire upon white fire, interpreted by Nahmanides in the Introduction to his commentary on the Torah as meaning that the whole revealed Torah (black fire) incorporates the literal level along with the written expression of the hidden name of God (white fire).

More radical kabbalistic works deconstruct the essentially dual meaning of the revealed and concealed facets of reality. They juxtapose its parts and establish the hidden 'doctrine of the tree of life' in contrast to the revealed 'doctrine of the tree of knowledge'.[32] Some describe the Torah in the present as 'the doctrine of the age of law [judgement]' characterized by commandments and laws and numerous strictures. This is juxtaposed with 'the doctrine of the age of mercy' which will be adopted in the future and in which there are no commandments or judgement, when all strictures will be abolished.[33] Some tell the story of creation in other worlds and in other languages in which the alphabet conveyed to us is reduced by a number of letters or enriched by an unknown letter. That a letter might be added or subtracted from the written version is a change that will overturn the biblical plain text, as has been said by the author of the exegesis of the fourteenth-century *Sefer hatemunah*: 'And there is a Torah in one additional letter missing now.'[34] This author presents very interesting ideas about the relativity of the plain meaning while he tells the story of the end of time as a story of the contraction of the letters of the language: 'The world is filled with great and beautiful trees illuminating like fragrant wood and cedar trees, and everything is like the deed of paradise and holy creatures are always singing endlessly, and they are pure and brilliant. . . . and it has . . . seven letters only. There will be one Torah with one additional letter that is missing at present.'[35]

---

[30] On *kelipah uferi* (fruit and shell) see Tishby (ed.), *Wisdom of the Zohar*; Tishby, *Doctrine of Evil*.

[31] *Zohar ḥadash*, Ruth, 83a.

[32] *Ra'aya mehemna*. On the doctrine of the 'tree of life' and 'tree of knowledge' see Scholem, *Major Trends*, 180; Scholem, 'Meaning of the Torah'; Scholem, 'Redemption through Sin'; Elior, 'Messianic Expectations'.

[33] *Sefer hatemunah* (1892), 41a; cf. Tishby (ed.), *Wisdom of the Zohar*, ß2, Divine Service, Tree of Life, and Tree of Knowledge, pp. 387–94 (Hebrew text).

[34] *Sefer hatemunah* (1892), 42b.

[35] Ibid. On *torat hashemitot* (the sevenfold cycles theory) see Scholem, *Kabbalah of Sefer hatemunah*; Scholem, *Origins of the Kabbalah*, 460–75; *Galya raza*, ed. Elior.

These and similar ideas concerning the relativity of plain meaning are summarized by the author of *Or hame'ir*: 'There is no doubt that there is no word in the Torah that does not hide wonderful awesome secrets.'[36] This suggests, therefore, that beyond the traditional position, which sanctified the plain meaning of the text, there were currents of thought that sought to liberate the text from its single meaning by reading within it a great many other possibilities. In other words, the search for 'hidden awesome secrets' displays a sceptical, critical, and subversive attitude towards reality.

In the kabbalistic tradition, the many-layered essence of the Torah, its revealed and hidden aspects, and its simultaneous existence in the upper and lower worlds, led to a complex use of letters and names. On the one hand, one reads the sacred text and uses letters and names in order to create a passage from the earthly to the heavenly, from the *yesh* to the *ayin*, in order to 'initiate emanation' of divine abundance and to influence the upper worlds. On the other hand, one does this in order to create a passage from the heavenly to the earthly, from the *ayin* to the *yesh*, to 'receive emanation' or divine effulgence and to influence the lower worlds. This process is tied to various chapters of the esoteric tradition, to 'descent to the chariot', 'bringing down the prince of the Torah', 'the use of names', 'drawing down of emanation', 'intentions', unifications, devotion, and 'the sparkling of letters and names' within the spirit of the kabbalist. There are those who identify these bi-directional intentions with mystical and magical activity and distinguish between the two, but strictly speaking distinguishing between these categories misses the deep relationship among the different uses of language that form a bridge between the divine and the human.

The first use is demonstrated in the writings of those kabbalists who infer from the double aspect of the sacred text and its relation to the upper worlds the need to obey commandments with devotion in this world for the sake of influencing, in hidden ways, the divine world: 'The kabbalist, while recalling these letters in his Torah or in his prayer below, shares and awakens the upper roots above', in the words of the sixteenth-century Safed kabbalist Elijah ben Moses de Vidas.[37]

The second use is demonstrated by the words of those kabbalists who prefer to focus on deconstructing the plain meaning of the biblical text and reconstructing it anew according to visionary inspiration. In the words of the thirteenth-century Abraham Abulafia, author of the *Ḥayei ha'olam haba*:

And begin to combine a few or many letters and overturn them and roll them rapidly until your heart becomes heated with their rolling . . . and you will understand from them new matters which you did not grasp in the human way and you did not know by yourself through logical study and already you are prepared to receive the divine

[36] Wolf, *Or hame'ir*, 177.   [37] *Reshit ḥokhmah*, 'Sha'ar hakedushah', ch. 10, §19.

abundance and the emanation emanates upon you . . . prepare your true thoughts to describe and picture the Name, may He be blessed, and His highest angels.[38]

The effort to reveal the hidden meaning of the literal text is linked to the promise of mystical exaltation, because exposure of the manifold facets of the Torah, in one of the many ways that the tradition offers, changes a human being from a 'passive' reader of the plain text into an 'active' listener to a mystery. This kind of active reading may create a metamorphosis in which a human being changes from being a reader of the univocal written version into being a listener to the multi-vocal word of the living God, which sometimes is 'engraved in his thought' and sometimes 'sparkles', 'illuminates', and 'speaks' within him. It seems that direct contact with the divine word and attachment to the upper worlds, for which the esoteric masters yearn and to which they attest, is simply a metamorphosis that takes place in the relations between the sacred text, holding the secret, and the decoding reader, who reinterprets the text and makes it speak in a new way in his imagination. Moses Hayim Luzzatto offers an illuminating exposition of the nature of the mystical study of the Torah:

Consider a coal that is not burning and the flame is hidden and closed inside. When someone blows upon it, then it spreads and flares and it continues to expand. Within this flame there are many different colors, which were not apparent initially; nevertheless, everything is coming from the coal.

So too with this Torah that is before us. Every one of her words and letters are like a coal. When one sets them out as they are, they appear like coals, somewhat dim. If an individual endeavors to study her, then from each letter a great flame bursts forth, filled with many colors. These are the data that are hidden in each letter. This was already explained in the Zohar concerning the alef beit. This is not an analogy, but literally something that is indeed essential, for all of the letters that we see in the Torah correspond to the twenty-two lights that exist above. These supernal lights shine on the letters. From here is derived the holiness of the Torah, the Torah scrolls, the tefillin, mezuzot and all sacred writings. According to the sanctity with which they were written, so too will grow the divine inspiration and illumination of these lights on the letters. Therefore a Torah scroll that has only one mistake is totally invalidated for there is not the appropriate illumination by reading from it, from which will flow sanctity to the nation.[39]

Blurring the boundaries between the plain and concealed meanings, or between the fixed written version from the past and the word heard anew in the present, characterizes mystical consciousness. It seems at times that cleaving, illumination, and exaltation are simply the direct contact between the reader who decodes the

[38] Quoted in Scholem, *Kabbalah of* Sefer hatemunah, 211. On the drawing down of divine abundance see Green, 'Typologies of Leadership and the Hasidic Zaddiq'; Elior, 'Between *Yesh* and *Ayin*'; Idel, *Hasidism*.

[39] Luzzatto, *Kuf-lamed-het pithei hokmah*; trans. Verman, *History and Varieties of Jewish Meditation*, 167. On the coal and the flame see *Sefer yetsirah* 1: 1.

mystery within the plain text and the hidden author of the revealed divine text whose voice is heard anew by the contemplative observer listening with his spirit. The use of letters and names to influence the upper worlds is connected to the ability of the kabbalist to illuminate letters and names with his spirit, a process connected to the dismantling of the boundaries of language and the boundaries of consciousness, which will be discussed below.

The esoteric master, who transcends the plain text and hears the infinite divine word, visualizes and inhabits the upper worlds, immersing himself in the study of names and spheres (*sefirot*), divine chariots (*merkavot*) and temples (*heikhalot*), cherubs and the Shekhinah, 'the orchard' (*pardes*), and 'the stature of God' (*shiur komah*), 'luminous spheres' (*tsaḥtsaḥot*) and 'sparks' (*nitsotsot*), 'fallow years' or eternal sevenfold cycles (*shemitot*), and 'countenances' (*partsufim*), and other creations of the mystical spirit. He may cross the boundaries of sensual reality and conventional consciousness, hear the divine voice that speaks in him beyond the plain written meaning and visualize the living revelation of concepts that express the hidden world.[40] He may even achieve the exaltation of imagination, the sparkling of letters or revelation of names, hearing the word of the Shekhinah, the conversation of angels and the words of heralds, and similar visionary revelations of the mystical language that is deconstructed and reconstructed anew.[41]

Many kabbalists and esotericists express interest in the hidden names of God, which are concealed in the sacred text and connected to the mystical and magical tradition.[42] The Torah is defined in their writings as a code of holy names that represent mutable divine forces. Many kabbalists and others focus on deciphering the symbolic meaning of esoteric midrashic traditions that were absorbed into the kabbalistic corpus, and the Torah is decoded in their works in relation to the world of the *sefirot*, a structured, symbolic representation of the hidden world.

The mutual relations between the Torah and the names of God in the mystical tradition are demonstrated by the words of the thirteenth-century Sephardi kabbalist Joseph Gikatilla in his book *Sha'arei orah*:

Since it was found that all the Torah in its entirety is woven from the appellations, and the appellations from the names, and the holy names, all of them, are contingent on the

---

[40] On hearing divine voices see Werblowsky, *Joseph Karo*; Aescoly, *Messianic Movements*; Elior, 'R. Joseph Karo'; Idel, 'Inquiries into the Doctrine of *Sefer hameshiv*'; Goldish (ed.), *Spirit Possession in Judaism*; *Jewish Mystical Autobiographies*, trans. Faierstein; Jacobs, *Jewish Mystical Testimonies*.

[41] On the mystical elevation and the hidden meaning of the literal dimension in different periods see Himmelfarb, *Ascent to Heaven*; Elior, *Three Temples*; Arbel, *Beholders of Divine Secrets* (in antiquity); Liebes, 'Messiah of the Zohar'; Idel, *Mystical Experience in Abraham Abulafia* (in medieval times). For the early modern period see Elior, 'R. Joseph Karo'; Fine, *Physician of the Soul*; Goldish, *Sabbatean Prophets*; Jacobs, *Jewish Mystical Testimonies*; *Jewish Mystical Autobiographies*, trans. Faierstein.

[42] On holy names see Urbach, *Sages*, ch. 7; Grözinger, 'Names of God'; Schäfer, *Hidden and Manifest God*; Idel, *Kabbalah: New Perspectives*; Gruenwald, 'Writing, Epistles, and the Name of God'; Elior, 'Mysticism, Magic and Angelology'; Lesses, *Ritual Practices*; Arbel, *Beholders of Divine Secrets*.

name of YHVH, and all of them are unified in Him, thus the whole Torah is found to be woven from the name of God . . .[43]

A different view, ascribing critical importance to the name of God, is articulated by Shemtov of Faro, the author of *Sefer hayihud*: 'Like a person drawing one thing with various colours, the Torah, from the beginning until it was seen by all Israel, is the form of the great and awesome name of God.'[44] A similar contention is found in the writing of Ramban: 'We have received a true tradition that the entire Torah consists of Names of the Holy One, blessed be He.'[45]

A different aspect of critical importance that arises from the mystical understanding of the Torah is concerned with the freedom of reading and interpretation. The assumption that an infinitude of meanings is concealed in the Torah in general, and in language in particular, by virtue of being the expression of God's infinitude, allows a person unlimited interpretative freedom, which expresses the infinitude of thought and the relativity of the concrete. The fundamental freedom that underlies Jewish mysticism is the freedom to read and interpret the different layers of meaning of the infinite text. This freedom allows one to retell the biblical story, create new worlds, fashion a renewed conception of divinity and a mutable conception of the human being, and offer an alternative reading of historical experience. This freedom offers limitless possibilities for interpretation in which the hidden illuminates the revealed and the mystic interprets common external experience according to a unique inner experience.

Included in mystical interpretation are the disclosures of hidden beings and paradoxical statements that broaden and intensify the meaning of human experience, because it seems that the words *sitrei torah* (the secrets of the Torah) may be interpreted as coming from *nistar* (hidden) as well as from *setirah* (paradox)— words that are formed of the same letters. The denial of common experience and immutable reality, on the one hand, and the exposure of the contradictions and secrets of both the divine creation and the human spirit, on the other, are reflected throughout the esoteric literature and express the freedom that is embedded in it.

The source of this position is the mystical conception that blurs distinctions and inverts existence when it forms God in the image of man and empowers man by ascribing to him a divine essence. The philosophical tradition distances man from God, points to their radical difference, and bases the relationship between them on negative attributes only. In contrast, the mystical tradition blurs the distinction between the human and the divine, draws them closer, and combines them in ties of flesh and soul, figure and imagination, symbol and myth, which weave into one the cosmic and the spiritual, the heavenly and the mundane. One of many examples of the contradictions that exist in the creation of higher worlds

---

[43] *Sha'arei orah*, Introduction.
[44] Quoted in Idel, 'Perception of the Torah', 63. Shem Tov (son of Jacob) of Faro wrote in the last decade of the 13th c.   [45] *Kitvei rabenu mosheh ben nahman* 1: 167.

in the image of the human is found in the words of Luria regarding the origins of the divine emanation:

And then ten *sefirot* were emanated in a direct manner in the image of a human being. And they are ten vessels in the likeness of a human being and in each vessel there is inwardness and outwardness . . . everything is done in a straightforward way in the image of a human being . . . It is clearly expounded that the ten *sefirot* are shaped as a person who has 248 limbs, known as vessels, and within them is contained the essence of the lights which is known as human soul. As the earthly person has body and soul, so the heavenly person is composed of ten *sefirot*, which are 'essence' and 'vessels'. The essence is concerned with inner lights that illuminate the vessels just as the soul illuminates the human body, as it is said: 'The life breath of a man is the lamp of the Lord.'[46]

The mystical relationship prevailing between the divine and the human is demonstrated in the enigmatic words of Akiva relating to the image of God, as quoted in *Heikhalot zutarti*. We see here the blurring of the separate domains, as differences and similarities become indistinct:

Rabbi Akiva said: it is as if He is like us, but He is greater than anything and that is his glory that is hidden from us . . . He himself is the glory that fills the world and everything in it. Like the sun and like the moon, and like the stars, like the face of a human, like the limbs of an eagle, like the claws of a lion, like the horns of a bull, the image of His face is like the image of the spirit and the form of the soul that no one can recognize, and His body like *tarshish* [ocean; precious stone], filling the whole world so that neither from nearby nor from afar can anyone see it. May His name be blessed for ever and ever.[47]

Sometimes it seems that in mystical thought each physical essence takes on a spiritual form, and each spiritual essence can be perceived by the senses, because mysticism unites situations and entities that essentially contradict each other when it mediates between the physical and the spiritual by means of visionary language. Incorporating angelic entities and heavenly mentors, who facilitate the visionary language and the new mystical insights into the spiritual life of the community, enabled the mystics to open new ways of reading and writing that transcended traditional conventions and challenged normative insights.

The language of the Zohar, which connects the upper world with the lower world in a daring anthropomorphic manner, demonstrates the expansion of the human horizon in a paradoxical way by ascribing physical form to the hidden world: 'We learnt that this world is in the image of the higher world, and everything that exists in this world exists in the higher world . . . follow what we have learnt: everything that the Holy One, blessed be He, did above and below, everything is within the mystery of male and female.'[48] Crossing borders between male

---

[46] Vital, *Ets ḥayim*, 25, 30.
[47] *Heikhalot zutarti*, ed. Elior, 25–6; *Synopse zur Hekhalot-Literatur*, ed. Schäfer et al., §356.
[48] Zohar II. 144: 1.

and female and between divine and human distinctions is introduced in various places in the mystical tradition. In a manuscript entitled R. Meshulam's Kabbalah or Kabbalah of R. Meshulam the Zadokite, written in the thirteenth century in Germany, we find the following tradition, reworking Ezekiel's vision and BT *Yoma* 54*a–b*:

Know, my sons, that *Hashmal* and *Arafel* (Ezek. 1) are two powers: male and female . . . Hashmal is the great cherub: sometimes it is transformed into a male and sometimes into a female. Accordingly, you will find in Ezekiel's prophecy both *ḥashmal* and *ḥash-malah*, which is the feminine. Concerning this word Moses said, 'the cherubs and the flaming sword that revolved' (Gen. 3: 24).[49]

In the sixteenth century the magid of R. Joseph Karo is described as the angel who is transformed from male into female,[50] following the description of the Shekhinah in the Zohar, where she is described as the redeeming angel who is transformed from male into female and vice versa (Zohar I. 232*a*, 'Vayeḥi').

The writings of the thirteenth-century Sephardi kabbalist Ezra of Gerona also contradict common experience and modify the human perspective: 'A human being is made out of all spiritual things . . . a human being is made out of all the things and his soul is coupled with the higher soul.'[51]

In contrast to the blurring of differences between the human and the divine, which gives the human being a new dimension, one can find statements in the kabbalistic and hasidic literature that nullify the human perspective. The Ba'al Shem Tov says: 'In juxtaposition to the higher world, the whole world is nothing but a mustard seed.'[52] And Shneur Zalman of Lyady writes: 'This world is nothingness and naught and all that we see is merely imaginary',[53] and elsewhere, 'All the worlds are an absolute lie'.[54]

MYSTICAL TRANSFORMATION IN
HISTORICAL PERSPECTIVE

Jewish mysticism saw itself as an ancient tradition, transmitted from generation to generation, parallel to the Written Torah and the Oral Torah, concealed in certain circumstances, and revealed as circumstances changed. This concept, which presented the 'new' as revealing the 'ancient', allowed, on the one hand, extraordinary innovations within the boundaries of tradition, and validated, on the other

---

[49] Quoted and translated in Verman, *Books of Contemplation*, 208 from MS Milan 62 F. 10913.

[50] Elior, 'R. Joseph Karo'.

[51] *Perush ha'agadot*, ed. Tishby, 5. On creating heavenly worlds in human form in late antiquity see Scholem, 'Shi'ur Qomah', and cf. Arbel, *Beholders*; Cohen, *Shi'ur Qomah*; in the early modern period see Elior, 'Metaphorical Relationship between God and Man'; Liebes, '"De Natura Dei"'.

[52] In *Tsava'at harivash* (1975), 226.

[53] *Tanya*, 219. Cf. Shneur Zalman of Lyady, *Boneh yerushalayim*, 54.

[54] *Torah or*, 'Ki Tisa' (1978), 172.

hand, the rigid performance of all the details of religious observance. The profund-
ity contained within and revealed by those who are inspired or who receive a
mystical revelation is ultimately always tied to the sacred text. Jewish mysticism
developed, as previously discussed, within a culture at the centre of which stood
the earthly/heavenly Torah embodying the word of God and transcending,
through its very essence, the boundaries of time and space.

The creators of the mystical tradition refer to a sacred textual sequence that is
repeatedly deciphered anew through iterated modes of interpretation. The integration of these interpretations establishes the Jewish mystical library. These
modes of interpretation deal with the changing image of God, the changing literary, visual, and historical image of the mystic, the image of the mystical group,
and the meaning of mystical ritual.

The changing image of God in the mystical tradition is revealed through a
series of names that both reveal and conceal his hidden essence: 'I am who I am'
(*ehyeh asher ehyeh*), 'the ineffable Name' (*hashem hameforash*) (Scripture); 'two
spirits' (*shetei haruhot*) (Qumran); *Adu'el* (2 Enoch); 'the stature of God' (*shiur
komah*) (*Shiur komah*; *Heikhalot*); 'ten *sefirot* of infinite nothingness' (*eser sefirot
belimah*) (*Sefer yetsirah*); 'Infinitude' (*ein sof*) and 'spheres' (*sefirot*) (kabbalah);
'nothingness' (*ayin*) (hasidic kabbalah); 'unique cherub', *hashmal* and *hashmalah*,
Tiferet and *Shekhinah* (Hasidei ashkenaz and thirteenth-century kabbalah); and
many other names that refer to changes in the concept of God and in the perception of the world of the divinity.[55] These changes are connected to a new, visionary perception of God, perceiving divinity as a process, and revealing new
mythical, mystical layers in the depth of the sacred text. Each one of these names
is the tip of the iceberg of a complete religious conception, explored in many
pages and books and describing a ritual and mystical tradition. This is a written
tradition of extreme spiritual changes related to direct contact with the divine
realm.

The literary, visual, and historical image of the mystic is repeatedly shaped
through a connection to one of the mystical or historical figures to whom the
Jewish tradition has ascribed direct contact with God. Figures such as 'Moses
who ascended to the heights', 'Enoch who was taken to God', Akiva 'who entered
the *pardes*' and descended to the *merkavah*, or Ishmael 'who entered into the
innermost holy sanctuary', crossed the boundaries between the real world and the
heavenly world in antiquity, and returned. Moreover, several pseudepigraphic figures from the Middle Ages such as Shimon bar Yohai, to whom the book of the
Zohar revealed itself through a divine utterance while he was hiding in a cave, or
Nehuniah ben Hakanah, who 'gazed upon the chariot' and at higher worlds, and
transcended boundaries between reality and imagination and the human and the
divine, all served as inspirations and models for mystics throughout the course of

---

[55] On the changing perception of God see Scholem, 'Shi'ur Qomah'; id., *Major Trends*; Elior,
'Changes in the Concept of God'; Green, *Keter*; Wolfson, *Through a Speculum*.

history. In the Renaissance and at the beginning of the modern period we find among others Solomon Molcho, Joseph Karo, and Isaac Luria, Hayim Vital, Moses Cordovero, and subsequently Shabetai Tsevi, Moses Hayim Luzzatto, the Ba'al Shem Tov, Jacob Frank, Nathan Adler, and Isaac Safrin of Komarno. These were all inspired people, who had direct contact with a higher world, who perceived themselves as recipients of divine revelation or angelic visitation and were perceived by their followers and contemporaries as recipients of heavenly teachings, and who internalized and identified with some of their historical and literary predecessors. These figures directly or indirectly personified the new reading of the sacred text by virtue of visionary inspiration and the extension of the text's meaning to unknown realms.[56] The meaning of the new reading stems from an autonomous and changing definition of the hidden will of God, which is revealed through explicit dicta and through the establishment of a new basis for reciprocal relations between God and human beings.

Another motif that recurs in the esoteric tradition pertains to a 'sacred society', a mystical group that communes with the masters of the holy spirit or those who decipher the sacred text by virtue of their immediate contact with the divine realm. Historical and literary examples of holy groups can be found in antiquity in the first and second centuries BCE. *Adat hayahad* (the holy congregation) in Qumran, for example, perceived itself in multiple roles: as unified with angels, as the congregation of 'the children of light' (*benei or*) that was fighting 'the children of darkness' (*benei hoshekh*) by virtue of apocalyptic prophetic truths; and as subordinate to the divine revelation of the Teacher of Righteousness (*moreh hatsedek*), who conveyed the meaning of biblical prophecies to his contemporaries. In Qumran we also find the congregation of 'the priests of *korev*' (*kohanei korev*) who, together with the angels in seven heavenly temples, sang the 'Songs of the Sabbath Sacrifice' (*shirot olat hashabat*) and regarded themselves as serving together with the angels in the heavenly temple.[57] Additional examples of mystical groups that conjoined the heavenly with the earthly (*elyonim vetaḥtonim*) in the first centuries CE can be found in the congregation of 'the descenders of the divine chariot' (*yoredei merkavah*), the members of which 'entered the *pardes*', 'ascended to the *heikhalot*', 'gazed upon the *merkavah*', and spoke with the children of heaven under the inspiration of Akiva, who 'entered the *pardes*' (BT *Ḥag.* 14*b*) and 'ascended to heaven', and Ishmael, who 'entered into the innermost holy sanctuary' (BT *Ber.* 7*a*). The 'descenders of the divine chariot' left in our hands hymns and songs that were inspired by angels and composed according to priestly patterns.[58]

---

[56] On the changing image of the mystic see Ch. 3.

[57] On the mystical associations and holy groups in Qumran in the last two centuries BCE (whose literary activity is reflected in the *Discoveries in the Judaean Desert*, vols. 1–39) see *Songs of the Sabbath Sacrifice*, ed. Newsom, introduction; *Megilat haserakhim*, ed. Licht; *Megilat milḥemet benei or*, ed. Yadin; Elior, *Three Temples*.

[58] In the first centuries CE the holy societies of the 'descenders of the chariot'. Their literary

In the Middle Ages, other groups created a kabbalistic tradition in Provence and Castile.[59] Among them were the circle of students around Nahmanides, the anonymous contemplation circle, the group that was named the 'circle of the unique cherub', and other groups in Europe. We can also find the group of the Master of the Zohar (*ba'al hazohar*) in Spain, which imagined a circle around Shimon bar Yohai to whom heavenly secrets were revealed. This group, which was called 'the holy circle' (*idra kadisha*) or 'the harvesters of the field' (*meḥatsdei hakla*), sought to reveal secrets and dedicated itself to the unification of the *sefirot* in order to bring abundance to the world through the study of kabbalah and 'the formation of intentions' (*kivun kavanot*).[60] During the Renaissance and at the beginning of the modern era can be found the group of Joseph Taitazak in Salonika, who dedicated themselves to dealing with the redemption of the Shekhinah; the 'holy groups' in Safed in the sixteenth century led by Joseph Karo, to whom a new divine voice named a 'preaching angel' appeared; his disciple Solomon Alkabets, who testified to a direct connection with the holiness of his teacher; and Alkabets's brother-in-law, Moses Cordovero, who assembled the esoteric tradition and testified about groups of kabbalists who 'took to the field' (to divorce themselves from everyday life).[61] All these holy groups in Salonika and Safed were influenced by a secretive literary group that is described in the Zohar as walking in the fields, contemplating secrets, studying and listening to inspired teachings embedded in the sacred text. The group perceived its master as endowed with divine knowledge and saw itself as illuminated by heavenly illumination emanating from paradise. They were involved in the revival of kabbalistic symbols, in establishing a holy space in which the divine utterance would reveal itself, and in reform and redemption of the Shekhinah from exile through the study of kabbalah and the focusing of intentions.[62] Following them we find Luria's group, which is described in the writings of Hayim Vital, the group of

activity is reflected in *Synopse zur Hekhalot-Literatur*, ed. Schäfer et al., and *Genizah Fragmente*, ed. Schäfer. They are discussed in Scholem, *Major Trends*, ch. 2; Scholem, *Jewish Gnosticism*; Dan, *Jewish Mysticism*, i: *Late Antiquity*; Schäfer, *Hidden and Manifest God*; Halperin, *Faces of the Chariot*; Elior, 'Merkabah Mysticism'; Elior, 'From Earthly Temple'.

[59] On the kabbalistic groups in the 13th c. and their spiritual creativity reflected in the origins of kabbalah, see Scholem, *Origins of the Kabbalah*; Dan (ed.), *Early Kabbalah*; Pedaya, *Name and Sanctuary*; Pedaya, *Nahmanides: Exaltation*; Verman, *Books of Contemplation*; Isaac of Acre, *Me'irat einayim*, ed. Goldreich; Idel, *Kabbalah*; Idel, *Mystical Experience*.

[60] On the holy associations that created the Zohar see Scholem, *Major Trends*, chs. 5–6; Liebes, 'How the Zohar was Written'; Liebes, 'Messiah of the Zohar'; Wolfson, *Through a Speculum*; Hellner-Eshed, *A River Issues Forth*.

[61] On the holy associations in Safed in the 16th c. see Schechter, 'Safed in the Sixteenth Century'; Werblowsky, *Joseph Karo*; Scholem, 'Deed of Association of Luria's Disciples'; Benayahu, 'In Praise of the Ari'; Ginsburg, *Sabbath in the Classical Kabbalah*; Zak, *In the Gates*; Meroz, 'Redemption in the Doctrine of R. Isaac'; Fine, *Physician of the Soul*; *Jewish Mystical Autobiographies*, ed. Faierstein.

[62] See above, n. 60 and Tishby (ed.), *Wisdom of the Zohar*; Hellner-Eshed, *A River Issues Forth*; *Zohar*, trans. Matt.

Sukat Shalom ('peaceful dwelling'), and the group of Ele'azar Azikri in the second half of the sixteenth century. All these groups have left written texts with
their teachings, which required ascetic measures and pietistic conduct and facili-
tated ecstatic moods and mystical revelations; some teachings are also described in
the writings of their peers. The different sources teach us the critical importance
of studying the kabbalah to influence higher worlds and fight the forces of evil,
and reveal the mystical and ritual corpus that was created amongst these 'holy
groups'.

In the seventeenth and eighteenth centuries one can find Shabatean groups,
such as the students and followers of Shabetai Tsevi and Nathan of Gaza, who
were followed by the eighteenth-century group called Hemdat Yamim ('beloved
days'), which initiated many mystical rituals, and the hasidic kabbalistic groups
that realized the world of kabbalistic imagery in their vision and sought to live
according to the tradition of Luria. Among the latter is the group of Moses
Hayim Luzzatto in Padua, which was active in the third and fourth decades of the
eighteenth century in a period that was marked by persecution of the Shabateans.
This group committed itself to the ceaseless study of the Zohar. The person who
headed it heard angelic teachings, wrote ceaselessly, and created a new Zohar,
influenced by heavenly revelations of 'souls' and a *magid* (angelic mentor), and
was persecuted and excommunicated because of it.[63] In addition, we find the
group of the Ba'al Shem Tov, which he called *anshei segulati* ('my exceptional
people'), and who regarded their leader as a person who 'lives above nature', and
who is granted colloquy with the inhabitants of higher worlds.[64] Many additional
hasidic-kabbalist groups, such as Nathan Adler's in Frankfurt at the end of the
eighteenth century, the Frankist group in Iwanie headed by Jacob Frank from
the middle to the end of the eighteenth century, and the kabbalist group the
'House of God' (*beit el*) in the nineteenth century, were also concerned with
studying the kabbalah and deciphering the hidden behind the revealed.[65] These
groups, headed by charismatic leaders endowed with divine revelation or immediate contact with angelic beings and heavenly knowledge, were united around the
study of the esoteric tradition; around the revival of mystical experience through
asceticism and 'intentions', prayers and visions, and rituals and illuminations; and

[63] On Luzzatto's holy association in Italy in the 18th c. see Ginzburg, *R. Moses Hayim Luzzatto*;
Bialik, 'The Young Man of Padua'; Tishby, *Kabbalah Research*, iii; Rubin, 'R. Moses Hayim Luzzatto
and the Zohar'. On the persecution of Shabateans in this period, see Carlebach, *Pursuit of Heresy*.

[64] On the hasidic holy societies in the 18th c. see *Shivḥei habesht*, ed. Mondshine; Dubnow, *History
of Hasidism*; Dinur, *At the Turn of the Generations*, trans. in Hundert (ed.), *Essential Papers on
Hasidism*; Weiss, 'Via Passiva in Early Hasidim'; Rosman, *Founder of Hasidism*; Rapoport-Albert
(ed.), *Hasidism Reappraised*, 76–140; Elior, *Mystical Origins of Hasidism*; *In Praise of the Baal Shem
Tov*, ed. and trans. Ben-Amos and Mintz.

[65] On the holy group of Nathan Adler of Frankfurt in the 18th c. see Elior, 'R. Nathan Adler'. On
the Frankist group see Balaban, *History of the Frankist Movement*; Scholem, 'Redemption';
Hakeronikah, ed. Levin; Elior, *Jacob Frank*.

around mystical goals and theurgies that were connected to the transformation of reality, the redemption of the Shekhinah, and the hastening of the coming of the messiah. Members of these groups, who constantly studied mystical texts and recited kabbalistic teachings, experienced heavenly revelations and an immediate contact with the holy that often produced new mystical literary creations that were shaped into sacred texts. The disciples themselves frequently became creative innovators who breathed new life, while awake or dreaming, into sacred texts and into the ceremonies that accompanied the study of those texts, thus creating new layers of the esoteric tradition while re-enacting the spiritual world of previous literary and historical groups.[66]

The members of the mystical brotherhood were committed to loving kindness and joint responsibility, which would inspire earthly unity that would generate unification in the heavenly world. Hayim Vital described the ideal that Isaac Luria, his teacher, set for his students, who were expected to integrate earthly love and human bonding with mystical prayer and heavenly restoration:

Furthermore, my teacher, of blessed memory, admonished me and all the companions who belonged to his group (*havurah*) that before the morning prayer we should accept for ourselves the positive commandment 'and you shall love your friend as yourself' (Lev. 19: 18). A person should intend to love every Jew like himself, for by this means his prayer will ascend, included with all Israel. It will be able to ascend and to bring about the restoration above. Especially important is the love of all our companions towards each other. Each and every one must include himself, such that he is one of the limbs of this fraternity.

My teacher, of blessed memory, especially admonished me concerning this matter. If, God forbid, any member is plagued by anguish . . . then one should join in his pain and pray for him. Thus in every matter one should join together with his companions.[67]

Mystical activity was woven into a life of companionship and was based on loving relations and mutual social responsibility among all the companions, who took upon themselves common missions in the heavenly realm and in the earthly community.

Yet another motif pertains to the meaning of mystical activity, which time and again fashions anew the ascending ladder that bridges the revealed and the concealed by means of a new reading of the canonical texts. Mystical activity, whether abstract or ritual, and usually aiming towards higher worlds, is grasped in Songs of the Sabbath Sacrifice (*shirot olat hashabat*) as an imitation of the angelic

---

[66] On the different patterns of mystical activity see Tishby (ed.), *Wisdom of the Zohar*; Tishby, *Doctrine of Evil*; Scholem, *On the Kabbalah*; Werblowsky, *Joseph Karo*; Ginzburg, *R. Moses Hayim Luzzatto*; Weiss, 'Mystical Hasidism'; Liebes, 'How the Zohar was Written'; Idel, *Kabbalah: New Perspectives*; Verman, *History and Varieties of Jewish Meditation*; Wolfson, *Through a Speculum*; Idel, *Studies in Ecstatic Kabbalah*; Jacobs, *Jewish Mystics*; Jacobs, *Jewish Mystical Testimonies*; *Jewish Mystical Autobiographies*, trans. Faierstein; Fine, *Physicians*; Hellner-Eshed, *A River Issues Forth*.

[67] Hayim Vital, *Sha'ar hagilgulim* (Gate of Reincarnations) (1912), fo. 53a.

service in song and praise. It is described in the Heikhalot literature as 'descending to the chariot' (*yeridah lamerkavah*), revelation of 'secrets of the world' (*razei olam*), 'the use of names' (*shimush beshemot*), and 'gazing at the king's beauty' (*tsefiyah bamelekh beyofyo*). Among the expressions that were coined in late antiquity to denote mystical activity that refers to high worlds and to the crossing of boundaries between the human and the divine, can be found 'entering the *pardes*', 'ascending to the *heikhalot*', 'using the Name', 'imagining the measures of our creator', and 'uncovering the mysteries of the world'. In the Middle Ages, the mystical act is grasped as 'union' (*yihud*) and 'cleaving' (*devekut*), 'ascending emanations' and 'descending emanations', as a two-way awakening that is referred to as divine arousal (*itaruta deleila*) and human arousal (*itaruta deletata*). In addition, it is grasped as combining and forming circular lines of letters (an activity that deconstructs daily consciousness and enables a glimpse into higher worlds), as raising a prayer to heaven (an activity that is connected with the unification of the *sefirot*), or as supporting the union and harmony of heavenly worlds. Among the phrases that describe the first activity are 'combining and forming circular lines of letters', and 'engraving, cutting off, and combining letters'. The second activity has to do with cleaving to letters, and the third activity is connected with the intention to unite the Holy One, blessed be He, and the Shekhinah, to raise 'female aspects', and for humans to use divine prerogatives.

From the sixteenth century to the nineteenth century, a whole new world of concepts was created to describe the mystical activity required to correct the disharmony of the upper worlds and to redeem the divine. Among the phrases describing the restoration of metaphysical reality and the redemption of the holy are: 'raising sparks', 'drawing down divine abundance', 'descending emanations', 'the redemption of the Shekhinah' 'descent to the evil forces', 'restitution' (*tikun olam*), 'sacrifice of the soul' (*mesirat nefesh*), 'consuming desire', 'contemplation', and 'divestment of corporeality'. Each of the concepts connected to the mystical act has a meaning at the heavenly level as well as at the earthly level, in the cosmos as well as in human consciousness. From the biblical period and continuing through the esoteric literature of each generation, the written tradition had provided a basis for the ritual revival of mystical language and the creation of renewed visions.

In the preface to his book *Ets hayim*, a late sixteenth-century text written in Safed and Damascus aiming to introduce the Lurianic kabbalah for the first time, juxtaposing it with the earlier kabbalistic tradition, Hayim Vital explains how all levels of being are wrapped one within another, creating a single chain from the top of the divine world to the bottom of the human world. From this he derives the relationship between the mystical dicta and their divine source throughout the esoteric tradition: 'Indeed it was the delight in the Torah of the Holy One, blessed be He, when He was creating the worlds out of it. His involvement with the Torah was in it as an inner soul, called the secrets of the Torah, and also called *ma'aseh merkavah*, that is the essence of the wisdom of the kabbalah, as known to those who know.'[68] In his mystical activity, the kabbalist imitates the 'delight of the Holy One in the Torah' because in his imagination he creates new worlds out of the sacred texts, testifying at one and the same time to the direct connection that existed in the past between God and the people of Israel, and to their renewed relationship in the mystical tradition.

The concepts of the mystical tradition mentioned above refer to the changing image of God, the image of the mystic, the essence of mystical activity, and the group that takes upon itself the mystical responsibility. These concepts have a common denominator: they all refer to the infinite creative power of language that is displayed in the infinite meanings contained in the secrets of the Torah and attest to the creative power of the religious imagination. These secrets revealed to inspired spirits transcend the literal version in order to decipher the hidden truth. They are decoded throughout history by different readers, who establish within their consciousness an ever-renewed continuity of the esoteric tradition.

[68] Hayim Vital, *Sha'ar hahakdamot* (Gate of Introductions), introduction to his *Ets hayim*.

THREE

The Mystic: Life without Limits

And he pressed on to the limits without limits,
where opposites unify.
And he pressed on further, and discovered the crooked
most straight of all paths,
And took it until he arrived some time at a place
without time and without place.

HAYIM NAHMAN BIALIK
'Hetsits vamet' ('He Glanced and Died')

W HO IS A MYSTIC? One who is gifted with spiritual greatness, vision, imagination, inspiration, and the ability to be exalted; one who is able, awake or
in dreams, to cross boundaries of consciousness and to experience a feeling of
immediate contact with higher worlds; one who experiences a transition from one
reality to another through visions or dreams. The mystic ascribes a profound
meaning to dreams and other manifestations of a personal inner world and regards
them as sources of inspiration. The mystic is able to decipher the complexities of
language and fathom the sacred text. By using mystical metaphors or kabbalistic
symbols he is able to reinterpret the literal meaning of the text. These symbols and
metaphors represent imaginative entities and invisible voices and intricately convey a reality that is invisible or beyond rational comprehension. The mystic is
capable of denying reality to a certain extent; this releases him from the constraints
of his time and place and enables him to offer an alternative reading of historical
circumstances. By virtue of inner illumination or inspiration and authority from
higher worlds, the mystic shatters existing frameworks, deconstructs established
distinctions, and lives in the enigmatic world of Torah mysteries. The mystic has
the courage to go beyond the bounds of the conventional point of view and the
determinate state of the world and to free reality from its inflexibility. He grasps
revealed and hidden reality in its ambiguity and multifariousness as an ongoing
process in which he perceives endless possibilities, meanings, and interpretations.

In the Jewish tradition people blessed with these qualities have been called
prophets, visionaries, masters of secrets, kabbalists, *tsadikim*, or holy people.
Their essential attributes were defined by a variety of concepts expressing the
blurring of boundaries and the transcendence of limitations. In his consciousness

and in the consciousness of those around him, a mystic 'transcends nature'.[1] He 'ascends to higher worlds',[2] 'enters the *pardes*',[3] and 'descends to the chariot'.[4] He is blessed by the 'ascent of the soul'[5] and 'the revelation of Elijah'.[6] He listens to heavenly mentors and to the 'voice of the Shekhinah'.[7] The mystic is able to describe the unseen entities revealed to him in a dream or while awake. He experiences meaningful contact with the other reality or can draw upon mystical moments from the past in a meaningful way which bridges the mythological past and the mystical experience of the present. The anonymous author of 1 Enoch in the second century BCE describes the moment of mystical metamorphosis, relating the story of Enoch son of Jared (Gen. 5: 21–4) and his ascension to heaven:

And behold I saw the clouds: And they were calling me in a vision: and the fogs were calling me: and the course of the stars and the lightnings were rushing me and causing me to desire, and in the vision, the winds were causing me to fly and rushing me high up into heaven. And I kept coming (into heaven) until I approached a wall which was built of white marble and surrounded by tongues of fire; and it began to frighten me. And I came into the tongues of the fire and drew near to a great house which was built of white marble, and the inner walls were like mosaics of white marble, and the floor of crystal, the ceiling like the path of the stars and lightnings between which (stood) fiery cherubim and their heaven of water; and flaming fire surrounded the walls, and its gates were burning with fire . . .'[8]

The mystic is able to perform wonders and interpret omens, and, directly or indirectly, orally or in writing, express the manifestations of his transcendent spirituality in a way that is significant to his generation. By virtue of his spiritual traits, a mystic might experience an imaginative rush, an inspiration, a dream, a transcending consciousness, or hear voices coming from the depth of his soul or from higher worlds. The mystic is a herald who sees ahead of and beyond his time, who opens the eyes and the minds of those incapable of seeing, or who has a prophetic vision releasing him from the limitations of conventional reality. The mystic dares to burst into unknown domains, to blur the boundaries between reality and imagination, to cross the demarcation between heaven and earth, holiness and impurity, the forbidden and the permitted. An anonymous author from the rabbinic and

---

[1] On 'one who is above nature' and on mystical 'ascent of the soul' see Elior, 'R. Joseph Karo'; Nigal, 'Ahijah the Shilonite'.

[2] See 1 Enoch 14: 8–15; *Heikhalot zutarti*, ed. Elior, 22–3.

[3] Tosefta *Ḥag.* 2: 3–4; BT *Ḥag.* 14*b*–15*a*; *Heikhalot zutarti*, ed. Elior, 23.

[4] See *Synopse zur Hekhalot-Literatur*, ed. Schäfer et al., §§1–20, 216, 344–8.

[5] See *Toledot ha'ari*, ed. Benayahu, 155.

[6] See Luzzatto, *Igerot*, ed. Ginzburg, 39, and Scholem, 'Religious Authority', 19–21.

[7] On revelation of angelic mentors see Karo, *Magid meisharim*; Werblowsky, *Joseph Karo*; Elior, 'R. Joseph Karo'; Benayahu, *Joseph, my Chosen*; Ginzburg, *R. Moses Hayim Luzzatto*; Scholem, 'The "Divine Mentor"'; Jacobs, *Jewish Mystical Testimonies*.

[8] Trans. Ephraim Isaac in *Old Testament Pseudepigrapha*, ed. Charlesworth, i. 20.

Heikhalot period retells the vision of Ezekiel within the context of the priestly concepts of seven firmaments and ministering angels:

Thus Ezekiel stood on the Chebar river and was gazing in the water when the seven heavens opened up for him and he saw the holy Glory and the holy Creatures and the ministering angels and the celestial hosts and the fiery angels and the winged beings attached to the Chariot. They were traversing Heaven and Ezekiel saw them in the water.[9]

The mystic is able to obscure the boundaries between the individual and the public domains, to express the loss of the border between the internal and the external, to obliterate the boundaries of past, present, and future. The medieval author of the Zohar offers a beautiful example of such obliteration, describing in the thirteenth century the moment of mystical transport that took place 1,300 years earlier when the high priest entered the Holy of Holies on Yom Kippur:

He took a further three steps, closed his eyes, and attached himself to the world on high. He then entered the place he had to enter, where he heard the sound of the wings of the cherubim and they sang and they beat their wings that were spread out above in unison. As he burned the incense, the sound of their wings ceased and they came together in a whisper. If the priest was worthy that there should be rejoicing on high, then here below, too, there came forth an illumination, expressing acceptance, sweetened from the hills of pure balsam on high.[10]

The mystic's activities may occur because of historical circumstances, which give rise to acute questions regarding the arbitrariness of a meaningless reality, or because of personal circumstances, involving hardship and unbearable pain or religious controversies and social disputes. All these factors widen the gap between the desirable and prevailing reality and intensify the desire to fathom the hidden meaning of the real world. The mystic, without being influenced by external circumstances, sometimes might accomplish all the above solely by virtue of his spiritual qualities, his inclination to the mysterious beauty of the sacred text, or his mystical talent. The latter is unique and inborn rather than an acquired skill.

In a moment of inspiration the mystic is able to transcend reality by a vision or a dream, after hearing a heavenly voice or *magid*, or voices from higher worlds, while studying sacred texts in this world. Similarly, he may use a special faculty to reanimate a written text with a penetrating dialectical observation, or with his unusual talent for linguistic analysis, or by his ability to narrate a dream or to recount stories and secrets that are revealed to him at the 'Heavenly School'.[11] He may be gifted with spiritual greatness, charismatic radiance, social sensitivity, or a sense of divine vocation and earthly mission that causes him to establish groups,

---

[9] *Re'uyot yehezkel* (The Visions of Ezekiel), ed. Gruenwald, 113–14. On the text see Gruenwald, *Apocalyptic and Merkavah Mysticism*, 134–41.

[10] Zohar III. 67a.   [11] See *Toledot ha'ari*, 155, 165.

sects, and congregations.[12] His observations might deviate from the norms of his time and place, by virtue of a unique understanding that is ahead of his time. Often he makes radical changes in the interpretation of reality by virtue of his charismatic religious authority, which has been acquired through contact with the inhabitants of higher worlds.[13]

Joseph Karo, in his mystical diary *Magid meisharim*, written between 1533 and 1575 in Turkey and Safed, demonstrates some of the fascinating aspects of this breaking of boundaries. While reciting *mishnayot* (paragraphs of the Mishnah), he hears in his imagination a divine voice, the voice of the Shekhinah speaking from within the Mishnah, which converses with him in Hebrew and Aramaic, the languages of the Zohar. The Shekhinah promises Karo that like Solomon Molcho (who had been burnt at the stake in Mantua in 1532 by order of the Catholic Church), he too will be privileged to sanctify the Holy Name and to ascend to higher worlds. In his mystical autobiography Karo describes the transition from being a reader of holy texts to becoming a vessel for the word of God. He records the words spoken to him by the Shekhinah/Mishnah regarding his present life and the future awaiting him:

I started to recite *mishnayot* and read five sections. While I was reading the *mishnayot* a voice began pulsing within my mouth, playing music by itself, and said: 'Wherever you go God is with you, and in anything you have been doing or will do God will make you succeed, as long as you cleave to me, my worship, my Torah, and my *mishnayot*. Your thought will not disengage from my Mishnah even for one minute. And behold, I put you in charge of my people . . . And I have warned you that you shall not disengage your thoughts from my worship and my Mishnah even for one minute, and you shall not drink or eat for pleasure at all . . . and shall only think that, had it been possible to maintain the body without any pleasure, you would have desired it very much. So just cleave to God, blessed be He, and you will be granted the ability to perform miracles as were performed by the *rishonim* [the early sages], and the people will know "that there is [a] God in Israel" (1 Sam. 17: 46) . . . and after all this I will award you the privilege of sanctifying my name by being burnt at the stake and all your transgressions and sins will be drawn out by the fire and you will leave this place for heaven like clean wool. And all the righteous people of paradise will come out to greet you with the Shekhinah at their head. They will greet you with songs and praises; they will treat you among them like a groom walking in front of them; and all of them will escort you to your *ḥupah* [bridal canopy]'.[14]

[12] See Schechter, 'Safed in the Sixteenth Century'; Werblowsky, *Joseph Karo*, 38–83; Ginzburg, *R. Moses Hayim Luzzatto*.

[13] See Scholem, 'Tradition and New Creation'; cf. Elior, 'Breaking the Boundaries'. In Coenen, *Ydele verwachtinge der Joden* (1669), 55, Shabetai Tsevi is said to have promised equality to Jewish women, telling them that he came into this world to redeem them from their punishment, enslavement to their husbands, and from any form of discrimination. The social innovation is based on his self-perception as endowed with divine revelation. See Scholem, *Sabbatai Sevi*.

[14] Karo, *Magid meisharim*, p. 8, 5–6. On the vision of Karo see Werblowsky, *Joseph Karo*; Elior, 'R. Joseph Karo'; Benayahu, *Joseph, my Chosen*.

Creation of a new perspective, shattering of boundaries of worlds, and foreseeing new horizons reflecting spiritual greatness are dependent on the breaking of norms and the transcendence of conventional ways of thinking. Such deconstruction and breaking of frameworks lacks external sources of authority. It therefore requires an internal validity and inner justification. This is obtained through mystical, ecstatic, or visionary experiences that are integrated into the traditional system, in order to gain legitimacy and authority.

Thus, great spiritual innovators, all of them reformers who transcended the constraints of tradition, needed either heavenly validation and proof from higher worlds or pseudepigraphic authority from the distant past. This led them to claim inspiration from heavenly mentors or angelic voices, visions, revelations of souls, prophets and sages from the past, and similar ecstatic phenomena, in which man did not control the content of speech but allowed it to flow out of his mouth unimpeded. Both 'inner speech' and higher inspiration were legitimate contemporaneous sources of validation for change. They were needed in order to shed new light on traditional modes of thought and change established conventions, a surprising phenomenon in a society that drew all its values from the past. Traditional society, which anchored its authority in the sanctified past and its eternal unchangeable values, resented innovation or social reform and denied meaningful changes that involved critical observations concerning its values. This society, which disapproved of changes and opposed novelties, did not validate revelations of the human spirit and rejected individual originality and autonomous thought as a source of authority. Hence, consciously or unconsciously, the innovators, the creators, and those who sought change projected their inner world onto higher worlds and attributed their spiritual experiences to the hidden world and its messengers or to the heavenly sources of the law. Therefore, their new insights, their yearnings for change and novelty, their hopes and fears, the flow of their creativity and doubts, as well as the source of their authority for an alternative perspective of the traditional world, were ascribed to heavenly beings who externalized what the mystics heard within.

The need for support from higher worlds or pseudepigraphic authority from the distant past is demonstrated by the lives of mystical creators and great spiritual innovators such as the Teacher of Righteousness (*moreh hatsedek*) of Qumran, who wrote in the second century BCE on the mystical space in which his spirit dwells: 'For you, O God, have hedged in its fruit on every side with the mystery of angels, mighty creatures, and of holy spirits, with a whirling, flashing fire.'[15] Paul, at the beginning of Christianity in the first century CE, wrote in the third person of his celestial ascension: 'I know a man . . . who fourteen years ago was caught up to the third heaven. Whether it was in the body or out of the body I do not know—God knows. And I know that this man . . . caught up to paradise.

---

[15] *Megilat hahodayot*, ed. Licht, 135.

He heard inexpressible things that man is not permitted to tell.'[16] The authors of
I Enoch in the second century BCE described the ascent to the heavenly sanctuary: 'fear covered me and trembling seized me. And as I shook and trembled . . .
and I observed and saw inside it a lofty throne—its appearance was like crystal and
its wheels like the shining sun; and I heard the voice of the cherubim; and from
beneath the throne were issuing streams of flaming fire.'[17] Other examples are the
author of the Book of Jubilees, who relied on the angel of the presence, and
the authors of the Heikhalot literature in antiquity, who ascended to the heavenly
sanctuaries; Isaac Sagi Nahor and Abraham Abulafia in the thirteenth century;
the anonymous authors of *Sefer habahir* in the twelfth century and the Zohar in
the thirteenth century; the author of the *Sefer hamalakh hameshiv* (Book of the
Answering Angel) in the fifteenth century; Solomon Molcho, Joseph Karo,
the anonymous author of *Galya raza*, Isaac Luria (the Ari), and Hayim Vital
in the sixteenth century; Shabetai Tsevi and Nathan of Gaza in the seventeenth
century; Moses Hayim Luzzatto (Ramhal), Israel Ba'al Shem Tov (the Besht), the
anonymous authors of *Ḥemdat yamim* (Beloved of Days), Jacob Isaac Horowitz
the Seer of Lublin, all in the eighteenth century, and Isaac Safrin (1806–74) in the
nineteenth century. Safrin, who was a hasidic master in Galicia, wrote in his diary
about his mystical initiation, which paved the way to his becoming a hasidic
mystic:

While studying Talmud, in the middle of the day, suddenly a great light fell on me. The
house became filled with light, a marvelous light, the Shechinah resting there. This was
the first time in my life that I had some little taste of His light, may He be blessed . . .
afterwards I fell down once again for a time so I came to realize that I must journey to the
saints who would draw down His light, blessed be He, upon me, since I already had a
refined vessel wherewith to receive the light.[18]

In each generation this need for divine support required the recognition of supernal heralds, the observation of visions, the sense of divine illumination, or the
hearing of voices of heavenly teachers.

   The persecuted Italian kabbalist Moses Hayim Luzzatto (Ramhal), in letters to
his friend the kabbalist Beniamin Hacohen, describes the moments of inspiration
involved in the transition from the revealed to the concealed:

On the first day of the month of Sivan, 5487 [1727], while I was reciting in order to
reach mystical meditation, I fell asleep and when I woke up I heard a voice saying: 'I am
descending to reveal hidden secrets of the Holy King.' I was standing and trembling for
a while and then I became composed. And the voice did not stop, and [he] told a secret as
he had said. The second day, at the same time, I was trying to meditate while alone in the
room and the voice returned and told another secret. Afterwards, one day, he told me

[16] 2 Cor. 12: 2–14 (New Testament, New International Version).

[17] I Enoch 14: 14–19; *Old Testament Pseudepigrapha*, ed. Charlesworth, i. 21.

[18] *Megilat setarim*, trans. Jacobs in *Jewish Mystical Testimonies*, 240.

that he was a herald sent from heaven and delivered to me specific mystical meditations to perform daily so that he would come. And I did not see him; I only heard his voice speaking through my mouth. Then he also permitted me to ask questions. And then, for three months, he gave me personal vigils to perform every day so I would be worthy of the revelation of Elijah, of blessed memory. And then he ordered me to write a book on Ecclesiastes, the verses of which he has been interpreting to me one by one. Then came Elijah and told the secrets that he told . . . and all these things I was doing while I was lying prostrate and I saw the holy souls in the image of man, as within a dream.[19]

The members of Luzzatto's circle used the expression 'the angel begins to reveal to him wonderful secrets' to describe this phenomenon. Luzzatto himself, however, skilfully describes the unclear nature of the highest being that reveals secrets to him while speaking through his mouth in a half-awake, half-asleep state, when he hears 'as if in a dream'. Joseph Karo's *magid* spoke through his mouth while he was in a trance and had no control over his words; as he said numerous times in his diary, *Magid meisharim*, using the words of the Song of Songs, 'the voice of my beloved is knocking [pulsing] speaking by itself'. In these instances the boundaries between the sacred texts being read in his own voice (while he was awake) and the higher voice heard through his mouth (rewriting these texts while he was half-awake, half-asleep) were blurred. Luzzatto's *magid* caused him to speak in the same way. In moments of inspiration the *magid* reanimated the written tradition with a new inner voice and ordered him to write a new Zohar. He too burst the boundaries of consciousness and blurred the distinctions between the revealed and the hidden, the writer and the written, the eternal and the temporal. Karo's *magid* confirmed his doctrine, and regarded Karo as the redeemer of the Shekhinah and as the mystical incarnation of Moses and Shimon bar Yohai, the prolific writers of the divine word in previous historical periods and the great liberators and freedom fighters. Similarly, Luzzatto's *magid* regarded him as the redeemer of the Shekhinah, just like Moses and Shimon bar Yohai, and commanded him to write like them legal and mystical treatises that would lead to liberation and redemption. Luzzatto heard the *magid* telling him:

Blessed are you and blessed is your share [in life]. You have been the Shekhinah's support through her exile. Now you will prepare for her a Throne of Glory to redeem her from her bondage. You will lead her . . . You have lit the light for her with your supreme light. She will ascend through it from her exile when [the] time for redemption comes. Blessed are you and blessed is your share. The mysteries of the world were revealed to you . . . The people who have been walking in darkness saw a great light—the light that will be revealed in your books.[20]

---

[19] Luzzatto, *Igerot ramḥal*, ed. Ginzburg, 39. On Luzzatto see Ginzburg, *R. Moses Hayim Luzzatto*; Bialik, 'Young Man of Padua'; Tishby, *Kabbalah Research*: Rubin, 'R. Moses Hayim Luzzatto and the Zohar'.   [20] Luzzatto's letter, as quoted in Bialik, *Collected Works*, 158.

The Shekhinah, being at the same time the spiritual entity representing the exiled community of Israel, the oral law, the Mishnah, and the human soul (*neshamah*), is the voice heard by the Jewish mystics living in exile, a voice embodied as 'the redeeming angel', the 'angelic mentor', or as the exiled bride or widow that has to be redeemed through the eternal process of reciting the Mishnah and the divine law. The mystical revelation is the revival of the eternal divine voice in its many manifestations in the sacred text and the human soul.

Luzzatto and Karo intensively experienced the divine presence through the material world and in their consciousness realized the transition between the material and the spiritual. Borrowing from Thomas Mann, we may say that the mystic is one who dives into 'the well of the past' and revives the images of the people there, or who soars from the real world to imaginary places that offer hope, comfort, and an alternative interpretation of reality. The mystic dares to break through the limits of the spirit and penetrate the depths of language, decode 'the mysteries of the world', and challenge the limits of consciousness and accepted norms. The mystic is not afraid of physical and mental experiences even though they sometimes involve exaltation and downfall, devotion and loss of control, madness and breaking through consciousness. This mental exaltation exacted a heavy price: in Molcho's case it led to persecution and death at the stake; in Ramhal's case it involved persecution and excommunication. In the case of Shabetai Tsevi it cost him imprisonment and enforced conversion; so too was the case with Jacob Frank, who was excommunicated and imprisoned. The hasidic mystical tradition ascribed the utmost importance to an ecstatic condition in which the human being allows the Shekhinah (which is referred to in kabbalistic literature as 'the world of speech') to speak through his mouth 'as a harp playing by itself'. This tradition examined the meaning of the annihilation of existence and the loss of control over consciousness, which enable the discovery of the divine element but also threaten madness:

Sometimes when the holy sparkle of the Shekhinah that exists in his soul expands, it really speaks the words in his mouth and it seems as if he does not speak but the words come out of his mouth by themselves. And this is a great achievement. And this is also what we see, on the other hand, in the insane.[21]

The hasidic authors of such traditions were persecuted and excommunicated by the Jewish community between 1772 and 1815. The spiritual innovations and mystical renaissance experienced by hasidic leaders who were inspired by what they had read in the diary of Karo and the letters of Ramhal in the eighteenth century met with enthusiastic responses in some quarters and with severe persecution in other parts of the traditional community.[22]

---

[21] Meshulam Feivush of Zbarazh, *Likutim yekarim*, sign 172. Cf. Schatz-Uffenheimer, *Hasidism as Mysticism*, ch. 8.

[22] See Elior, *Mystical Origins of Hasidism*, chs. 3 and 7. Cf. Wilensky, *Hasidim and Mitnagdim*. A number of the hasidic masters were labelled as insane. Israel Ba'al Shem Tov, the founder of the

The Heikhalot tradition is linked to the 'four who entered the *pardes*'.[23] Three of the four paid with their lives or sanity for observing the hidden world. Their story gives us a glimpse of the experience of transcending consciousness, the dangers of doing so, and the reasons it is forbidden. That experience is described from the point of view of the mystic, who ascends to the upper worlds, observes what is beyond observation, and listens to the forbidden:

Who can be compared to our Creator, who can be compared to our Lord, who is like Him among the angels who crown Him? In six voices the bearers of His glorious throne, the cherubim, the *ofanim*, and the holy creatures sing His attributes aloud before Him. Each voice differs from and improves upon the previous one: the first voice drives the listener out of his mind, trembling and falling. The second voice immediately causes the listener to go astray and never come back. The third voice causes convulsion and the listener dies instantly. The fourth voice immediately breaks the listener's skull and his ribs and body fall apart. The fifth voice melts down the listener and he is covered in blood. The sixth voice causes his heart to pound and his excitement causes him to vomit and his blood runs cold, becoming like water, as it is said: Holy, Holy, Holy, Lord of Hosts. All those hymns Rabbi Akiva heard, while descending to the chariot, and obtained them from the angels singing in front of the throne of Glory, and from whom he learnt them.[24]

These heavenly hymns, which expel the listener from the realm of sanity and cast him into the realm of confusion and madness, describe the fear of being in the presence of the terrible sublime (called by Rudolf Otto 'mysterium tremendum', deriving from the Latin root *tremere*, to tremble, to lose control of the body). Another testimonial from this tradition, describing an ascent to heavenly temples, also expresses the intensity of the mystical experience and the breaking of the limitations of conventional conceptions: 'Rabbi Ishmael said about the angelic prince Mishtak who stood at the first entrance and attended the main gate: "When I saw him my hands burned, and I was standing without hands or feet." '[25]

The pre-eminent reality in the mystic's world is his own internal reality, which is informed by the infinite horizons of the mysterious hidden realm revealed in his spirit. There he exposes new layers of meaning through his visions, dreams, and

hasidic tradition, had periods of 'losing his mind', and this was also the case with his grandchild R. Nahman of Bratslav and with the Rabbi of Kotsk and the Seer of Lublin. On madness in the hasidic leadership see Mark, *Mysticism and Madness*; Elior, 'Changes in Religious Thought'; Green, *Tormented Master*.

[23] On 'the four who entered the orchard' see Tosefta *Ḥag.* 2: 3; Hai Gaon, *Otsar hage'onim*, ed. Levin, iv. 14; Scholem, *Jewish Gnosticism*, 14–19; Liebes, *Sin of Elisha*; Elior, 'Mysticism, Magic and Angelology'. On the Heikhalot tradition see Scholem, *Major Trends*, ch. 2; Scholem, *Jewish Gnosticism*; Dan, *Jewish Mysticism*, i: *Late Antiquity*; Gruenwald, *Apocalyptic and Merkavah Mysticism*; Schäfer, *Hekhalot-Studien*; Elior, 'Merkabah Mysticism'; Halperin, *Faces of the Chariot*; Elior, 'From Earthly Temple'; Schäfer, *Hidden and Manifest God*; Elior, 'Concept of God'.

[24] *Synopse zur Hekhalot-Literatur*, ed. Schäfer et al., §§103–4.

[25] *Heikhalot zutarti*, ed. Elior, 36.

poetic consciousness. In the tenth-century Geonic responsa literature that was published in *Otsar hage'onim* (The Geonic Treasury, originally written as an answer to a question about the essence of Heikhalot literature and the meaning of the heavenly ascent described in this literature), a striking account is offered of this internal reality: 'It is not that they ascend to heaven, but that they look and see within their heart, as one looks and sees with his eyes a clear thing, and they hear and say and speak as those who see through the holy spirit.'[26] This inner reality may be expressed by extraordinary phenomena, which demonstrate exceptional spirituality in an overwhelming or frightening way. It may also have charismatic manifestations, which serve as a source of assertion and authorization for the novelties immanent in these insights, which are the focus of hostility, criticism, and even persecutions and excommunication.

Phenomena that do not accord with standard behaviour are usually interpreted according to the status of the individual involved and the cultural norms of the place and time. The fine distinctions between prophecy, divine inspiration, and dream on the one hand and hallucination, derangement, and mental disturbance on the other, or between a mystic who sees visions and hears supernal heralds and the prophet who is regarded as a fool or insane, are often defined by the public according to the identity of the specific prophet, his social status, and the circumstances of his time and place. The determining factor lies within the cultural milieu and not in the content or meaning of the person's message. One should bear in mind that many cultures regard exceptional people, even the mentally ill, as holy people, and the development of physical and mental abnormalities as symbols of the transition between the profane and the holy. The mystical tradition teaches that experiencing prophecy, the revelation of the Shekhinah or the visitation of Elijah, divine and angelic visitations, or the hearing of heavenly heralds usually occurs in a situation in which the person has lost self-control or full consciousness. These experiences were regarded in certain periods as completely plausible and highly desired for some kabbalists and masters of secrets, and they were the accepted religious-cultural norm. In contrast, there were other periods in which the evaluation of these phenomena went to the opposite extreme, and visionary revelation was considered illusion, hallucination, false prophecy, or even mental illness.[27]

The mystic demonstrates that divine language is not mute. He disproves the assumption that heavenly visions have been blocked and the divine word sealed. He claims that revelation, along with continuous observation of heavenly visions

---

[26] Hai Gaon, *Otsar hage'onim*, iv. 61.

[27] On the essence of the mystic in different cultural traditions see Scholem, *On the Mystical Shape of the Godhead*, 88–139, 251–74; Weber, *On Charisma*; James, *Varieties of Religious Experience*; Erikson, *Young Man Luther*; Louth, *Eros and Mysticism*; Buber, *Ecstatic Confessions*; Werblowsky, *Joseph Karo*; Jacobs, *Jewish Mystics*; Liebes, 'Messiah of the Zohar'; Idel, *Mystical Experience in Abraham Abulafia*; Bilu, *Without Bounds*; Scharfstein, *Mystic Experience*; Elior, 'Between *Yesh* and *Ayin*'; Elior, 'R. Joseph Karo'; Green, 'Zadik as Axis Mundi'; Green, 'Typologies of Leadership and the Hasidic Ẓaddiq'; Dan, *On Holiness*.

and listening to the divine word, is ongoing and he defies any counter-argument. The mystic does not regard divine revelation as a single occurrence that took place at Sinai at a specific historical moment in biblical times alone, but rather as an event that might reoccur in the consciousness of unique individuals across various historical periods and changing circumstances. The mystic defies the invalidation of 'a divine voice'.[28] He disagrees with the statement that the prophetic period is over and the holy spirit no longer inspires.[29] The mystic cannot share the assumption that messengers of God do not reveal themselves anymore, because he hears angels, listens to supernal heralds, and sometimes even hears the word of God and sees in his mind new divine texts inspired through prophecy or by the Shekhinah. The mystic prophesies through the holy spirit and sees heavenly visions through his own spirit. In the words of the Ba'al Shem Tov, 'The soul becomes a throne for the light of the Shekhinah above the head. And it is as if the light spreads round him and he is within the light, sitting and trembling with joy'.[30] The mystic seeks the continuation of religious creativity, which relies on revelation or on direct contact with the upper world, offering an alternative perspective on the revealed and concealed reality.

This mystical assumption, that revelation continues for extraordinary people who are capable in their imagination and through their spirit of gazing at the *merkavah*, 'entering the *pardes*', experiencing visions, or hearing voices, is demonstrated in the Heikhalot tradition by the testimonies of Ishmael and Akiva.

Mystical conversion, initiating the adept into the pathways of heaven or the depth of his illuminated heart and soul, is described both as an illumination and as an experience of rebirth:

Rabbi Ishmael said in the name of Rabbi Nehuniah ben Hakanah, my master: 'When I was engaged in observing the *merkavah*, I saw exalted glory, the inner sanctum, awesome princes, the most pious, who were burning and fearful, their fire burning and their fear frightening . . . since I heard this message from Rabbi Nehuniah ben Hakanah, my master, I stood up and I asked him all the names of the ministering angels of wisdom, and from the question I asked my heart was lit up as the brightness of heaven . . . and since I heard this great mystery my eyes lit up . . . and my world was renewed in purification and it was as if I came from a new world . . .' Rabbi Ishmael said: 'Since my ears heard this great mystery my world has changed to become purified and my heart felt as if I came to a new world, and every day it feels like when I stood before the throne of Glory.'[31]

Rabbi Akiva said: 'When I ascended to the chariot a voice came out from under the throne speaking Aramaic. And in that language it said: "Before God created heaven and

---

[28] 'The Torah has already been given to Israel and one does not bring testimony based on a divine voice'; BT *Ber.* 52*a*.

[29] 'Since the latter prophets—Haggai, Zechariah, and Malachi—the holy spirit ceased to inspire Israel'; Tosefta *Sot.* 13: 4.   [30] *Keter shem tov*, 48, §§192–3.

[31] *Synopse zur Hekhalot-Literatur*, ed. Schäfer et al., §§309, 579–80, 680.

earth He installed a path to the firmament to enter and to exit it. And He installed a permanent entrance by which anyone can enter." '32

A thousand years later the medieval poet Judah Halevi describes the 'ladder of ascent' or the 'path to the firmament':

> Go outside at midnight in the footsteps of the men of renown,
> Upon their lips are praises;
> They embody neither guile nor extortion.
> Their nights are devoted to prayers;
> Their days to fasts.
> Their hearts are pathways to God.
> There are places for them in His throne.
> Their way—a ladder upon which to ascend to God, our Lord.33

R. Jacob Joseph of Polonnoye sums up the mystical perception of his teacher Israel Ba'al Shem Tov in the eighteenth century in relation to the ladder of ascension: 'Man is a ladder planted on earth whose head reaches heaven and the angels of God ascend and descend it.'34

This enigmatic testimony, which describes in a mystical legendary style the experience of hearing heavenly voices and seeing higher worlds, refers to the variety of experiences that deviate significantly from the biblical tradition and are called arcana, ascents, revelations, or mysteries. This testimony clearly shows that the mystic, in his imagination, in his heart, or in his spirit, comes and goes through the gates of heaven. He is able to see or hear the hidden world; he experiences the elimination of time and space in his consciousness. He ascribes a decisive importance to his psyche and his dreams and utilizes them to break through conventional limitations. He does this by virtue of thinking that he has direct contact with the holy and higher worlds, through prophetic revelation, mystical exaltation and divine inspiration. He does this also by virtue of being acknowledged by others for his exceptional spirituality and charisma, which grant him 'divine visions' or a revelation that casts a new light on reality. In the tradition of the *geonim* (the heads of the Babylonian academies, from the end of the sixth century until the middle of the eleventh), a fascinating description of the essence of the ascent is offered: 'And they do not ascend to heaven but watch and understand the wisdom of the heart as a person who looks and sees in a mirror that does not shine.'35

An example of what they 'watch and understand [in] their heart' can be found in the mystical hymns of *Heikhalot rabati* that describe the splendorous beauty of the heavenly sanctuary that is revealed to the 'descender of the chariot' who is ascending on high and sees the invisible beauty of the divine realm:

[32] *Heikhalot zutarti*, ed. Elior, 23, 63.

[33] Schirmann, *Hebrew Poetry in Spain and Provence*, 518.   [34] *Toledot ya'akov yosef*, 50.

[35] See above, n. 26.

when [the man who has made the ascent] stands before the throne of glory, he begins by reciting the hymn that the throne of glory sings each day:

King of Kings, God of Gods and Lord of Lords, encircled by wreaths of crowns, surrounded by boughs of glowing princes—He who covered the heavens with His glorious bough and appeared from the heights in His majesty. The deeps were set ablaze by His beauty, the firmaments were kindled by his radiant stature. The proud angels burst out of His stature, the mighty explode from His crown, the precious erupt from His garment. And all the trees rejoice in His word, the grasses exult in His joy, and as He speaks perfumes flow forth.[36]

The multi-sensory experience that takes place in the 'other reality' includes seeing, hearing, and smelling and is available to the mystics who alienate themselves from the sensory reality of this world and concentrate on the 'understanding of the heart'. The description of the heavenly sanctuary and its splendorous beauty is recited after the destruction of all earthly expression of divine worship in the Jerusalem Temple in 70 CE. The mystical transformation of the lost temple and the priestly service was one of the ways of defiance against the arbitrary conquest and the catastrophic results of the 'Hurban'. The two 'earthly' heroes of Heikhalot literature, R. Akiva and R. Ishmael, are the renowned sages who continued to teach when the Romans prohibited teaching the Torah and both sanctified God's name and were martyred in 135 CE as a result of the Roman persecution that followed Bar Kokhba's rebellion. (See the poem 'Eleh ezkerah' (These shall I mention), recited on Yom Kippur.)

The Besht's words in *Igeret hakodesh*, written in the middle of the eighteenth century as a private letter to his brother-in-law, the kabbalist Gershon of Kutow (then living in the Land of Israel), reveal something of the hidden meaning of the understanding of the heart (i.e. intuitive observation), incorporating textual tradition, ritual memory, and mystical experience informed by transformations of the lost past and hopes for eternal continuity in heaven of what was lost on earth.[37] These words explain the essence of the self-observation of the mystic who ascends through his spirit from the earthly to the heavenly and gains direct contact with the inhabitants of higher worlds at the time of 'spiritual ascent':

What will certainly amaze and please you, as it amazed me, regarding the vision that God showed me through my ascents, are the wondrous things one knows through spiritual ascents. I saw wondrous things that I have not seen since I reached maturity. What I have seen and learnt while ascending there is impossible to tell or to discuss even face to

---

[36] *Synopse zur Hekhalot-Literatur*, ed. Schäfer et al., §253. English translation in *Penguin Book of Hebrew Verse*, 200. Cf. Scholem, *Jewish Gnosticism, Merkabah Mysticism*, 20–30.

[37] On Israel Ba'al Shem Tov see *Shivḥei habesht*; Dubnow, *History of Hasidism*; Kahana, *Rabbi Israel Ba'al Shem Tov*; Scholem, 'Historical Image of Israel Ba'al Shem Tov'; Dinur, *At the Turn of the Generations*, trans. in Hundert (ed.), *Essential Papers on Hasidism*; Rapoport-Albert (ed.), *Hasidism Reappraised*; Rosman, *Founder of Hasidism*; Idel, *Hasidism*; Elior, 'R. Joseph Karo'; Elior, *Mystical Origins of Hasidism*; Etkes, 'Magic and Masters of the Name'; id., *The Besht*.

face. But while returning to the lower Garden of Eden I saw a few souls of the living and the dead known to me as well as countless unknown to me, and some were running back and forth with great happiness, [trying] to ascend from world to world by means of the pillar known to those who are acquainted with the hidden wisdom [*kabalah*]. It would be tiring for the mouth to tell and difficult for the physical ear to hear . . . And the pleasure, which cannot be achieved physically, is as great as at the revelation at Mount Sinai. And I was frightened and shocked by this vision because I thought maybe this was done for my sake and the time had arrived, God forbid, to leave this world. And perhaps because of that [my approaching death], it should have been done and a hint is enough. And I felt sorry for my soul and for my friends who died abroad until I came and entered the King Messiah's palace and I saw face to face that which I have not seen from the time I reached understanding until now. And I was told revelations that I cannot share with you and also they revealed to me awesome wonderful things within the depths of the Torah that I have neither seen nor heard nor has any ear heard for some years. And it occurred to me in my heart and in my mind to ask him [the messiah] whether this great happiness is taking place in expectation of his arrival. I asked: 'And when will you be coming, sir?' And his exalted answer was: 'No, it is impossible to reveal. By this you will know, when your teaching is spread and discovered by the world and your springs gush forth [your name will go forth], and [by] what I taught you and you understood. And they will also be able to achieve ascensions and mystical meditations as you have, and at that time all the evil forces will be annihilated and it will be an age of favour and redemption.' I felt great sorrow about the length of time and I was wondering when it could possibly come to pass. But because of what I have heard, the three words, *segulot*, and three holy names, which are easily learnt and interpreted, my mind cooled off. And I thought that it was possible by this for precious people of my circle to come to my level and be like me, that is, be able to exalt [their] spirit to heaven and study and understand as I do. And permission was not given to reveal it as long as I live. And I requested [permission] to teach you and they absolutely did not permit it and I am sworn by them and I am bound by this. And this is the information I deliver and may God be with you and be aware of your virtues . . . And particularly in this world while you pray and study, in each word and utterance you will intend mystical meditation because in each letter there are worlds and spirits and divinity which ascend and connect and unify with each other and with God and then connect and unify the letters and become a word and they absolutely unify with God and your soul will be included in it in each and every aspect of the aforementioned. And all the worlds are unifying together and ascend and become a measureless joy and pleasure . . . This vision occurred while awake and not in a dream, in a vision and not in riddles.[38]

[38] 'Igeret aliyat haneshamah' (Letter Concerning the Ascent of the Soul), in *Sefer shivḥei habesht* (The Praises of Israel Ba'al Shem Tov), ed. Mondshine, 233–6; see also the discussion on pp. 229–42. On the 'Holy Epistle' see Scholem, 'Historical Image of Israel Ba'al Shem Tov'; Kahana, *Rabbi Israel Ba'al Shem Tov*, 44–5; *Shivḥei habesht*, ed. Mintz; Rosman, *Founder of Hasidism*, 99–113; Elior, *Mystical Origins of Hasidism*, 41–58; Jacobs, *Jewish Mystical Testimonies*, 148–55, offers another English translation of *Igeret aliyat haneshamah* according to its first printed version (Korets, 1781).

The complex words of the Besht clearly attest to the transformation that occurs in the psyche of someone who experiences a passage from one reality to another through 'an ascent of the soul', a vision or a dream. They reveal something of the new world-view that follows the experience of a heavenly revelation. They also show the critical importance that the Besht ascribes to his personal revelations, to the enigma of the destiny of his people reflected in the depths of his soul, and to the arcane world of his dreams.[39] His words demonstrate the blurring of the distinctions between the upper worlds and the lower worlds that takes place during mystical exaltation. They also reveal the yearning to merge the eternal and the earthly by exposing the divine character of language. The Besht's words are a complex combination of new insights with transfigurations of previous mystical traditions of heavenly ascensions that he read and internalized and relived in his being. An example of this kind of metamorphosis can be found in his references to 'the lower Garden of Eden', 'the pillar known to the kabbalists',[40] and 'the revelation at Sinai', and also in the link between his words and the description of the soul's ascent which Isaac Luria, the Ari, was granted two centuries before him in Safed:

Also [Luria] had the privilege that each night his soul would ascend to heaven. And ministering angels would come and accompany his soul to the school of heaven and would ask him to which school he wanted to go. Sometimes he would say to the school of Rabbi Shimon bar Yohai or to the school of Rabbi Akiva or of Rabbi Eliezer the Great or other *tana'im* and *amora'im* [sages of the mishnaic and talmudic periods] or prophets (*nevi'im*) and he would be led to the school of his choice and on the following morning he would tell the sages what he had received at that school.[41]

These hagiographic narrative traditions about the spiritual ascent of Luria to higher worlds circulated in both manuscript and print, throughout the Jewish world from the beginning of the seventeenth century, in works like *Shivḥei ha'ari* (Praises of the Ari) or *Toledot ha'ari* (Biography of Isaac Luria).[42] It is hard to doubt that they influenced the Besht, who internalized the mystical figure of Luria and the heavenly sources of his doctrine and relived the stories connected with them. Joseph Karo provided detailed descriptions in his mystical diary, written between 1533 and 1575 and published in the early seventeenth century, of his nocturnal ascent to heavenly schools and conversations with supernatural figures

[39] On the role of dreams in the world of the Besht see the testimony of his grandson, Moses Hayim Ephraim of Sudylkov, in his book *Degel maḥaneh efrayim*, 282–5. On the role of dreams in mystical thought see Dodds, *Greeks and the Irrational*, 102–34; Elior, 'Reality in the Test of Fiction'; Oron, 'Dream, Vision, and Reality'; Jacobs, *Jewish Mystical Testimonies*; *Jewish Mystical Autobiographies*, ed. Faierstein.

[40] On 'ascending the pillar known to the masters of mystery' see the 'Holy Epistle' in *Shivḥei habesht*, ed. Mondshine, 229–42; and *Toledot ha'ari*, ed. Benayahu, 155, 165.

[41] *Toledot ha'ari*, ed. Benayahu, 155.

[42] On *Shivḥei ha'ari* and *Toledot ha'ari* see Benayahu, 'In Praise of the Ari'.

associated with the Shekhinah. In these descriptions the Shekhinah makes him promises referring to his future and to the dissemination of his teachings and his books using the language of the verse mentioned in the *Igeret hakodesh*: 'and your springs gush forth'.[43] These descriptions nourished the Besht's imagination; they influenced the illuminations he experienced and the messianic mission that he accepted on behalf of heavenly revelation.

Hayim Vital's detailed spiritual portrait of his teacher Luria in the introduction to his book *Ets ḥayim* (written in the sixteenth century)[44] demonstrates the essence of mystical perception from the perspective of an outsider who regards those who had achieved such spirituality as 'men of great holiness'. His testimony defines the ideal image of the mystic for generations to come:

And behold today I will utter enigmas and wonders . . . because in each generation God has been amazingly generous to us and he showed us his grace by remnants that God calls on . . . and he pitied his people and sent us an angel and holy person who came down from heaven, the divine great rabbi, the righteous one, my master and rabbi, our teacher our rabbi the Rabbi Isaac Luria Ashkenazi [the Ari], may his memory be alive in the next world, crammed with Torah as a pomegranate [is with seeds], filled with Bible, Mishnah, Talmud, dialectics (*pilpul*), Midrash, and legends, *ma'aseh bereshit* (the deed of creation), *ma'aseh merkavah* (the deed of the mystical speculations of the *merkavah*), competent in the language of trees, in the language of birds, in the language of angels, familiar with the discipline of physiognomy . . . familiar with all that human beings have done and will do, who knows the intentions of human beings before they act on them, who knows the future and everything that exists on the Earth and everything that has been determined in heaven, who is acquainted with the transmigration of souls old and new . . . is able to read wonderful things in the flame of a candle and the flame of a fire, looks at and observes with his eyes the spirits of the former (*rishonim*) and latter (*aharonim*) holy people (*tsadikim*) and studies kabbalah (*ḥokhmat emet*) with them . . . and my eyes, and not [the eyes of] an alien, saw frightening things that have not been seen nor heard in the whole universe from the time of Rabbi Shimon bar Yohai, may he rest in peace, until today . . . all this he achieved by himself, by his piety and his asceticism, after occupying himself for days and years with books old and new, dealing with the discipline of kabbalah, and in addition, piety and asceticism and purity and holiness which brought him to the prophet Elijah, who always revealed himself to him and used to speak to him face to face and taught him this discipline . . . and even if prophecy ceased, the holy spirit through Elijah did not cease.[45]

[43] Interestingly, to Karo, who was a prolific writer, the Shekhinah promised that his books would be widely spread and well accepted. To the Ba'al Shem Tov, who did not write down his teachings, the messiah promised that his teachings would be widely spread.

[44] On the introduction to *Ets ḥayim* see Elior, 'Messianic Expectations'; Avivi, 'R. Hayim Vital's Writings on Lurianic Kabbalah'.

[45] *Ets ḥayim*, 'Hakdamat sha'ar hahakdamot' (introduction to the 'Gate of Introductions'), 8. On the end of prophecy see Urbach, 'When did Prophecy Cease?'; Elior, *Three Temples*, 214. For further descriptions of the extraordinary knowledge of Luria see Vital, *Sefer haḥezyonot*.

The outstanding qualities ascribed to Luria in this hagiographic testimony and the proclamation of the heavenly source of his doctrine portray him as a charismatic superhuman or as a man who transcends the boundaries of knowledge as well as the limits of time and space. These qualities correspond to the definition of charisma given by Max Weber: 'Charisma is the quality of an individual's personality by virtue of which he is separated from ordinary mortals and is treated as if he were endowed with supernatural, superhuman qualities, or at least with specific extraordinary qualities.'[46] These qualities attribute to him a divine perspective, a unique timeless insight, and hidden knowledge. This knowledge establishes a new perspective and grants mystical authority to reinterpret heavenly and earthly reality. Luria is a model of the mystic who dares to penetrate the forbidden domain by means of his imagination, 'to enter the *pardes*', 'to descend to the *merkavah*', to observe 'higher palaces', to mingle with high angels, and to decode hidden mysteries. He is able to establish contact in his imagination with a world of angels, to listen to heavenly voices referred to as *magidim*, and to be granted a 'spiritual ascent' or 'revelation of Elijah'. He is privileged to hear the words of the Shekhinah or see the messiah, to receive teachings from heavenly teachers, dream about studying the secrets of the Torah in heavenly schools, and see angels. He is privileged to understand the conversation of birds and palm trees, to experience speech speaking by itself or writing written by itself, and to experience other interactions between this world and worlds beyond it, which take place through asceticism and the study of legendary traditions and holy texts that bridge heaven and earth.

From another perspective it might be noted that Luria is the first mystic known to us in Jewish history whose mystical biography was told in great detail by a pupil who devoted his life to editing the oral teachings of his master and recounting his spiritual life. Lurianic kabbalah and Luria's mystical biography are the result of two and a half years' encounter between Luria and Vital in 1572–5 in Safed. Vital's writing created Lurianic kabbalah and the pattern of mystical behaviour that to a great extent shaped many later developments in the following centuries.[47]

The study, reading, and memorization of mystical works, recitation of halakhic and aggadic books, as well as prayer and ritual imbued with mystical intentions, induce new life in mystical symbols and in hidden beings. These activities occur during wakefulness or in a dream, in conjunction with seclusion, mortification, abstinence, and purification. They disengage the visionary from daily routines and create a holy space in which spiritual experiences take place. Study and seclusion turn the archaic written text into a 'speaking text' which one hears, experiences or envisages in one's mind. This turns ancient symbols into a contemporary living speaking being. One example of how the study of a sacred text brings about

---

[46] Weber, *Theory of Social and Economic Organization*, 258–9.
[47] See Scholem, *Major Trends*, ch. 7; Fine, *Physician*.

a deep metamorphosis in the scholar's soul can be found in the words of the thirteenth-century Spanish kabbalist Abraham Abulafia:

And I, while in Barcelona at the age of 31, was awakened by God from my sleep and studied *Sefer yetsirah* with its commentaries, and the word of the Lord came to me, and through it I wrote a book of wisdom and books of wondrous prophecies, and my spirit was revived and the spirit of the Lord reached my mouth and a spirit of holiness rose in me and I saw many and wondrous awesome visions through miracles and omens.[48]

The mystic in whom 'a holy spirit arose' is one who revives and reanimates the entities described in the written traditions. He listens to their words and observes their revelations recreated in his soul. In his imagination he causes a transition from a subject–object relation between separate things (reader/text) to a reflexive relation (the text 'speaking' within the reader). That is to say, he experiences the transition from reading and praying about the messiah to listening to the messiah's words directly or sometimes becoming the messiah himself, from reading about the *merkavah* or enquiring into it to observing it and hearing its singing, from reading about 'the pillar known to the kabbalists' in the Book of Splendour, relating to the pathway to the heavenly world, to ascending it, or from praying to the Shekhinah to being in direct contact with its words. These encounters of consciousness (which are nurtured by the reanimation of prophetic and written mystic traditions and by their renewed dramatization and unique verbalization in the mind of the visionary) inspire him and grant him new insight and hidden knowledge. This knowledge provides a new perspective and grants mystical authority to overturn traditional modes of thinking by virtue of direct contact with the upper worlds.

It appears that the mystic projects the depths of his soul and the powers of his imagination onto the divine being and internalizes God's attributes within a human being. These two dialectical aspects in the image of the mystic express the creativity shared by God and man in mystical thought.[49] Just as God creates through his spirit—creating worlds through language, commanding and decreeing, exercising an infinite, multidimensional mastery of freedom, transcending distinctions and boundaries, unifying opposites and reconciling oppositions—so, to a great extent, does the mystic create through his imagination. He too creates new worlds through his spirit, in his thoughts, and in his soul. He too creates and decrees, examines and knows, bursts finite boundaries, unifies opposites, overturns principles, interchanges divine and human, inner and outer, creates and forms metamorphoses, and in his spirit continually renews the work of creation.

---

[48] *Otsar gan eden haganuz* (Treasure of the Hidden Paradise), quoted in Scholem, *Kabbalah of Sefer hatemunah*. On Abulafia see Scholem, *Kabbalah of* Sefer hatemunah; Idel, *Mystical Experience*; Wolfson, *Through a Speculum*.

[49] On the two faces of the mystic see Elior, 'Metaphorical Relationship'; Jacobs, *Jewish Mystics*; Jacobs, *Jewish Mystical Testimonies*.

The creation of the world according to mystical thought is, to a great extent, creation by the poetic spirit shared by God and man. This is a creation free of the conventional limitations of time, space, reality, plain meaning, realistic awareness, and rational judgement.

An example of the creative spirit of the mystic can be found in the description of the throne addressing God in one of the Heikhalot hymns, described by Gershom Scholem in the following words: 'Their immense solemnity of style is unsurpassed in Hebrew hymnography.'[50] One may add that their wondrous heavenly beauty is in complete contrast to the devastation of the priestly lore on earth after the destruction of the Jerusalem Temple.

King of miracles, King of power, King of wonders, King of marvels: Your throne hovers yet does not move, ever since You set the peg of the loom which fixes the world's course and its perfection, all these many years and endless generations. Your throne has never set foot on the floor of the seventh heaven, but hovers like a bird and does not move. The proudest of the proud, adorned with crowns, and all the royal living creatures whom You created stand close together beneath Your throne of glory, bearing it with might, strength, and power. They too have never set foot upon the floor of the seventh heaven, but hover like a bird and do not move. Thrice daily Your throne of glory prostrates itself before You and says: 'Zohariel, Adonai, God of Israel, sit upon me in glory, resplendent King, for Your burden is most dear to me and does not weigh me down.'[51]

A mystic who has been granted contact with the upper worlds might become a person who recognizes a secret in everything or a visionary who postulates a hidden perspective on plain reality that bestows an unknown meaning upon human experience. This meaning arises from the assumption that, behind revealed mundane reality, there is a hidden mystery. Beyond meaningless arbitrary time, eternity unfolds. Beyond human existence limited by time and space, an abstract metaphysical existence of the human soul continues. Even more so, beyond a meaningless history, which seemingly is the result of the arbitrary actions of man, and is reflected in the exile, there is hidden a meaningful metahistory guided by God towards redemption. And beyond meaningless commandments in this world lies hidden decisive metaphysical meaning in the upper worlds. It often seems that in mystical consciousness, unity behind the distinction between God, the world, and the human being is revealed. Beyond apparent reality, its mythical being and its mystical meaning are concealed. Beyond the concrete exile, a hidden redemption exists. Beyond the destroyed temple and the abandoned priesthood, the heavenly eternal *merkavah*, the singing throne, and the angelic priesthood exist for ever. Beyond the arbitrariness of the physical world, which is ruled by demonic

---

[50] Scholem, *Jewish Gnosticism*, 21.

[51] *Synopse zur Hekhalot-Literatur*, ed. Schäfer et al., §98. Trans. Carmi in *Penguin Book of Hebrew Verse*, 198–9.

powers that bring destruction, exile, misery, and death, exist angels and heavenly creatures that foster eternity, redemption, and hope for the continuity of life and faith. Beyond the husks of mundane reality, sparks of holiness exist. Beyond the spoken language exists a hidden language of holy names and letters. Beyond the revealed 'harsh judgement' there is hidden 'divine mercy'. Beyond the mythical catastrophe that shaped history, known as the 'destruction of the world', there is the mystical hope known as 'the repair of the world'. Beyond the reality of endless exile ruled by 'the forces of darkness' exists the world of the 'forces of light' that symbolize the coming redemption. The transition from the revealed aspects of reality to its hidden yearned-for aspects is carried out within the spirit of the mystic, who blurs the sharp distinctions between imagination and reality on the one hand, and the divine and the human on the other, and offers a new vision that gives meaning to arbitrary human experience. The mystic experiences the hidden reality through his spirit by reinterpreting revealed reality, redeems it from its chaotic arbitrariness, grants it meaning, vision, and structure, endows it with mysterious beauty, and connects past, present, and future through hope and purpose.[52] The study of mystical literature often shows that phenomena and facts that might be considered by most people as insignificant, fragmented, and arbitrary are turned by the mystic into visionary materials and metaphors representing alternative existence, yearning and desires, or mainstays of personal and collective memory.

The anonymous author of *Galya raza*, a mystic from the first half of the sixteenth century who lived in the shadow of the horrors of the expulsion from Spain and who yearned for redemption, demonstrates the new insights that arise from blurring the distinctions between the heavenly and the earthly. He does it by studying the secrets of the numbers and measures mentioned in the Bible and the Mishnah and connects the present and the future by examining the revealed and hidden meanings of the measures of the *mikveh* (240 *kabin*).[53] In his vision he sees the transition from earthly time and space to eternity, and observes the moment when the Land of Israel floats on the surface of the waters free of the constraint of time towards the consolation of eternity. He describes the change in the regulation of the world and explains the connection between numbers relating to a ritual reality (measurements of the *mikveh*) and mystical reality (*shiur komah*), or the way in which the hidden reality explains the revealed reality:

And it has been discovered that the measurements of the ritual bath suggest that the number of years since the beginning of the world is 6,000 years minus 240 years,[54] because in those years there is no procreation and no ploughing and no harvesting and

---

[52] On hidden reality beyond revealed reality see Elior, 'Doctrine of Transmigration'; Goldish (ed.), *Spirit Possession*; Chajes, *Spirit Possession*.

[53] A unit of measurement of liquid volume.

[54] 6000 − 240 = 5760, referring to the 240 years before the end of the present cycle that is expected to come to an end in the year 6000 of the Hebrew calendar.

only the completely righteous who have repented will survive and there will be no rein-carnation any more. And those who survive in those 240 years are called the family of *resh-mem*,[55] such as Abraham Amram Elihu from the family Ram [see Job 32: 2]. During those 240 years the lower waters will rise and cover the whole earthly world and nothing will remain except the Land of Israel by itself in its borders 400 parasangs by 400 parasangs,[56] and it will float on the water like Noah's ark, and it will come close to the earthly Paradise where the four rivers emerge. And those who are named after the family Ram [will] immerse themselves in the river and purify themselves and become spiritual. And this is what *resh-mem* suggests: it is 240 [*resh-mem*] *kabin* that shows that they are purified by a material *mikveh* and a spiritual *mikveh*, where they immerse themselves in a river of fire and enter the seventh millennium . . . and stand in the earthly Paradise.[57]

The numerical value of letters and biblical names becomes closely affiliated in the mystical imagination that strives to transcend borders of time and constraints of space. The story of the Flood and the end of the world are associated with the idea of purity by water and its transformative effect. The defiled world of exile will drown and the new world of redemption will be created in paradise, containing only the Holy Land from the past and the holy people who can enter the new sev-enth millennium. Only the depth of misery of the historical reality of the perse-cuted Jews can yield such an apocalyptic vision that foresees the drowning of the world as we know it and creation of a new time and a new place that will retain only the Holy Land and a fraction of the Jewish people from the previous existence.

The combination of the real visions that the kabbalist carefully describes and the academic abstractions that grow out of them sometimes engenders visions that are spectacularly beautiful and mesmerizingly profound. The beginning of the deciphering of secrets hidden in being is often connected to the deconstruc-tion of the plain text, by reducing it to letters, names, and numbers that turn into objects of devotion through recombination. The mystical way is nourished by the investigation of the mysteries of numbers, letters, and the hidden layers of language, which bridges the upper and lower worlds by its revealed and hidden combinations. The way the mystical point of view is established is described in the words of two thirteenth-century Sephardi kabbalists, Azriel of Gerona, the author of *Perush ha'agadot* (Commentary on the Aggadot of the Talmud),[58] and Abraham Abulafia, the author of *Or hasekhel* (Light of the Mind):

The most important part of the service of the enlightened and those who contemplate His name is: [And you shall] Cleave to Him. And this is an important principle in the

---

[55] The numerical value of the Hebrew equivalent is 240; the letter *resh* is 200 and the letter *mem* is 40.   [56] A parasang is about 3¼ miles.

[57] *Galya raza*, ed. Elior, 56–7. On the mystical concepts 'immersing in the river of fire' and 'gazing on the beauty of the king' see *Heikhalot zutarti*, ed. Elior; *Synopse*, ed. Schäfer et al.; *3 Enoch*, ed. Alexander.

[58] On R. Ezra and R. Azriel see R. Azriel, *Perush ha'agadot*, ed. Tishby; Scholem, *Origins of Kabbalah*; Pedaya, *Name and Sanctuary*.

Torah for prayers and blessings to combine one's thought and belief as if they have cleaved to God, and to compose the name through its letters and to include in it the ten *sefirot* as the flame is connected to the burning coal; with his mouth he shall remember Him by His [pronounced] name [*adonai*] and in his heart he shall compose Him through the [possible] structural combinations of [the letters of] His written name [YHVH].[59]

When you wish to mention this glorified name engraved above with its vowels, adorn and seclude yourself in a special place so that your voice will not be heard by anyone else, and purify your heart and soul of any thoughts of this world. Then you should think that your soul separates from your body and you are dead as far as this world is concerned, and you live for the next world, which is the source of the life that exists and is scattered in all that lives, which is wisdom . . . and is in the image of the King of Kings.[60]

The mystic often displays mythic traits by being able to transcend boundaries between the living and the dead, to move between textual reality and physical reality, and to live through his consciousness simultaneously within the present, the past, and the future. These features can be found in myths about overcoming death by descending to and returning from the world of the dead, and about the struggle against the forces of evil by descending to the world of husks or the world of demons beneath the earth and returning after their defeat. Other characteristics are presented in myths about a hero who ascends to the upper worlds and returns with hidden knowledge acquired through risk and struggle, which he bequeaths to his contemporaries and future generations, or the hero who struggles with angels who revile man in the upper worlds, and who is transformed from a human being into a superhuman creature transcending his time and place.

The description of the exaltation of Enoch, who was taken to heaven by God (Gen. 5: 23–4) and transformed into the angel Metatron, illustrates the crossing of boundaries and the mystic metamorphosis connected with it, as conceived by the authors of the Merkavah tradition.[61] The following segment from *Sefer heikhalot* (Book of Heavenly Sanctuaries = 3 Enoch) describes the conversion of holy fire as a metaphor for the transition from earth to heaven and from the domain of mortals to the domain of immortals:

> Rabbi Ishmael said:
> Metatron, the ministering Angel of the Countenance
>   who resides above all, told me:
> because the Holy One, blessed be He,
>   took me by fire to serve the Throne and the wheels of
>   the chariot and the needs of the Shekhinah

---

[59] *Perush ha'agadot*, ed. Tishby, 16.

[60] *Or hasekhel*, 62, cited in Scholem, *Kabbalah of* Sefer hatemunah, 62.

[61] On the elevation of Enoch-Metatron see *3 Enoch*, ed. Odeberg; *Synopse zur Hekhalot-Literatur*, ed. Schäfer et al., §§1–80; *Geniza Fragmente*, ed. Schäfer, 105–10; Scholem, *Jewish Gnosticism*; Halperin, *Faces of the Chariot*; Elior, 'From Earthly Temple'; Elior, *Three Temples*, 88–110.

immediately my flesh turned into a flame
and my veins into a burning fire
and my bones into hot coals of a broom tree
and the light of my eyes into the splendour of lightning
and the orbs of my eyes into a torch of fire
and the hairs of my head into a blaze and flame
and all my limbs into wings of burning fire
and all my body into blazing fire
and on my right burning flames of fire
and on my left a burning torch
and around me stormy gusty winds were blowing
and clamorous sounds in front of me and behind me.[62]

The Heikhalot tradition describing apotheosis and 'angelification' by divine eternal fire alludes to a holy fire, a purification in fire, the eternal sacred fire of the Temple, the fire and lightning during the revelation at Sinai, and the *ḥashmal* (light or fire) and torches in the vision of Ezekiel. Here, it describes a kind of 'projection' of the mystical conversion that is taking place within the mystic, when his mythical counterpart Metatron describes the transformation he went through when he was summoned to serve in heaven and turned into a blazing immortal. A later description, which interprets the Merkavah tradition from a kabbalistic point of view, demonstrates the mystical metamorphosis that occurs through studying and the ecstatic experience that follows. While studying the *merkavah*, the mystic transcends his physical being, concentrates on upper worlds, turns into an atemporal being surrounded by a blazing fire, and secrets are revealed to him, as described in the Midrash and in *Perush ha'agadot* by Azriel of Gerona:

Ben Azai used to sit and study while the fire blazed around him (*Shir hashirim rabah* 1: 2 (10)) . . . Because he used to sit and study and concentrate his thought on what is above, the awesome words were engraved in his heart, and because of that emanation and the concentration of that mind the words accumulated and expanded, and out of that joy they were revealed to him.[63]

With respect to the blazing fire, the *midrash* links Ben Azai's story to the revelation at Sinai:

And the fire blazes around them and the words were joyful as if they had been given at Sinai, because was it not the fire in which they were given at Mount Sinai that was the most important? As it is written: and the mountain burned with fire to the midst of heaven. Ben Azai was sitting and studying and the fire blazed around him.[64]

The language describing Ben Azai alludes to the angels in Psalms, 'His ministers are a blaze of fire' (Ps. 104: 4), and to the holiness of the inner sanctum as it is

---

[62] *Synopse zur Hekhalot-Literatur*, ed. Schäfer et al., §19.
[63] R. Azriel, *Perush ha'agadot*, ed. Tishby, 40.   [64] *Shir hashirim rabah* 1: 2 (10).

described in the Jerusalem Talmud: 'A fire came out of the Holy of Holies and blazed around him.'[65] Ben Azai, who studies the *merkavah* while 'the fire is blazing around him', relives and revives the divine revelation at Sinai, its heavenly succession in angelic being, and its earthly continuation in the Holy of Holies, all of which are connected to the *merkavah*. Ben Azai, about whom it was said in the story about the four sages who entered paradise (*pardes* = orchard = Garden of Eden) 'he glimpsed and died',[66] turns into a prototype of the mythic mystic who encounters the holy and timelessly unites within himself heavenly and earthly holiness. An ancient poetic priestly tradition from the beginning of the second century BCE conveys the moment of illumination that followed the encounter with the holy. The most sacred place—the Holy of Holies—and the most sacred time, Yom Kippur, are associated with the divine service of the high priest, who emerged glowing with the exquisite beauty surrounding him from the Holy of Holies:

> Chief among his brethren and pride of his people,
> Simeon son of Yohanan the priest in whose time the House
> was repaired and in whose days the Temple was fortified . . .
> How glorious he was as he looked out
> from the Tent of the Presence, as he emerged
> from the curtained shrine!
> Like a star shining through the clouds,
> or the full moon on feast days.
> Like the sun glittering on the king's palace
> or the rainbow seen in the cloud:
> like a blossom on the bough at spring time,
> or a lily by a flowing stream.
> Like a flower of Lebanon on a summer day,
> or the fire of frankincense upon the offering . . .
> when he clothed himself in his splendid robes
> and put on his glorious diadem;
> when he ascended the majestic altar
> and filled the Temple Court with his splendour . . .[67]

The poetical mystical depiction of the sacrificial service on Yom Kippur in the Temple of Jerusalem is closely associated with the tradition of the *merkavah* because the cherubim in the Holy of Holies (1 Chron. 28: 18, 2 Kgs. 7–8) were the earthly representation of the glowing cherubim in the heavenly chariot and the divine throne (Ezek. 1: 10) as well as of the awesome cherubim of paradise (Gen. 3)—the heavenly domain which the high priest was entering on Yom Kippur (Zohar III. 67*a*), according to the mystical tradition. When the high priest enters the Holy of Holies on Yom Kippur,

---

[65] JT *San.* 10: 52.   [66] Tosefta *Ḥag.* 2: 2.   [67] Simeon Ben Sira: *Ben sira* 50: 1–14.

he hears the sound of the wings of the cherubim, who sing and beat their wings that are stretched out towards the heavens. He burns the incense-offering; the sound of their wings subsides and they cleave together in silence . . . When he has finished, the cherubim lift up their wings as they did before and begin to sing. Then the priest knows that it has been accepted, and it is a moment of joy for all.[68]

Mystics are those who mediate in their dreams and visions, in their thoughts and consciousness, in their soul and spirit, in their poetry and ritual, between the fire blazing at Sinai and the fire blazing around the beholders of the *merkavah*, between the fire of the angels and the heavenly fire that envelops Ezekiel's chariot. The mystics connect the Holy of Holies and the heavenly temples; the human temporal world associated with the mystical priestly service and the timeless world of the angels; the cherubim of the Holy of Holies, the cherubim of the Garden of Eden, the cherubim of the heavenly chariot and the blazing fire of Sinai. They are mediators between the world of emanation and the world of man, the world of the dead and the world of life, ancient days and the end of time, mythical time and real time. They also mediate in their imagination and consciousness between utopian yearnings and earthly reality, revealed and hidden souls, the world of demons and the world of man, and the realm of holiness and the realm of husk. They do all this because they are able to ascend spiritually to 'the world of emanation', or descend to the world of the dead and return, to ascend to the Garden of Eden and return to see in their imagination the world of 'the children of light' through the world of 'the children of darkness'. By means of their spirit they are able to hear angels, enter the *pardes*, ascend and observe the heavenly sanctuaries, the divine chariot, the cherubim of paradise, the chariot of the cherubim in the Holy of Holies, which is described in Ezekiel's vision of the heavenly chariot. These are all associated with the heavenly pattern of cherubim that Moses saw at Sinai (Exod. 25) and that the high priest saw in the Holy of Holies on Yom Kippur when he entered the earthly sanctuary and the heavenly sanctuary simultaneously. The mystic was able to see and hear with closed eyes and open heart/mind the cherubim and the Shekhinah. He was able to foresee the future and proclaim it, speak with Abraham, Moses, and Ahijah, with Elijah and Akiva, with Metatron and Shimon bar Yohai. In his imagination he is able to make the Shekhinah and the messiah speak; listen to angels and heralds in heavenly schools; speak with living and dead souls, with 'transmigrating souls' and 'transformed souls'; descend to the husk and raise himself above it; conjure the souls of the dead and return to the world of the living; wander in the heavenly temples; observe the mystical worlds of 'emanation, creation, action'; observe the depths of 'the light that does not contain thought' and 'the light that contains thought'; 'ascend the middle pillar known to the masters of secrets' and join together with holy association. He was able to 'ascend to the chariot' and 'descend into the

---

[68] Tishby (ed.), *Wisdom of the Zohar*, iii. 92–3.

abyss' and return; be in immediate contact with textual realities; connect in his mind the different worlds of imagination and reality; peruse in his imagination the secrets of human experience and thought, and tie them to both their historicity and their metaphysical meaning.

Mystical literature depicts the mediating ability of the mystics, their mythical traits, and the transcendent meaning of their experience. It includes the complex images of their imagination and their heavenly counterparts. These earthly and heavenly figures, by means of their spirit, break through the confines of human existence and establish new interrelations between the human and the divine. Often these mystical figures display penetrating observation of the psyche, careful attentiveness to the secrets of language, and profound observation of mysteries of the upper worlds, and they hearken to new divine, angelic, and human voices. Some of the outstanding characters among them are described in the Ethiopic and Slavonic books of Enoch from late antiquity (1 and 2 Enoch).[69] These characters were transformed from human beings into angels living in heaven, combining the human and the angelic. These books, which tell of the ascent of a human being to heaven, what he heard, and what was revealed to him by God and His angels, offer new insights into heaven and earth, mysticism and ritual, God in the image of man and man in the image of God. They suggest a totally new conception of God, a totally new creation story, a complex myth about the revolt of the angels against God, a detailed description of the solar calendar that is contradictory to the accepted lunar calendar,[70] a concept of the human being that differs from its biblical counterpart, a description of the angelic liturgy in the upper world, and many other topics that convey a sense of disagreement, struggle, defiance, and criticism of sanctified values and a reawakening that formulates new insights in an ancient mythic language.[71] Enoch plays an important role in the Book of Jubilees, where he is the incarnation of knowledge imparted by the angels to a man taken into paradise (Jubilees 4).[72] The figure of Enoch in the priestly mystical literature unites within himself the characteristics of knowledgeable man, priest, seer, mystic visionary, and scribe, a messenger who brings from heaven all the divine knowledge pertaining to the priestly service—numbers and calendar; letters and history; singing and liturgy; incense and books; records and laws. Enoch-

---

[69] On 1 (Ethiopic) Enoch, found among the Dead Sea Scrolls and in the Pseudepigrapha see *Books of Enoch*, ed. Milik; VanderKam, *Enoch and the Growth of an Apocalyptic Tradition*; id., *Enoch, a Man for All Generations*; *1 Enoch*, trans. Black; *1 Enoch*, ed. Charlesworth, 5–89. On 2 (Slavonic) Enoch see *Old Testament Pseudepigrapha*, ed. Charlesworth, i. 91–222; Böttrich, *Weltweisheit*; VanderKam, *Enoch, a Man for All Generations*; Nickelsburg, '1 Enoch'; Orlov, *The Enoch–Metatron Tradition*.

[70] On the significance of Enoch in the priestly literature that associated him with a holy calendar see Elior, *Three Temples*, chs. 4–5; on Enoch's significance in apocalyptic and mystical literature see Collins, *Apocalyptic Imagination*; Gruenwald, *Apocalyptic and Merkavah Mysticism*; VanderKam, *Enoch, a Man for All Generations*.

[71] On Enoch's role in mythical literature see Arbel, *Beholders of Divine Secrets*.

[72] See Elior, *Three Temples*, 99–110, and 'From Earthly Temple to Heavenly Shrines'.

Metatron in 3 Enoch, composed after the destruction of the Temple and the abolition of the priestly service on earth, when all aspects of Temple worship were transformed into the heavenly sanctuaries known as *heikhalot*, unites within himself the characteristics of God, man, and angel and, amazingly enough, regards all three of them from the point of view of suffering, vulnerability, and punishment, ascribing to them mythical aspects and human traits.[73] Metatron transforms into a mediating entity, communicating among the human, the divine, and the angelic, for he is known as 'the little Yahweh' whose 'name is as his Lord's',[74] and 'his crown is as his King's crown'.[75] Enoch was a human being who was taken to God (Gen. 5: 24), set in paradise as a scribe, and was renamed by the sages as the angel Metatron, who was punished by fire because of the sin of Elisha.[76] But he is also a heavenly character who resembles God to such an extent that God fears him and tells the descender to the chariot 'Don't worship him'[77] and 'Don't replace me with him'.[78]

Similarly, the historical and pseudepigraphic figures of the *tana'im* Akiva and Ishmael in the Merkavah literature, who 'descend to the *merkavah*', 'ascend to heaven', 'observe the King in his beauty' in upper sanctuaries, and 'enter the *pardes*' and 'the innermost place of the sanctuary', testify to the deep meaning of the crossing of boundaries between the revealed and the hidden, the real and the imaginary, the ritual and the mystical, and the physical and the spiritual. In addition, they unite human and angelic existence, crossing boundaries between heaven and earth by serving in the earthly temple, which continues to exist only in their memory, and in the upper sanctuaries, eternalized in their imagination.[79]

If Jewish mysticism in late antiquity and during the Byzantine period was focused on the glorious lost past, on the mystical transformation of the lost Temple and the abolished service, transforming them into heavenly sanctuaries, heavenly chariots, and ministering angels, the next stage of Jewish mysticism was focused on the future, that is, on redemption, on the messianic redemption, and on the hidden schemes and structures that will hasten redemption and the return to the Holy Land.

The mythological accounts of the literary protagonists of antiquity and the Middle Ages, mystics such as Nehuniah ben Hakanah in *Sefer habahir* or Joseph

---

[73] On 3 Enoch see *3 Enoch*, ed. Odeberg; *3 Enoch*, ed. Alexander. On Enoch-Metatron cf. BT *Ḥag.* 14*b*–15*a*. [74] *Synopse zur Hekhalot-Literatur*, ed. Schäfer et al., §19.

[75] *Geniza Fragmente*, ed. Schäfer, 105.

[76] BT *Ḥag.* 14*b*–15*a*; *Synopse zur Hekhalot-Literatur*, ed. Schäfer et al., §§1–20. Cf. Scholem, *Jewish Gnosticism*, 14–19, 43–55. [77] *Geniza Fragmente*, 105.

[78] BT *San.* 38*b*. Elisha ben Avuyah's sin was substituting Metatron, the angelic entity, for the divine entity. BT *Ḥag.* 14*b*–15*a*.

[79] On the role of Akiva and Ishmael in the mystical tradition see Scholem, *Major Trends*, ch. 2; Scholem, *Jewish Gnosticism*, 14–19; Urbach, 'The Traditions about Merkabah Mysticism'; Gruenwald, *Apocalyptic and Merkavah Mysticism*; Dan, *Jewish Mysticism*; Halperin, *Faces of the Chariot*; Schäfer, *Hidden and Manifest God*; *Heikhalot zutarti*, ed. Elior.

della Reina in the magical narratives referring to him, were all concerned with the upper worlds and the revelation of secrets learnt therein, often pertaining to the secrets of redemption. Moreover, these accounts significantly influenced the formation of the mystical portraits of various kabbalists (some known to us by name and others only through their anonymous works).[80] Sixteenth-century figures— Solomon Molcho in *Ḥayat hakaneh*, Solomon Turiel in *A Sermon on Redemption*,[81] Joseph Karo in his mystical diary *Magid meisharim*, and the anonymous author of *Galya raza*, who in their life and action maintain a reciprocal relation with visible and audible heavenly entities revealing to them the secrets of redemption and the mysteries of the hidden divine plans for changing the course of history—well express the mythical and mystical characteristics of the mystic in the Jewish tradition. They illustrate the meaning of life within a textual reality unlimited by time, space, rational thinking, or physical reality, informed mainly by memories of the lost past and hopes and yearning for a redeemed future. The meaning of mystical transcendence, the merging of the written text with the revived text within the reader, and the blurring of distinctions between the imaginary and the real and between the temporal and the atemporal in their experience are clearly demonstrated by the anonymous authors of *Sefer hamalakh hameshiv*, *Galya raza*, and *Avodat hakodesh* (Holy Worship) in the first half of the sixteenth century, and the charismatic hagiographic figures of Luria in the introduction to Hayim Vital, *Ets ḥayim*, and in Vital's *Sha'ar hagilgulim* (Gate of Reincarnations) and *Sha'ar ruaḥ hakodesh* (Gate of the Holy Spirit), of Moses Cordovero in *Sefer gerushin* (Book of Banishments), and of Vital in *Sefer haḥezyonot*, in the second half of the century.

The literary portraits of Nathan of Gaza and Shabetai Tsevi in the seventeenth-century Shabatean literature and the biographies of their followers, Barukhyah Russo, Samuel Primo, Abraham Michael Cardozo, Mordecai Ashkenazi, and Jacob Frank, are similar examples of mystics who perceived themselves and were often perceived by their contemporaries as liberators, redeemers, or messianic figures who were able to alter the course of the history of the exile and promote or facilitate earthly/heavenly redemption. They too demonstrate the variety of concepts that mediate and connect times, spaces, and archetypal figures linked to the revival of the mystical tradition in the spirit of its creators and students. In general, it is possible to say that the mythical portrait serves as the strongest source of validity for introducing new ideas regarding the hidden world and its relation to the revealed world. Mystical themes—concerning the worlds of *sefirot* and souls, the end of the exile and the time of redemption, reincarnation, apotheosis, the world of the angels, the solar calendar, the heavenly sanctuaries, the secrets of Torah, the coming of the messiah, the defeat of the forces of evil and the redemption of the Shekhinah, the Divinity that creates itself, and the

---

[80] On the characteristics of the mystics, the kabbalists, and the 'descenders of the chariot' see the Appendix, which includes bibliographical references.

[81] See Scholem, 'A Homily on Redemption'.

human being created in its image—these themes are all validated by their linkage to mythical figures and their association with memories of the glorious past and yearned-for future. Those figures ascend to the upper worlds and transcend the limitations of time and space. They bring from there the previously unknown insights that reshape the concepts of time and space. That is to say, the atemporal mythical garment is a cover for mystical renewal that simultaneously takes place within the boundaries of time and space and transcends them.

The exceptional portrait of Moses Hayim Luzzatto (emerging from his letters to his contemporaries in the first half of the eighteenth century) and the autobiographical descriptions of the Besht in *Igeret hakodesh*, written in the middle of the eighteenth century, demonstrate the internalization of the images of the mythical protagonists who wish to hasten redemption and to bring the messiah, the new era of liberation and the revival of the mythical kabbalistic tradition. These descriptions reflect the moulding of the writers' images in relation to mythological figures and voices from the upper worlds that were revealed to them in a dream or while awake. Similarly, the autobiographical testimonies of Mordecai Ashkenazi in the notebook of his dreams, of Jacob Isaac Horowitz of Lublin in the volume of his sermons, *Zot zikaron* (This to Remember), and Isaac Safrin of Komarno in his book *Megilat setarim* (Scroll of Secrets)—referring to visions, to voices that spoke through their mouths, and words of Torah that were divulged to them from heaven—reveal the complex relations with the written mystical tradition that reappeared and was revived in their visions and dramatized in their imagination. The biographical sketches of Nahman of Bratslav in *The Life of my Teacher Rabbi Nahman*, of Nathan Adler in *Ma'aseh ta'atuim* (Deed of Mischief), of Jacob Frank in *Divrei ha'adon* (Words of the Lord), of Jacob Wazana in *Lelo meitsarim* (Beyond Boundaries)—as well as the images of additional mystics drawn from autobiographical notes, dream books, scholarly letters, and biographical descriptions which are hagiographical, historical, and literary—attest to the complexity of those who live in the presence of the holy, who mediate between the hidden and the revealed and unite within themselves earthly and heavenly entities. These writings likewise reflect the lack of demarcation among those qualities representing the literary, mythic, mystical, fictional, imaginary, and real. The overwhelming majority of the written mystical documents that have come down to us describe changes in the creative imagination that give rise to previously unknown beings and alternative categories. These changes take place when the mystic opens the written word to new meanings connecting past and future and turns the sacred words and symbols into living entities and uncovers the reciprocal connections between the written text and its hidden meaning and between inner consciousness and memories and the divine, as a depository of hopes and yearnings attached to the literary memories of the past.

A comparative study of these biographies and autobiographies often shows that the inner link among them has been created by internalization that is revealed through the obvious similarities between fictional literary images and historical realistic figures. In many works of mystical literature the extraordinary identification with earlier mystical figures, both real and literary, is manifested by the inclusion of visionaries from the past in the portrait of the contemporary mystic, and by the adoption of the language and doctrine of previous mystical authorities in the new doctrines. This kind of internalization, incorporation, and identification between past and present establishes contact with the holy and is a source of primary inspiration and authorization for new conceptions. In the Book of Ezekiel the prophet-priest (who lived in the sixth century BCE at the end of the First Temple period) describes visions concerning the heavenly chariot, the true Temple, and the priests descended from Zadok. Inspired by those visions, the Teacher of Righteousness of Qumran (*moreh hatsedek*), in the second Temple period (second century BCE), a time of crisis and dispute, sees himself as a chosen one who has been granted prophecy and revelation of supernal mysteries. He internalizes the image of the prophet Ezekiel and polemically describes the future of the cult and its ritual practice. He praises the priests descending from Zadok and writes mystical poetry on heavenly sanctuaries and angelic service around the heavenly chariot. The anonymous authors of the Heikhalot literature (who lived in the first centuries CE after the destruction of the Second Temple and saw themselves as being granted heavenly revelation) identified with Akiva, who 'ascended to the *pardes*', as described in BT *Ḥagigah* 14a, and with Ishmael, the high priest who entered 'the Holy of Holies', as described in BT *Berakhot* 7a. These two traditions, which were based on Ezekiel's vision, demonstrate the eternalization of the heavenly Temple in contrast to the destruction of the earthly Temple and depict Akiva and Ishmael as Moses and Aaron, the symbols of prophecy and priesthood, in relation to the divine chariot, *merkavah*, and the angelic liturgy.[82] These traditions became a foundation for the exaltation of the mystic in the Heikhalot literature, which eternalized in heaven that which had been destroyed on earth.

In addition to the mystic figures of the two *tana'im*, the authors of the Heikhalot literature also developed the many-faced figure of Enoch-Metatron, the mortal man who turned into an immortal angel, escaped from time into eternity, and was exalted into a figure who united the divine, angelic, and mythic with the human, priestly, and mystical. Upon completion of the apotheosis, Enoch-Metatron is given seventy names, among them 'Little Yahweh', 'For my name is within him', and 'Michael, high priest who sacrifices on the altar of heaven'. They portrayed him in the image of the hidden God and the high priest in the heavenly Temple.[83]

---

[82] On the mystical metamorphosis of the priesthood and the temple rites see Elior, 'From Earthly Temple'; *Songs of Sabbath Sacrifices*, ed. Newsom; Himmelfarb, *Ascent to Heaven*; Morray-Jones, 'Paradise Revisited'; id., *A Transparent Illusion*.

[83] See *3 Enoch*, ed. Odeberg; Scholem, *Jewish Gnosticism*, 43–55; *3 Enoch*, ed. Alexander; VanderKam, *Enoch, a Man for All Generations*; Nickelsburg, '1 Enoch'; Elior, 'You Have Chosen Enoch'; Himmelfarb, *Ascent to Heaven*; Orlov, *Enoch–Metatron Tradition*.

This apotheosis is tied to their self-conception as guardians of the mystical tradition of ascent to heaven and the priestly tradition of the open pathways between the earthly Temple and upper temples on Yom Kippur. While in antiquity mystical revelations are connected with a heavenly metamorphosis of priesthood, ritual, the Temple, the liturgy, and the angels, in the Middle Ages and the beginning of the modern period they are strongly connected with exile and redemption and the multifaceted figures of the Shekhinah and the messiah. The Shekhinah represents the earthly and heavenly congregation of Israel on different levels—mystical and ritual, spiritual and textual—linked to the burden of exile and the hope of redemption.[84] The messiah represents the heavenly entity who promises redemption and eternal continuity.

In medieval mystical writings, a masculine–feminine archetypal conception stands out, based on the mythical-mystical identity of the cherubim in BT *Yoma* 54*a–b* and *Bereshit rabah* 21: 24.[85] This conception sees the divine realm as having both male and female aspects that are manifested in the following couples: the Holy One, blessed be He, and the Shekhinah; Glory and Kingdom; Messiah and the Shekhinah; Moses and the Torah; Bridegroom and Bride, *hashmal* and *hashmalah*: 'This is its sign: "cherub, lions and palms according to the spacing of each, and wreaths encircling" (1 Kgs 7: 36). There is in this the secret of the cherubs: an allusion to . . . "male and female He created them" (Gen. 5: 2).'[86] 'Know, my sons, that *Hashmal* and *Arafel* are two powers: "male and female He created them." *Hashmal* is the great cherub; sometimes it is transformed into a male and sometimes into a female. Accordingly you will find in Ezekiel's prophecy [both] *Hashmal* and *Hashmala*, which is the feminine.'[87]

Many symbols, images, visions, and biblical and midrashic figures are connected with masculine (the redeemer) and feminine (the one who is in exile) elements. In the kabbalistic literature the mystic often sees himself linked to the male figure (the redeemer and legislator, representing the eternal continuity and stability from the past to the future) and to the female figure (the one who is in exile, representing changes and transformations, oppression and yearnings, who is being redeemed), thus containing within himself both aspects. Moses, the archetype of mystic ascension, associated with prophecy, law, divine covenant, and redemption, represents the male aspect of divinity. The Shekhinah represents the feminine aspect and is linked to the Torah, the congregation of Israel, the experience of exile, and the yearning for redemption, memories of the 'daughter of Zion' who is in exile according to the biblical tradition, and hopes for restitution and transformation, liberation and redemption.

---

[84] On the mystical metamorphosis connected to the Shekhinah and to redemption see Werblowsky, *Joseph Karo*, 9–23, 206–33; Scholem, 'Shekhinah'; Ginsburg, *Sabbath*; Elior, 'R. Joseph Karo'; Green, *Keter*; Wolfson, *Through a Speculum*.

[85] *Bereshit rabah*, ed. Theodor-Albeck, 3 vols. (Berlin, 1912), i. 203.

[86] Verman, *Books of Contemplation*, 203; cf. 207, 208. [87] Ibid. 208.

Moses, who came closer than any other mortal to the divine realm, serves as an archetype for many mystics throughout the ages. In their imagination the mystics follow his footsteps. Moses ascended to heaven and returned with the word of God. They too ascend to heaven, seeking the word of God and returning with new doctrines. According to the mystical tradition the following verses refer to Moses, who ascended to heaven from Mount Sinai (Exod. 19–25): 'God's chariots are myriads upon myriads, thousands upon thousands; the Lord is among them as in Sinai in holiness. You went up to the heights, having taken captives, having received tribute of men . . .' (Ps. 68: 18–19).[88] These verses combine the revelation at Sinai, Ezekiel's chariot, the ascent to heaven, and the return with gifts for men.[89] The author of the Zohar identifies with the messianic and mystical figure of Shimon bar Yohai, which was constructed in the image of Moses. The highest moments in the life of Moses and Shimon bar Yohai are associated with the holiday of Shavuot, the time of the Sinai revelation, according to the mystical tradition that was interested in re-enacting the covenant between heaven and earth. *Ra'aya mehemna*, from the medieval Zohar literature, refers to Moses, 'the faithful shepherd'[90] and connects him with the new mystical messianic figure of Bar Yohai. Joseph Karo, at the beginning of the modern period, internalizes Moses, the legislator, redeemer, and carrier of the word of God. Karo interprets the verse 'For I will speak to him face to face' as referring to himself and ascribes to himself the revelation of the Shekhinah, the hearing of the divine voice, who beseeches him to settle in the Land of Israel, to redeem the Shekhinah, and to reinterpret the laws and the commandments while he is engaged in the comprehensive codification of Jewish law in *Beit yosef* and *Shulḥan arukh*, thinking of himself as the new Moses.[91] Moses Hayim Luzzatto, who makes the connection between Moses and his own name, and marries a woman named Zipporah out of identification with his biblical counterpart, internalizes the image of Karo's *magid*, who requires that he compose a new Torah and redeem the Shekhinah from her exile. Luzzatto too says about himself in the name of his angelic mentor: 'you [Luzzatto] have been a support for the Shekhinah in her exile. Now you will prepare for her a throne to redeem her from her bondage.'[92]

Solomon Molcho identifies with the prophet Daniel and his visions of redemption when he unfolds his own messianic vision and the calculation of the designated messianic era in his book *Ḥayat hakaneh* (Creature of the Reeds). Luria and Luzzatto deeply identify with the mystic and messianic image of Shimon bar Yohai and, inspired by him, they write a new Zohar and continue to cultivate

---

[88] On the heavenly ascent alluded to in Ps. 68: 18 and the chariot tradition see Halperin, *Faces of the Chariot*, 171–5 and 355.

[89] On the Sinai revelation and the chariot tradition see ibid. 262–89; Elior, 'Earthly Temple', and *Three Temples*, 136–7, 143, 154–61.

[90] See Liebes, 'Messiah of the Zohar'; Hellner-Eshed, *A River Issues Forth*.

[91] See Jacobs, *Jewish Mystical Testimonies*, and Werblowsky, *Karo*.

[92] Bialik, 'The Young Man of Padua', 158; *Igerot ramḥal*, 408–9.

hopes for redemption. The *magid*'s words to Luzzatto clearly reflect this link: 'And the enlightened shine as the splendour of heaven [*zohar harakia*]—the two enlightened ones: the one, Rabbi Shimon bar Yohai, the holy light, and the other, you, the holy *ḥasid* (pious disciple). Each one in his own splendour [*zohar*]: this one, the beginning, and this one, the end.'[93] The Besht internalizes both the image of Joseph Karo, who transcended boundaries and regarded his innovations as the outcome of a heavenly *magid*'s revelation (as suggested in his book *Magid meisharim*), and the charismatic figure of Isaac Luria, who attributed his doctrine to Elijah's revelation (as is suggested in the book *Shivḥei ha'ari*). Like Karo, Luria, and Luzzatto, the Besht also sees himself as one who ascends to heaven and regards his doctrine as delivered to him in the upper worlds by the messiah during an 'ascent of the soul' and as given through the 'world of speech'.[94] Jacob Frank, who regards his words as based on a revelation of the Shekhinah (to whom he refers as 'Rachel'), identifies with the biblical figure of Jacob who struggled with God and men and bested them and with the figure of his brother Esau. He also identifies with Shabetai Tsevi and Barukhyah Russo, the Shabatean-mystical redeemers, and, indirectly, with Jesus and the Virgin Mary, all of whom break conventions.[95] The Seer of Lublin internalizes in detail two figures: that of Joseph Karo, who referred to the divine voice that he heard as 'a voice of my beloved beating in my mouth, a harp playing by itself', and that of Moses, the faithful shepherd who inspired his hasidic doctrine of the *tsadik*. The Seer uses Karo's language to describe the illumination granted to him as 'the voice of my beloved beating within my mouth' (in his book *Zot zikaron*), and also regards himself as 'the tabernacle of testimony', a spokesman who speaks words (of Torah) from Heaven, a religious renewer, a redeemer, and a faithful shepherd.[96] Mordecai Joseph Leiner of Izbica, author of *Mei hashilo'aḥ* (Waters of Shiloah), in turn identifies with the Seer of Lublin.[97]

Jewish mysticism shows not only how one mystic is influenced by an earlier mystic and shaped in his image, but how the vision of a previous mystic returns and is revived by a later one. The visionary reads and internalizes visions from the sacred literary text, inserts new imagery into the original visions, and thus transforms them into a living reality within himself. In addition, the mystical tradition

[93] *Igerot ramḥal*, 409.

[94] On the mystical hasidic tradition that considered ecstatic states as the highest spiritual achievements and described them as 'the world of speech', 'the speech of the Shekhinah', and 'a violin singing by itself' see Schatz-Uffenheimer, *Hasidism as Mysticism*, chs. 8–9; Weiss, 'Via Passiva'; Elior, 'Between *Yesh* and *Ayin*'; Idel, *Hasidism*. On the mystical ascent of Israel Ba'al Shem Tov, see above, n. 40.

[95] On Jacob Frank see Elior, 'Jacob Frank's *Divrei ha'adon*'; Scholem, 'Redemption through Sin'. On the interiorization of Shimon bar Yohai, the messiah of the Zohar in Shabatean imagery, see Scholem, *Sabbatai Sevi*; Goldish, *Sabbatean Prophets*.

[96] On the mystical life of the Seer of Lublin see Elior, 'Between *Yesh* and *Ayin*'.

[97] On Mordecai Joseph Leiner see Weiss, *Studies in East European Jewish Mysticism*, 209–48; Elior, 'Changes in Religious Thought of Polish Hasidism'; Faierstein, *All is in the Hands of Heaven*.

demonstrates how a vision or a mythological concept, which functions in the sacred text as a multilayered symbol, a visionary reality, or a kabbalistic metaphor, becomes the object of a mystical experience of the author of another text. This tradition shows that the mystic draws from his historical, literary, and visionary predecessors in a manner that allows him to rely on voices from the heavenly school.[98] Reliance on the voices of Metatron, Shimon bar Yohai, the Shekhinah, Elijah, the redeeming angel, the responding angel, the *magid*, or the messiah and the other residents of the heavenly schools (*metivta direkia*) exempts the mystic from reliance on an earthly authority and from being evaluated according to accepted traditional norms. This reliance on 'answers from heaven' allows him to establish new concepts that are interwoven with heavenly revelation and divine authority.

During the course of ancient history extraordinary changes occurred in the meaning and focus of mystical expressions involving the *merkavah* (from Ezekiel's vision of the chariot)—'visions of *merkavah*', and 'the cherubs' *merkavah*', 'descenders to the *merkavah*', 'pattern of the *merkavah*', 'gazing upon the *merkavah*', 'one should not expound the *merkavah*', 'one should not *lehaftir bamerkavah*' (conclude the reading of the Shavuot Torah portion with Ezekiel's chariot, i.e. Ezekiel 1 and 10)—as well as 'entering into paradise' and ascending to the 'Throne of glory'. These changes attest to the complex transitions between ritual reality and written, experienced, visionary, and mystical reality. The full range of mystical terms that were renewed during the Middle Ages within mystical circles also demonstrates the personifications of God and the abstractions of divinity as 'ten *sefirot* of infinite nothingness ending where they begin', 'splendorous brilliant light', the 'voice of the Shekhinah' and the 'speech of the Shekhinah', 'the world of speech', 'the revelation of the Shekhinah', 'redemption of the Shekhinah', 'kingdom', '*kelipot*' (the evil realm), 'sevenfold cosmic cycles' and 'emanation', 'primordial man', 'big image' and 'small image', 'father' and 'mother', 'conception' and 'suckling' in divinity, 'the tree of souls', 'infinitude and spheres', as well as 'the sanctuary of the bird's nest' (*heikhal ken tsipor*), the heavenly residence of the messiah and the depth of the Shekhinah, the abyss or *nikbat tehom rabah*. All these concepts, which are revived by the kabbalists by using the sacred texts and reinterpreting them according to their own visions and understanding, together with the ongoing modification of the images of Moses, Enoch, Metatron, Shimon bar Yohai, Elijah, Ahijah, and many others, reflect the dialectical process of creating new concepts from remnants of ancient ones. This process sanctifies the traditional text, deconstructs and reconstructs it anew by inspiration, exaltation, and vision, internalization, and by the profound analysis of language and the unrestrained poetic mystical creative insight and impulse to write. In addition, these

---

[98] On heavenly voices as the new source of authority see Scholem, 'Religious Authority and Mysticism'; Scholem, ' "Divine Mentor" of Rabbi Yosef Taitazak'; Idel, 'Inquiries into the Doctrine of *Sefer hameshiv*'.

concepts demonstrate the complex meaning of the revival and internalization of a living mystical tradition, released from the limitations of time and space, taking off on the wings of imagination.

In Jewish mysticism we witness a repetitive twofold mythical pattern—on the one hand the ascent to heaven and direct contact with the holy, and on the other the return with a new vision or with the previously unknown Torah, which has been revealed to the visionary in the upper worlds. Moses, who 'went up' and returned with the Ten Commandments, serves as a prototype. Among those who exemplify this pattern are the following: Akiva, who ascended to the upper world, entered the *pardes*, and returned with the Oral Torah and the Merkavah tradition; Enoch, who was taken to heaven and returned with the book of Enoch, the priestly tradition, and the solar calendar; and Shimon bar Yohai, who exalted himself by his asceticism in the cave through which he was granted a divine revelation and wrote the Zohar, a revelation that he shared with his followers, named in the zoharic tradition as 'the workers of the field'.[99] Others are Solomon Molcho, who was awarded a visionary exaltation and as a result wrote *Ḥayat hakaneh*; Joseph Karo, who through his vision exalted himself to the upper worlds and heard the voice of the *magid* and as a result wrote his book *Magid meisharim* and parts of his halakhic works; and Moses Hayim Luzzatto, who was granted a revelation from a *magid* and as a result wrote *Adir bamarom* and his Zohar-related mystical works. Additional mystical figures act in accordance with this model; among them are Isaac Luria, Shabetai Tsevi, Israel Ba'al Shem Tov (the Besht), and the Seer of Lublin. Charisma, the direct contact with the divine that takes place in the mystic's consciousness and is validated by his circle, may be interpreted in many ways and can be expressed in a variety of ways.[100] However, the new doctrines, implicit and explicit, and the new rituals are almost always sanctified and become obligatory. This type of consciousness, independent of external recognition, often exists in contrast to conventional legitimacy, established rabbinic authority, and accepted customs.

Often by dint of charisma the mystic modifies the tradition by which he has been nourished. Sometimes he does so in the name of the upper worlds. Extreme modifications and meaningful changes are demonstrated by the following examples: the names of the angels in the tradition of the priestly cult of the Judaean desert, the struggle over the solar calendar and its modification in the mystical writings found at Qumran, and 'beholding the *merkavah*' according to the cult of the Judaean desert.[101] The relation between the earthly and the divine was viewed

---

[99] On the mystical meaning of 'the workers of the field' in the Zohar see Liebes, 'How the Zohar was Written', and 'Messiah of the Zohar'.

[100] See Weber, *On Charisma* and *Theory of Social and Economic Organization*; Otto, *The Idea of the Holy*.

[101] On legal and spiritual changes in Qumran derived from mystical inspiration see *Songs of Sabbath Sacrifice*, ed. Newsom, 59–73; Suessmann, 'Research on the History of Halakhah'; Elior, *Three Temples*.

from a new perspective, causing a profound debate on the ritual of divine service during the Second Temple period. This change was influenced by the Teacher of Righteousness (*moreh hatsedek*), 'the priests of *korev*', or 'the people of the unification' (*anshei hayahad*), priests who viewed themselves as united with the angels, and the 'beholders of the *merkavah*', who wrote the *Songs of the Sabbath Sacrifice* (*shirot olat hashabat*) before the Common Era and the hymn of the *merkavah* and *heikhalot* after the destruction of the Temple. The relation between the earthly and the heavenly was grasped from a new perspective owing to written testimony following heavenly revelations, which stirred a fierce debate on the services performed during the Second Temple period and on the nature of the sacred calendar that was the basis of the eternal cycles of rituals. The extreme changes that occurred in the concepts of God and angels in Heikhalot circles influenced prayer. The purpose of these changes was to perpetuate the Temple service in the common prayer of the Jewish people.[102] Expressions of these changes in the medieval period can be found in: (i) modification of the reasons for the divine commandments (*ta'amei hamitsvot*) in the kabbalistic tradition, the spread of the *sefirot* doctrine, and the rise of the status of the Shekhinah, following the increased popularity of the Zohar, and (ii) the modification of the practice of ritual slaughter and the concepts of *yibum* and *halitsah*[103] in kabbalistic and hasidic circles in accordance with the doctrine of reincarnation that was popular in the kabbalistic tradition.[104]

In a similar way the vigil of Shavuot (*tikun leil shavuot*), midnight vigil (*tikun hatsot*), *kabalat shabat* (welcoming the sabbath), and *melaveh malkah* (literally 'accompanying the queen', a ceremonial conclusion of the sabbath) in Safed kabbalah are novelties that were introduced following a new conception that was mystically inspired. This conception equated God with the Shekhinah, Moses with the Torah, and the mystic with both the earthly and the heavenly congregation of Israel. The mystic who is engaged in Torah study unites with the Shekhinah and redeems the heavenly congregation of Israel. The terms 'devotion', 'prayer', 'vigil', '*tikun*' (rectificatory prayer), 'mystical meditation', and 'unification', commonly used in kabbalistic language, are concerned with combining within the mystic the two redemptive mystical aspects of the deity—the redeeming male and

---

[102] See Elior, 'From Earthly Temple'.

[103] *Yibum* is levirate marriage, the practice of a childless widow being married to her late husband's brother in order to perpetuate his memory by giving birth to a child; if the widow (or the brother) do not wish to do this, the brother must perform the *halitsah* ceremony, in which the widow unties his shoe and spits as a ritual expression of disdain for his neglect of his duty to his dead brother. The origin is biblical: Deut. 25: 7–10.

[104] On substantial changes introduced in the mystical tradition as a result of mystical revelations see Scholem, 'Tradition and New Creation'; Tishby (ed.), *Wisdom of the Zohar* (on the new meaning of the commandments); Gottlieb, *Studies in Kabbalah Literature*, *vikuah hagilgul* (on the transmigration of souls); Ginsburg, *Sabbath*; Scholem, *Sabbatai Sevi*; Wirschowsky, 'Shabatean Ideology of the Messiah's Conversion'; Liebes, *Secret of Shabatean Faith*; Wirschowsky, 'Shabatean Theology of Nathan of Gaza'; Elior, 'R. Nathan Adler'.

the redeemed female. Innovations introduced by dint of the mystical tradition include modification in dress and in the mode in which the tefillin are tied, following the customs of the Ari; the cancellation of the Tishah Be'av fast (mourning the destruction of the First and Second Temples) within Shabatean circles, following the assumption that the Shekhinah has been resurrected; annulment of the thirty-six transgressions punishable by excommunication or death (*karet*) in Shabatean circles, on the premiss that the messianic age has arrived, and with it also the promise 'that a new law will proceed', meaning that laws that prohibit and permit are inverted. The modifications of liturgical patterns and leadership within hasidism, and the modifications of the meanings of the prohibition of incest in Shabateanism and Frankism, which had extreme social and religious ramifications, stem from the clash between mystical authority and the establishment.

The mystic is made capable of this kind of change through inspiration from the hidden world structure revealed to him, by the autonomous power of determination which he adopts through his direct contact with upper worlds, or by the sense of transcending boundaries that characterizes mystical inspiration and prophetic revelation. Indeed, an anarchic, antinomian, revolutionary potential is embedded in the mystical tradition, which strives to attain the hidden worlds and ascribes only relative importance to the revealed world. The mystic expresses an anarchic position regarding reality and an antagonistic attitude that subverts the absolute validity of sanctified establishments. This type of mystic believes that the world is close to its end and that its institutions are worthless in comparison with the new world that is to come. The anarchic position towards reality is expressed in various ways: 'everything is divinity' or 'the world is nothing but a grain of mustard' (as the Besht said in the *Tsava'at harivash*), or 'all the worlds are an absolute lie' (as Shneur Zalman of Lyady said in *Torah or*). Those supporters of the messianic mystical position fought over the truth of their conception and its advantages, and demonstrated in the course of history the anarchic subversive quality arising from their vision. The most extreme antinomian examples and anarchic positions are to be found in the words of the eighteenth-century Shabatean teacher Jacob Frank in his autobiography 'The Words of the Lord' (*Divrei ha'adon*): 'I came to destroy all laws' (§890); 'You should [he is addressing his followers] step and trample on all the commandments, the laws, and the religious customs' (§724). In compensation for this blunt antinomianism he says 'I promise you eternal life' (§408).[105] The messianic hopes for a new world and a new era are the background for the above contentions, which reflect the misery of living in exile and alienation from the entire symbolic order and traditional norms. The communities' reactions—polemics and opposition, persecutions and excommunications, book burning and denunciations to the authorities—often attest to the ways in which the mystic potential was sometimes interpreted by the religious establishment. The mystic

[105] See Scholem, 'Redemption through Sin'; Elior, 'Jacob Frank's *Divrei ha'adon*'.

threatens the social order, both actually and symbolically, and often creates a desire to impose supervision on him, limit his authority, and restrict his influence. The history of Jewish mysticism is marked by a continual confrontation of mystics (beholders of mysteries, visionaries, prophets, and innovators inspired by divine revelation) with the guardians of convention and tradition (the rabbinic leadership or other members of the religious establishment). The persecutions and excommunications of some of the most outstanding teachers and creators of Jewish mysticism demonstrate the explosive and anarchic potential embedded in mystical thought.[106]

Drawing their inspiration for exceptional innovation from upper worlds and direct contact with supernatural entities, many of these dreamers, prophets, and mystics demonstrate by their often tragic lives the destiny of those who actualized the yearning to observe the forbidden and reveal that which should be left unseen. They ruptured the norms of their time and place and, consciously or unconsciously, threatened the social order and the foundations of the symbolic order, for which they paid a heavy price more than once. The Teacher of Righteousness was persecuted mercilessly in the second century BCE.[107] The *tana* Shimon ben Azai 'glimpsed [into the forbidden realm] and died'. His friend Ben Zoma 'glimpsed and was injured' (became insane). Elisha ben Avuyah, known as Aher ('the Other'), denied the uniqueness of God as a result of a mystical experience and was excommunicated after he perceived two powers in heaven.[108] Akiva and Ishmael were martyred in sanctification of the divine name.[109] Enoch–Metatron was punished with *pulsa de nura* (smitten with fire).[110] All the biographies, historical, literary, or legendary, of these figures (from the second century BCE to the second century CE) attest to the price paid for crossing boundaries and being an outsider. The bitter fates of Jesus and Paul probably belong to this category as well. The anonymity of many writers of the mystical tradition in various centuries probably signifies the sense of danger and threat that those who had these experiences encountered.

The lives of many figures from the thirteenth to the eighteenth centuries illustrate the meaning of breaking down normative conventions and the personal and public price paid for it. The author of the *Sefer habahir* chose anonymity in the twelfth century.[111] Abraham Abulafia was excommunicated in the thirteenth century.[112] The author of *Ra'aya mehemna* (fourteenth century) chose anonym-

---

[106] On the history of the persecuted mystics and the excommunicated writers in the Jewish mystical tradition see the Appendix, especially the articles about Solomon Molcho; Abraham Abulafia; Nathan Adler; Moses Hayim Luzzatto; Jacob Frank; Shneur Zalman of Lyady; Jacob Isaac Halevi Horowitz, the Seer of Lublin; Menahem Mendel Morgenstern of Kotsk; and Mordecai Joseph Leiner of Izbica.

[107] See Vermes, *Complete Dead Sea Scrolls*, 49–67.

[108] See Urbach, 'Traditions'; Liebes, *Sin of Elisha*.

[109] BT *Ber.* 5*b* for the Day of Atonement, lamentation 'Eleh ezkerah'.   [110] BT *Ḥag.* 14*b*–15*a*.

[111] See Scholem, *Origins of the Kabbalah*.

[112] See Scholem, *Major Trends*, 126–55; Idel, *Mystical Experience*.

ity,[113] and the author of *Sefer hameshiv* (fifteenth century) hid under the cover of angelic pseudepigrapha.[114] Asher Lemlein, who prophesied on redemption, was persecuted in the fifteenth century.[115] Solomon Molcho was burnt at the stake in Mantua in 1532, after being informed on by his Jewish opponents, who were worried about the consequences of his messianic propaganda in the Christian world and their effect on the Italian Jewish community living there.[116] The author of *Galya raza* hid under cover of anonymity because of opponents and scoffers during the middle of the sixteenth century.[117] Similarly, Joseph della Reina was punished by Satan or by God for his efforts to hasten redemption,[118] and Luria died at an early age as punishment because he revealed secrets, according to the kabbalistic tradition of his disciples.[119] The fates of Shabetai Tsevi, Nathan of Gaza, and Luzzatto also testify to the price paid by mystics who experience in their consciousness direct contact with the upper worlds, are granted celestial visions, break through the boundaries of accepted norms, and threaten the existing order. Shabetai Tsevi was a manic-depressive and spent the last part of his life in prison. Nathan of Gaza suffered from epilepsy.[120] Both were persecuted, incarcerated, and excommunicated in the seventeenth century.[121] Similarly, Luzzatto was excommunicated and persecuted throughout Europe and in the 1730s was forced to be present while his books were burned in front of him.[122] There are legendary traditions related to the Besht suggesting that he was persecuted and also that he suffered from 'weakness of the brain' (first half of the eighteenth century).[123] Jacob Frank, who saw himself as the follower of Shabetai Tsevi and Barukhyah Russo, was persecuted and incarcerated in the second half of the century, and eventually converted to Islam and then to Christianity as a way to find refuge from the persecution of the Jewish community.[124] During the course of the controversy between the hasidim and their opponents at the end of the eighteenth century, which in a sense was a dispute between mystical innovators and the leaders of the rabbinical establishment, Shneur Zalman of Lyady was incarcerated as a result of being denounced by his opponents in Russia,[125] and Nathan Adler from Frankfurt was excommunicated and persecuted in Germany.[126] At the turn of the nineteenth century, in the course of the internal hasidic disputes over the

[113] Giller, *Enlightened Will Shine.*
[114] See Scholem, '"Divine Mentor"'.
[115] See Kopfer, 'Visions of Asher'.
[116] See Aescoly, *Messianic Movements.*
[117] See *Galya raza*, ed. Elior.
[118] See Dan, 'Story of Joseph della Reina'.
[119] See Liebes, '"Two Young Roes"'.
[120] On him see Wirschowsky, 'Shabatean Theology of Nathan of Gaza'.
[121] See Scholem, *Sabbatai Sevi.*
[122] See Tishby, *Paths of Faith and Heresy.*
[123] See Dov Ber of Linitz, Eng. trans. by Ben-Amos and Mintz, *In Praise of the Baal Shem Tov*; Dubnow, *History of Hasidism.*
[124] See Elior, 'Jacob Frank's *Divrei ha'adon*'; Kraushar, *Jacob Frank*; Balaban, *History of the Frankist Movement.*
[125] Mondshine, *Kerem Habad*; Hilman, *My Master's House*; Wilensky, *Hasidim and Mitnagdim.*
[126] Elior, 'R. Nathan Adler'.

succession of leadership and over conflicting mystical and social ideological positions, Moses, the son of Shneur Zalman of Lyady, converted to Christianity,[127] as did Wolf, the son of Jonathan Eibeschutz, who was a Shabatean kabbalist, persecuted in the eighteenth century.[128] Nahman of Bratslav was persecuted and became ill,[129] the Seer of Lublin suffered 'a fall',[130] Menahem Mendel of Kotsk went out of his mind and isolated himself from his followers,[131] and Mordecai Joseph Leiner of Izbica, the author of *Mei hashilo'aḥ*, was silenced, persecuted, and excommunicated and his book was burnt upon its publication in Vienna in 1860.[132] In the early part of the twentieth century R. Abraham Isaac Hakohen Kook, who was a renowned mystic and a rabbinic authority, was severely persecuted by the religious establishment in Jerusalem,[133] and the followers of the messianic leader Menahem Mendel Schneersohn, the Lubavitcher Rebbe, were excommunicated and persecuted by fellow Jews in the USA, who resented his halakhic tolerance and visionary broadmindedness, which informed each other.[134]

This shows the price of the confrontation between those who defended the norms and those who challenged them. It also demonstrates that what one person regards as the holy spirit or divine inspiration another may regard as madness that endangers the community.[135] The historical and social contexts of the mystical corpus and its creators' fates reveal new considerations that have not always been taken into account. It should be pointed out that the evaluations of many of the aforementioned cases have been reversed during the course of history.[136] Many of those visionaries and innovators who were excommunicated while alive were regarded as respected kabbalists, founders of intellectual movements and leading spiritual innovators after their death. Sometimes their followers tried to defend them by publishing their works and by bringing to light their true intentions. Sometimes other independent spirits, such as writers and poets who identified

---

[127] Elior, 'The Controversy over Habad's Legacy'.   [128] See Liebes, *Secret of Shabatean Faith*.

[129] See Green, *Tormented Master*.

[130] On his biography see Elior, 'Changes in Religious Thought'.   [131] Ibid.

[132] See Faierstein, *All is in the Hands of Heaven*.   [133] Schatz-Uffenheimer, *Messianic Idea*.

[134] Berger, *The Rebbe, the Messiah, and the Scandal of Orthodox Indifference*.

[135] On mysticism and madness see James, *Varieties of Religious Experience*; Dodds, *Greeks and the Irrational*, 64–101; Geertz, *Interpretation of Cultures*; Mark, *Mysticism and Madness*.

[136] On later changes in attitude towards the excommunicated mystics see Bialik, 'Young Man of Padua' (on Luzzatto); J. Katz, *Halakhah and Kabbalah*, 356–61 (on Adler); Elior, 'R. Nathan Adler'; Aescoly, *Messianic Movements*; Molcho, *Ḥazon shelomoh molkho ḥayat hakaneh*, ed. Aescoly; Idel, 'Solomon Molcho as a Magician'; Scholem, 'Redemption through Sin'; Kraushar, *Jacob Frank*; Balaban, *History of the Frankist Movement*; Elior, 'Jacob Frank's *Divrei ha'adon*'; Scholem, *Studies in Shabateanism* (on Frank); Wilensky, *Hasidim and Mitnagdim* (on Levi Isaac of Berditchev and Shneur Zalman of Lyady; Elior, *Paradoxical Ascent*; Hilman, *My Master's House* (on Shneur Zalman of Lyady); Weiss, 'Question in Rabbi Nahman of Bratslav's Doctrine'; Green, *Tormented Master* (on Nahman of Bratslav); Elior, 'Changes in Religious Thought of Polish Hasidism'; Brill, *Thinking God: Mysticism of Rabbi Zadok of Lublin* (on Leiner) ; Elior, 'Controversy over Habad's Legacy' (on Moses, the son of Shneur Zalman); Emden, *Megilat sefer* (on Eibeschutz); Liebes, *Secrets of Shabatean Faith*.

with those who were persecuted, came to their rescue. Sometimes the people's opinion brought about the change, and sometimes further investigation changed the public perception of those who had formerly been excommunicated. Those actions and changes did not reduce the suffering of those who were persecuted, but the lesson to draw from this historical injustice is that changes in the public arena can be very slow. While public reaction is swift and rigid in opposing any attempt to undermine conventional norms, to threaten or break down boundaries, it is very slow to adjust to novelties and accept extraordinary spirituality. Historical distance allows one to re-examine from a different perspective the positions of both the 'innovators', who relied on heavenly revelation and the holy spirit's illumination, and the 'guardians of the city', who tried to support earthly existence and maintain the social order and the boundaries of tradition. All this demonstrates the relativity of 'absolute truths' in changing historical, social, and cultural circumstances.

At the base of cultural and religious conceptualization and the foundation of reality are several sharp distinctions between heavenly and earthly, divine and human, hidden and revealed, internal and external, life and death, temporal and eternal, present, past, and future, as well as the unequivocal distinctions between permitted and forbidden, the religious duty of observing the divine commandments (*mitsvot*) and transgression. The abrogation of these dichotomies or their shift from absolute to relative, along with the blurring of other distinctions and the adoption of the principle of metamorphosis, may shatter the foundations of reality and break down its accepted boundaries. Drawing distinctions by means of laws, norms, regulations, conventions, religion, and language shapes important aspects of human life and, to a great extent, defines its destiny. The blurring of dichotomies, the shattering of accepted categories, and the establishment of passages (whether clear or obscure) among the different domains are forbidden for earthly creatures and are the privilege solely of the inhabitants of heaven. Sometimes, however, the narrators of myths, people blessed with creative imagination, liberators, innovators, and freedom lovers, those gifted with exceptional spirituality, people with profound human understanding and great social sensitivity, prophets and mystics, thinkers, visionaries and dreamers, poets and preachers, free themselves from established dichotomies and deviate from traditional laws, rules, and norms in order to participate in changes and metamorphoses, in mystical meditations, combinations, and reincarnations, and the fluctuations of 'fixed distinctions'.

The mystical tradition demonstrates the extraordinary ramifications of the ability to redefine the reasoning behind religious acts and to reposition the boundaries of the traditional world in the light of a changing mystical reality. The mystic tries to free himself from cultural and social conventions. He outlines the relation between actual historical reality and mystical reality (the hidden structure of the world). Sometimes the mystic feels free to interpret the relation between

past divine revelation and its modified meaning in the present and to decide inde-
pendently what the implied will of God is and how to respond to it.[137]

In some schools of mystical thought there is a discrepancy between God's will
as it had been revealed in the past and His will as revealed to the mystic. In the
past, God's will was embedded in a single historical revelation and reflected in the
plain meaning of a sacred canonical text and in commands that required obedi-
ence and fear. God's hidden will, disclosed to the mystic as part of an ongoing
process of revelation, is not based on a written text but on a new divine voice
heard in the spirit of the mystic. It requires a new response of love, the shattering
of boundaries, and the creation of a new text. Through his connections with both
the sacred text and the new revelations he experiences, the mystic eliminates the
dimension of time in the relation between God and man and establishes ongoing
direct contact with God. This position is best attested in Mordecai Joseph
Leiner's *Mei hashilo'ah*, burnt immediately upon its publication in Vienna in
1860.

The mystic also establishes new ties between the present and the future—an
outcome of the distinction between different cycles of time and the consequent
modification of eternal commands according to time and circumstance. Examples
can be found in the distinctions between the following pairs: the plain meaning of
the text as known in the present and its secret meanings that will be revealed in the
future; the 'doctrine of the Tree of Knowledge' as known in the present and
the 'doctrine of the Tree of Life', which will be valid in the future; the 'Torah of
Creation' and the 'Torah of Emanation' (presented in *Ra'aya mehemna*); the
Torah that was revealed in Ancient Days in the 'Age of Judgement', and the Torah
that will be revealed in the End of Days in the 'Age of Mercy' (as discussed in the
'*Shemitah* Treatise' in *Sefer hatemunah*); the 'World of Disruption' (*shevirah*,
Breaking of Vessels) and the 'World of Reformation' (*tikun*, Restitution of the
Broken Vessels, described in Lurianic kabbalah); 'shade' (seemingly literal truth
as perceived by human beings) and 'depth' (a complex divine perspective of reality) (discussed by Leiner in *Mei hashilo'ah*); and 'the worship in fear' and 'the
worship in love' (related to traditional worship and mystical worship), which are
part of the doctrine of the Seer of Lublin. All these distinctions belong to categories that refer to the 'relative eternity' of the tradition, the assumed unequivocal meaning of the Torah and its actual multiplicity of meaning, and the many
changes that take place in the meaning of the divine word, which is recognized as
thus reinterpreted by mystics and masters of secrets in different periods.

A few examples of new categories created by the mystics can be found in antiquity in the distinction between an enslaved existence and a redeemed existence
in connection with the war between 'the children of light and the children of
darkness'. A new religious and social meaning was given to existence as a whole by

[137] On new categories comparing indirect revelation in the past and an ongoing direct revelation in
the present see Elior, 'Changes in Religious Thought'; Faierstein, *All is in the Hands of Heaven*.

the Teacher of Righteousness, who aspired to the End of Days and to the return of the rightful priests to power—those priests who will reinstate in the Jerusalem Temple the sacred solar calendar of 364 days that was replaced wrongly with a lunar calendar of the usurping priesthood of the Hasmonean period. Time and space acquired new meanings in the world of the descenders to the *merkavah*. A new conception of God connected to 'God's stature' (*shiur komah*) was established and in the angelic world a new ladder of ascent was created to bridge the hidden and the revealed, the prayer of angels and that of humans, which are described in the Heikhalot literature. During the Middle Ages the doctrines of the *sefirot* and reincarnation and the concepts of the Shekhinah and the tree of souls were developed in *Sefer habahir* and the mythological world of the Zohar.

The Zohar describes the domains of the holy and the evil as worlds embodied respectively in two couples, God and the Shekhinah, Satan and Lilith. The female aspects of divinity known as the Shekhinah or Kingdom symbolize the feminine exiled part of the Godhead, and her evil counterpart, Lilith, symbolizes the feminine destructive power of the other side. The gazelle (or the queen) symbolizes the Shekhinah, and the *kelipah* (husk) symbolizes Lilith. The king (or the lover) symbolizes the holy male powers, and the snake and the crocodile symbolize the evil male powers. The relations between these powers are dialectical, with the world of holiness 'hanging down and emanating from the crocodiles' fins'. In addition, the book *Ra'aya mehemna* describes the differences between the 'Torah of redemption', Torah that will be revealed in the future, as against the present 'Torah of exile'. This is also the time when kabbalists create the world of spheres as a new foundation for the religious world and the worship of God, as suggested by the author of *Mare'ot hatsove'ot* (The Reflecting Mirrors), David ben Judah Hehasid, and the fourteenth-century kabbalist Menahem of Recanati, the author of a commentary on the Torah. Both the fallow year treatise in *Sefer hatemunah*, which describes alternative worlds that operate according to a different temporal system, and God's direct speech in *Sefer hameshiv*, which draws an alternative image of God, belong to the fourteenth and fifteenth centuries.

In the sixteenth century, in the books *Sefer ḥayat hakaneh* and *Sefer hamefo'ar* Solomon Molcho reinterprets the reasons for the commandments and the kabbalistic metaphysical requirement hidden within them in the light of an ascetic perception of the human being and a mythical conception of the messianic vision. Joseph Karo, in *Magid meisharim*, redefines asceticism and ecstasy, the death of the body and the birth of the spirit, as the basis for mystical worship—following Molcho's death at the stake and the revelation of the Shekhinah he was granted. Solomon Alkabets creates new rituals for the redemption of the Shekhinah and the hastening of the arrival of the messiah.[138] Solomon Turiel has visions of the End of Days. The author of *Galya raza* describes the struggle between holiness

---

[138] See Kimelman, *Lekha Dodi*; *Safed Spirituality*, trans. Fine.

and impurity and the secrets of reincarnation as the key to decoding the dates of the exile and redemption.[139] Moses Cordovero, the author of *Pardes rimonim*, presents a systematic mystical world based on the Zohar's philosophy and Lurianic kabbalah, distinguishing among contraction, destruction, and restoration as fundamental categories of the conceptions of God's creation and divine worship.[140] These mystics, who see themselves as the redeemers of divinity, and the divinity as the redeemed Shekhinah, and regard themselves as the decipherers of the Torah's secrets who have influence in the upper worlds, create and establish new categories for the relations between God and humans. They reshape the mutual relations between the revealed and the concealed, and redefine the active role of the human being in the process of Jewish history and its development from exile to redemption.

Proceeding to the modern era, in the seventeenth century Shabetai Tsevi and Nathan of Gaza define the boundaries of the permitted and the forbidden. They believe that the messianic era has commenced and the time has come for a new Torah, superseding the old one.[141] After them, in the first half of the eighteenth century, Luzzatto is granted supreme revelations, writes a new Zohar, hears within himself 'an angel who reveals wonderful secrets to him', and arranges his marriage to the Shekhinah, and because he believes that the End of Days is close, he nourishes messianic hopes.[142] At about the same time, the Besht argues that 'everything is divinity', and that everyone is expected to worship God in every way, because 'God wants to be worshipped in all possible ways'.[143] Also at this time Dov Ber, the Maggid of Mezhirech, formulates the principles of hasidism based on the assumption that 'one should release oneself from any materiality to the extent that it will allow one to ascend through all the worlds and be united with the Holy One, blessed be He, and only when one is released from reality will he be called a human being'.[144] Jacob Frank, during the second half of the eighteenth century, preaches nihilism and destruction in *Divrei ha'adon* (The Words of the Lord) in the name of an anarchic messianic vision, following a blend of wrathful prophecies in the style of the Zohar and Shabatean antinomian traditions. He illustrates the argument that the mystic may highlight as meaningless not only the conventions of his time, but also the established classifications commonly used in the Jewish social-religious tradition and in the surrounding Christian culture.[145]

At the end of the eighteenth century, Jacob Horowitz, the Seer of Lublin, demonstrates the norm and the way to break through it with respect to the con-

---

[139] See Elior, 'Doctrine of Transmigration'.

[140] On Cordovero see Ben-Shelomoh, *Theology of Moses Cordovero*; Zak, *In the Gates*.

[141] See Scholem, *Sabbatai Sevi*; Goldish, *Sabbatean Prophets*.

[142] See Tishby, 'The Messianic Agitation'.

[143] See Rosman, *Founder*; *Die Geschichten vom Ba'al Schem Tov*, ed. and trans. Grözinger.

[144] *Magid devarav leya'akov*, ed. Schatz-Uffenheimer, 38–9.

[145] See *Hakeronikah*, ed. Levin; Elior, 'Jacob Frank's *Divrei ha'adon*'; Balaban, *History of the Frankist Movement*; Scholem, 'Redemption through Sin'.

cepts of 'fear' and 'love'. He argues in favour of 'a religious act achieved through transgression' and of 'a transgression done for the sake of God's name'. He formulates the doctrine of the *tsadik* with regard to spiritual and physical matters, and offers new categories for an autonomous social leadership.[146] In the nineteenth century in Nahman of Bratslav's teaching, found among the hasidic writings in Bratslav, there is the term *kushya* (a question), which requires doubting conventional conceptualization and known reality.[147] In the hasidic writings of Mordecai Joseph Leiner of Izbica one can find the terms 'depth' and 'shade', 'scepticism' and 'tranquillity', which distinguish between the hidden and the revealed, require a critical sceptical stance towards the tradition, and establish new categories of freedom and autonomy.[148]

The mystic is free to determine God's will in his time as well as the appropriate response to it. He is free to determine his relationship to the divine will embedded in the commonly accepted norms and based on divine revelation in the past. He reinterprets the sacred texts in the light of his own vision and outlines how actual reality relates to the desired mystical reality. A clear example of a person who sees himself as a vessel serving God is provided by the Seer of Lublin. He reminds himself in his diary that what gives him the autonomy to make independent decisions and enables him to mould new religious patterns—the extraordinary spirituality granted to him—was not given to him for his own sake but for the community's: 'It should be permanently in your heart that you reached this point not because of your righteousness but because of the kindness of God, who helps those whose aim is to purify.'[149] In addition, the Seer tells himself in circular reasoning that he should speak only under ecstatic inspiration, endowed from heaven when he imagines himself speaking to the holy creatures in Ezekiel's vision (Ezek. 10):

[The phrase] 'The speaking burning holy living creatures' means that one should not speak unless by the vitality of the Torah and the ecstasy of the love of the Creator, blessed be He, and the fear of Him, which is called the flame of God which is love and fear from God which generate human vitality from above, meaning that one should not speak until reaching the great vitality and ecstasy endowed by God that is the creatures uttering fire fiercely.[150]

The Seer feels free to define himself as the tabernacle for the essence of divinity, a status he was granted (according to him) to help all of Israel in physical and spiritual matters: '[The phrase] "the tabernacle of testimony" means also that

---

[146] On the theory of the *tsadik* in general see Green, 'Typologies of Leadership and the Hasidic Ẓaddiq'; Green, 'Zadik as Axis Mundi'; Rapoport-Albert, 'God and the Zaddik'; on the theory of the *tsadik* in the writings of the Seer of Lublin and his mystical perception see Elior, 'Between *Yesh* and *Ayin*'. [147] See Weiss, *Studies in East European Jewish Mysticism*.

[148] Ibid.; Schatz-Uffenheimer, *Hasidism as Mysticism*; Faierstein, *All is in the Hands of Heaven*; Elior, 'Changes in Religious Thought'. [149] *Zot zikaron*, 25–6. [150] Ibid. 18.

[God] dwells in us in order to perform miracles and wonders for the sake of Israel and this is testimony to the inspiration of the Shekhinah within us that responds to all of our calls.'[151] His contemporary Solomon of Lutsk, a student of the Maggid of Mezhirech and an eminent publisher of hasidic books in Korets, regards the *tsadik* as a medium for divine revelation in the present, or as the expression of God's will revealed in the world through a human being:

He is called a *tsadik* because through him the abundance of the divine blessing and His vitality are drawn. And He contracts His glory, blessed be He, in this world and lets His divinity in this world be known . . . Through Him the existence in the whole world of the Creator, blessed be He, will be revealed . . . The rule that follows is that the *tsadik* has to know and to let all of this be known, which means that the Holy One, blessed be He, creates and maintains everything to make His lordship and authority known and His name will be blessed in the universe.[152]

In the name of this new understanding regarding the relations between God and man, the Seer of Lublin redefines the limits of his religious duty as the leader responsible for the redemption of Israel:

For the *tsadik* has to be careful about two things: one, that his soul is always pure and free of any sin . . . in order to be prepared for the inspiration of the holiness of God, blessed be He, on him and within him; and in addition, he has to take actions to fulfil God's will, to ensure that His holiness is magnified, blessed be He, in the universe and to act for the redemption of Israel and [for] miracles and wonders.[153]

After reading these works of mystical literature, it often seems that the mystic's experiences precede those of the general public. The reason is that the mystic is anxious to be 'prepared for the inspiration of the holiness of God, blessed be He, on him and within him', and yearns to explore the limits of his psyche and establish the truthfulness of its unique faculties. Mystical experience is the seedbed of the recognition of many voices in the human spirit, the discovery of opposites, multiplicities, and different identities within one psyche at one and the same time. It also underlies the awareness of the capability of consciousness and creative imagination to break through the boundaries of conventional limitations of time and space. Mystical experience, which involves inspiration or idiosyncratic observation and imaginative interpretation, is the origin of the recognition of the profound linkage between the human psyche and the secrets of the divine being and of the complex relations between the inner dimensions of man and outer reality. The awareness of the relativity of concepts to place and time, the changing conceptions of God and man, the place of dreams and thoughts in an associative sequence, the freedom to create, and the absence of an unequivocal authority can also be traced to mystical experience. The same is true for the acknowledgement of the decisive importance of scepticism and questioning, the importance of per-

---

[151] *Zot zikaron*, 73.   [152] *Divrat shelomoh*, 'Mikets', 33.   [153] *Zot zikaron*, 73.

sonal criticism of accepted authority, the significance of autonomous decision-making, and the freedom of the imagination to create alternative worlds and idiosyncratic language. It is the mystical literature that accepts, for the first time, a relativistic reading of traditional obligations, the autonomous spirit granted to unique individuals, the relativity of reality, and the possibility of alternative worlds, and even a different concept of man. Within the framework of the traditional world, it was mystical thought that accepted irrational expressions, extraordinary experiences, transcendance of conventional borders, and subversive ideas.

FOUR

Mystical Language and Magical Language

*'Though I speak with the tongues of men and of angels . . .
and though I have the gift of prophecy and
understand all mysteries . . .'*

Rabbi Israel Ba'al Shem Tov, may he rest in peace, taught: An opening for light
shalt thou make for the ark, for in each and every letter there are worlds and souls
and divinity.
Tsava'at harivash (The Testament of the Besht), §75

Bezalel was able to combine letters through which heaven and earth were created.
BT *Berakhot* 55a

The Names are like keys to each and every thing that a human being needs for any
matter or issue in the world.
GIKATILLA, *Sha'arei orah*

He is His Name and His Name is Him. He is in Him and His Name is in His
Name. Song is His Name and His Name is song.
Synopse zur Hekhalot-Literatur, §588

I
N MYSTICAL THOUGHT the basic assumption for understanding reality is that
the upper and lower worlds are joined and related. The hidden world is implied
in the revealed world and is seen in its unity despite its various contrasts, whereas
the revealed world reflects in its variety the hidden world and draws its life and
essence from it. Everything is included in everything else, and every aspect has
depths of reflections and endless reciprocal interrelations.

This reciprocity is based on language, which according to the mystical point of
view has a divine source whose existence is multifaceted.[1] Speech is the unfolding
of the divine being in language, and reality, as we know it, is simply the unfolding and revelation of the divine word. Divine language is thus a revelation in perceptible concepts of the infinite power of God within creation, understood by

---

[1] On the mystical language see Bialik, 'Language Closing and Disclosing'; Scholem, 'Meaning of
the Torah'; Scholem, 'Name of God'; S. Katz, 'Language, Epistemology, and Mysticism'; Dan, *On
Holiness*.

mystical doctrine as an infinite stream of letters or as a chain of letters and divine names whose links are connected from the highest level of the unknown being down to its revealed end.[2] The letters are thus understood as a 'ladder placed on earth whose top touches heaven'. Creative power is embodied in the letters of the sacred divine language, which constitute the building blocks of being and join one another in the process of creation. Each letter is a doorway to one of the upper worlds, which are successively connected in revelation and concealment to all the other worlds.

According to Jewish mysticism, language develops in two opposite directions: (i) it constructs (or synthesizes) from the abstract to the concrete in the creation of the material world, and (ii) it deconstructs (or analyses) from the concrete to the abstract in the process of stripping away the material world. It is thus a two-way bridge that embraces all opposites and connects God and man, the hidden and the revealed, the infinite and the finite, the past and the present. Cleaving to the letters provides an opportunity for the enclosure of the upper worlds and for the human spirit to adhere to them.

The early mystical work *Sefer yetsirah* discusses the divine meaning of letters and numbers, which form a bridge between the Creator and the created and are understood as the basis and secret of being. This work begins with a statement that points out the essential role of the letters in the creation process in both its concealed and revealed stages:

In thirty-two wondrous paths of wisdom engraved YH the Lord of Hosts, God of Israel, the Living God, El Shadai, high and exalted, dwelling all the way to the heights, whose name is holy, and he created his world through three books (*sefarim*) of *s-f-r*: through *sefer* (book) and *sefor* (number; or *sefar*, counting) and *sipur* (story). Ten *sefirot* of infinite nothingness and twenty-two elemental letters.[3]

The mystical tradition, early and late, sought to express both the infinite divine revelation embedded in the Holy Scriptures and the power of the perpetual presence of God. The tradition combined the twenty-two letters of the holy language into the ten spheres (*sefirot*). These were interpreted in their unity as *sefer* (the Torah), the eternal divine language composed of written letters, *sipur* (the story or the history of the creation of the world, of language, and of men by God according to the biblical tradition composed of written letters as elements of eternal being), *sapir* (the translucent reflection of the divine—the reference is to the word *sapir*, usually translated 'sapphire', which appears in two places in connection with a vision of the

---

[2] On names and letters in the mystical tradition see *Sefer yetsirah* 1: 1; Talmage, 'Apples of Gold'; Fine, 'The Contemplative Practice of Yiḥudim in Lurianic Kabbalah'; Idel, *Golem*; Green, *Keter*; Gruenwald, 'Writing, Epistles, and the Name of God'; Grözinger, 'Names of God'; Zak, *In the Gates*; Lesses, *Ritual Practices*; Arbel, *Beholders*.

[3] *Sefer yetsirah*, 1: 1. In Hebrew the words 'book', 'number', and 'story' share a common root; see above, Ch. 1 n. 85. On *Sefer yetsirah* see Aloni, 'Date of *Sefer yetsirah*'; Dan, 'Religious Significance of *Sefer Yetsirah*'; Gruenwald, 'A Preliminary Critical Edition of Sefer Yeẓira'; Liebes, *Creation Doctrine of Sefer Yetsirah*.

divine, Exod. 24: 10 and Ezek. 1: 26), and *mispar* (the ten elements of being corresponding to ten *sefirot*).[4] The mystical tradition explained their divine source and creative power: 'And why are they called *sefirot*, because it has been written in Psalm 19: 2 that the heavens declare [*mesaperim*] the glory of God.'[5] 'The meaning of the word *sefirah* [first mentioned in *Sefer yetsirah*] was understood as "counting", based on *mispar* [number], and there are those who say it stems from *sapirut* ['sapphirehood'] and clarity, as suggested in the commentary, that it is a work of the stone of sapphire.'[6] 'And as I have heard . . . that God, blessed be He, made a book which is the world and the commentary on that book is the Torah, because the Torah is like an interpretation of the possessions of God, blessed be He, within creation.'[7]

This description of creation by letters (the interpretation of which is based on the common meaning of letters and 'coming', as in the phrase *yeteh veyavo*, which means 'coming all the time'; see Isa. 21: 12, Deut. 33: 2, Isa. 44: 7, Job 3: 25) and *sefirot* (the interpretation of which is based on all the derivations of the root *s-f-r*) demonstrates the nature of mystical language as a language that crosses boundaries or as a language of mirrors and reflections that culture holds up to itself. While the concepts of creation commonly used are limited by their application to a single occurrence, in contrast an ongoing creation is suggested by means of a hidden cosmic reflection through the images of mystical paths, spheres (*sefirot*), books (*sefarim*), numbers (*sefar*) and sapphire (*sapir*), which shed new light on ordinary understanding, which distinguishes among them. The linguistic reflection of a hidden reality, where letters and numbers, spheres and paths of wisdom, books and divine creation are united in an eternal ongoing process, is juxtaposed with revealed reality, where the creative process is associated with language, numbers, and letters, with books and human wisdom. The mirror of a mythical past and a mystical present is held up to a particular present reality. The reflection of the vastness of the creative divine language is contrasted with human speech and human thought.

This conception of mystical language is based on the dialectical assumption that language is a limited physical revelation of the infinite abstract being of God, which needs to be concealed and contracted in order to be revealed. According to this conception, the concealed divine being animates the revealed language and eternalizes it by giving it many layers and infinite meaning:

And God enacted a covenant [with Abraham] . . . and it is the holy language. He tied twenty-two letters in his tongue. And God revealed to him their secret, he moistened them in water, enflamed them with fire, whirled them with wind, enflamed them in seven stars, led them in twelve signs of the zodiac. (*Sefer yetsirah* 6: 8)

---

[4] On the numerical value of letters, note that the arabic numbers that we use today to signify numbers are a late historical development. In the Jewish tradition letters signify the numerical value in calculations of dates from antiquity to the present. The first ten letters denote the first ten numbers; the next nine letters denote the decades starting with 20, 30, etc.; the last three letters denote 200, 300, 400.

[5] *Sefer habahir*, §125.   [6] R. Shem-Tov, *Sefer ha'emunot*, Gate 4, ch. 4, p. 28*b*.

[7] Zadok Hakohen of Lublin, *Tsidkat hatsadik*, 216.

The source of mystical language is divine and its letters and words are divine names, signs, hints, meanings, and secrets, which conceal depths of meaning. This language is understood to be the essential representation of the reciprocal link between the divine and the human. This link in turn is understood as a unity of opposites, such as being and nothingness, ebb and flow, elusive appearance and essential reality, the physical and the abstract, the finite and the infinite. It is the source of the influence that places its stamp on all of being and its representations in language. These opposites exist in a regular dialectical relation in which the existence of the revealed is contingent upon the concealed nothingness, and the revelation of the abstract nothingness is contingent upon physical existence.[8] That is to say, the revealed parts of language are nothing but a cover over its hidden and divine essence. The revelation of the divine essence of language in turn is contingent upon its contraction into words and its concealment in letters.

The following quotation from Israel Ba'al Shem Tov cogently expresses the double meaning of language, in which every unit and word reflects at one and the same time nothingness and being, or the hidden divine infinitude and the revealed material finitude: 'Rabbi Israel Ba'al Shem Tov, may he rest in peace, taught: An opening for light shalt thou make for the ark [*tevah*, which also means 'word'] [Gen. 6: 16] . . . [which] teaches that in each and every letter there are worlds and souls and divinity.'[9] In the mystical tradition language blends metaphysical and real essences, units of thought, speech, writing and reading, pronunciation and signifying. These form a bridge between human experience and its divine source. The mystic translates the reality beyond language into a linguistic reality and deconstructs linguistic reality into its generative elements—letters, units, names, words, numerical values, musical notes, signs, and meanings. Like a musician who puts life into the score, the mystic is an inspired artist who animates the written text to express the power of the hidden divinity embodied in the revealed language. The physical and abstract dimensions of the letters and words, their animating power and cosmic existence, their sacred character and their hidden communicative essence (which exists at one and the same time in heaven and on earth) have been extensively interpreted throughout the mystical literature: in explicit studies, in visionary illuminations, and by means of suggestive poetic and symbolic methods. In 3 Enoch, written between the third and sixth centuries CE, one of the first stages of the mystical path is presented.[10] During this stage linguistic principles familiar from earthly reality simultaneously gain an animating divine power, a visual appearance, and a cosmic existence. This transformation

---

[8] On the dialectic relation between the divine and the human in the hasidic tradition see Elior, *Paradoxical Ascent to God*.

[9] [Israel Ba'al Shem Tov], *Tsava'at harivash* (The Testament of the Besht), §75. On this work see Dubnow, *History of Hasidism*, 387–8 and index; Gries, *Book, Author, and Story in Early Hasidism*.

[10] On 3 Enoch see *3 Enoch*, ed. Odeberg; *3 Enoch*, ed. Alexander; *Synopse zur Hekhalot-Literatur*, ed. Schäfer et al., §§1–80; Dan, *Jewish Mysticism*, i: *Late Antiquity*; Elior, *Three Temples*; Gruenwald, *Apocalyptic and Merkavah Mysticism*; Arbel, *Beholders of Divine Secrets*.

takes place during the course of a poetic description of the animating letters guarded in heaven, which are shown by Enoch–Metatron to Ishmael as he ascends to heaven:

Rabbi Ishmael said: 'Metatron said to me: "Let me show you letters out of which heaven and earth were created. Letters out of which oceans and rivers were created. Letters out of which mountains and hills were created. Letters out of which trees and grass were created. Letters out of which the stars and constellations, the moon and the sun, Orion and the Pleiades and all kinds of lights of the firmament were created. Letters out of which the ministering angels were created, each letter flashed time after time like bolts of lightning, time after time like torches, time after time like flames, time after time like the rising of the sun, moon, and stars." I approached him, and he seized me with his hand, lifted me with his wings, and showed me all those letters that were engraved with a pen of fire on God's throne, and fiery sparks and lightning were coming out of them and covering all the chambers of the seventh heaven.'[11]

Through their animating power these glowing letters testify to the precedence of divine language over human language and to the divine and non-communicative source of language. They are not only cosmic entities or divine animating forces latent in the fundamentals of creation, but also form a creative conceptual essence and a creative human category. This is because the letters, or their symbolic representations, single out human beings who are familiar with the letters' physical and abstract qualities, as readers and writers, speakers and thinkers, who use them creatively in their thought, speech, and action by abstracting and realizing, building and destroying, representing and decoding, annihilating and commemorating.

The world of kabbalists and mystics is a world of language and speech, revelation and concealment, names and letters. At times it is the world of those who create being out of nothingness, those who seek a new language capable of expressing a previously unknown reality, a reality for which the commonly used language is too narrow and which it is incapable of containing or expressing. It is the world of those who expose the deep meanings that resonate within language. The hidden private language of the mystics and beholders of secrets draws from the psyche and the realm of holiness. Their language creates a world of its own and interprets reality according to its own principles. In contrast, conventional language is based on tradition and existing reality and defines its meaning according to social conventions of communication. The mystic rebels against what seems to him to be imprisonment by the denotative language, which defines and limits. Often he tries to create a new language that interprets the world as a symbolic or metaphoric system or a system of mirrors and reflections. The mystic is an idiosyncratic creator who sees the brightness of the sapphire (*livnat hasapir*) through number (*mispar*), and 'worlds, souls, and divinity' through the letters, and who 'blows the letters back up to their source'. He sometimes enflames and illuminates the letters or

---

[11] *Synopse zur Hekhalot-Literatur*, ed. Schäfer et al., §59. Cf. *3 Enoch*, ed. Alexander, 265–6.

engraves them in his spirit or combines letters like Bezalel, 'who was able to combine the letters through which heaven and earth were created'.[12] He sometimes believes that 'the names are like keys to each and every thing that a human being needs for any matter or issue in the world'.[13] Sometimes the mystic expresses himself in an obscure language—a language of symbols and allusions—and sometimes he penetrates to the depth of a meaningless language, decodes its secrets, and, by illuminating its hidden meanings, forms a new creation, and sometimes he exclaims: 'The Torah and the souls and the *sefirot* are all one thing.'[14]

The mystical tradition regards the letters involved in thinking, reading, writing, speaking, praying, and intending as a bridge between what is above and what is below. It presents language as 'a ladder placed on the earth whose top reaches heaven and angels of God are ascending and descending on it' (Gen. 28: 12). This is because the divine word, which constitutes the 'forms of the Name, blessed be He' and is delivered through language, is embodied in the letters of the Torah, and transmitted to humans as the ever changing abstract spirit along with the unchangeable concrete form:

And here, all the letters of the Torah, in their forms, in combinations and separately, entangled, crooked and distorted, added and missing, small, big and crowned, and the letters' calligraphy, and the closed, open, and arranged portions are [the forms of the Name, blessed be He] the patterns of the ten *sefirot* . . . because in its entirety it is a divine structure, carved in the name of the Holy One, blessed be He . . . in addition all of the Torah is the names of the Holy One, blessed be He, and therefore it is forbidden to add to it or to subtract from it, even one letter.[15]

According to *Sefer yetsirah*, God engraves, carves, and brings down an infinite stream of letters throughout the creation process. By combining letters he transforms the abstract into the material, the infinite into the finite, and the spiritual into the physical. By means of a linguistic whirlpool that blends the metaphysical and the physical, voice, sound, and form, he creates the material world. In contrast, a human being 'turns the material into the abstract' or 'divests corporeality' from its physical constraints: he deconstructs and separates, analyses and distinguishes, studies and decodes the combinations, in his quest for the common linguistic element that exists beyond distinctively material being. He abstracts and elevates letters and combinations of names according to their roots in a process of exaltation, and creates new combinations and beings in his imagination. In contrast to God, who perpetually creates the world through letters and combinations, going from nothingness to being, the human strips off materiality, using letters and combinations, going from being to nothingness. Shneur Zalman of Lyady described it as follows: 'but here we see a kind of annihilation of being into

---

[12] BT *Ber.* 55*a*.   [13] Gikatilla, *Sha'arei orah*, 88.   [14] Moses Cordovero, *Or yakar*, iv. 36*a*.
[15] Menahem of Recanati, *Commentary on the Torah*, 'Lekh lekha'; corrected according to Milan, Biblioteca Ambrosiana, MS num. 62, p. 113*b*.

nothingness in all that was created, which is the opposite of creating being out of nothingness'.[16] The letters are the dialectical creative element shared by God and man. The detachment of the letters from the word (*tevah*) of the written canonized text, and their devoted recitation in thought and speech (in such a way that 'the word [*tevah*] becomes an illuminating opening'),[17] revive their animating power and influence the upper and lower vitalities. Following Ezekiel's vision, the dialectical creative element is referred to as 'the vitality running back and forth' (derived from Ezek. 1: 14). It includes abstraction and concretization, creation and annihilation, obfuscation and clarification, and this is an infinite thinking process that abstracts materiality and materializes the abstract:

When a human being recalls the letters he shakes the upper vitality. And when he wholeheartedly cleaves in his mind to the Name, blessed be He, he reanimates the vitality that has been emanating from the highest thought until it is ready to be spoken and put in the mouth of the human, and through the words of the prayer he yearns for the Name, blessed be He, and by it he blows the letters back up to their source.[18]

The poetical words of Judah Halevi express the vocalization of the letters, offering the mystic the unifying moment that he is yearning for:

> I sought You,
> With all my heart I called out to You.
> When I sought You,
> I discovered You seeking me.[19]

Throughout its history, mystical thought has been based on the assumption that the world as perceived through language is the unfolding of the divine being through the Hebrew language. The language, however, has two poles: the concealed, which is inaccessible and connected to the divine name, and the revealed, which is accessible and connected to the letters. Often in mystical literature it seems that everything exists within a dynamic process that revolves around a linguistic reality revealed in the letters and a reality, hidden in the names, that goes beyond the language. According to this tradition the world was created out of letters: 'everything was created according to the Torah, into which the Holy One, Blessed Be He, looked as if into a blueprint while he created the world. Thus, the letters of the Torah exist in everything in the world.'[20] The author maintains that the letters are the divine element sustaining all creation and argues that human duty is to decipher the divine letters in every corporeality.[21] In the Heikhalot literature God's hidden image (known as *shiur komah*) is depicted as an infinite body

---

[16] Shneur Zalman of Lyady, *Torat ḥayim*, fol. 1ᵛ.

[17] [Israel B'al Shem Tov], *Tsava'at harivash*, §75.

[18] Meshulam Feivush of Zbarazh, *Likutim yekarim*, 132b.

[19] Judah Halevi, 'Yah, 'anah 'emtsa'akha', *Shirim nivḥarim*, p. 8.

[20] Ze'ev Wolf, *Or hame'ir*, a sermon for Shavuot, 170a, 186b; see *Bereshit rabah* 1: 1; cf. Zohar I. 134a, II. 161a.   [21] Wolf, *Or hame'ir*, 84a, 28a, 131a, 139.

covered with letters which compose divine names ascribed to separate limbs of the divine stature.[22] The ineffable name of God in the biblical tradition is a mysterious combination of letters. God is 'The Name'. The power of 'The Name' in the ritual tradition is described in a prayer recited on Rosh Hashanah and Yom Kippur interchanging the ritual past and the mystical present:

> The Name of God is a tower of strength. By means of it the righteous can run and be exalted. Master of the universe, from the day the Temple was destroyed we have nothing that promotes atonement: no sacrifices, priestly garments, grain offering, slaughtering, and no altar—only Your great Name sustains us. (*Maḥzor rabah*, 207)

In the introduction to his commentary on the Torah, Nahmanides argues that the whole Torah is the hidden name of God. The letters are the limbs of the Shekhinah, which is referred to as the 'world of speech'.[23] The 'garment', another divine concept in kabbalah, is an entity woven out of all the letters of the alphabet, and exists between the worlds of emanation and infinitude.[24] *Sefer hatemunah* interprets the phrase 'He sees the likeness of God' to refer to the form of the letters and the form of the name of God. Many other kabbalistic traditions would agree with the sixteenth-century kabbalist Joseph Ibn Tabul that 'the whole emanation doctrine is the name of God'.[25]

Within the mystical tradition the holy language consists of 'lower, second, and third' levels. There are letters that join together into meaningful words, creative clarifying materializing elements that turn chaos into creation and establish being. In contrast to this, there are letters that join into meaningless words and hidden and abstract elements, that turn creation back to chaos and 'blow the letters back up to their source'. Mystical language is concerned with the letters that join into words of infinite meaning, while magical language is concerned with the letters that merge into meaningless names. These two languages function alongside the language of human communication. The mystical language expands human knowledge, consciousness, and meaning by creating a new vocabulary that affects human creativity and imagination. The magical language gives up on all these realms, resorting to meaningless combinations of letters, which are considered to be understood beyond the human realm and believed to be effective for human needs. The mystical language adds on to the conventional language, expanding human expression. The magical language is sometimes associated with the ritual language, which is not preconditioned by understanding.[26]

The relation between the mystical and conventional languages, on the one hand, and the magical and ritual languages, on the other, is the relation between a

---

[22] On *shiur komah* see *Shiur komah*, in *Synopse zur Hekhalot-Literatur*, ed. Schäfer et al.; Cohen (ed.), *Shi'ur Qomah*; Scholem, 'Shi'ur Qomah'; Farber-Ginat, 'Studies in Shi'ur Komah'; Arbel, *Beholders*.   [23] See Ch. 3 n. 94.

[24] On the 'garment' see Cohen-Alloro, 'Magic'.   [25] Joseph Ibn Tabul, *Derush ḥeftsivah*, p. x.

[26] See Austin, *How to Do Things with Words*; Betz, *Greek Magical Papyri in Translation*, Introduction.

creating language and an annihilating language, or a spoken language and a mute language. Mystical language deciphers the hidden reality of heaven and earth. Conventional language evaluates meaning according to comprehensibility and expressed intentions. In contrast, the magical and ritual languages are mute languages of names. Humans cannot evaluate them according to their comprehensibility, because they do not have a revealed explicit meaning and do not relate to immediate reality. The reciprocal relation between the mystical and conventional languages, on the one hand, and the magical and ritual languages, on the other, reflects the divine 'running back and forth'.[27]

If we look at the relation between mystical language and magical language as the relation between creation and destruction, or as the relation between construction and deconstruction, then, by any meaningful naming, claiming, defining, distinguishing, or construing of words or sentences, we move from chaos to creation. That is to say, by naming, by establishing distinctive physical or abstract entities, one limits chaos or participates in the process of moving from nothingness to being. This process involves the 'growing of letters from their roots', a meaningful naming or apprehensible embodiment that defines borders and meaning. In contrast, by deconstructing one strips the sentence of its meaning, erases the word, the name, and the distinct existence, and participates in the process of moving from being back to nothingness. The process of 'unnaming', disembodiment, and disclaiming blows the letters back up to their source and moves creation back to chaos, the state in which nothing is limited by words.

Mystical literature specifies the holy names.[28] These names are combinations of letters that have a mystical and magical meaning but lack a communicative meaning. This literature includes the letters of the ineffable name of God and the tradition of the explicit names. These names have a visual combination of letters as signs, icons, or symbols, but do not have a sound or a comprehensible meaning that can be explained or translated. Creative letters are mentioned, as well as 'sealing' letters, 'binding' letters, and 'connecting' and 'conjuring' letters, and letters functioning as containers and units of the divine word. Mystical writings mention combinations of letters capable of creating, destroying, adjuring, blessing, and cursing. This literature contains different traditions referring to the formulation of adjurations, divine names, magic words, amulets, and linguistic traditions connected to the creation of a *golem*[29] and the ascent to the upper worlds. Many

---

[27] On magical and ritual language, see Tambiah, 'A Performative Approach to Ritual'; Austin, *How to Do Things with Words*.

[28] On the holy names see Urbach, *Sages*, ch. 7; Grözinger, 'Names of God'; Elior, 'Mysticism, Magic and Angelology'; Elior, 'From Earthly Temple'; Schäfer, *Hidden and Manifest God*. For examples of the use of holy names see *Synopse zur Hekhalot-Literatur*, ed. Schäfer et al.; *Geniza Fragmente*, ed. Schäfer, concordance under *shem*, *shemot* (name, names); *Heikhalot zutarti*, ed. Elior. For English translations of adjurations in the Heikhalot literature, see Lesses, *Ritual Practices*, 63–101, 161–73, 412–25; cf. Arbel, *Beholders*.

[29] A *golem* is a magical figure invented in the writings of the medieval German-Jewish pietists. It is

mystical traditions deal with Holy Names, and many writings begin in a way similar to the beginning of *Heikhalot rabati*: 'This is a book of seven sanctuaries of holiness in which the seventy Holy Names are specified.'[30] The holy names comprise strings of letters that do not have any communicative or semantic meaning. But just because of their incomprehensible combinations as meaningless names, they become identical to the creative infinite divine being that is beyond comprehension.

The early mystical tradition of the Heikhalot literature identified the hidden God with his revealed name:[31] 'He is His Name and His Name is Him, He is in His Name and His Name is Him';[32] 'His Name is in His Might and His Might is in His Name, He is His Strength and His Strength is His Name'.[33] God's essence is identical with His Name. Therefore knowing the names means knowing His essence. This knowledge, which humans cannot understand, is dangerous, as is reflected in the following warning: 'The one who uses the crown [the names of God] will vanish [from the world].'[34]

The hidden Name is one of the attributes of the divine essence and possesses creating and annihilating powers. Because of its overwhelming power as well as its ability to empower, it is desirable and dangerous.[35] The ineffable Name represents the mystical-magical element of the divine essence in its manifestation in language. It is obtained from a heavenly source such as an angelic revelation or through a mystical revelation to a human being ascending to heaven and gazing upon the upper sanctuaries. Obtaining the Name enables a human being, on the one hand, to control the domain of his heavenly revelation and to become a magical instrument in the recurring human ascent to heaven, and on the other hand to bring upper powers down by the withdrawal of discursive understanding and consciousness.

The divine Name contains an infinite essence and a finite meaningless embodiment. It is a morphologically inexplicit assembly of letters, which paradoxically is

created through a mixture of letter magic and meditative practices aimed at producing ecstatic states of consciousness. The *golem* came to life only while the ecstasy of his creator lasted. The creation of the *golem* was considered a sublime experience felt by the mystic who became absorbed in the mysteries of the alphabetic combination described in the *Sefer yetsirah*. Pseudo-Sa'adiah, in his commentary on the book, says that recitation of the alphabets of the book has the God-given power to produce a *golem* and to give it vitality and soul. MS Munich 40, as quoted by Scholem, *On the Kabbalah*, 192.

[30] *Heikhalot rabati*, in *Synopse zur Hekhalot-Literatur*, ed. Schäfer et al., §81.

[31] On the identity between the hidden God and the revealed name of God in Heikhalot literature see Schäfer, *Hidden and Manifest God*; Elior, 'Mysticism, Magic and Angelology'; Elior, 'Concept of God'.

[32] *Ma'aseh merkavah*, in *Synopse zur Hekhalot-Literatur*, ed. Schäfer et al., §588.   [33] Ibid. 557.

[34] *Heikhalot zutarti*, ed. Elior, 26 and 68. Cf. *Pirkei avot* 1: 3. *Avot derabi natan* 12: 13. Cf. the author of *Sha'arei tsedek* on the danger of death to the student of mysticism engaged in the ineffable Name (Scholem, *Kabbalah of Sefer hatemunah*, 249).

[35] On the bitter destiny of people who use divine names see *Heikhalot zutarti*, ed. Elior; Urbach, *Sages*, ch. 7; Dan, 'Story of Joseph della Reina'; Scholem, *Kabbalah of Sefer hatemunah*, 249–53.

called the Explicit Name (*hashem hameforash*). However, since there is no tradition of vocalization of this name, it is an ineffable name or names—one may write it but not pronounce it. Mystics, who believe that, in spite of being meaningless, name and power are synonyms, try to discover the holy names, which are connected with the upper worlds and a reality surpassing language. They look for names that emerge from the hidden divine language, in spite of the dangers attached to breaching boundaries, and in spite of explicit threat:

When you wish to mention this glorified name engraved in heaven with its vowels, ornament yourself and meditate in a special place, so that your voice is not heard by anyone else, and purify your heart and soul of any earthly thoughts. Imagine that at that time your soul separates from your body and dies in this world to live in the next world, which is the source of the existing life that is scattered in all that lives, and it is the intellect . . . and is in the image of the King of Kings.[36]

Magical language is mystical language whose meaningful functional dimensions have been suppressed in order to express meaningless intentions that draw from ritual and magical traditions. The magical tradition, like the mystical tradition, is based on the assumption that letters and words possess a wondrous creative power.[37] This power is ascribed to the divine and human word alike. Nevertheless, while the mystical tradition relates to the formative elements of what is hidden, symbolic templates, and visionary paradigms of the concealed reality, the magical tradition relates to meaningless names, meaningless phrases, meaningless unifications, adjurations, circles of letters, angelic language, magic words, amulets, and other context-free combinations of letters that do not convey any semantic meaning. While the mystical tradition refers to a system that has a hierarchy and semantic meaning that can be linguistically conveyed, the magical tradition gives expression to a chaotic system that avoids terminological crystallization. An example of both languages is found in *Heikhalot rabati*:

when a person wishes to descend to the *merkavah* he should call to Suriaa, the prince of the countenance, and adjure him one hundred and twelve times by TWTRWSYY YWY who is called TWTRWSSYY . . . the God of Israel.[38]

He should not add to the one hundred and twelve times nor should he take away from them—his blood is on his head. His mouth brings out the names and the fingers of his hand count one hundred and twelve. Immediately he descends and rules over the *merkavah*.[39]

---

[36] Abraham Abulafia, *Or hasekhel*, Munich MS 62, cited in Scholem, *Kabbalah of* Sefer hatemunah, 225; cf. 210–11.

[37] On mysticism and magic see Scholem, *On the Kabbalah*; Betz, *Greek Magical Papyri*; Cohen-Alloro, 'Magic and Sorcery in the Zohar'; Dan, 'Story of Joseph della Reina'; Gruenwald, 'Magic and Myth'; Gruenwald, 'Writing, Epistles, and the Name of God'; Schäfer, 'Jewish Magic Literature'; Idel, *Golem*; Swartz, *Scholastic Magic*.

[38] *Synopse zur Hekhalot-Literatur*, ed. Schäfer et al., §204.   [39] Ibid. §§204–5.

The words in small capitals, which cannot be translated because they lack semiotic meaning, reflect the magical language, while the rest of the text conveys mystical language.

Magical language uses names and meaningless words to create a connection with a supernatural power. One calls out for God by pronouncing his Explicit Name (an act that is forbidden) and his names that seem to be explicit but in reality are hidden.[40] These names are created by an infinite combination of letters. One calls upon the spirits ('winds' in Hebrew) by using the language of winds—a construction of vowels without consonants.[41] One calls upon the angels by meaningless names constructed of consonants without vowels.[42] This meaningless language is tied to God's Name and to different combinations of the letters of the alphabet. The assumption behind the meaningless language is that, although it is unintelligible in this world, it is decoded and intelligible in the upper worlds, and it influences the upper powers to carry out the person's request. In the Heikhalot literature, which includes a variety of magical elements, examples can be found of the use of this kind of language: 'These are the twenty-two letters that are twenty-two names [made out of] one letter of the Torah. ZYXW VTSR QPN MLKJ HGFE DCB. KI BIH COR OLMIM ADONAI AH YHA HAYU YAH VHI VHI VH YAH HAYAH YAH . . . This is the crown of the explicit name.'[43]

No specific date or distinctive religious-cultural place can be assigned to the magical way of thinking. Magical language belongs to the most ancient and sacred domains of the religious corpus. It is constructed out of sacred names, which are not evaluated according to their intelligibility to human beings but rather by their power to influence the upper worlds. Magical language may also include names that convey a sacred ritual tradition that empowers its users with the knowledge of the past and the future and enables them to control hidden beings. The users of magical language give up any syntactic structure and semantic meaning in order to participate in the language used by the inhabitants of upper worlds, or to influence hidden beings through meaningless language:

This is the sword of Moses [= the hidden name] that was given to him in the burning bush, and was revealed to Rabbi Ishmael son of Elisha in the Deed of the Chariot and this is the procedure: First call upon Malkiel . . . PATW AYR AMTDAL SRWPA GRA GTI TLBI . . .[44]

These meaningless names are called secrets, divine names, and adjurations, and are often connected to Metatron, the heavenly high priest:

---

[40] For examples of the language of holy names see ibid. §§655, 569, 657, 629, 580, 636; cf. *Heikhalot zutarti*, ed. Elior; Lesses, *Ritual Practices*, 69, 381–425.

[41] See e.g. the incomprehensible names in the adjuration 'its explanation in the language of purity with *yod he* how it is said: YHWH YW YHWY WW YHWH HW HW YHWH YH HYH YHWH HY WHYY HYW HYH YH YH HHW YH YYH . . .'. *Synopse*, §673.

[42] See Lesses, *Ritual Practices*, 72.   [43] *Synopse*, §364.   [44] Ibid. §598.

Rabbi Ishmael said: 'Any scholar who understands this great mystery . . . will state and explain and adjure and remind and decree and fulfil by the name HVZYAH ZHVBD YHVH YYAH MN MH, which is the name referring to Metatron. MRGVYEL is Metatron, SASGIRIA is Metatron, SNDIA is Metatron, PZKK is Metatron . . .

And one called to the other and said: Holy, holy, holy is the Lord of hosts. The whole earth is full of his glory. And he decreed decrees over them.'[45]

Dialectically, it is the giving up of meaning and intelligibility, context and intention, that allows a deeper knowledge, drawing from heavenly forms and projecting them onto the earthly level. This process also uncovers unknown powers in the human psyche and the divine being. The person who uses this language chooses to give up meaning and intelligibility in order to control, in a formulaic meaningless mode, hidden powers that might affect the revealed realm through invocations and adjurations. The hidden names, connected to the secrets of creation and cosmic powers, are obtained from angels or during mystical ascent to heaven, as is depicted in the First Book of Enoch, written in the circles of separatist priests in the second century BCE:

This is the order of Kazvi'el, the minister of oaths, which he showed to the angels when he gloriously dwelt in heaven . . . He told Michael to show him the hidden name, so that he might mention it in an oath and make them tremble at the name and the oath, those who showed mankind everything that was hidden. And this is the power of this oath that is huge and enormous, and he put the oath in Michael's hand. And these are his secrets in this oath and he is powerful by his oath, and by it heaven has been created since the creation of the world to eternity. And by that oath the ocean was created . . . and by that oath the depths have been fortified and fixed to their place without moving from eternity to eternity.[46]

Meaningless names and powerful oaths, in the possesion of angels and delivered to human beings during a mystical revelation or through magical tradition, control the hidden world because the names and the oaths represent the secrets of the eternal creative element that captures, binds, and dominates being.

Magic deals with the dialectical relation between unintelligible expression in the earthly world and its desired interpretation in the heavenly world. It is interested in the relation between 'deconstructed' language (combinations of letters that are meaningless in standard language and can be found in magical texts), which has been delivered to mankind in secrets, adjurations, and unifications, and language that is decoded and fully coherent only in the upper world. As previously said, in magical speech, poetry, ritual, or writing there is a process of dis-

---

[45] *Synopse*, §682.
[46] 1 Enoch 69: 13–14. On the quotation from Enoch cf. *Old Testament Pseudepigrapha*, ed. Charlesworth, i. 48–9, which offers a different version. The dating of the different sections of 1 Enoch is a subject of scholarly controversy. On the section that this quotation is taken from see Nickelsburg, '1 Enoch'.

mantling constructed beings, or essentializing meaning from a comprehensive sentence to a single word, or from a word to a letter. The language created by letters of the alphabet that do not combine into meaningful words or units is the language of secrets, unifications, or adjurations.[47] Using this language can cause the disintegration of consciousness that is followed by the deconstruction of being. Both losing control over consciousness and using meaningless speech in magical language are found throughout the mystical-magical tradition from antiquity to the present. Hayim Vital, the sixteenth-century kabbalist, gives us an unusually nuanced description of an internal and external disintegrative experience. In his diary, published as *Sefer hahezyonot* (The Book of Visions), Vital attests to the 'confusion of the mind' or the disintegration of consciousness that he experienced through unification and its magical language, and to the loss of physical and mental control. He learnt the art of unification from his teacher, Isaac Luria.[48] The unification was tied to the transcendence of time and place and prostration on the graves of the righteous (*tsadikim*) in order to connect with their souls in the upper worlds:

In Tamuz 5331 [=1571] I asked my teacher to teach me a unification in order to reach a mystical experience. He told me I was not ready yet. I begged him and he gave me a short unification. And I got up in the middle of the night and I used it. And I felt a shock in my body and my head became heavy and I was losing my mind and my mouth was twisted to one side and I stopped performing the unification.[49] On the first day of the month of Elul 5331 [=1571] my teacher, of blessed memory, sent me to the cave of Abaye and Raba. And I prostrated there on the grave of Abaye, of blessed memory, and I first unified the unification of the mouth and the nose of the ancient divinity,[50] and sleep overtook me and I woke up and saw nothing. Then I prostrated again on Abaye himself and unified the unification written by the hands of my teacher, may he rest in peace. While I was composing and combining the letters of [the name] *hvyh* and the name of God *'dnvt*[51] and the name *'dny* as *y'hdhvny*, as it is known, my mind became confused and I could not compose them . . . and I stopped thinking while composing that composition, and then it appeared to me in my mind as if a voice was telling me: 'Reconsider, Reconsider' many times . . . and here, all this appeared to me at that time in my mind, and then a great fear fell upon me, and all my body was shaking enormously and my hands were shaking. Also my lips were shaking unusually, and moving rapidly and frequently, running anxiously as if a voice was sitting on my tongue between my lips, saying anxiously over a hundred times these words: what shall I say, what shall I say. And I have been holding myself and my lips to prevent them from moving without being able to

---

[47] On mysteries and adjurations see *Sefer harazim*; Lesses, *Ritual Practices*; Swartz, *Scholastic Magic*.

[48] On unifications see Vital, *Shemonah she'arim*, 'Sha'ar ruah hakodesh' and 'Sha'ar hayihud'; Jacobs, *Jewish Mystical Testimonies*; *Jewish Mystical Autobiographies*, trans. Faierstein; Fine, *Physician of the Soul*; *Safed Spirituality*, trans. Fine.   [49] Vital, *Sefer hahezyonot*, 237.

[50] A unification referring to the anthropomorphic picture of God in Lurianic kabbalah.

[51] A combination of the letters of the name *hvyh*.

calm them down at all . . . And then a voice has been blasting in my mouth and on my tongue saying: 'Wisdom, Wisdom', over twenty times . . . and all this happened very quickly, a wonderful thing, many times, while awake, while I was prostrating in the cave of Abaye.[52]

Paraphrasing Paul Valéry, it can be said that magical language creates a world of words, the logic of which is not semantic but phonetic, that is, the words do not serve to represent a distinct meaning but a distinct sound. Dialectically, the names of these sounds denote their opposite: 'explicit names', 'unifications', 'combinations', 'holy names'. Often, these names do not have a vowel system or a phonetic tradition or earthly meaning. Therefore it is to a great extent a silent ritual language. The users of this language are participants in a process of deconstructing the language and disintegrating consciousness and reality. They turn creation back from the defined stage to the abstract stage, from the spoken language to the ancient language of sounds, recited or sung as rituals lacking meaning. It is not surprising that in many languages 'chant', 'enchantment', 'canto', and 'incantation' belong to the same semantic field.

The deviation of magical language from the limits of existing standards is suggested in the biblical descriptions of prophets in a trance, where they are referred to as people out of their minds, or people invaded by spirits: 'every man who is demented and considers himself a prophet' (Jer. 29: 26); 'The prophet is a fool, the spiritual man is insane' (Hos. 9: 7). This deviation is fascinatingly expressed in ancient Greek. 'Our greatest blessings', says Socrates in the *Phaedrus*, 'come to us by way of madness' (Plato, *Phaedrus* 244 A), 'provided the madness is given us by divine gift.'[53] The word denoting insanity in Greek (*mainomai*) is the same word for the utterances of the oracle at Delphi, the mystical sayings of the priestess and the Sibyls, and the enthusiastic followers of Dionysus while in a prophetic trance.[54] All of them are referred to after the Common Era as 'speaking in tongues', following Paul's words to the Corinthians: 'Though I speak with the tongues of men and of angels' (1 Cor. 13: 1–2; cf. 1 Cor. 14: 23). 'Speaking in tongues' is the uttering of meaningless sounds and is not an outcome of intentional thought but is created through a different process, sometimes described as the Holy Spirit, that is not part of discursive thought. In this process, of 'speaking in tongues' or glossolalia or *mania* or *mainomai*, man serves as a passive vehicle for automatic uncontrolled speech in an unintelligible language, as described in the story of the apostles: 'And they were all filled with the Holy Spirit and began to speak with other tongues, as the Spirit gave them utterance' (Acts 2: 4), or in the previously cited testimony of Hayim Vital. The magical meaning of this kind of speech rests on the assumption that through it one is able to participate in what is explicit and implicit in the

---

[52] *Sefer haḥezyonot*, 170–1.   [53] See Dodds, *Greeks and the Irrational*, 64–82.

[54] In Greek *mania* and *mainomai* denote one who was taken over by a deity and refers to manic prophecy. See Dodds, ibid. 70–4, 85.

language used by the inhabitants of the upper worlds. Following this logic, if intelligible and controlled rational speech relates to human language and to the revealed world, unintelligible, irrational, and uncontrolled speech relates to God's language and the hidden world.

The dialectical kabbalist tradition stipulates that 'each creation is a judgement [= limit]' and each 'being' is limited by words and 'dressed in letters', while 'the nothingness' exists 'beyond the reason that is obtained through letters', as formulated by Shneur Zalman of Lyady (*Tanya* 165). If the 'running' (*ratso*) is the transition from nothingness to being, culminating in *yesh*, being, and the 'back' (*shov*) is the transition from being to nothingness (culminating in *ayin*, nothingness), then 'nothingness' refers to the limitless undefined realm, rich in its infinitude and obtainable through the magical and ritual language, and 'being' refers to the defined, limited, finite, and double-sided realm, which is reached by conventional and mystical language. The boundless spirit returning to its divine source relates to the magical language, which transforms the concrete into the abstract, while the creative language, which flows from the divine to the human, and transforms the abstract into the concrete, relates to the mystical language. Magical and ritual language, which covers everything from divine inspiration to mental derangement,[55] may relate to the realm of nothingness with the intention of influencing being, and conventional and mystical language, which covers everything from creation to annihilation, relates to the realm of being in order to reveal its divine aspects.[56]

The bi-directional language, which stems from a source that is divine, that is, infinite, eternal, multidimensional, multilayered, and ambiguous, turns into a ladder of ascent from materiality to divinity. The deconstructed words are released from their fixed denotations and open up to infinite new possibilities in their reassembled forms. Concepts limited by words are released from their experienced materiality and enriched by additional meanings latent in thought. In his book *Or hame'ir*, Ze'ev Wolf of Zhitomir, a late eighteenth-century hasid, clearly expresses the freedom embedded in this way of seeing the infinite meanings of language.[57] He also clarifies the dynamic relation between the letters of the holy language and the plain meaning of the text, on the one hand, and the freedom to create and retell the story anew, on the other:

The truth of the matter is that the Torah as a whole is nothing but letters, and any one of Israel, according to his understanding and ability, forms combinations of the letters. And behold, these combinations recreated now through his [the person's] talent and the depth of his understanding were latent in the letters from the beginning, waiting to be formed by a person enlightened by his enormous knowledge and effort in the worship of the Creator.[58]

[55] See Tambiah, 'A Performative Approach to Ritual'.

[56] See Elior, *Paradoxical Ascent*, 25–30, 63–73, 127–38.

[57] On the freedom of interpretation in mystical literature see Elior, 'Changes in Religious Thought'.   [58] *Or hame'ir*, 'Vayeḥi', 38*b*.

The magical-mystical relation to the letters is a relation of deconstruction (*peruk*) and reconstruction (*tseruf*). Deconstruction means the separation of language from its conventional common meaning and the separation of consciousness from its conventional limitations. It also means cutting off ties with revealed reality and its plain literal expressions in order to participate in a hidden reality reflected in secrets. Reconstruction and transposition mean creating new linguistic combinations that illuminate the depth of the language and stipulate new meanings, thus reaching new levels of consciousness. An example of mystical language reconstructing a new reality hidden from the eye is to be found in the hymns of thanksgiving from the Dead Sea Scrolls:

> [I thank Thee, O God,
> for] Thou hast placed me beside a fountain of streams
> in an arid land,
> and close to a spring of waters
> in a dry land,
> and beside a watered garden
> [in a wilderness].

> [For Thou didst set] a plantation
> of cypress, pine, and cedar for Thy glory,
> trees of life beside a mysterious fountain
> hidden among the trees by the water,
> and they put out a shoot
> of the everlasting Plant.
> But before they did so, they took root
> and sent out their roots to the watercourse
> that its stem might be open to the living waters
> and be one with the everlasting spring.
> And all [the beasts] of the forest
> fed on its leafy boughs;
> its stem was trodden by all who passed on the way
> and its branches by all the birds.
> And all the [trees] by the water rose above it
> for they grew in their plantation;
> but they sent out no root to the watercourse.

> And the bud of the shoot of holiness
> for the Plant of truth
> was hidden and was not esteemed;
> and being unperceived,
> its mystery was sealed.
> Thou didst hedge in its fruit, [O God],
> with the mystery of mighty Heroes
> and of spirits of holiness

and of the whirling flame of fire.
No [man shall approach] the well-spring of life
or drink the waters of holiness
with the everlasting trees,
or bear fruit with [the Plant] of heaven,
who seeing has not discerned,
and considering has not believed
in the fountain of life,
who has turned [his hand against] the everlasting [bud].[59]

In the mystical dialectical language deconstruction is called *yiḥud* (unification), and refers explicitly and implicitly to magical language. For example:

These are the codes, combination, utterance, sum, and computation of the explication of the Ineffable Name—unique in the branches of the root of vocalization that is magnified in the thirteen types of transformation. How is the code accomplished? It derives the word through the utterance and the utterance through the word . . . the sum through the computation and the computation through the sum. Until all the words are positioned in the font of the flame and the flame in the font—until there is no measuring or quantifying the light that is hidden in the superabundance of the secret darkness.[60]

Reconstruction is called *devekut* (adherence) and refers to the mystical language. The deconstruction of the infinite word of God represents by itself the freedom of interpretation—the reader's freedom to ignore the plain meaning, reject it, replace it, and fill in the text with new content. The principles of mystical language, which are based on deconstruction and reconstruction, and on the ongoing dynamics of meaning, reflect the desire to go beyond the plain meaning of the Torah, and, analogously, to rescue reality from its limitations, that is to say, to grasp the hidden content of the Torah, and to reveal its metaphysical meaning and its intricate relation to upper worlds.

Mystical freedom is anchored in the belief that an infinite number of combinations exist in each word. Thus nothing is closed or permanent. This freedom stems from the certainty that each being is made of a spiritual essence and a physical garment, and the relations between the two fluctuate and alternate. The intellectual power of mystical thought, which perceives the divine as a dialectical process of unity of opposites, lies in its deconstruction of the univocality of material revelation, and the infinite reconstruction of new spiritual essences. The fluidity of letters that are perpetually combined and taken apart in the human mind is nothing, then, but an imitation of the divine unity of opposites, which unites within the infinite process of creation: expansion and annihilation, revelation and concealment, covering [= materializing] and uncovering [= abstracting]. In his mind, the human being, who uncovers [= abstracts, divests] the single meaning of

---

[59] Vermes, *Dead Sea Scrolls in English*, 213–14.

[60] *Ma'ayan ḥokhmah* (The Fountain of Wisdom), trans. Verman in *Books of Contemplation*, 50–1.

the plain text and covers [= invests, concretizes] it with new combinations, imitates the word of God, which covers and uncovers being all the time:

Whoever possesses the knowledge of God and puts his effort into learning Torah for its own sake really understands that the Torah is nothing but combinations of names, holy appellations. And as we mentioned above with regard to the book named 'The Two Tables of the Covenant', the Torah is called *pekudei YHVH* because the main issue written about in the Torah from the beginning until its revelation to the eyes of Israel has been entrusted (*pekudah* and *pikadon*) and hidden in the name *HVYH* . . . and the righteous one through the depth of his comprehension strips off the fables she [the Torah] puts on herself, and clothes her in spiritual forms, heavenly lights, and supernal mysteries made out of holy names suggested in these stories . . . The Torah is called *pekudei YHVH*, because it means a deposit [*pikadon* in Hebrew], that is, that the Torah as a whole, from the beginning until its revelation to the eyes of Israel, is nothing but holy names, whose purpose is to indicate the substance of *HVYH*, blessed be He. In that name the principles and the details of the matters are hidden and deposited . . . because in this holy name all the Torah is deposited and hidden . . . and everyone is free to choose if one improves and straightens his ways and grasps the clothing of God by contracting His holy and pure dimensions. If so he is able to divest the Torah of its materiality and clothe it in spirituality and form combinations as incumbent upon him through his talent . . . The obligation is laid upon everyone of Israel to divest the letters of the Torah of their materiality and to raise them to their source, that is to say, to form holy combinations within the Torah and the liturgy.[61]

The kabbalist who discovers within his mind the divine foundation of material reality—the letters—the one who deconstructs and reconstructs language, or the one who regards all the elements of being as details capable of being reconstructed, breaks through the limits of time and space: 'And behold, the God-fearing righteous person . . . remembers in each and every minute before whom he is standing, and he strips himself of materiality, as if he is above this world beyond the rule of time.'[62] If the principle of enveloping the infinite divine light within the confines of the finite, permitting the manifestation of the world, is the main principle of the relation between God and reality, then for the mystical consciousness, the principle of 'uncovering', the stripping off of materiality, follows for the mutual relations among man, God, and the world. These two principles also apply to the relations between God and the Torah (covering—the concealment of God in the revealed) and between man and the plain meaning of the text (uncovering—abstracting the revealed to expose the concealed). These two principles are embodied in the Torah, which reflects the covering and the uncovering and demonstrates the process by which God at one and the same time is revealed in creation and in the plain text and is concealed 'in wonderful hidden secrets': 'There is no doubt that there is not a word throughout our holy Torah that does

---

[61] Wolf, *Or hame'ir*, Ruth, 175*a*; 'Vayeḥi', 38–9; Ruth, 178*a*.   [62] Ibid., 'Vayeḥi', 39*b*.

not hold hidden awesome wonderful secrets, ideas that the human heart cannot grasp, for who can penetrate the secrets of God, and who will find them, so deep and profound are they.'[63]

Mystical literature, which is founded to a great extent on penetrating contemplation into the depth of language and the ancient memories embedded in it, and on deciphering its mysteries and uncovering hidden dimensions, includes many genres and a rich variety of forms of expression, relying on unique names and combinations that are perpetually deconstructed and reconstructed. It contains side by side unrestricted automatic spontaneous writing, writings influenced by the subconscious and myth, and visionary writings that reflect dreams and revelations. Often one can find in mystical literature a new reading of a well-known text that dismantles the conventional frameworks and reconstructs new combinations that create beautiful as well as unclear linguistic forms. In addition, this literature includes unexpected confessions in poetical language as well as autobiographical writing, anonymous pseudepigraphical writing, meaningful imaginative stories retelling well-known texts, rigid frameworks for codification, and systematic rational writing, which explains abstract mystical concepts within the framework of traditional commentary on the reasons for the commandments. It includes visionary, didactic, and magical writing, provocative and anarchic writing presented as commentary, and nihilistic writing that rejects the yoke of the Torah.[64]

Sometimes mystical language is metaphoric or synecdochic. It represents the obscure totality by an unconventional detail, and blends realistic and imaginary entities, as suggested in *Sefer habahir*:

The Holy One, blessed be He, has one tree in which there are twelve diagonal borders, an east–north border, an east–south border . . . and they widen for ever, and these are the arms of the world, and within them there is the tree. And what is that tree that you mentioned? These are the forces of the Holy One, blessed be He, one on top of the other, and they resemble a tree. As this tree produces fruits the Holy One, blessed be He, by water strengthens the tree. And what is the water of the Holy One, blessed be He? It is wisdom and the souls of the righteous who fly from the spring to the great pipe that ascends and clings to the tree.[65]

This text joins together elements from the *Sefer yetsirah* and from the Midrash but creates a new world and a new conceptual language that has no objective correlative—it has only mythical associations and mystical combinations.

---

[63] Ibid., Ruth, 177*a*.

[64] For examples of anarchic and nihilistic Jewish mystical literature see Atiash, Scholem, and Ben-Tsevi (eds.), *Songs and Praises of the Shabateans*; Frank, *Divrei ha'adon*; Aaron b. Moses Halevi Horwitz of Starosielce, *Sha'arei ha'avodah*; Mordecai Joseph Leiner, *Mei hashilo'aḥ*. On their historical context in Shabateanism, hasidism, and Frankism see Scholem, 'Redemption through Sin'; Atiash, Scholem, and Ben-Tsevi (eds.), *Songs and Praises of the Shabateans*; Elior, *Theology in the Second Generation*, 244–88; Kraushar, *Jacob Frank*; Balaban, *History of the Frankist Movement*; Elior, 'Jacob Frank's *Divrei ha'adon*'; Faierstein, *All is in the Hands of Heaven*; Brill, *Thinking God*.

[65] *Sefer habahir*, §95; §119. See Scholem, *Origins of the Kabbalah*.

Mystical language, which combines the hidden and the revealed, renews itself through visions and dreams that go beyond the limits of reality and expose previously unknown layers of language. Sometimes the renewal occurs through unifications, adjurations, and situations of loss of control, and sometimes through the study of sacred texts that requires the utterance of the renewed version of the written text and its transformation into 'a speaking word'. Mystical language renews itself through the unique experience of the mystic, who finds through his imagination new meanings in previously known concepts, and who revives popular symbols. A mystical poetical tradition mentioned in the Talmud (BT *Avodah zarah*) relating to the Ark of the Covenant that was made of acacia wood (Exod. 25: 10) is revived in a third-century *merkavah* hymn, part of *Heikhalot rabati*, which speaks of a mystical transformation of the Ark of the Covenant, turned into a singing heavenly throne:

Sing, oh sing, acacia tree, ascend in all thy gracefulness. With golden weave they cover thee, the *Devir* palace hears thy eulogy, with diverse jewels art thou adorned. (BT *Avodah zarah* 24*b*)

Rejoice, rejoice, throne of glory, sing for joy, seat of the Most High! Exult, exult, O precious vessel, so marvellously fashioned! You will gladden the king upon you, as a bridegroom is gladdened in his bridal chamber.[66]

The unique experience that is embedded in the assumption 'that each [deliverance] of his imagination is true, because the purpose of creation was to reveal his Divinity, blessed be He, precisely through the imagination',[67] and the transformations of the sacred text into a new speech are regarded as the revelation of the word of God. 'The source of the word that comes to humans is the Shekhinah.'[68]

Mystical visions are often tied to a translinguistic experience stemming from a sacred textual system that had been deconstructed and reconstructed, becoming a new text. They may also be tied to an actual experience that had been deconstructed in the visionary's imagination, gone through a visual metamorphosis, and been re-experienced and rewritten. In contrast, the symbol in mystical thought is the representative of a concept, substance, or process, which by itself is not revealed in any way and cannot be expressed in any conventional way. The mystic defines it arbitrarily or in accordance with a mystical interpretative tradition. Alongside the popular symbols in the written tradition, a mystic creates images, detailed visionary descriptions, poetic expressions, and new combinations that are revealed in visions, which blend reality and imagination to create a new reality.

An example of a mystical description of a new reality, relying on the deconstruction and reconstruction of a biblical text, can be found in a segment of the

---

[66] *Synopse zur Hekhalot-Literatur*, ed. Schäfer et al., §260.

[67] Aaron b. Moses Halevi Horwitz of Starosielce, *Sha'arei ha'avodah*, Preface.

[68] Elijah b. Moses de Vidas, *Reshit ḥokhmah*, ch. 10, §24.

'Songs of the Sabbath Sacrifice'.[69] This work was written by the priests of Qumran, who left the Temple in Jerusalem in the second century BCE because of disagreements over important questions regarding the order of service, the true calendar, and rights to the priesthood.[70] Each word in this song is familiar, but almost none of its combinations are otherwise known. It combines a visionary tradition linked to Ezekiel's chariot with angelic-priestly traditions related to the Temple:

For the Master.
Song of the burnt offering of the twelfth sabbath on the twenty-first of the third month.
Praise the God of cycles of wonder and exalt Him.
Glory is in the tabernacle of the God of knowledge.
The cherubim fall before Him and bless Him.
As they rise the sound of divine stillness [is heard] .
There is a tumult of jubilation;
as their wings lift up the sound of divine stillness [is heard].
The cherubim bless the form of the chariot throne [which is] above the firmament of
    the cherubim;
and they sing and praise the splendour of the luminous firmament, [which is] beneath
    His glorious seat.
And when the wheels move, the holy angels return. They emerge from his glorious
    wheels
like sights of fire, spirits of the holy of holies round about, between the appearance of
    [mighty] streams of fire like *ḥashmal.*
And there is radiance, embroidery of glorious and wonderful colours, wondrously hued,
    a pure blend.
The spirits of living godlike beings which move continuously with the glory of the won-
    drous chariots.
There is a still sound of blessing amid the roar of their
Movement; they praise His holiness as they return to their paths.
As they ascend they ascend wonderfully, and when they settle, they stand still.
The sound of joyful praise falls silent. There is a stillness of divine blessing in all of the
    camps of godlike beings;
Sound of praises. . . . [coming] from among all their divisions.
On their sides each of their number in his turn praises while passing by and all their
    mustered troops rejoice, each one in his station.[71]

The fragmented text, through its exalted celestial language, focusing on praises raised to the Lord from every corner of his heavenly Temple by all his angels, clearly reveals that the praising, singing, blessing, and joy in the heavenly Temple

[69] See *Songs of the Sabbath Sacrifice*, ed. Newsom; Elior, *Three Temples.*
[70] On the priests from Qumran see *Megilat hahodayot*, ed. Licht; *Megilat haserakhim*, ed. Licht; *Songs of the Sabbath Sacrifice*, ed. Newsom, 1–80; *Pesher ḥavakuk*, ed. Nitzan.
[71] 4Q 405 20 ii–22: 6–14, in *Songs of the Sabbath Sacrifice*, ed. Newsom, 303.

are ascribed to cherubim, chariot throne, spheres, wheels, spirits of the living God, and chariots of wonder. In other words, in the vision of the priests of Qumran, the earthly service of the earthly Temple is released from its earthly limits and is reconstructed anew garbed in its heavenly form—a new mystical poetry sung by angels.[72] This text alludes to Ezekiel's chariot, the biblical tradition of the angels' chanting, and the glory of the inhabitants of heaven.

It is possible that these poems, some of which are enigmatic, were influenced by the ancient tradition of magical names, which was connected to priestly traditions during the First Temple period.[73] In the biblical tradition priestly magic is related primarily to holy and explicit names, which are always treated with awesome reverence. These ineffable names are partially derived from the priestly ritual tradition of the Temple[74] and the priestly mystical tradition concerning the angelic world.[75] Later mystical tradition refers in a suggestive manner to the antiquity of the tradition of names, while alluding to the high priest's breastplate and *Sefer yetsirah*:

These are the twelve precious, illuminated, explicit names of Israel's twelve tribes . . . all of which are included in the thirty-two [paths] of heaven and are divided into twenty-four names; male and female are included and counted in Teli [a heavenly constellation], wheel and heart, and they are the source of wisdom.[76]

From Ben Sira and Philo to the Mishnah and the Talmud, Jewish literature has explicitly taught us that the tradition of engraved ineffable names is a priestly tradition connected to the tradition of God's name. It is related to the explicit name that was forbidden to be pronounced, the explicit name that the high priest used to pronounce in the Holy of Holies on Yom Kippur that could not have been heard by others, the priestly benediction used at the Temple to bless in the name of God, the name that was engraved on the ornament the high priest wore, and the names connected to taking an oath, writing, and uttering God's name both within the Temple and outside it.[77] One example that combines the tradition related to the Explicit Name, the priestly benediction,[78] and the mystical-magical tradition is found in *Sefer habahir*:

---

[72] On the angelic liturgy as mystical poetry see *Songs of the Sabbath Sacrifice*, ed. Newsom; Elior, 'From Earthly Temple'; Elior, *Three Temples*, 165–200.

[73] On the connections between the Temple and the tradition of holy names see Urbach, *Sages*, ch. 7; Elior, 'From Earthly Temple'; Lesses, *Ritual Practices*.

[74] See the biblical and mishnaic-talmudic tradition about God's name on the crown of the high priest. The priests are pronouncing God's name in the priestly blessing in the Temple; the high priest is pronouncing the Name of God on Yom Kippur in the Temple. See Urbach, *Sages*, ch. 7.

[75] Elior, 'Mysticism, Magic and Angelology'.   [76] *Sefer habahir*, §§111, 112.

[77] On the centrality of Temple worship as reflected in the 'halakhic' literature in Qumran see Suessmann, 'Research on the History of Halakhah'; on its centrality in the mystical literature see Elior, *Three Temples*.

[78] On the priestly blessing and the tradition of holy names see Urbach, *Sages*; Elior, 'From Earthly Temple'.

Rabbi Ahilai sat and taught: why is it written God is Ruler [*melekh*], God has been ruling [*malakh*], God will be ruling for ever and ever [*yimlokh*]. Because this is the explicit name, which we are permitted to use and mention in combinations, as it is written: 'Thus they shall link my name with the people of Israel, and I will bless them' (Numbers 6: 27). And it is a name of twelve letters [which is included] in the priestly benediction— The Lord bless you etc.—which are three, and they are twelve . . . and if one sacredly and purely guards and mentions it, all his prayers are accepted, and as if this were not enough, he is loved in the lower [world] and the upper [world], desired in the lower [world] and the upper [world], attended and helped immediately. This is the explicit name written on Aaron's forehead. And in the explicit name there are seventy-two letters. And the explicit name, which is twelve names, was delivered by the Holy One, blessed be He, to the angel Masmeryah, who had been standing in front of the curtain, and he delivered them to Elijah on Mount Carmel, and by them he was elevated and did not experience the taste of death.[79]

In the writings of the German pietists of the twelfth to thirteenth centuries there are various traditions of the transmission of the divine names. In the book *Sodei razaya* of R. Ele'azar of Worms (*c*.1165–1230) the ritual of transmission is described as follows: 'The one who deals with the *merkavah* or with the honoured name should go, he and his student, to whom he wishes to transmit the name, and they should wash in water and cleanse all their body in water . . . and immerse themselves in the water . . . they should immerse their bodies and dress in white clothes and stand in water up to their thighs.'[80]

Significant parts of the tradition of names are connected to the world of the angels who serve in the upper sanctuaries, who are the mystical counterparts of the priests who served in the earthly Temple. There are no doubts regarding the priestly identity of the circles in which the hymns of the Sabbath sacrifice were composed,[81] and the tradition described by Josephus, Joseph ben Matityahu, ascribes to them a special interest in the names of angels. It is interesting that the prayer of sanctification (Kedushah), sung by humans and angels alike in the upper and lower worlds praising the name of God, exists in different forms in Qumran and the Heikhalot literature. If one part of the tradition of names is connected to the Temple ritual, priesthood, and angels of upper temples in charge of the divine worship and heavenly liturgy, then a second part is connected to the benefits for humans as explicitly expressed in the previously quoted promise to the guardians of the names: 'And if one sacredly and purely guards and mentions it, all his prayers are accepted, and as if this were not enough, he is loved in the lower [world] and the upper [world], desired in the lower [world] and the upper [world],

---

[79] Ibid., §111. The name of seventy-two letters is discussed in *Bereshit rabah* 44: 19; the names of twelve letters and of forty-two letters are mentioned in BT *Kid.* 71*a*. Cf. Rashi, commentary on BT *Suk.* 45*b*.

[80] Ele'azar of Worms, *Sefer sodei razaya*, 149–50; see Dan, *Occult Theories*, 74–5.

[81] *Songs of the Sabbath Sacrifice*, ed. Newsom, 1–80; Elior, *Three Temples*, ch. 8.

attended and helped immediately.' These versions can be found for the first time in the texts of *Shiur komah*, written in the early centuries of the Common Era, which directly tie the knowledge of God's names to benefits for humans, such as the ability to control nature.[82]

The link between the knowledge of names, which were connected with the priestly blessing and divine grace, and 'being attended and helped immediately' applies to all human needs, especially for the healing of the body and the soul. This link is clearly reflected in all magical literature starting with the Heikhalot literature, fragments of the Genizah, and *Sefer harazim*, through *Ma'ayan haḥokhmah* (Fountain of Wisdom) and *Shimushei torah* (Uses of the Torah), and concluding with Abraham ben Isaac of Granada's *Berit menuḥah, Shivḥei habesht*, and dozens of volumes in between of amulets, adjurations, and magical formulas.[83] One should not be surprised by this link, for the magical ritualistic language is grasped as the path to the concealed, the hidden knowledge, the mysteries of controlling the heavenly world, and also regarded as a source of power, knowledge, and benefit in the earthly world.[84] From the beginning, magical language has been connected to rituals, mysteries, adjurations, blessings, and ceremonies in the domain of the Temple priests. This language has also been linked to medicine and magic,[85] witchcraft and spells, and the total complex of rituals capable of interfering with natural causality, and not confined to a ritual centre such as the Temple. The use of magical language takes place through the conviction of the few who believe in their ability to impose human will on heavenly powers, and through those around them who believe in the power of names they possess.

Mystical language is often a poetic language that connects the earthly and the heavenly, as is expressed clearly in the opening of *Heikhalot rabati*: 'What makes it unique? By poetry one descends to the *merkavah*. One starts by saying poetical praises.'[86] This is obvious in *Songs of the Sabbath Sacrifice*, which describe the singing of the angels in a mysterious place in which 'all those who are present in

---

[82] See Cohen, *Shi'ur Qomah*.

[83] For examples of magical literature see *Sefer harazim* (Book of Secrets), ed. Margaliot (magical tradition and Heikhalot literature, according to Genizah manuscripts from the talmudic period). *Heikhalot zutarti, Shimushei tehilim, Sefer haḥeshek, Ma'ayan haḥokhmah*, and *Ḥarba demosheh* are examples of books which contain magical traditions. On these books see Dan and Liebes (eds.), *Library of Gershom Scholem*. On these texts see Scholem, *Jewish Gnosticism*, 75–83, 94–100; *Synopse zur Hekhalot-Literatur*, ed. Schäfer et al.; *Geniza Fragmente*, ed. Schäfer; Schäfer, 'Jewish Magic Literature'; Swartz, *Scholastic Magic*; *Ḥarba demosheh*, ed. Harari; Lesses, *Ritual Practices*; Idel, 'Perception of the Torah'; Grözinger, 'Names of God'.

[84] On the role of magic in Jewish tradition in different periods see Scholem, *On the Kabbalah*; Betz, *Greek Magical Papyri*; Schäfer, 'Jewish Magic Literature'; Swartz, *Scholastic Magic*; Elior, 'Mysticism, Magic and Angelology'; Cohen-Alloro, 'Magic and Sorcery in the Zohar'; Dan, 'Story of Joseph della Reina'; Gruenwald, 'Magic and Myth'; Idel, *Golem*; Gruenwald, 'Writing, Epistles, and the Name of God'; Idel, *Hasidism*; Etkes, 'Magic and Masters of the Name'; Lesses, *Ritual Practices*.

[85] On magic and healing see Bilu, *Without Bounds*, and Lesses, *Ritual Practices*.

[86] *Synopse zur Hekhalot-Literatur*, ed. Schäfer et al., §81.

the *devir* [Holy of Holies] feel the wonderful praises in a wonderful *devir*, from *devir* to *devir* in a voice full of holiness . . . together they praise the chariots of his *devir*.[87] The poetic mystical language which enlarges the scope of human horizons constructs the hidden heavenly sanctuary. The purpose of using the magical ritual language of names (which gives up on human understanding) through invocations, adjurations, and unifications is to obtain either knowledge hidden in the world of the dead or the eternal world of the angels or the secrets that control the upper and lower worlds, by stripping language of its content. The magical names are derived from combinations of letters beginning or ending verses, by a numerological principle. For example, the name containing seventy-two letters, which is mentioned in *Bereshit rabah* 44: 19 and explained by Rashi in his commentary to BT *Sukah* 45*b*, is derived from the vertical reading of three consecutive verses, each one containing a total of seventy-two letters, mentioned in Exodus 14: 19–21. Another name of forty-two letters is derived from the first letters of all the verses in one of the prayers. Many other names are obtained by rearranging the letters in the biblical names of God. The unintelligible language, constructed of meaningless or imperceivable names in the human domain which are fraught with hidden meaning in the divine realm, becomes numinous, divine, powerful, and frightening because of the unexplained powers it holds: 'and you should attest according to the book *Shimushei torah*, which extracts a number of names from a number of Torah portions and changes the letters' order and combinations until one works awesome deeds by means of them'.[88] Magical language achieves this status by returning language to its primal stratum, the stratum of heaven, in a mythological time preceding distinct categories of time and space, context and meaning. It transcends rational thought and returns, as it were, to the depth of consciousness that precedes rational distinctions. Magical literature clearly shows that one seeks power and influence over, and contact with, supernatural entities through both intelligible and unintelligible language. An example of using the Holy Name and the preconditions for its proper use are found in the magical chapters of Heikhalot literature, where the adjuration of angels through holy names, fasting, and praying is described:

R. Ishmael said: I sought this secret and I sat twelve days fasting. When I saw that I was not able [to persevere in the fast], I made use of the great name of forty-two letters and PDQRS the Angel of the Countenance descended in anger so that I trembled and fell back.

He said to me: Son of the stinking drop . . . you made use of the great name, you took for yourself the orders of the Torah. I will not give it to you until you sit forty days in fast.

Immediately I hastened and pronounced three letters and he ascended: ZH BR BYH greatness TYTBYT. I sat forty days in fast and prayed three prayers in the morning and

---

[87] 4Q403 1 ii 13–15, in *Songs of the Sabbath Sacrifice*, ed. Newsom, 226, 229.

[88] Matitiyah Delacrut, commentary on *Sha'arei orah* (Jerusalem, 1960).

three prayers in the afternoon and three prayers in the evening . . . and I mentioned twelve words at every one. On the last day I prayed three times and I mentioned twelve words and PDQRM the Angel of the Countenance descended and with him angels of mercy and they caused wisdom to settle in the heart of R. Ishmael.

R. Ishmael said: I myself sealed seven seals at the time that PDQRS the Angel of the Countenance descended. Blessed are you, YY, you who created the heaven and the earth in your wisdom and your understanding. Your name is forever. HYWP SYSY PYYW LWSM BY KYY TNYY name of your servant.[89]

As the visionary literature shows, contact with such entities occurs within mystical language or dreams, which are free to recombine the perceptible and the abstract without being restricted by reality. One example of the way in which secrets are revealed through the inspiration of dreams and 'visions of the night while half-awake, half-asleep' can be found in the testimony of the anonymous author of the mid-sixteenth century *Galya raza* or *Raza gali* (the Revealer of Mysteries), who links his mystical revelation to a mission imposed on him by heaven:

Blessed be the Lord God of Israel, who revealed to me these secrets of the uppermost that until now had never been revealed to a human being in this generation since the shining light [= Rabbi Shimon bar Yohai] disappeared from this world . . . And all this that I wrote was awakened in my heart to write and publish [because I] was awakened from heaven as I was on my bed, and through visions of the night while half-awake, half-asleep they put in my mouth to say . . . And in the morning, when I returned from the synagogue, I sat and wrote what they summoned me to put in my heart . . . because Gabriel is in charge of dreams and his name is *Raza gali* (Revealer of Mysteries) . . . Therefore, I named my work the Revealed Secret, because through dreams at night and sometimes while awake I composed all the compositions that I made.[90]

The feeling of approaching the end of days often causes the kabbalist to break the restrictions of esotericism and write down his words. Solomon Almoli, in sixteenth-century Istanbul, ascribed his heavenly revelations to the approach of the messiah and to divine inspiration, probably influenced by the Zohar tradition, which links the approach of redemption to the revelation of secrets:

And I realize that by God's mercy secrets and wonderful teachings were revealed to me, which had never been revealed, so much so that it makes me wonder, who am I and what is my life that I am worthy of this. It must be the sign of our redemption and the salvation of our souls . . . And this composition is completely new because all its teachings . . . came to me through profound and vigorous study by the providence of God, blessed be He, who bestowed them upon me.[91]

---

[89] *Synopse zur Hekhalot-Literatur*, ed. Schäfer et al., §§565–6. On the text see Lesses, *Ritual Practices*, 420; Janowitz, *Poetics of Ascent*, 48.

[90] *Galya raza*, 15–16. Cf. Elior, 'The Doctrine of Transmigration in *Galya Raza*'.

[91] *Sha'ar adonai heḥadash*, 13a; 2a.

The content of the revelation can be mystical and abstract, embedded with messianic hopes for the benefit of the entire exiled community, or magical and ritual, intended for the benefit of the individual who wishes to gain power or knowledge. The words 'secrets and mysteries' refer to both mystical and magical language, and their content might be revealed in a dream or in a vision. Sometimes mystical language is prosaic and philosophical in an attempt at exaltation through systematic analysis and scholarly observation, as is reflected in the kabbalistic works of the medieval anonymous author of *Ma'arekhet elohut* (System of Divinity) and the sixteenth-century author of *Pardes rimonim*, Moses Cordovero, and the books of Shneur Zalman of Lyady, his student Aaron Halevi Horwitz of Starosielce, and his son Dov Ber of Lubavitch in the eighteenth and nineteenth centuries. Sometimes it is a magical language that tries to reach exaltation by giving up meaning and using meaningless names and fixed formulas, as one can see in the Heikhalot literature, in the *Shiur komah* texts, and in *Sefer harazim* from late antiquity and the Byzantine period. Sometimes it is a symbolic language that through mystical symbols expresses attributes and entities that are unreachable through the senses. These different aspects of mystical language refer to the hidden divine being, the beginning of time, unknown periods, *shiur komah*, *merkavot*, worlds that were destroyed, and worlds conceived in thought, the revelation of the Shekhinah, the singing of the angels, the different 'faces' of the divinity that creates itself, and much more. These expressions, which refer to the prehistory and metahistory of the divine and human world, are expressions of the inner world of man, who is revealed through language and exposed through his unique experience of worlds that transcend the constraints of materiality.

A meaningful mystical work enables the reader to experience the decoding of hidden meanings through the exposure of different layers of language. This is possible because of the infinitude ascribed to the divine text, the decoding of which is an ongoing process, and the complexity of terms, images, and pictures used by a mystical text, which embodies additional terms, images, and pictures from earlier periods. Key mystical concepts often touch the depths of myth, the heart of the biblical tradition, the mysteries of priestly traditions connected to holy names, angels, and heavenly chariots, and the secrets of the aggadic tradition, in which the immediate and the distant, the yearned-for and the lost in history are united. Surprisingly, these concepts suggest, symbolize, or apply universal human concepts to the divine realm and project divine concepts onto human reality. They sometimes express the mythologization and mystification of ordinary concepts, which turn into mythical and cosmic concepts such as 'eternal life', 'metempsychosis', 'sing, oh sing, acacia tree', or 'tree of souls'. They sometimes personify divine powers such as 'the redeeming angel who is sometimes male and sometimes female', or 'incest is the king's sceptre', referring to an exceptional prerogative in heavenly realms which is prohibited in earthly society. These kinds of concepts demonstrate 'a condensed concept'. They offer a multilayered associative fabric that reflects the abstraction of a ritual and textual tradition on the one hand, and the materialization of mystical and mental symbols on the other. Both are embedded in collective memory attested in written texts and ancient ritual-liturgical tradition and both are connected to unexpected domains of the concealed and the revealed. Mystical concepts par excellence previously mentioned, describing the hidden world as 'seven words of wonder', 'seven temples', 'ten *sefirot* of infinite nothingness', 'thirty-two mystical paths of wisdom', 'emanation', 'ancient man' or 'primordial man', 'countenances', 'breaking of the vessels', 'the death of kings', and others, illustrate the mixture of the perceptible and the imaginary, the lost and the invented, the poetical and the mystical, the mythical and the historical, the human and the divine. Mystical concepts, describing God as 'beauty that sets depths on fire' and 'a face in the image of spirit and soul', when no earthly representation of the divine presence is available any more, and defining the desired future in a language of defiance and hope as 'the land of Israel floating on water' or 'the yearned-for age of mercy', or as a language that will have one new letter which will transform accepted definitions and will take on reality in a new era, demonstrate that fundamental concepts of mysticism often 'project' feelings, contexts, and meanings from one domain onto another, and establish new perspectives with respect to hidden and revealed reality. Mystical metaphor symbolizes and condenses popular concepts, and deepens their associative space. It refers to the beginning of days, the end of days, the passages among worlds, the depths of the human soul, the infinity of language, and the relations between God and the world in a language of freedom which defies any earthly constraints, and offers alternatives to existing order. The image of God as a being without shape, as spirit without a body, as creative power with no borders, the decoding of the hidden world—its mythic creation and its mystical principles, the reciprocal relations between the upper and lower worlds, the application of the principle of opposites to the human soul and to the divine being, destruction and redemption, the beginning of the soul and its end—are all described by concepts rich in meaning, through metaphors, names, and secrets that illustrate the ability to interpret the text from a different point of view, initiating a new and powerful dialogue between the concrete and the abstract.

*

Jewish mysticism, written across three millennia in numerous places, demonstrates a remarkable chapter in the history of freedom, where people who suffered from the arbitrary hardship of history challenged the loss of the Temple and the continuous exile, the ongoing persecutions, and the recurrent expulsions by anchoring their hopes and yearnings in the heavenly domain, where memories of the lost glorious past could be deposited (from Temple to chariot to sanctuaries; from priests to angels), where ongoing creative freedom was secured ('in thirty-two paths of wisdom . . . in book, story, and number . . . God created his world'), where lost bodies could be transformed into eternal souls (the 'tree of souls' theory of reincarnation), and where structure, meaning, order, and purpose could be established as against chaos, meaningless catastrophe, and suffering in historical reality. In the mystical tradition there are always numbers and structures (ten *sefirot*; thirty-two paths of wisdom; seven sanctuaries; four faces of the chariot; twelve diagonal borders) and there is always an active plan which assists commemoration of the lost past or assists activation of the hoped-for future. The former was embedded in the mystical liturgy of the Merkavah tradition that transformed the lost priestly venue on earth into seven heavenly sanctuaries where the eternal divine service is performed by the angels, and the chariot of the cherubim is glowing and singing as if there were never a destruction on earth. 'Descenders of the chariot' and mystical adepts describe in detail the hidden heavenly world of the *merkavah*, where the Temple worship was continuously performed for close to a thousand years. The latter, the activation of a hoped-for future, took place for 800 years, from the twelfth-century *Sefer habahir* to the twentieth century. The Book of Splendour and *Magid meisharim*, *Ets ḥayim*, and the vast kabbalist–hasidic library participate in building the passage from the past to the future. They further elaborate on the passage from exile to redemption through contemplation and unification, free interpretation and mystical ascension, revival of prophetic inspiration and renewal of messianic hopes, and alternative perceptions of existence. The new perceptions of language ('in every letter there are world, souls, and divinity') and the new perception of the deity (Shekhinah and *Kudsha berikh hu*; ten *sefirot*, *adam kadmon*, the responding angel, the messiah in heaven), where distinctions between the divine spirit and the human spirit are blurred and erased, paved the way to new avenues in the history of freedom, where human beings succeeded in changing the course of history against all odds and managed to transform historical exile into different forms of human liberation.

Historical and Literary Figures, Kabbalists, and Mystics Mentioned in Jewish Mystical Literature

ALL AUTHORS are listed under their first name, with the anonymous authors first.

Anonymous author of *Avodat hakodesh*

An anonymous kabbalist of the sixteenth century who wrote, according to his testimony, under the inspiration of 'the holy spirit and the angel of the covenant'. His book *Avodat hakodesh* (Holy Worship) was written in Italy between 1564 and 1567 and is devoted to messianic expectations of the imminent redemption in 1575 in the light of the torments of exile of the previous decades, which were interpreted as pre-messianic tribulations. On the book see Tamar, *Studies in the History of the Jews*.

Anonymous author of *Galya raza*

An anonymous kabbalist who lived in the sixteenth century, presumably in the Byzantine Christian culture within the Ottoman Empire. In his book, written in 1552, he struggled to establish the superior status of the kabbalah, which he linked with the approaching messianic era. He ascribed significant importance to theories of reincarnation and transmigration of the soul and tied the theories of transmigration to eschatological calculations alluded to in Scriptures and corroborated in the Zohar. The author, who describes himself as persecuted and mocked by his contemporaries owing to his concern with kabbalah, was particularly interested in the stories of sinners in the Bible in general and of forbidden marriage (incestuous relations) in particular, stories he associated with the pre-determined messianic scheme according to dreams and visions that he integrated with the mystical tradition of the Zohar. On *Galya raza* see the edition by Elior; Elior, 'Doctrine of Transmigration'; Tishby, 'On the Problems of the Book'.

Anonymous authors of Heikhalot literature

An anonymous circle of mystics who lived in the land of Israel in the early centuries CE, after the destruction of the Second Temple. They left rich mystical and poetic literary traditions written in beautiful Hebrew which describe heavenly sanctuaries and celestial servants, modelled after the earthly Temple and its priestly and levitical servants. These mystical circles, which described themselves as *yoredei hamerkavah* (descenders to the chariot or masters of the chariot) and left many prayers inspired by the angelic liturgy, were familiar with the liturgical and mystical traditions of the Qumran priests (Zadokite priests), and like their priestly predecessors they expressed profound interest in Enoch son of Jared, the hero of the ancient priestly tradition (see below, Enoch); they most probably had a priestly identity and affiliation. Among their writings are *Heikhalot rabati* (Greater Heikhalot = heavenly sanctuaries), *Heikhalot zutarti* (Lesser Heikhalot), *Ma'aseh merkavah* (Deed of the Chariot), *Sefer heikhalot* (= 3 Enoch), *Shivḥei metatron* (Praises of the Angel Metatron, prince of the countenance, known originally as Enoch son of Jared), and *Shiur komah* (Stature of the Godhead). On Heikhalot literature see Scholem, *Major Trends*; id., *Jewish Gnosticism*; Dan, *Jewish Mysticism*; Gruenwald, *Apocalyptic and Merkavah Mysticism*; Elior, 'Concept of God'; Elior, 'Mysticism, Magic and Angelology'; Elior, 'From Earthly Temple'; Schäfer, *Hidden and Manifest God*; *Synopse zur Hekhalot-Literatur*, ed. Schäfer et al.; *Geniza Fragmente*, ed. Schäfer; Halperin, *Faces of the Chariot*; Elior, *Three Temples*; Cohen, *Shi'ur Qomah*; Arbel, *Beholders of Divine Secrets*; Janowitz, *Poetics of Ascent*; Swartz, *Mystical Prayer*; Lesses, *Ritual Practices*.

Anonymous author of *Sefer hamalakh hameshiv*

An anonymous kabbalist who lived at the end of the fifteenth or the beginning of the sixteenth century and wrote a voluminous mystical manuscript entitled *Sefer hameshiv* or *Sefer hamalakh hameshiv* (The Book of the Answering Angel), of which major parts were written in 'automatic writing', including visionary inspiration and prophetic revelation, calculations for the end of days, and messianic dreams. On the anonymous author and his manuscript see Scholem, *Kabbalah Manuscripts*; id., ' "Divine Mentor" of Rabbi Yosef Taitazak'; Idel, 'Inquiries into the Doctrine'.

Anonymous author of *Sefer hatemunah*

An anonymous kabbalist who probably lived in the fourteenth century. His book elaborates the doctrine of the recurring sevenfold cycle of fallow years (*shemitah*), expressing the temporal and spatial dimensions of the seven spheres in the mystical history of creation. The book develops an interesting theory of language based on the secret meaning of the letters which the author associates with the sevenfold division of the spheres. On this book see Scholem, *Kabbalah of* Sefer hatemunah; Gottlieb, *Studies in Kabbalah Literature*.

Aharon Halevi Horwitz of Staroselye or Aaron ben Moses Ha-Levi Horwitz of Starosielce (1766–1828)

The most prominent student of Shneur Zalman of Lyady, founder of Habad hasidism and a leader of a group of hasidim who saw him as the true heir of the Habad heritage. The two decades after the death of Shneur Zalman were marked by profound controversy between his son Dov Ber and his student R. Aaron. Both wrote about their theological differences and personal encounters in their books (see Elior, 'The Controversy over Habad's Legacy'). Horwitz wrote *Sha'arei hayihud veha'emunah* (Shklov, 1820) on the second part of the book of his teacher, *Tanya: Sha'arei ha'avodah* (Shklov, 1821), on the mystical framework of divine worship, and *Avodat halevi* (Lemberg, 1842; Warsaw, 1866), a compendium of sermons, letters, and miscellaneous works. On him see Elior, *Theology in the Second Generation*; Elior, *Paradoxical Ascent to God*; Jacobs, *Seeker of Unity*; Hilman, *My Master's House*; Loewenthal, *Communicating the Infinite*.

Abraham Abulafia (1241–after 1292)

A controversial kabbalist who was born in Spain and wandered in Greece, Italy, and the land of Israel. He is the founder of the method of the 'prophetic kabbalah', which is concerned with the perception of the prophetic spirit attained by delving deeply into letters and holy names. Abulafia, who wrote on eschatology, was persecuted and banned by his contemporaries, among them Solomon ibn Aderet, one of the major religious authorities of his time. Abulafia's books were banned by some later eminent kabbalists such as Judah Hayat but were studied by others. Among his books are *Sefer ha'ot* (Book of the Letter), *Sitrei torah* (Secrets of the Torah), *Hayei ha'olam haba* (Life of the Next World), *Or hasekhel* (Light of the Mind), *Imrei shefer* (Good Words), and *Zot liyehudah* (This is for Judah). Many of his books remained in manuscript and some were published in other books without mentioning their author. On him see Hayat, *Minhat yehudah*, published in the anonymous book *Ma'arekhet elohut* (Mantua, 1558) as a commentary; Scholem, *Kabbalah of* Sefer hatemunah; id., *Major Trends*; Aescoly, *Messianic Movements*; Idel, *Mystical Experience in Abraham Abulafia*; id., *Studies in Ecstatic Kabbalah*; id., *Kabbalah: New Perspectives*; Wolfson, *Abraham Abulafia*; Jacobs, *Jewish Mystical Testimonies*, 56–72.

Abraham Michael Cardozo (1626–1706)

A Shabatean mystic, son of a Spanish 'Marrano' family. He emigrated to Italy in 1648, and there returned to Judaism. In 1664 he moved to Tripoli in Libya, where he experienced mystical visions, and from that year on was an adherent of Shabetai Tsevi. His book *Boker le'avraham* and other writings were banned and burned. On him see Scholem, *Sabbatai Sevi*; Liebes, *Secret of Shabatean Faith*; Yosha, 'Philosophical Background'; Goldish, *Sabbatean Prophets*.

Ahijah the Shilonite

A biblical prophet mentioned in the time of King David (1 Kings 11: 29; 12: 15; 15: 29) who in the mystical tradition became the divine mentor of the founder of eighteenth-century hasidism, Israel Ba'al Shem Tov. Ahijah is described as his guide in the ascents to the upper worlds. His mystical reputation derives from the midrashic tradition, which states that Shimon bar Yohai (see below) once claimed that he could hasten the time of the coming of the messiah if Ahijah the Shilonite would join him (*Bereshit rabah* 35: 2). The different talmudic traditions describe Ahijah as a figure who transcends borders of time and place—he is simultaneously present and active in such distant historical periods as the Exodus from Egypt, the court of King David, and the time of Elijah (Ahijah is introduced as his teacher). These instances, and others mentioned in various sources, which made him one of the few people whose consecutive life spans cover all of historical time (the others are Adam, Methusaleh, Shem, Jacob, Serah the daughter of Asher, Amram, and Elijah) influenced his mystical role as the heavenly teacher of Israel Ba'al Shem Tov (BT *Sanhedrin* 102a; BT *Bava batra* 121b). On him see Maimonides, *Mishneh torah*, introduction; Jacob Joseph of Polonnoye, *Toledot ya'akov yosef*, 'Balak' 156a; Elior, 'R. Joseph Karo'; Nigal, 'Ahijah the Shilonite'; Liebes, 'Messiah of the Zohar'.

Akiva

A renowned sage (*tana*) born in the last third of the first century CE. He was one of the greatest teachers of the Mishnah, who died as a martyr in the second century, one of the ten sages who were killed and tortured by the Romans because of their insistence on carrying out their religious duties, forbidden by the authorities. Akiva is associated with the mystical tradition through the tale of 'The four who entered Paradise' (*pardes* or paradise is the Greek translation of the biblical Garden of Eden in the Septuagint, third century BCE) (Tosefta *Ḥagigah* 2: 3–4; BT *Ḥagigah* 14b; JT *Ḥagigah* 2: 1; *Otsar hageonim* (B. M. Levin), *Ḥagigah*, p. 31; *Heikhalot zutarti*, pp. 23, 62). There it is mentioned that Akiva is the only one who 'entered in peace and came out in peace' (in a parallel version 'ascended in peace and descended in peace'), formulas associated with the high priest's entrance into the Holy of Holies in the Temple on Yom Kippur, before the destruction of the Temple in 70 CE. Akiva's association with the mystical tradition is also mentioned in *Avot derabi natan*, ch. 6 (in the second addition to the first version), 'things hidden from all humans were revealed to Rabbi Akiva' (cf. the fifth-century midrashic work *Pesikta derav kahana*, §4). In the mystical tradition of the talmudic period known as the Heikhalot literature, a section known as *Heikhalot zutarti* (Lesser Heikhalot) is attributed to him as well as an esoteric tradition concerning the divine stature known as *Shiur komah*. Akiva is the colleague and companion of Ishmael in various traditions recorded in Heikhalot literature and he is introduced as the mystical adept who ascends to heaven and upon his return to earth brings with him the heavenly liturgy sung by the angels and the mysterious tradition of the *merkavah*—the world of the Divine Chariot. On him see Scholem, *Jewish Gnosticism*; Urbach, 'Traditions about Merkabah Mysticism'; Dan, *Jewish Mysticism*; *Heikhalot zutarti*, ed. Elior; Elior, *Three Temples*, 232–65; Halperin, *Faces of the Chariot*; Liebes, *Sin of Elisha*; Morray-Jones, *Transparent Illusion*; id., 'Paradise Revisited'.

Asher Lemlein

A kabbalist who lived in Germany and northern Italy at the end of the fifteenth and first half of the sixteenth century. Following the horrors of the expulsion from Spain in 1492 and the rise of expectations for immediate redemption, he generated messianic agitation among the Jews of Italy by announcing the imminent coming of the messiah in the year 1500. The Jews of Italy, who were expecting the event in accordance with the prophecies of the renowned Spanish Jewish leader Isaac Abravanel (1437–1508), the author of *Yeshuot meshiho* who wrote comprehensive messianic literature in Italy after the expulsion, and forecast redemption in the year 1503, accepted Asher Lemlein's gospel, and some saw in him the herald of the messiah. Scholars argue about the precise background of Lemlein's prophecy but agree on his influence at the turn of the sixteenth century. On him see Scholem, *Sabbatai Sevi*; Kopfer, 'Visions of Asher ben Me'ir'; Aescoly, *Messianic Movements*; Idel, introduction to Aescoly, *Messianic Movements*.

Azriel ben Solomon of Gerona (beginning of the 13th c.)

A Spanish kabbalist, among the most important of Gerona's kabbalistic school. His teachings deal with the idea of the infinite divine being and the division of the ten spheres (*sefirot*) and are elaborated as an interpretation of legends of the Talmud and include a series of questions and answers on theological issues. Among his writings are *Sha'ar hasho'el* (Gate of the Inquirer), on the *sefirot*; a commentary on *Sefer yetsirah* (Book of Creation); and commentary on talmudic *agadot*, *Perush ha'agadot*, ed. Tishby. On him see Scholem, *Origins of the Kabbalah*; Pedaya, *Name and Sanctuary*.

Barukhyah Russo (1677–1720)

The leader of an extremist antinomian group within the Shabatean movement, called 'Doenmeh', in Salonika. ('Doenmeh' = Turkish Jews who converted voluntarily to Islam at the end of the seventeenth century, influenced by the enforced conversion of Shabetai Tsevi in 1666.) Barukhyah, who followed Shabetai Tsevi (see below) and headed the movement from the end of the seventeenth century, maintained that the new messianic Torah, called *torah de'atsilut* (Torah of Divine Emanation), which rules the world since the messianic revelation of Shabetai Tsevi, engendered the annulment of the thirty-six prohibitions on incest

(Leviticus 18–20); thus his followers were encouraged to free themselves from traditional restrictions and celebrate the freedom of the new messianic era. He further adhered to the belief that the time had arrived to transform the prohibitions into positive commandments. Barukhyah developed a radical mystical concept according to which he and Shabetai Tsevi were the incarnations of God on earth, and he maintained that the annihilation of the Torah was actually its fulfilment. Barukhyah had a profound influence on Jacob Frank (see below), who came to see himself as his successor. On him see Scholem, *Sabbatai Sevi*; id., 'Barukhia Russo'; Liebes, *Secret of Shabatean Faith*; Atiash, Scholem, and Ben-Tsevi, *Songs and Praises of the Shabateans*; Elior (ed.), *Dream and its Interpretation*.

Dov Ber Schneersohn of Lubavitch (1773–1827)

Known as Dov Ber the son of Shneur Zalman of Lyady (d. 1813) and as 'der mittle rebbe' (the middle rabbi). He was a hasidic leader involved in the conflict concerning the leadership of Habad. His rival for leadership, R. Aaron Halevi Horwitz (1766–1828), saw himself as the true interpreter of the teachings of Shneur Zalman. Dov Ber wrote *Kuntres hahitpa'alut* (Tract on Ecstasy) and *Kuntres hahitbonenut* (Tract on Contemplation) expressing his opinions about the right interpretation of Habad esoteric teachings. He settled in Lubavitch while his opponent, R. Aaron, settled in Starosielce. Both wrote extensively on the right way to communicate the esoteric teachings of Habad to society as a whole. On him see Jacobs's edition, *Tract on Ecstasy*; Loewenthal, *Communicating the Infinite*; Elior, *Theology in the Second Generation*; Elior, 'The Controversy over Habad's Legacy'; Elior, 'Dov Ber Schneersohn's *Kuntres hahitpa'alut*'; Asaf, 'Apostate or Saint'.

Dov Ber the Maggid of Mezhirech (1710?–1772)

A hasidic mystic and prominent disciple of Israel Ba'al Shem Tov (1700–60) and a disseminator of his teachings. He combined the Ba'al Shem Tov's teachings with the kabbalistic tradition and created new mystical concepts that influenced hasidic thought. He founded a new hasidic *beit midrash* in Volhynia and surrounded himself with disciples who spread the hasidic mystical thought and way of life. His teachings were edited by his disciples and published in the books *Magid devarav leya'akov*, *Or torah*, and *Or ha'emet*. Among his disciples were the eminent authors of hasidism Shneur Zalman of Lyady, Levi Isaac of Berditchev, Ze'ev Wolf of Zhitomir, Jacob Isaac Horowitz of Lublin, Hayim of Amdor, and Elimelekh of Lyzhansk. On him and on his teaching see Schatz-Uffenheimer, *Hasidism as Mysticism*; Dov Ber, *Magid devarav leya'akov*, ed. Schatz-Uffenheimer; Rapoport-Albert, *Hasidism Reappraised*; Elior, *Mystical Origins of Hasidism*.

Ele'azar Azikri (1533–1600)

A kabbalist who lived in Safed in the sixteenth century. He wrote the mystical-ethical book *Sefer ḥaredim* (Book of the Devout). He also wrote the *piyut* (liturgical poem) 'Yedid nefesh' (Friend of my Soul) and a mystical diary entitled *Milei deshamaya* (Celestial Words) in which he described his mystical experiences. On him see Ele'azar Azikri, *Milei deshamaya*, ed. Fechter; *Safed Spirituality*, trans. Fine.

Eliezer the Great

A sage who lived in the mishnaic period and was involved in various disputes on the nature of authority (cf. BT *Bava metsia* 59*b*). The ancient mystical tradition of the Heikhalot literature (see above) associated him with the drawing down of angels and the revelation of 'The angelic prince of the Torah'. The midrashic work ascribed to him which is known as *Pirkei derabi eli'ezer* has interesting mystical traditions. On him see 'Sar torah', in *Heikhalot rabati*, in *Synopse zur Hekhalot-Literatur*, ed. Schäfer; Dan, *Jewish Mysticism and Jewish Ethics*; Stein, *Maxim, Magic, Myth*.

Elijah de Vidas

A kabbalist who lived in Safed in the sixteenth century. He is the author of the kabbalistic ethical-mystical book *Reshit ḥokhmah* (Beginning of Wisdom), which is known to have had a vast influence on the mystical hasidic movement. The author was a disciple of Moses Cordovero (see below), and perhaps of Isaac Luria (the Ari). On him see Schechter, 'Safed in the Sixteenth Century'; *Safed Spirituality*, trans. Fine.

Enoch-Metatron, 3 Enoch; see below under Metatron.

1 Enoch

Enoch son of Jared, a biblical figure who became the major hero of the mystical priestly tradition. Enoch is the seventh in the list of the world's patriarchs introduced in the Bible (Genesis 5: 18, 21–4). He is described in an exceptional way, significantly different from the stereotypical characterization of the other biblical figures in the historical list. He is unique since he did not die as all men but was 'taken' to God while still alive: 'And Enoch walked with God . . . and all the days of Enoch were three hundred sixty and five years. And Enoch walked with God and he was not for God took him' (Gen. 5: 18, 23–4). Since it was believed that he entered paradise while he was still alive, and it was written that he lived on earth for 365 years (the number of days of the solar calendar) and was the seventh of the world patriarchs, he became a major figure in the priestly Enochic literature and Qumran scrolls, written in the last centuries before the Common Era, which took particular interest in these numbers. His figure was related to the traditions that dealt with the solar calendar containing 364/365 days, and to the priestly tradition that sanctified the number seven as the foundation for all holy divisions of time. In his complex identity as priest, prophet, timeless witness, celestial author, and boundless mystic Enoch exemplifies piety that transcends borders. An extensive literature became associated with his name: 1 Enoch = Ethiopian Enoch from the second to third centuries BCE; 2 Enoch = Slavonic Enoch from the first century BCE to first century CE; 3 Enoch = *Sefer haheikhalot* from the tannaitic and talmudic periods (see the Bibliography). His figure as the first man who learnt to read and write appears in the Book of Jubilees 4, in *Genesis Apocryphon*, in the Wisdom of Ben Sira, and in various fragments of the Qumran scrolls. The different books of Enoch recount the story of his ascent to heaven, his vision of the heavenly chariot, and his return to earth with the books containing celestial doctrines relating to the solar calendar, which he imparts to his descendants, the priests. He brought divine instructions that their authorship was ascribed to angels and their teaching kept and imparted by the priests. On Enoch and his books see *3 Enoch*, ed. Odeberg; *Books of Enoch*, ed. Milik; *Old Testament Pseudepigrapha*, ed. Charlesworth; Collins, *Apocalyptic Imagination*; Gruenwald, *Apocalyptic and Merkavah Mysticism*; *Book of Enoch*, trans. Black; Himmelfarb, *Ascent to Heaven*; Elior, *Three Temples*; VanderKam, *Enoch*; *Qumran Cave 4.XXVI* (DJD 36); Arbel, *Beholders of Divine Secrets*; Alexander, 'Historical Setting'.

2 Enoch or (Slavonic) Enoch

Enoch son of Jared, whose story is retold at the turn of the first century CE in Greek, presumably in Egypt, and translated into many languages, notably Slavonic, in which this book has come down to us. The new depiction has a complex character and original religious perceptions are devised in new terminology. The book has detailed angelology as well as detailed priestly genealogy. It also has a new creation story, a new perception of God that unfolds in a unique dialogue between God and Enoch, and a new anthropology recounted to Enoch in his celestial tour; its image of Enoch is exceptional in the conceptual world of the time. On 2 Enoch, see 2 Enoch, in *Old Testament Pseudepigrapha*, ed. Charlesworth; Böttrich, *Weltweisheit, Menschheitsethik, Urkult*; Orlov, *EnochMetatron Tradition*; and the bibliography below.

Ezra ben Shelomoh of Gerona (?–1245)

A Spanish kabbalist, one of the first creators of kabbalah. He composed a kabbalistic commentary on the Song of Songs and on talmudic legends that had a great influence on the Spanish kabbalists. On him see Azriel of Gerona, *Perush ha'agadot*, ed. Tishby (where the traditions ascribed to R. Ezra are brought together with those ascribed to R. Azriel); Scholem, *Origins of the Kabbalah*; Pedaya, *Name and Sanctuary*, 154–60, 198–212.

Hayim Vital (1543–1620)

A prominent kabbalist and a prolific writer who lived in Safed and Damascus and was active in the last decades of the sixteenth century and early decades of the seventeenth. Vital was a prominent disciple of Luria, and later recorded his master's teachings. Vital's principal writings presenting Lurianic doctrine are *Ets ḥayim* (Tree of Life) and *Shemonah she'arim* (Eight Gates). In his youth he studied alchemy and then devoted himself to kabbalah. After Luria's death in 1572, Vital became the leader of a group of kabbalists in Safed and saw himself as a messianic precursor—messiah son of Joseph. He wrote an exceptional composition, a mystical autobiography devoted to his dreams and visions entitled *Sefer haḥezyonot* (Book of Visions). The main part of this book was written in 1608–10 and reflects the cultural world of Safed in the last third of the sixteenth century. See *Sefer haḥezyonot*, ed. Aescoly and Ben-Menahem; Scholem, *Major Trends*, ch. 7; id., 'Deed of Association'; Werblowsky, *Joseph Karo*; Elior, 'Messianic Expectations'; Fine, *Physician of the Soul*; Meroz, 'Redemption in the Doctrine of R. Isaac Luria'; Avivi, 'R. Hayim Vital's Writings on Lurianic Kabbalah'; Idel, *Kabbalah: New Perspectives*; Goldish (ed.), *Spirit Possession*; Oron, 'Dream, Vision, and Reality'; *Jewish Mystical Autobiographies*, ed. Faierstein; Jacobs, *Jewish Mystical Testimonies*, 123–35.

Isaac ben Samuel of Acre (last third of the 13th c. to mid-14th c.)

A kabbalist, he studied in his youth in Acre in circles that were opposed to the philosophical conception of Judaism. He arrived in Spain in 1305, settled in the region where the Zohar was written, and attempted to analyse the manner in which it was composed. His writings include *Me'irat einayim* (Enlightenment of the Eyes); *Otsar ḥayim* (Life's Treasure), a mystical diary in manuscript; a commentary on *Sefer yetsirah* (Book of Creation). On him see Tishby (ed.), *Wisdom of the Zohar*; Gottlieb, *Studies in Kabbalah Literature*; *Sefer me'irat*, ed. Goldreich.

Isaac ben Solomon Luria (1534–1572)

The Ari (acronym for 'the divine rabbi Isaac' or for the 'Ashkenazi rabbi Isaac'). A kabbalist of major influence, Luria was born in Jerusalem. After the death of his father he was taken as a child to his mother's family in Egypt. He practised kabbalah from a very young age and was gifted with exceptional spiritual virtues. In 1570 he settled in Safed and studied for a short period under Moses Cordovero. He was recognized by his contemporaries as possessing the holy spirit (*ruaḥ hakodesh*) and as gifted with the 'revelation of Elijah' (*gilui eliyahu*). In his brief years in Safed he gathered around himself a circle of disciples, and after his death his teachings were recorded by his followers, Hayim Vital and Joseph Ibn Tabul. His teachings are to be found, among others, in Hayim Vital, *Ets ḥayim* (Tree of Life), *Sefer haḥezyonot* (Book of Visions), *Shemonah she'arim* (Eight Gates), and *Derush ḥeftsivah*. His kabbalistic doctrine, known as Lurianic kabbalah, formulated a new image of God depicted with human qualities and a new perception of men endowed with divine facets, and had a profound influence on his listeners. A biographic-hagiographic mystical portrait is found in the preface to *Ets ḥayim*, in *Sefer haḥezyonot*, in *Toledot ha'ari*, and in *Shivḥei ha'ari*. On him and his doctrine see Scholem, *Major Trends*, ch. 7; Tishby, *Doctrine of Evil*; *Toledot ha'ari*, ed. Benayahu; Meroz, 'Redemption in the Doctrine of R. Isaac Luria'; Elior, 'The Metaphorical Relationship between God and Man'; Elior and Liebes, *Lurianic Kabbalah*; Fine, *Physician of the Soul*.

Isaac Judah Jehiel Safrin of Komarno (1806–1874)

A hasidic master, known as Rabbi Isaac Eizik of Komarno, son of the founder of the Komarno hasidic dynasty, Alexander Sender, and one of the most important kabbalists among the hasidim. He lived and worked in Galicia and was closely associated with his uncle Rabbi Tsevi Hirsch Eichenstein of Zhidachov, who was a famous kabbalist. He inscribed dreams, visions, and messianic ideas in his book *Megilat setarim* (Scroll of Secrets), ed. Ben-Menahem (Jerusalem, 1944) (trans. Faierstein in *Jewish Mystical Autobiographies*) and he wrote the books *Zohar ḥai* (Living Zohar), *Netiv mitsvoteikha* (Path of your Commandments), and *Otsar haḥayim* (Treasure of Life). He identified with Israel Ba'al Shem Tov and relived his exceptional spiritual heritage in his book *Zohar ḥai*. On him see the preface of Ben-Menahem to *Megilat setarim*; *Jewish Mystical Autobiographies*, trans. Faierstein; Jacobs, *Jewish Mystical Testimonies*, 239–44.

Isaac the Blind (Sagi Nahor) (1160?–1230?)

The son of Abraham ben David of Posquières, he was the founder of kabbalah in Provence, and the teacher of Ezra and Azriel of Gerona. Isaac was blind from birth and the kabbalistic tradition ascribed to him a high spiritual degree known as *gilui eliyahu* (the revelation of Elijah). He was one of the originators of the kabbalistic distinction between Ein Sof (the hidden God) and *sefirot*, manifested dimensions of the deity. He was also one of the formulators of the emanation (*ha'atsalah*) process, which binds the divine entity with the mundane. In all the aspects of existence he saw the embodiment of the divine speech and infinite language and from this concept he developed a doctrine of intentions (*torat kavanot*) and dealt with the metaphysics of language. Kabbalistic tradition ascribes to him the transformations of traditional prayers and blessings into their mystical versions. On him see Scholem, *Origins of the Kabbalah*; Pedaya, *Name and Sanctuary*.

Ishmael ben Elisha

A sage of priestly origin who lived at the end of the first century and the first third of the second century. He died as a martyr and is remembered in the ten martyrs tradition, notably in the dirge 'Eleh ezkerah', read on Yom Kippur. Ishmael was a prominent figure among the sages appearing in the Mishnah and among the 'descenders of the chariot' in the ancient mystical tradition known as the Heikhalot literature. His connection with mystical literature emerged with the description of him as a high priest (*kohen gadol*) (BT *Berakhot 7a*) who entered the inner sanctuary of the Temple (*lifnei velifenim*) when the latter no longer existed. He was known as a companion of Akiva (see above), who is described as one who entered 'Paradise' (BT *Ḥagigah* 14*b*–15*a*; Mishnah *Ḥagigah* 2: 3). Ishmael's mystical character is described in *Ma'aseh merkavah* (Work of the Chariot), as well as in 3 Enoch and in *Heikhalot rabati*, all belonging to Heikhalot literature. On him see *3 Enoch*, ed. Odeberg; Scholem, *Major Trends*; *Synopse*, ed. Schäfer; Elior, *Three Temples*; Halperin, *Faces of the Chariot*; *3 Enoch*, ed. Alexander; Wolfson, *Through a Speculum*, 74–124.

Israel Ba'al Shem Tov, the Besht (1700–1760)

Founder of the hasidic movement. A charismatic healer, kabbalist, and mystic who appeared to others to possess exceptional qualities. In a letter ascribed to him entitled *Igeret hakodesh* (published in the end of the book of Jacob Joseph of Polonnoye, *Ben porat yosef* (Korets 1781)), his mystical self-perception is described. The hasidic sources perceive him as a spark (*nitsots*) from the soul of Shimon bar Yohai, the hero of the Zohar. His mystical teachings were compiled by his disciples Jacob Joseph of Polonnoye and Dov Ber of Mezhirech. His realistic and fictional portrait may be found in his disciple's books that were printed in the eighteenth century, his grandson's book *Degel maḥaneh efrayim*, and the book *Shivḥei habesht* (In Praise of Israel Ba'al Shem Tov) that were printed at the beginning of the nineteenth century and influenced the formation of the hasidic movement. On him see Dubnow, *History of Hasidism*; Dinur, *At the Turn of the Generations*; Scholem 'Historical Image'; Elior, 'Karo'; Elior, *Mystical Origins*; Kahana, *Rabbi Israel Ba'al Shem Tov*; Rosman, *Founder of Hasidism*; Etkes, 'Magic and Masters'; Etkes, *The Besht*.

Jacob Frank (1726–1791)

A Shabatean leader. He was born as Jacob Leibowitsch in Galicia. In his youth he lived in Korolowka, Bucasz, Bucharest, Constantinople, and Salonika, where he met with the followers of Shabetai Tsevi and was influenced by the successors of the Shabatean movement and by the members of the 'Doenmeh' sect (see above, Barukhyah Russo). He saw himself as the reincarnation and successor of Shabetai Tsevi and Barukhyah Russo, the two previous Shabatean leaders. He founded a messianic-antinomian sect in Poland in 1755 and was banned by the rabbinical authorities in 1756 after they were informed about his disconcerting behaviour (dancing with his followers around a naked woman with the crown of a Torah scroll on her head). In 1757 he converted to Islam to escape Jewish persecution, and in 1759, together with his followers, he converted to Christianity in order to live a free life of the messianic age under *torah de'atsilut*—a Torah without restrictions. He was convicted of heresy and fraud by the Church and was imprisoned in the Częstochowa fortress in 1760–72 when the Church realized that his conversion was not truly intended and was meant only as a cover for his mystical-messianic beliefs, centred around himself. With the Russian conquest of

Poland in 1772 he was released and he went to Austria, Moravia, and Germany, surrounding himself with supporters from the Shabatean remnants, and gathered around himself followers from all over Europe who believed in his promise of eternal life for those who would obey him. He was a charismatic leader, a visionary (*ba'al halomot*), healer (*ba'al shem*), and storyteller who was able to blur the boundaries of reality and imagination and create around himself a new kabbalistic-messianic syncretistic mythology. Through his mythical powers, as conveyed by stories and mystical teachings, he transgressed the boundaries of custom and tradition. His life, teachings, and world-view are described in *Hakeronikah* and in his autobiographical book *Divrei ha'adon* (Words of the Lord). On Jacob Frank and his writings see Kraushar, *Jacob Frank*; Balaban, *History of the Frankist Movement*; *Hakeronikah*, ed. Levin; Scholem, 'Redemption through Sin'; Elior, 'R. Nathan Adler'; Elior, 'Jacob Frank's *Divrei ha'adon*'; Elior (ed.), *Dream and its Interpretation*; Rapoport-Albert, 'On the Position of Women'.

Jacob Isaac Halevi Horowitz, the Seer of Lublin (1745–1815)

A disciple of the Maggid of Mezhirech and of Elimelekh of Lyzhansk, he was one of the founders of the hasidic *tsadik* doctrine and one of the main disseminators of hasidic thought in Galicia and Poland at the end of the eighteenth and beginning of the nineteenh century. His mystical theories and social concepts achieved eminent influence, engendering whole-hearted approval or absolute rejection by the Przysucha, Kotsk, and Izbica hasidic circles. His books are *Divrei emet* (Words of Truth) (Zolkiew, 1808 [1831]); *Zot zikaron* (This to Remember) (Lvov, 1851); *Zikaron zot* (This is the Memory) (Warsaw, 1869). On him see Elior, 'Between *Yesh* and *Ayin*', and 'Changes in Religious Thought'.

Jacob Wazana (first half of the 20th c.)

A Jewish folk healer from the region of the western Atlas mountains of Morocco. He was believed to be endowed with magical healing forces and to be in contact with occult worlds, both positive and negative. On him see Bilu, *Without Bounds*.

Joseph della Reina

A mystic-magic literary character living towards the end of the Middle Ages. He was associated with the folk kabbalistic tale of the attempt to overcome the devil and to hasten the redemption. His story was retold in the sixteenth century. On him see Scholem, *Sabbatai Sevi*; Dan, 'The Story of Joseph della Reina'.

Joseph Gikatilla (1248–1325)

One of the most prominent kabbalists in Spain, he was among the disciples of Abraham Abulafia and was related to Moses de Léon, the author of the Zohar. Gikatilla inclined to thematic explanations of the kabbalistic concepts of prayer intentions and was interested in the systematic representation of the ten spheres and their symbols. Among his books are *Ginat egoz* (Garden of Nuts), on the kabbalistic meaning of letters; *Sha'arei orah* (Gates of Light), on the symbolism of the ten *sefirot*; *Sha'arei tsedek* (Gates of Justice), on the doctrine of the spheres and vision of God. On him see Scholem, *Major Trends*; Gottlieb, *Studies in Kabbalah Literature*; *Sha'arei orah*, ed. Ben-Shelomoh; Idel, *Kabbalah: New Perspectives*.

Joseph Ibn Tabul (16th c.)

A disciple of Isaac Luria, he composed an original version of his mentor's doctrine in *Derush heftsivah*, printed under the name of Hayim Vital at the beginning of the book *Simhat kohen* of Masud Hakohen el-Hadad (Jerusalem, 1921). On him see Scholem, 'The Deed of Association'; Tishby, *Doctrine of Evil*; Rubin, 'Sermon on Dragons by Rabbi Joseph Ibn Tabul'.

Joseph Karo (1488–1575)

The pre-eminent halakhic authority and important kabbalist from the generation of the Spanish expulsion. He composed the renowned legal codes *Shulhan arukh* and *Beit yosef* (1542) and was known primarily as an important halakhic authority. Nevertheless, he was also a prominent kabbalist who was endowed with the 'revelation of the Shekhinah' and the 'words of a *magid*' (angelic mentor), as is demonstrated in his autobiographic composition *Magid meisharim* and noted by his contemporaries. In his influential halakhic work *Beit yosef*, which includes all the *halakhot* mentioned in the Jerusalem and Babylonian Talmuds as well as a variety of later sources, he took account of rulings of the Zohar in halakhic matters where there was such a possibility. Karo, who was exiled from Spain as a child in 1492, spent forty years in Turkey; there he probably met Solomon Molcho, whose execution by fire in 1532 in Italy left a deep impression on him. In 1536 he immigrated to the land of Israel after he had a divine revelation of the Shekhinah, which was related to Molcho's fate and to his immigration to the land of Israel, and he founded the kabbalist settlement in Safed, where he became the head of a large yeshiva. Among his colleagues and disciples were Solomon Alkabets, Moses Cordovero, and Moses Alsheikh. On him see Werblowsky, *Karo, Lawyer and Mystic*; Benayahu, *Joseph, my Chosen*; Katz, *Halakhah and Kabbalah*; Elior, 'Karo'; Jacobs, *The Jewish Mystics*, 98–122; Jacobs, *Jewish Mystical Testimonies*, 98–122.

Joseph of Hamadan

A kabbalist of the end of the thirteenth century and the beginning of the fourteenth century who probably lived in Spain. Around 1300 he wrote a large treatise on the Torah portion 'Terumah' and on the Song of Songs, mostly in the characteristic language of the Zohar. He also composed the book *Ta'amei hamitsvot* (Reasons of the Commandments), which includes important kabbalistic teachings on kabbalistic divine worship. A part of his book was printed in *Sefer hamalkhut*

(Book of Monarchy). His books demonstrate his interest in reincarnation theories as part of the punitive system in the afterlife, and were probably the first to use the Hebrew term *gilgul* to describe the return of the soul after death to a second lifetime in another body. He interpreted the mystical connotation of the commandments (*ta'amei hamitsvot*) in relation to the doctrine of reincarnation as part of the reward and punishment that transcend the borders of this world. He was also probably the first author to use the term *adam kadmon* (primordial man), frequently used by later kabbalists. His theories were disseminated through Menaham Recanati's kabbalistic interpretation of the Bible and reasons for the commandments. His writings were printed and reprinted in the twentieth century. On him see Gottlieb, *Studies in Kabbalah Literature*; Meier, 'Joseph of Hamadan'; Elior, 'Doctrine of Transmigration'; Zwelling, 'Joseph of Hamadan's Sefer Tashak'.

Joseph Taitazak (1487–1546)

Rabbi and kabbalist, he was most influential among the first generation after the expulsion from Spain who settled in the Ottoman Empire. One of the most important figures among the rabbinic authorities of his time, he was associated with Solomon Molcho and with Joseph Karo, who was influenced by his ascetic measures and mystical orientation. The kabbalistic tradition ascribes to Taitazak the revelation of an angelic mentor known as a *magid*. On him see Scholem, ' "Divine Mentor" '; Idel, 'Inquiries into the Doctrine of *Sefer hameshiv*'; Zak, *In the Gates*.

Menahem Mendel Morgenstern of Kotsk (1787–1859)

One of the prominent leaders of the hasidic movement in Poland in the nineteenth century, he was the disciple of Jacob Isaac, the Seer of Lublin, Jacob Isaac, the Holy Jew of Przysucha, and Simhah Bunem of Przysucha. After the death of Simhah Bunem in 1827 he became the rabbi of Kotsk, the leader of the majority of Przysucha hasidim. He gathered around himself an elite group of hasidim who maintained an ascetic way of life and were often separated from their families for long periods of time. He emphasized the principle of one absolute truth. His disciple Mordecai Joseph Leiner of Izbica (see below) disagreed with him, separated from him in 1839, and established his own hasidic court. Against the concept of single truth of his master, Leiner developed in his book *Mei hashilo'ah* a concept of many doubts and relative perspectives of truth in a reality which is predetermined by divine will and shaped by changing human choice. In consequence, Menahem Mendel shut himself away for twenty years and refused to see his followers; nevertheless, he was still admired despite his seclusion and idiosyncratic manners. On him see Elior, 'Changes in Religious Thought'; Faierstein, *All is in the Hands of Heaven*; Magid, *Hasidism on the Margin*.

Menahem Recanati (14th-c. Italy)

An Italian writer who collected different kabbalistic traditions and presented them in his *Perush al hatorah* (Commentary on the Torah) (Venice, 1503) and in his book *Ta'amei hamitsvot* (Reasons of the Commandments) (Constantinople, 1544). His books, which appeared before the Zohar was first printed (1558), had a vast influence on the dissemination of kabbalah, and the versions of the kabbalistic texts that were printed in his writings are of major importance since they were collected many years before the first printed versions appeared. On him see Rubin, *Quotations from the Zohar in the Torah Commentary of Menahem Recanati*; Idel, *Rabbi Menahem Recanati*.

Metatron

The angelic name of Enoch son of Jared (see above), who became a celestial prince in the Enochic literature written in the early centuries of the Common Era, who instructs the 'descenders of the chariot' and was encountered by the 'four who entered Paradise' (BT *Ḥagigah* 15a). The name Metatron appears in *Sefer heikhalot*, written between the third and fifth centuries CE, as well as in various midrashic, targumic, talmudic, and magical traditions of the same period pertaining to Enoch, who was taken to heaven as a human witness (Gen. 5: 24; 1 Enoch 14), where he served as an angel and a heavenly priest. His figure preserves different aspects of the character of the first and second Enoch (see above) and is drawn in an angelic-priestly form, unifying in its essence divine God-like traits as well as human-priestly and angelic characteristics. Metatron is the eminent figure appearing in the book known as 3 Enoch (= *Sefer heikhalot*; *Synopse*, ed. Schäfer, §§1–80) and in the composition *Shivḥei metatron* (*Synopse*, §§384–406, 468–79). He plays a central role in the magical and angelic tradition and is a central figure in the priestly tradition, in the conflict between priests and sages, and in the Jewish–Christian debate. On Metatron see *3 Enoch*, ed. Odeberg; Alexander in *Old Testament Pseudepigrapha*, ed. Charlesworth, i. 223–315; *Synopse*, ed. Schäfer; *Geniza Fragmente*, ed. Schäfer; Scholem, *Jewish Gnosticism*; Dan, *Jewish Mysticism*, i: *Late Antiquity*; Elior, *Three Temples*: Elior, 'From Earthly Temple'; Halperin, *Faces of the Chariot*; Segal, *Two Powers in Heaven*; Swartz, *Scholastic Magic*; Orlov, *Enoch-Metatron*.

Mordecai Ashkenazi

A Shabatean kabbalist who lived in the seventeenth and eighteenth centuries. He was the disciple of the Italian kabbalist Abraham Rovigo, author of *Eshel avraham* on the Zohar. Ashkenazi was known to have had an angelic mentor, or *magid*, who appeared to him in his dreams and taught him kabbalistic secrets. He and his teacher were covert Shabateans and immigrated to the land of Israel in 1702. On him see Scholem, *The Dreams of R. Mordekhai Ashkenazi*.

Mordecai Joseph Leiner of Izbica (1800–1854)

A controversial hasidic leader who was considered to be the spiritual successor of the Seer of Lublin's mystical teachings. He was one of the disciples of Simhah Bunem of Przysucha and Menahem Mendel of Kotsk. He saw himself as the spiritual disciple of the Seer of Lublin, who taught two ways of divine worship, love and awe, and as a result he was opposed to the position of his teacher, the rabbi of Kotsk. His turbulent separation from his rabbi in 1839 is considered to be the cause of Menahem Mendel of Kotsk's twenty-year seclusion. After the separation there was acute hostility between the hasidic followers of Kotsk and Izbica. His main composition, *Mei hashilo'aḥ* (Waters of Shiloah), based on autonomous decisions pertaining to moral issues founded on a mystical vision and on freedom of interpretation of the divine commandment, in changing circumstances, as well as on the obligation to doubt all things, was banned and burnt when it was published in Vienna in 1860. On him see Elior, 'Changes in Religious Thought'; Elior, *Mystical Origins*; Faierstein, *All is in the Hands of Heaven*; Magid, *Hasidism on the Margin*.

'Moreh hatsedek', the Teacher of Righteousness

The name is attributed to the priestly leader of the Qumran community (led by the priests from the house of Zadok) in the second century BCE. His persecution by the Hasmonaean priests of Jerusalem is described in *Pesher ḥavakuk*. From the writings ascribed to him, such as the Thanksgiving Scroll, he apparently perceived himself as being endowed with divine revelation and as an opponent of the incumbent priesthood of his time (*Pesher ḥavakuk*; *Miktsat ma'asei hatorah* (MMT)). He held to the ancient biblical tradition of the Zadokite priests and cultivated different priestly legal and ritual perspectives from those that were accepted at the time by the Hellenized and Hasmonean priests who took his place. Scholars attribute to him the hymns of *Megilat hahodayot* (Thanksgiving Scroll) and relate them to the descriptions in *Megilat hapesharim* of being persecuted. On him see *Megilat haserakhim*, ed. Licht; *Megilat hahodayot*, ed. Licht; Suessmann, 'Research on the History of Halakhah'; Nitzan (ed.), *Pesher ḥavakuk*. For the texts ascribed to him in English translations see Vermes, *Complete Dead Sea Scrolls*.

Moses ben Nahman, Nahmanides, Ramban (1195–1270)

A rabbi, talmudic commentator, doctor, religious philosopher, and kabbalist. He was born and lived in Gerona in Spain. Nahmanides came to Jerusalem in 1267 after he was sentenced to be exiled owing to his participation in a public Jewish–Christian religious debate in Barcelona in 1263. He was concerned with the renewal of Jewish settlement in Jerusalem and built there a synagogue and a yeshiva. In his important *Perush al hatorah* (Commentary on the Torah) he included kabbalistic traditions. On him see Scholem, *Origins of the Kabbalah*; Idel, *Absorbing Perfections*; Wolfson, *Through a Speculum*; Pedaya, *Nahmanides*.

Moses Cordovero (1522–1570)

One of the leaders of the kabbalists in Safed in the sixteenth century. He was the disciple of Joseph Karo in halakhah and of Solomon Alkabets in kabbalah. He was a major contributor to the systematic theoretical integration of kabbalistic theories with the systematic definition of the mystical doctrines of the ten spheres. His main compositions are *Pardes rimonim* (Orchard of Pomegranates); *Elimah rabati*; *Or ne'erav*; *Tomer devorah* (The Palm Tree of Deborah, trans. Jacobs); and *Or yakar* (Glorious Light), his voluminous interpretation of the Zohar, which remained in manuscript until the second half of the twentieth century. His autobiographical book *Sefer gerushin* (Book of Excursions) describes his mystical way of life in Safed. On him see Ben-Shelomoh, *Theology of Moses Cordovero*; Scholem, 'Kabbalah'; Zak, *In the Gates*; Schechter, 'Safed in the Sixteenth Century'.

Moses de León

A Spanish kabbalist who lived in the thirteenth century, author of a number of Hebrew books on kabbalah and the alleged author of the Zohar (The Book of Splendour), ascribed to the second-century sage Shimon bar Yohai (see below). The authorship of the Zohar has been discussed by a great number of scholars with regard to other books written by Moses de León. See Scholem, *Major Trends*, chs. 5–6; Tishby (ed.), *Wisdom of the Zohar*, introduction; Liebes, 'How the Zohar was Written'; Wolfson, *Through a Speculum*; Cohen-Alloro, 'Magic and Sorcery in the Zohar'.

Moses Hayim Luzzatto, Ramhal (1707–1747)

A kabbalist, poet, playwright, mystic, and inspired author of ethical and mystical books. He was born in Padua in Italy. In his consciousness he was endowed with celestial revelations, mystical inspiration, and messianic aspirations, and he was concerned with eschatological calculations and writing mystical texts. His books, which were considered to have been written by a celestial angelic mentor, *magid*, were treated as a new Zohar. He was suspected of Shabatean tendencies by the 'Shabatean hunter' Moses Hagiz, was persecuted and excommunicated, and his books were banned all over Europe. He was prohibited from teaching or writing kabbalah in Italy and his books were burned and buried in the Frankfurt cemetery. In 1743 he emigrated with his family to Acre and died there during a plague. Among his writings are the well-known ethical book *Mesilat yesharim* (Path of the Upright) and the introduction to kabbalah, *Kuf-lamed-het pithei hokhmah* (138 Gates of Wisdom). His kabbalistic composition *Perush al idra rabah* (a commentary on a central portion of the Zohar) was printed under the title *Adir bamarom* (Mighty in Heaven) (Warsaw, 1886). Luzzatto, in his short lifetime, was a prolific writer and in addition to the kabbalistic texts written under heavenly inspiration, he wrote ethical tracts, poems, grammar books, and plays. On him see Bialik, 'Young Man of Padua'; Tishby, *Kabbalah Research*; Ginzburg, *R. Moses Hayim*

Luzzatto (in English as *Life and Works of Moses Hayyim Luzzatto*); Rubin, 'R. Moses Hayim Luzzatto and the Zohar'.

Nahman of Bratslav (1772–1810)

A hasidic *tsadik* in Ukraine, the great-grandson of Israel Ba'al Shem Tov, the founder of hasidism. His grandmother was Odel, the daughter of Israel Ba'al Shem Tov. Nahman was the founder of Bratslav hasidism and was endowed with mystical inspiration; he was a prolific writer, with an original imaginative style, and messianic aspirations which are expressed in various books. Nahman was known for his unique patterns of leadership and provoked antagonism owing to the messianic elements in his teachings, which opponents alleged were associated with Shabateanism. In his short and tormented life, which was marked by sickness, madness, and inspiration, he developed a unique perception of himself as *tsadik hador* (righteous man of the generation), owing to which no heir was elected after his death and his followers remained attached to his memory; his hasidim are therefore called the 'dead hasidim'. His writings, *Likutei moharan* (Collections of the Sayings of R. Nahman) and *Sipurei ma'asiyot* (Hasidic Tales), were collected by his disciple and scribe Nathan Sternhartz of Nemirov (1780–1845). On Nahman see Weiss, *Studies in East European Jewish Mysticism*; Weiss, 'Mystical Hasidism'; Green, *Tormented Master*; Mark, *Mysticism and Madness*; Rapoport-Albert (ed.), *Hasidism Reappraised*; Magid (ed.), *God's Voice from the Void*; Urban, *Hermeneutics of Renewal*.

Nathan Adler (1741–1800)

A renowned rabbi, head of a yeshiva in Frankfurt in the second half of the eighteenth century, a mystic and teacher of kabbalah and halakhah. Adler was recognized as the admired rabbi and teacher of Moses Sofer, the 'Hatam Sofer' (the later leader of Orthodoxy) and at the same time Adler was banned and excommunicated in his town. He established one of the kabbalistic pietistic circles that was close to the Ba'al Shem Tov's hasidism in spirit and adopted some of its mystical practices inspired by the Lurianic literature. He adhered to the kabbalistic-hasidic world-view in his method of ritual slaughtering and in his manner of prayer, inspired by the tradition of Safed kabbalists. Adler was excommunicated and persecuted by the Jews of his community for his mystical and ritual tradition, his exceptionally pious manners, and his establishment of a separate prayer quorum—all of which were suspected to be associated with Shabateanism, which was a considerable threat in the second half of the eighteenth century. Jacob Frank, who had converted to Christianity in 1759 in Lvov, came to live in Offenbach, near Frankfurt, in 1786. The proximity of the threat generated suspicion against Adler and persecution. Adler ascribed major importance to dreams and to the ritual-kabbalistic tradition. The circumstances surrounding his excommunication are described in the book *Ma'asei ta'atuim* (Deeds of Mischief). On him see Elior, 'R. Nathan Adler and the Frankfurter Pietists'; Katz, *Halakhah and Kabbalah*, 353–86.

Nathan of Gaza (1643?–1680)

A rabbi and a kabbalist who was born in Jerusalem and resided in Gaza. His prophetic visions persuaded him to convince Shabetai Tsevi (see below) to declare himself as the messiah. After Shabetai Tsevi converted to Islam, in 1660 Nathan, whose father Elisha Ashkenazi converted to Christianity, created a complex messianic theology, which sheds a mystical light on the act of conversion and its hidden rationale in the messianic process. On him see Scholem, *Sabbatai Sevi*; Wirschowsky, 'The Shabatean Ideology of the Messiah's Conversion'; Wirschowsky, 'The Shabatean Theology of Nathan of Gaza'; Liebes, *Secret of Shabatean Faith*; Goldish, *Sabbatean Prophets*.

Nehuniah ben Hakanah

A sage in the mishnaic period whose vague figure in the talmudic literature became a principal character in the mystical tradition. He is mentioned in the Heikhalot literature as part of the tradition of contemplating the heavenly chariot and as the mentor of Ishmael (*Heikhalot rabati*). In the Middle Ages he figures as a prominent mystical character, to whom many anonymous compositions are ascribed. The books *Sefer habahir*, *Sefer hatemunah*, *Sefer hakanah*, all anonymous and pseudepigraphical mystical compositions, were ascribed to him. On him see Scholem, *Origins of the Kabbalah*.

Rashbi, *see* Shimon bar Yohai.

Samuel Primo (1635–1708)

A rabbi, kabbalist, and Shabatean leader who was born in Cairo. In 1665 he met Shabetai Tsevi in Jerusalem and became one of his supporters, remaining with them in Gaza and Constantinople. He was Shabetai Tsevi's scribe while the latter stayed in the Gallipoli fortress, and transcribed his pamphlets on the messiah. He remained loyal to Shabetai Tsevi after his conversion to Islam, although he avoided saying so publicly. Later he was a rabbi in Adrianople. On him see Scholem, *Sabbatai Sevi*; Liebes, *Secret of Shabatean Faith*.

Shabetai Tsevi (9 Av 1626–Yom Kippur 1676)

A mystic and kabbalist, founder of a messianic movement claiming that redemption had started and the new messianic law was to be obeyed. He was born in Izmir (Smyrna). He was attracted from a young age to kabbalah and to the occult. In 1648, when he was 22 years old, following the horrors of the Chmielnicki persecutions in the Ukraine, where a hundred thousand Jews were murdered by the Cossacks (as he learnt from the book of a witness, Nathan Neta Hanover, *Yeven metsulah* (Venice, 1653)), he revealed his messianic tendencies and ambitions for the first time, and was excommunicated by the Jewish community. In 1665 he proclaimed himself messiah, with the encouragement of Nathan of Gaza, who publicized his name in letters and sermons and inflamed the passion of thousands in Jewish communities in the East and in the West. Around this time he was arrested by the Turkish authorities and coerced to convert to Islam or face execution. His enforced conversion in 1666 created a major upheaval among his followers and led to a mass conversion among those who elected to follow the way of their master. (Doenmeh was the name of his followers who converted to Islam.) As a consequence of Shabetai Tsevi's conversion a complex messianic-kabbalistic theology was created to explain the conversion as a necessary stage in the process of the elevation of fallen sparks of the soul of the messiah. The principal ideas of his doctrine are to be found in the book *Raza dimeheimanuta* (in Aramaic: The Secret of the Faith), which he dictated to one of his followers before his death. On him see Scholem, *Sabbatai Sevi* and 'Sabbatai Sevi'; Wirschowsky, 'Shabatean Ideology'; Wirschowsky, 'Shabatean Theology'; Liebes, *Secret of Shabatean Faith*; Goldish, *Sabbatean Prophets*.

Shimon bar Yohai

A mishnaic sage living in the second half of the second century, a disciple of Rabbi Akiva, and one of the most important teachers of halakhah in the Mishnah, also known by his acronym of Rashbi. He founded a yeshiva in Meron. He became a key figure in the pseudepigraphical mystical tradition of the Zohar, written a thousand years after his lifetime. According to the aggadah, during the time he fled from the Roman persecutions he hid in a cave with his son Ele'azar for thirteen years and at this time divine secrets were revealed to him, which he wrote down as the Book of the Zohar. The authentic author of the Zohar, Rabbi Moses de León, who lived in the thirteenth century (see above), combined the aggadic tales that are concerned with bar Yohai and his support for the messianic movement of Bar Kokhba in the second century CE with new mystical messianic insights pertaining to the second millennium, although the medieval book was ascribed to the mishnaic period by its author. The mythical and mystical aspects of Shimon bar Yohai's character, which are related to Moses and the messiah, to the revelation of celestial secrets and to redemption, and to a playful and mysterious interpretation of the sacred tradition, have been a fertile ground for generations of students of mysticism. On him see Scholem, *Major Trends*; Tishby (ed.), *Wisdom of the Zohar*; Liebes, 'Messiah of the Zohar'; Liebes, 'How the Zohar was Written'; Hellner-Eshed, *A River Issues Forth*; *Zohar*, trans. Matt.

Shneur Zalman of Lyady (1745–1813)

The founder of Habad hasidism in White Russia, a disciple of Dov Ber, the Maggid of Mezhirech. Shneur Zalman combined a profound mystical perceptiveness with methodical theosophical thought and his writings inspired the

Habad Lubavitch movement. His mystical theosophy, which reflects an intense experience of divine presence and a profound sense of ecstatic rapture, is concisely formulated in *Sha'ar hayiḥud veha'emunah* (Gate of Unity and Faith) in the *Tanya*. Among his writings are *Tanya, Likutei amarim* (Collections of Sayings); *Sidur tefilah shel harav* (The Rabbi's Prayer Book); *Torah or* (Light of Torah); *Shulḥan arukh harav* (a code of law). His mystical theosophy, along with his teachings in hasidism, his mystical-halakhic books, and the broad public support he attracted provoked persecution by the mitnagedim (the opponents of the hasidic way) and the fury of the hasidim. He was arrested and imprisoned by the Russian authorities after defamation by the mitnagedim, involving perjury. He was often at the centre of internal hasidic disputes concerning his position on the broad dissemination of kabbalah. On him see Hilman, *My Master's House*; Wilensky, *Hasidim and Mitnagdim*; Elior, *Paradoxical Ascent*; Loewenthal, *Communicating the Infinite*; Orent, 'Ethical and Mystical Elements'. His book *Tanya* has been translated by Mindel, Posner, and Schochet.

Solomon Alkabets (1500–1576)

A kabbalist and a poet who was born in Turkey. He learnt Torah from Joseph Taitazak (see above). Alkabets moved to Adrianople, where he met Joseph Karo, joined his kabbalistic circle, and made public Karo's mystical insight. Alkabets emigrated to the land of Israel together with Karo around 1535–6. He was active in Safed with his mentor in spreading kabbalah and, finally, was the head of a kabbalistic yeshiva. He was the teacher of Moses Cordovero, his brother-in-law, who describes in his books Alkabets's ritual and mystical customs. He renewed, with other members of this circle, the kabbalistic rituals and composed the famous mystical sabbath *piyut* 'Lekha dodi'. He wrote kabbalistic commentary on some of the biblical books and on the Passover Haggadah. Among his books are *Ayelet ahavim* (Venice, 1552), on the Songs of Songs; *Berit halevi* (Lemberg, 1862), on the Passover Haggadah; *Manot halevi* (Venice, 1585), on Esther; *Shoresh yishai* (Venice, 1561), on Ruth; *Tikun tefilot*, in *Sefunot*, 6 (1962), 135–82. A collection of his prayers has been preserved in Moscow, MS Ginzburg 694, and Paris, Bibliothèque nationale de France, MS 198. On Alkabets see Werblowsky, *Karo, Lawyer and Mystic*; Ben-Shelomoh, *Theology of Moses Cordovero*; Zak, *In the Gates*; Kimelman, *Lekha Dodi*; Schechter, 'Safed in the Sixteenth Century'; *Safed Spirituality*, trans. Fine.

Solomon Almoli (before 1490–1542)

A fruitful author on dreams who was born in Spain and expelled as a child. He was a doctor, philologist, and scientist. Almoli lived in Constantinople in the sixteenth century, where he was a member of the community court. He dealt with the investigation and interpretation of dreams. He wrote books concerning dreams, among them *Sefer ha'ahlamah . . . inyan pitron ḥalomot* (Concerning the

Interpretation of Dreams), *Kitsur misefer pitron ḥalomot* (The Interpretation of Dreams, condensed version) (Salonika, 1556), and *Mefasher ḥelmin* (Interpreter of Dreams), also known as *Pitron ḥalomot* (Solving Dreams) (Salonika, 1516).

Solomon ben Shimon Turiel

A kabbalist who is reputed to have been numbered among the Safed kabbalists of the sixteenth century. He wrote a commentary on *Sefer yetsirah* entitled *Eshet ne'urim* (Wife of Youth) and composed a sermon regarding salvation in the seventh decade of the sixteenth century. On him see Scholem, 'Homily on Redemption'.

Solomon of Lutsk (b. 18th century, d. 1813)

A disciple of Dov Ber, the Maggid of Mezhirech. He was a key figure in the publishing of kabbalistic and hasidic books, including the books of Jacob Joseph of Polonnoye and of Dov Ber of Mezhirech in the early 1790s in Korets and Parizk. He composed an important homily book entitled *Divrat shelomoh* (Speech of Solomon) (Zolkiew, 1848). On him see Schatz-Uffenheimer, *Hasidism as Mysticism*; Gries, *Book, Author, and Story*; Elior, 'The Paradigms of *Yesh* and *Ayin*'.

Solomon Molcho (1500–1532)

A kabbalist, a mystic who had visions, an author of kabbalistic books, and a founder of a messianic movement. Molcho, born as a Christian son of a Marrano family and named Diego Perez, was a secretary of the King's Council in Portugal. In 1525 he converted to Judaism after he met David Reuveni, a messenger from the Jews of Christian Ethiopia, who arrived in Portugal in 1524 (Portugal had established a naval base in Ethiopia in 1522). Reuveni wanted to offer military help on behalf of the Jews to the Christians led by the Habsburg emperor in their fight against the Ottoman Turks in return for royal and papal permission to allow Jewish settlement in the Land of Israel after the victory over the Ottomans. Molcho, taken by Reuveni's ideas, circumcised himself, learnt Hebrew, and received visions; he left Portugal and wandered among different Jewish communities, spreading the resurgence of messianic beliefs. In 1529 he published his book of homilies *Sefer hamefo'ar* (The Glorious Book), in which he proclaimed the coming of the messiah in the year 1540, and was in contact with kabbalistic circles in Salonika. In 1529, when he heard that the army of the emperor Charles V had conquered Rome, he went to Italy and convinced many listeners that the fall of Rome (Edom) announced the coming of the messiah. He predicted some eschatological events, among them flood in Rome and earthquake in Portugal, which were fulfilled within the time he had claimed, a fact that gave him a special position in the papal and royal courts. He saw himself as the herald of the messiah, hinted in his visionary autobiographical book *Ḥayat hakaneh* (Creature of the Reeds), which greatly influenced the kabbalistic circles of the sixteenth century. Molcho attempted to advise Pope Clement VII and the Habsburg emperor Charles V concerning political and military plans that were related to his messianic visions, and to the Portuguese presence in Ethiopia in that period. Together with Reuveni, he offered assistance to the Christian emperor in his war against the Turks and in return he requested an imperial document granting permission to the Jews to emigrate to the Land of Israel after such a victory. His plans failed, as a defamation by the Italian Jewish doctor Jacob Mantino brought about his detention by the Inquisition. This court tried him and sentenced him to execution by burning for his refusal to acknowledge the veracity and superiority of the Christian religion, into which he had been born as a Marrano and from which he converted to Judaism. In November 1532 he was burnt at the stake in Mantua and died as a martyr. His life, books, and deeds had crucial influence on Joseph Karo in his mystical awakening. On Molcho see Aescoly, *Messianic Movements*; *Ḥazon shelomoh molkho ḥayat hakaneh*, ed. Aescoly; Idel, 'Solomon Molcho as a Magician'; Elior, 'R. Joseph Karo').

Yohanan ben Zakai (1st c. CE)

He was the leading sage at the end of the Second Temple period, known for his interest in mystical matters. The Talmud records that, during the siege of Jerusalem by the Romans, he escaped from the city and obtained permission to live in Yavneh, where he set up an academy that became the centre of rabbinic activity after the destruction of the Temple. In the mystical tradition he is associated with the expounding of the divine chariot and with exceptional knowledge in esoteric lore (BT *Sukah* 28a; BT *Ḥagigah* 14b).

Zadok Hakohen (1823–1900)

A leading disciple of Mordecai Joseph Leiner of Izbica, author of *Mei hashilo'aḥ* (see above), he was a prolific hasidic author, halakhic writer, and a mystical teacher. He wrote on his dreams in the book *Resisei lailah* (Night Dew) and in the tract *Divrei ḥalomot* (Words of Dreams) (Lublin, 1903). On him see Brill, *Thinking God*; Magid, *Hasidism on the Margin*.

Ze'ev Wolf of Zhitomir (b. 1730? died between 1795 and 1799)

One of the most important disciples of the prominent hasidic teacher the Maggid of Mezhirech. Ze'ev Wolf wrote one of the early hasidic books, *Or hame'ir* (Shining Light), between 1780 and its publication in Korets in 1798. The book reflects major developments in hasidic thought and deals with the letter-combination theory (*tseruf*) and the significance of linguistic deconstruction (*peruk*). He wrote on the intense experience of the divine presence and on the infinite creative power of language, and he elaborated on the doctrine of the Shekhinah, 'the world of speech', and its hasidic interpretation. On him see Tishby, 'The Messianic Idea'.

Bibliography

In the Primary Sources, references are listed under the author's name; anonymous works are listed under the title. The first modern edition cited is the one used in the book.

PRIMARY SOURCES

ABRAHAM BEN ISAAC OF GRANADA (Avraham Hasefaradi; Merimon), *Berit menuḥah* (Covenant of Rest) (Amsterdam, 1648; Jerusalem, 1979). Partial translation in Jacobs, *Jewish Mystical Testimonies*, 87–97.

A late medieval kabbalistic text discussing holy names and angels. The book was highly regarded by sixteenth-century kabbalists.

ABULAFIA, ABRAHAM, *Ḥayei ha'olam haba* (The Life of the World to Come). Manuscripts in Paris and Oxford. Quoted in Scholem, *Kabbalah of* Sefer hatemunah. Partial translation in Jacobs, *Jewish Mystical Testimonies*, 56–72, and in Scholem, *Major Trends*, 136–7. On him and his book see Scholem, *Major Trends*, ch. 2; Idel, *Mystical Experience in Abulafia*.

—— *Or hasekhel* (Light of the Mind), manuscript, cited in Scholem, *Kabbalah of* Sefer hatemunah, 62.

Prophetic kabbalah of the thirteenth century.

—— *Otsar gan eden haganuz* (The Treasure of the Hidden Paradise), in Scholem, *Kabbalah of* Sefer hatemunah.

Prophetic kabbalah of the thirteenth century.

AGNON, SHMUEL YOSEF, 'Hasiman' (The Sign), in *The Fire and the Woods: All of S. Y. Agnon's Stories* [Kol sipurav shel shemuel yosef agnon: ha'esh veha'etsim] (Tel Aviv and Jerusalem, 1974), 283–334. English translation by Arthur Green in *Response: A Contemporary Jewish Review*, 19 (1973), repr. in *A Book that was Lost*, ed. A. Mintz and A. G. Hoffman (New York, 1995).

Mystical account in an autobiography written as a response in heaven to the holocaust on earth and published in 1944.

ALMOLI, SOLOMON, *Sha'ar adonai heḥadash* (New Gate of the Lord) (Salonika, 1516).

Sixteenth-century dreams.

Avodat hakodesh (Holy Worship), anonymous, reprinted in David Tamar, *Studies in the History of the Jews in the Land of Israel and Italy* [Meḥkarim betoledot hayehudim be'erets yisra'el ve'italyah] (Jerusalem, 1973), 20–38.

Kabbalah, Italy, sixteenth century.

AZIKRI, ELE'AZAR, *Milei deshamaya* (Celestial Words). Ed. Mordechai Fechter (Tel Aviv, 1991).

A mystical-ethical autobiography of a late sixteenth-century kabbalist, the author of *Sefer ḥaredim* (Book of the Devout).

—— *Sefer ḥaredim* (Book of the Devout) (Jerusalem, 1981).

The book reflects ideas that were formed in societies of mystical piety in Safed in the second half of the sixteenth century.

AZRIEL OF GERONA, *Perush ha'agadot* (Commentary on the *Aggadot* of the Talmud). Ed. Isaiah Tishby (Jerusalem, 1945).

Spanish thirteenth-century kabbalah of the students of Isaac the Blind.

BA'AL SHEM TOV, ISRAEL, *Igeret hakodesh* (The Holy Epistle). Different versions in Jacob Joseph of Polonnoye, *Ben porat yosef* (Korets, 1781); *Shivḥei habesht*, ed. Benjamin Mintz (Jerusalem, 1969), 167–9; 'Igeret aliyat haneshamah', in *Shivḥei haba'al shem tov: A Facsimile of a Unique Manuscript*, ed. Yehoshua Mondshine (Jerusalem, 1982), 229–38.

A letter written by the founder of hasidism in the mid-eighteenth century relating his ascent to heaven and conversation with the messiah. English translation: Jacobs, *Jewish Mystical Testimonies*, 148–55; Rosman, *Founder of Hasidism*, 97–113.

BEN SIRA, Ecclesiasticus, see *Wisdom of Ben Sira*.

Book of Jubilees, in *Old Testament Pseudepigrapha*, ed. Charlesworth, ii. 35–142, trans. O. S. Wintermute.

Priestly tradition, written in the middle of the second century BCE. Biblical history from the creation to the Sinai revelation as retold by the 'Angel of the Presence who sees God' (*malakh hapanim*) to Moses in a new alternative order. The history is told in a sevenfold structure of 'weeks of years' and jubilees, which are based on the solar calendar of 364 days, fifty-two weeks, and sevenfold divisions. The book's alternative history focuses on the commandments which connect the life of the Patriarchs and the 'appointed times of the Lord' according to the solar calendar. The holiday of Shavuot is a central topic. It is dated to the fifteenth of the third month, the date of all the covenants in the priestly tradition.

The Books of Enoch: Aramaic Fragments of Qumran Cave 4, ed. Jozef T. Milik (Oxford, 1976). Re-edited in Discoveries in the Judaean Desert, 36 (Oxford, 2000).

Oldest version of the Enoch tradition pertaining to heavenly ascent, angelic knowledge, and the solar calendar.

CARDOZO, ABRAHAM MICHAEL (who ascribed it to Shabetai Tsevi), *Raza demeheimanuta* (The Secret of Faith), in Nehemiah Hayon, *Oz lelohim* (Berlin, 1713).

Sabbatical text that generated great controversy and brought upon its author persecution and excommunication. On Cardozo, see Yosha, *Cardozo*.

COENEN, THOMAS, *Ydele verwachtinge der Joden getoont in den Persoon van Sabethai Zevi, haren laetsten vermeynden Messias* (Amsterdam, 1669); trans. into Hebrew by

A. Lagawier and E. Shmueli as *Tsipiyot shav shel hayehudim kefi shehitgalu bidemuto shel shabetai tsevi* (Vain Hopes of the Jews as Revealed by the Figure of Shabetai Tsevi) (Jerusalem, 1998).

The earliest eyewitness testimony to Shabetai Tsevi in Turkey in the last third of the seventeenth century.

CORDOVERO, MOSES, *Or yakar* (Glorious Light), on *Zohar ḥadash*, Song of Songs, 17 (Jerusalem, 1989).

—— *Pardes rimonim* (Orchard of Pomegranates) (Kraków, 1592; Munkacs, 1906).

Safed kabbalah, sixteenth century; systematic exposition of the Zohar and the Spanish kabbalistic tradition.

—— *Sefer gerushin* (Book of Banishments) (Venice, 1602; Shklov, 1792).

A mystical autobiographical diary of Cordovero, a prominent kabbalist from Safed, describing the mystical circle of his time and its central interest in the Shekhinah and the mystical identity of the companions who identified with her destiny.

—— *Tomer devorah* (The Palm Tree of Deborah), trans. Louis Jacobs (London, 1960).

Safed kabbalah; a sixteenth-century combination of moral and mystical literature.

DAVID BEN JUDAH HEHASID, *Mareot hatsove'ot* (Reflecting Mirrors), in Daniel Matt, 'Mareot hatsove'ot' (Ph.D. diss., Brandeis University, 1978).

Fourteenth-century kabbalah.

DOV BER, MAGGID OF MEZHIRECH, *Magid devarav leya'akov* (Telling his Words to Jacob) (Korets, 1781). Ed. Rivka Schatz-Uffenheimer (Jerusalem, 1976; repr. 1990).

Eighteenth-century hasidism; a major text in consolidating hasidic mysticism.

DOV BER OF LINITZ, *Shivḥei habesht* (In Praise of Israel Ba'al Shem Tov), ed. Israel Yaffe of Kapost (Kapost, 1814). Ed. Benjamin Mintz, *Sefer shivḥei habesht* (Jerusalem, 1969); ed. Yehoshua Mondshine, *Shivḥei haba'al shem tov: A Facsimile of a Unique Manuscript* (Jerusalem, 1982); Abraham Rubinstein, *Sefer shivḥei habesht* (Jerusalem, 1993). Ed. with a German translation in *Die Geschichten vom Ba'al Schem Tov, Schivche ha-Bescht*, ed. and trans. K. E. Grözinger (Wiesbaden, 1997). English translation: *In Praise of the Baal Shem Tov: The Earliest Collection of Legends about the Founder of Hasidism*, ed. and trans. D. Ben-Amos and J. R. Mintz (Bloomington, Ind. and London, 1970).

Hasidism; history, literature and hagiography; written at the end of the eighteenth century, edited and published at the beginning of the nineteenth. The text reflects the perspective of the Besht's contemporaries in the middle of the eighteenth century as well as later traditions. On the book see *Die Geschichten vom Ba'al Schem Tov*, ed. and trans. Grözinger; Gries, *Book, Author*; Rosman, *Founder*.

ELE'AZAR OF WORMS, *Sefer sodei razaya* (Secrets of Mysteries) (Bilgorei, 1936; Jerusalem, 1988).

Thirteenth-century German Jewish pietistic mystical literature. On the author see Dan, *The Occult*.

EMDEN, JACOB, *Megilat sefer, korot ḥayav vezikhronotav shel rav ya'akov emden al pi ketav yad oksford* (Biography and Memories of Rabbi Jacob Emden According to an Oxford Manuscript), ed. Avraham Bick (Jerusalem, 1979).

1 Enoch, in *The Old Testament Pseudepigrapha*, ed. Charlesworth, i. 5–89, trans. E. Isaac. *The Ethiopic Book of Enoch*, trans. R. H. Charles (Oxford, 1893). Matthew Black republished it in 1985 with a new translation *The Book of Enoch, or, I Enoch*, trans. Matthew Black (Studia in Veteris Testamenti Pseudepigrapha, 7; Leiden, 1985).

1 Enoch, or Ethiopic Enoch, was written close to the Hasmonean period in the second century BCE; it is called Ethiopic after the place where the manuscript was discovered in 1796, and for the Ethiopian Semitic language, Ethiopic or Ge'ez, into which it was translated from Aramaic. The book reflects the priestly tradition of the solar calendar that was revealed to Enoch in his heavenly ascent (Gen. 5: 24) and various traditions of the angelic world.

2 Enoch, in *The Old Testament Pseudepigrapha*, ed. Charlesworth, i. 91–222.

Slavonic Enoch was written in the first century CE and is called Slavonic after the language into which it was translated from Greek; the manuscript was found in Belgrade in 1886. The book reflects priestly traditions on the solar calendar and on Enoch the founder of priestly tradition and his heavenly ascent.

3 *Enoch: The Hebrew Book of Enoch*, ed. Hugo Odeberg (Cambridge, 1928; repr. New York, 1973 with prolegomena by Jonas Greenfield). Republished and interpreted by Philip Alexander in *The Old Testament Pseudepigrapha*, ed. Charlesworth, i. 223–315. Manuscripts transcribed in *Synopse zur Hekhalot-Literatur*, ed. Schäfer et al., §§1–80.

The Hebrew Book of Enoch was composed during the talmudic period; the name of the composition is *Sefer heikhalot* or *Sefer shivaah heikhalot* (Book of Seven Sanctuaries). It was called Third Enoch by its first editor, Hugo Odeberg. The book discusses the life of Enoch, who was transformed into an angel, Metatron, and his conversation with the mystical adept R. Ishmael, who ascended into the heavenly sanctuaries and the world of the angels.

FEIVUSH, MESHULAM, OF ZBARAZH, *Likutim yekarim* (Precious Collections) (also known as *Yosher divrei emet*) (Lemberg, 1792; Jerusalem, 1974).

Eighteenth-century hasidism, including autobiographical testimony.

FRANK, JACOB, *Divrei ha'adon* (Words of the Lord). A partial English version, translated from Polish, is to be found in *Sayings of Ya'akov Frank*, trans. Harris Lenowitz (Berkeley, 1978). A Hebrew translation by Fania Scholem, edited by Rachel Elior, in an interim edition (Jerusalem, 1997), has been placed in the Scholem collection in the National Library in Jerusalem; see Elior (ed.), *Dream and its Interpretation*. A printed edition of the Polish manuscript was first published by Jan Doktór as *Księga Słów Pańskich: Ezoteryczne wykłady Jakuba Franka*, 2 vols. (Warsaw, 1997).

An autobiographical statement that was related in Yiddish, written in Hebrew, and translated into Polish by Frank's disciples at the beginning of the nineteenth century.

Galya raza (Revealed Secrets), anonymous, ed. Rachel Elior (Hebrew University, Jerusalem, 1981).

Sixteenth-century kabbalah, discussing the reincarnation of the soul and messianic theories after the expulsion from Spain, based on angelic visions and heavenly dreams according to the author, who wanted to hasten redemption.

Geniza Fragmente zur Hekhalot Literatur, ed. Peter Schäfer (Tübingen, 1984).

Parts of the Heikhalot literature that were found in the Cairo Genizah. The Hebrew texts are from the tenth and eleventh centuries. The texts are concerned with the heavenly sanctuaries and their angelic residents.

GIKATILLA, JOSEPH, *Sha'arei orah* (Gates of Light) (Mantua, 1561). Ed. Yosef Ben-Shelomoh (Jerusalem, 1970). Trans. A. Weinstein as *Gates of Light* (San Francisco, 1994).

Thirteenth-century kabbalah. A systematic introduction to the symbols of the *sefirot* in the Zohar.

R. HAI GAON, *Otsar hage'onim lemasekhet ḥagigah* (The Responsa of the Geonim on the Tractate Ḥagigah), ed. Binyamin Menasheh Levin, in *Otsar hage'onim: teshuvot ge'onei bavel uferusheihem al pi seder hatalmud* (The Geonic Treasury: The Responsa of the Babylonian Geonim and their Interpretations according to the Order of the Talmud), iv (Jerusalem, 1934).

Hakeronikah: te'udah letoledot ya'akov frank utenu'ato (The Chronicle: A Document Regarding Jacob Frank and his Movement), ed. Hillel Levin (Jerusalem, 1984).

A translation from Polish to Hebrew of an eighteenth-century Frankist biographical-historical document relating to the life of Jacob Frank, founder of a mid-eighteenth century Shabatean movement, Frankism, in Poland.

HALEVI, JUDAH, *Shirim nivḥarim* (Selected Poems) (Jerusalem, 1950). Ed. Haim Schirman (Jerusalem, 1952).

Ḥarba demosheh (The Sword of Moses), ed. and annotated by Gershom Scholem, *Tarbits* (1982); transcribed from manuscript in *Synopse zur Hekhalot-Literatur*, ed. Schäfer et al., §§598–622. Re-edited by Yuval Harari, *Ḥarba demosheh* (Jerusalem, 1997).

A magical composition from the end of the Roman period.

HAYAT, JUDAH, *Minḥat yehudah* (Judah's Offering), ed. Immanuel of Benvenuto (Mantua, 1558; Jerusalem, 1963).

A book of sixteenth-century kabbalistic commentary on a thirteenth-century anonymous kabbalistic text, *Ma'arekhet ha'elohut*, written by Judah Hayat at the end of the fifteenth century and the beginning of the sixteenth. Hayat was among the exiles from Spain and Portugal (1492–7) and describes in his introduction the bitter fate of the exiles.

Heikhalot rabati (Greater Heikhalot), anonymous, attributed to Rabbi Ishmael. *Synopse zur Hekhalot-Literatur*, ed. Schäfer et al., §§81–306. Portions are translated into English in Gershom Scholem, *Jewish Gnosticism*, and David R. Blumenthal, *Understanding Jewish Mysticism: A Source Reader*, i (New York, 1978), and Halperin, *Faces of the Chariot*.

Heikhalot literature, relating to BT *Berakhot* 7a, including numinous hymns and martyrology, heavenly sanctuaries, angels, and prayers of the heavenly world.

Heikhalot zutarti (Lesser Heikhalot), anonymous, attributed to Rabbi Akiva. Ed. Rachel Elior, *Jerusalem Studies in Jewish Thought*, app. 1 (Jerusalem, 1982).

Heikhalot literature related to the tale of 'the four who entered paradise' (BT *Hagigah* 14a–15a), including mystical poetry and magical texts centred around holy names and visions of the divine chariot.

Hemdat yamim (Beloved of Days) (Smyrna, 1731–2). See Fogel, 'The Sabbatian Character of *Hemdat yamim*'.

Deals with the mystical reasons of the commandments according to Lurianic kabbalah as well as with moral instructions and ethical discussions, kabbalistic customs, prayers, and mystical intentions. It was condemned as heretical by the Ba'al Shem Tov, yet it does not quote any Shabatean source.

HOROWITZ, JACOB ISAAC, the Seer of Lublin, *Zikaron zot* (This is the Memory) (Munkacs, 1942). On the book see Elior, 'Changes in Religious Thought of Polish Hasidism'.

Eighteenth-century Polish hasidism, including autobiographical notes.

—— *Zot zikaron* (This to Remember) (Lvov, 1851; Munkacs, 1942).

Eighteenth-century Polish hasidism, including autobiographical notes.

HORWITZ, AARON B. MOSES HALEVI, of Starosielce, *Sha'arei ha'avodah* (Gates of Worship) (Shklov, 1821). Ed. A. M. Kraus (Jerusalem, 1988).

Mystical teachings of Habad hasidism, early nineteenth century.

—— *Sha'arei hayihud veha'emunah* (Gates of Unity and Faith) (Shklov, 1820). Ed. A. M. Kraus (Jerusalem, 1988). On the book and its author, see Elior, *Theology in the Second Generation*, and Jacobs, *Seeker of Unity*.

Mystical teachings of Habad hasidism, early nineteenth century.

ISAAC OF ACRE, *Me'irat einayim* (Enlightenment of the Eyes) (Leipzig, 1853; repr. Jerusalem, 1975). Ed. Amos Goldreich, *Sefer me'irat einayim shel r. yitshak demin ako* (Jerusalem, 1981). His teachings are discussed in Gottlieb, *Studies in Kabbalah Literature*.

Thirteenth-century kabbalah.

—— *Otsar haḥayim* (Treasure of Life), Ginzburg MS 775, Moscow, quoted in Gottlieb, *Studies in Kabbalah Literature.*

A mystical diary of the fourteenth-century kabbalist.

JACOB OF MARVÈGE, *She'elot uteshuvot min hashamayim* (Responsa from Heaven) (Venice, 1818), ed. Reuven Margalyot (Jerusalem, 1988).

JACOB JOSEPH OF POLONNOYE, *Toledot ya'akov yosef*. The first hasidic book, printed in Korets in 1780.

The book records the teachings of his teacher, Israel Ba'al Shem Tov. It had a great influence on dissemination of hasidism in the end of the eighteenth century and parts of it were abbreviated as instructions for hasidic ways of life in the last decade of the eighteenth century.

Jewish Mystical Autobiographies: Book of Visions and Book of Secrets, trans. Morris Faierstein (New York, 1999).

JOSEPH OF HAMADAN, *Ta'amei hamitsvot* (Reasons of the Commandments). Partially published in Meier, 'Joseph of Hamadan'.

Fourteenth-century kabbalah expressing a special interest in reincarnation.

KARA, AVIGDOR, of Prague, *Sefer hapeliah* or *Sefer hakaneh* (Book of Wonder) (Korets, 1784).

Fourteenth- to fifteenth-century kabbalah. On the book, see Oron, *Hapeliah vehakaneh.*

KARO, JOSEPH, *Magid meisharim* (Upright Sayings) (Lublin, 1648; Jerusalem, 1960). Ed. Yehiel bar Lev (Petah Tikvah, 1990). Parts of the book are translated into English in Werblowsky, *Joseph Karo*, and in Jacobs, *Jewish Mystical Testimonies*, 98–122. On Karo see Werblowsky, *Joseph Karo*; Benayahu, *Joseph, my Chosen*; Elior, 'R. Joseph Karo'.

The first mystical autobiography, written between 1533 and 1575 by a sixteenth-century kabbalist and a major halakhic authority in the Jewish world. It influenced many kabbalistic circles and affected the founder of eighteenth-century hasidism.

Keter shem tov: Anthology of the Sayings of R. Israel Baal-Shem Tov, ed. R. Aharon Hakohen (Brooklyn, 1984).

KOOK, ABRAHAM ISAAC HAKOHEN, *Arpilei tohar* (Clouds of Purity) (Jaffa, 1914). The book was published only in part and was concealed by the heirs of the author and censored. A complete edition was published in Jerusalem in 1997.

Mystical writings of a prominent halakhic authority and notable mystic of the early twentieth century, inspired by Habad hasidism and the mystical tradition. On the different dimensions of his mystical creativity see Garb, *Yeḥidei segulah.*

LAVI, SIMEON, *Ketem paz* (Pure Gold) (Livorno, 1795; repr. Jerusalem, 1981). On the book see Hus, *On Golden Foundations.*

Sixteenth-century kabbalah; exegesis on Zohar retaining important traditions not connected to Safed kabbalah.

LEINER, MORDECAI JOSEPH, of Izbica, *Mei hashilo'aḥ* (Waters of Shiloah) (Part 1, Vienna, 1860; Part 2, Lublin, 1924). English translation of parts of the book in Faierstein, *All is in the Hands of Heaven*.

Nineteenth-century Polish hasidism. The book provoked great controversy upon publication and was burnt by its opponents. On its contents and the reasons for the controversy see Elior, 'Changes in Religious Thought'.

LUZZATTO, MOSES HAYIM (RAMHAL), *Adir bamarom* (Mighty in Heaven) (Warsaw, 1886).

A kabbalistic composition written in Italy in the first part of the eighteenth century under mystical inspiration. The book is introduced as a continuation of the Zohar. See Ginzburg, *R. Moses Hayim Luzzatto*.

—— *Igerot ramḥal* (Letters of M. H. Luzzatto). Ed. Simeon Ginzburg (Tel Aviv, 1937). Also available in English: Ginzburg, *Life and Works of Moses Hayyim Luzzatto*.

A collection of letters and documents of Moses Hayim Luzzatto and his contemporaries, in the first half of the eighteenth century, including detailed elaborations of dreams and visions and details on his persecution.

—— *Kuf-lamed-ḥet pitḥei ḥokhmah* (138 Gates of Wisdom) (Jerusalem, 1961). Partial trans. in Verman, *History and Varieties of Jewish Meditation*.

Ma'arekhet ha'elohut (System of Divinity) (Ferrara, 1558; Mantua, 1558).

A kabbalistic book written in the thirteenth century dealing with the emanation of the ten spheres and the kabbalistic significance of various talmudic traditions. It was first published in the sixteenth century in Italy as part of the struggle on the status of kabbalah.

Ma'aseh merkavah (Work of the Chariot), in Scholem, *Jewish Gnosticism*. Translation into English in Janowitz, *Poetics of Ascent*, and Swartz, *Mystical Prayer*. The Hebrew text is available in *Synopse zur Hekhalot-Literatur*, ed. Schäfer et al.

One of the poetical-mystical compositions of the Heikhalot texts describing the ascent and descent to the chariot.

Ma'asei ta'atuim (Deeds of Mischief) [Loeb Wetzler] (Frankfurt, 1789). Ed. Yekutiel Gruenwald (Budapest, 1922).

A sharp polemical writing against Nathan Adler of Frankfurt; the end of the eighteenth century. On the book and the polemical circumstances of its publication see Elior, 'R. Nathan Adler'.

Ma'ayan haḥokhmah (Fountain of Wisdom) (Venice, 1601; Warsaw, 1863; Jerusalem, 1968). English translation in Verman, *Books of Contemplation*, 49–64.

Medieval Jewish anonymous mystical writing, belonging to the Circle of Contemplation that emerged around 1230 and was concerned with the secrets of the divine world and the explication of the Ineffable name. The anonymous author represents mystical secrets transmitted by the angel Michael to the mysterious angel Pe'eli to

Moses pertaining to the process of cosmogony, i.e. how the universe came into being. Gershom Scholem noted that the printed Hebrew editions are corrupt and the text is unintelligible (Scholem, *Origins of the Kabbalah*).

Marot hatsoveot, ed. and trans. Daniel Matt (Chico, Calif., 1982).

Megilat hahodayot (The Scroll of Thanksgiving Psalms), ed. Ya'akov Licht (Jerusalem, 1957). English translation in *Qumran Cave 4, XX: Poetical and Liturgical Texts*, ed. Esther Chazon, Eileen Schuller, et al. (Discoveries in the Judaean Desert, 29; Oxford, 1999).

Poetic mystical text ascribed to the deposed high priest known as the Teacher of Righteousness, written in the mid-second century BCE.

Megilat haserakhim (The Rule Scroll: A Scroll from the Wilderness of Judaea 1Qs 1QSa 1QSb), ed. Ya'akov Licht (Jerusalem, 1965). English translation in *Qumran Cave 4, XIX: Serekh Ha-Yahad and Two Related Texts*, ed. P. S. Alexander and G. Vermes (Discoveries in the Judaean Desert, 26; Oxford, 1998).

Legal and mystical-poetic writings by the deposed priests, the sons of Zadok, mid-second century BCE.

Megilat milhemet benei or bivenei hoshekh (The Scroll of the War of Sons of Light with Sons of Darkness), ed. Yigael Yadin (Jerusalem, 1957).

Mystical description of the heavenly and earthly struggle between the righteous and the powers of evil. Angelic assistance is promised the former to fight the demonic strength of the latter. Written by priestly circles in the second or first century BCE.

MOLCHO, SOLOMON, *Hazon shelomoh molkho hayat hakaneh* (The Vision of Solomon Molcho, Creature of the Reeds) (Amsterdam, 1660). Ed. Aharon Ze'ev Aescoly (Jerusalem, 1939). Also ed. Yehudah Edri (Jerusalem, 1989). The first editor was Abraham ben Joseph Rotenberg, in the 1660s.

Hayat hakaneh is a visionary text concerned with redemption inspired by the Book of Daniel; the author was born a Marrano and reconverted to Judaism in the decade that he wrote the book.

—— *Sefer hamefo'ar* (The Glorious Book) (first published in Turkey in 1529).

A book of kabbalisic sermons written at the end of the third decade of the sixteenth century.

MOSES HAYIM EPHRAIM of Sudylkov, *Degel mahaneh efrayim* (Korets, 1810; Jerusalem, 1963).

Hasidic teachings written by the grandchild of the founder of hasidism, containing family memories and quotations from Israel Ba'al Shem Tov's teachings and dreams.

NAHMAN OF BRATSLAV (1772–1810). See Green, *Tormented Master*; Mark, *Mysticism and Madness*; David Assaf, *Bratslav: An Annotated Bibliography. Rabbi Nahman of Bratslav, his Life and Teachings, the Literary Legacy of his Disciples, Bratslav*

Hasidism in Context [Bratslav: bibliografiyah mu'eret. R. naḥman mibratslav, tole-dotav umorashto hasifrutit, sifrei talmidav vetalmidei talmidav, ḥasidut bratslav usevivoteiha] (Jerusalem, 2000).

NAHMANIDES, *Kitvei rabenu mosheh ben naḥman al pi kitvei yad udefusim* (Writings of Nahmanides), ed. Hayim Dov Chavel, 2 vols. (Jerusalem, 1964–5).

—— *Perush al hatorah* (Nahmanides' commentary on the Torah). Ed. Hayim Dov Chavel (Jerusalem, 1976).

Kabbalah and exegesis of the Torah written in Spain in the thirteenth century.

The Old Testament Pseudepigrapha, ed. J. H. Charlesworth, 2 vols. (Garden City, NY, 1983–5) (an English translation of the Pseudepigrapha, including priestly mystical traditions such as 1 Enoch, 2 Enoch, 3 Enoch, Jubilees, Testament of the Twelve Tribes, Testaments of Levi, Joseph, and Asenath).

Pesher ḥavakuk (Commentary on Habbakuk), ed. Bilha Nitzan (Jerusalem and Tel Aviv, 1986).

Polemical text found among the Dead Sea Scrolls describing the difference between the deposed priests from the house of Zadok and the usurper priests from the house of Hasmonai.

Qumran Cave 4, XXVI: Cryptic Texts and Miscellanea, part 1, ed. Stephen J. Pfann, Philip Alexander, et al. (Discoveries in the Judaean Desert, 36; Oxford, 2000).

Includes parts of the Aramaic Book of Enoch.

Ra'aya mehemna (Faithful Shepherd). See below, Zohar, and Isaiah Tishby (ed.), *Wisdom of the Zohar*.

A medieval text from the fourteenth century included in the Zohar literature; the date of its composition is later than that of the Zohar itself. The book is concerned with the mystical image of Moses, the faithful shepherd.

RECANATI, MENAHEM BEN BENJAMIN, *Perush al hatorah* (Recanati's Commentary on the Torah) (Venice, 1503; Basle, 1581).

Fourteenth-century kabbalah, retaining important kabbalistic traditions.

—— *Ta'amei hamitsvot* (Reasons of the Commandments) (Constantinople, 1544; Basle, 1581). Ed. S. B. Libermann (London, 1969).

Kabbalah, thirteenth and fourteenth centuries.

Reshit ḥokhmah hakatsar (Summary of 'Beginning of Wisdom'). Trans. M. Perelman (Brooklyn, NY, 1979).

A shorter version of a major kabbalistic text, *Reshit ḥokhmah*, written by Elijah de Vidas in Safed in the sixteenth century.

Re'uyot yehezkel (The Visions of Ezekiel), ed. I. Gruenwald = *Temirin*, 1 (Jerusalem, 1972), 101–39.

An anonymous treatise on the visions of Ezekiel written in the talmudic period.

Safed Spirituality: Rules of Mystical Piety, the Beginning of Wisdom, trans. and introd. Lawrence Fine, preface by Louis Jacobs (New York, 1984).

SAFRIN, ISAAC JUDAH YEHIEL, of Komarno, *Megilat setarim* (Scroll of Secrets). Ed. Naftali Ben-Menahem (Jerusalem, 1944; repr. Brooklyn, 1985). English trans. in *Jewish Mystical Autobiographies*, trans. Faierstein. Partial trans. in Jacobs, *Jewish Mystical Testimonies*, 239–44.

A mystical messianic autobiography of a nineteenth-century hasidic teacher.

SCHNEERSOHN, DOV BER, *Kuntres hahitbonenut* (Tract on Contemplation). See *Ner mitsvah vetorah or. Kuntres hahitpa'alut* (Tract on Ecstasy), trans. Louis Jacobs, *Tract on Ecstasy* (London, 1965).

An internal Habad debate on divine worship and the succession of spiritual authority after the death of Shneur Zalman of Lyady, the Habad founder, in 1813. On this debate, see Elior, *Theology in the Second Generation*; Loewenthal, *Communicating the Infinite*; Jacobs, *Jewish Mystical Testimonies*, 224–38.

—— *Ner mitsvah vetorah or* (Lamp of the Commandment and Light of Torah) (Kopyst, 1820; New York, 1974) [includes *Sha'ar hayihud* (Gate of Unity) and *Kuntres hahitbonenut* (Tract on Contemplation)]. Partial English translation in Jacobs, *Seeker of Unity*.

Habad hasidim; an intra-hasidic debate on the succession of the spiritual leadership of Habad after the death of Shneur Zalman of Lyady in 1813, and on divine worship in the nineteenth century.

Sefer habahir (The Book of Elucidation), anonymously written in the twelfth century, attributed to the second-century CE sage Nehuniah ben Hakanah (Amsterdam, 1651). Ed. Reuben Margaliot (Jerusalem, 1948); ed. Daniel Abrahams (Los Angeles, 1995).

Among the founding texts of the kabbalistic tradition, introducing a new perception of the heavenly world, the human soul, the theory of transmigration, and the dual perception of reality. On the book see Scholem, *Origins*; Dan, *Jewish Mysticism*.

Sefer ha'iyun (The Book of Contemplation). Verman, *Books of Contemplation*.

A short theosophical-mystical treatise written anonymously around 1230 in western Europe, ascribed to Rabbi Hammai (Aramaic seer or visionary), discussing the mystery of the divine realm. The treatise, considered one of the seminal texts of the Jewish mystical tradition, circulated throughout Spain and Provence and within a few decades dozens of texts were composed reflecting the unique terminology of the book and its idiosyncratic doctrine. It has become a scholarly convention to refer to all of these works as 'circle of contemplation'.

Sefer hamalakh hameshiv (Book of the Answering Angel), or *Sefer hameshiv*, anonymous. In Scholem, 'The "Maggid" of R. Yosef Taitazak'.

The anonymous text presents itself as written automatically, dicated by an angel. The dating of the text is debatable, and is discussed in Scholem's book and in Idel, 'Inquiries into the Doctrine of *Sefer hameshiv*'.

Sefer harazim (Book of Mysteries), ed. Mordecai Margaliot (Jerusalem, 1967). Edition and English translation by Michael Morgan, *Sefer harazim: The Book of the Mysteries* (Chico, Calif., 1983).

Magical tradition and Heikhalot literature, according to Genizah manuscripts from the talmudic period.

Sefer hatemunah (Book of the Image), anonymous, written in the fourteenth century, attributed to the second-century sage Nehuniah ben Hakanah and to Ishmael the high priest (Korets, 1784; Lemberg, 1892; Tel Aviv, 1972). On the book see Scholem, *The Kabbalah of* Sefer hatemunah.

Fourteenth-century kabbalah.

Sefer yetsirah (Book of Creation) (Mantua, 1562; Jerusalem, 1989). Ed. Gruenwald in 'A Preliminary Critical Edition'. English translation by Aryeh Kaplan, *Sefer Yetzirah: The Book of Creation* (rev. edn., York Beach, Me., 1997). On the book see Liebes, *Creation Doctrine*, and Dan, 'The Religious Significance of *Sefer Yetsirah*'.

A basic book in the mystical tradition concerning a new perception of the deity as expressed in the creative process through language, letters, and numbers, ascribed by scholars to different dates from the first century CE to the Islamic period. The anonymous author initiated the concept of ten spheres (*sefirot*) and twenty-two elemental letters, which profoundly affected the Jewish mystical tradition.

SHEM-TOV IBN SHEM-TOV, *Sefer ha'emunot* (Book of Beliefs) (Ferrara, 1556; Jerusalem, 1969).

Kabbalah. On him see Gottlieb, *Studies in Kabbalah Literature*, and David Ariel, *Shem Tov ibn Shem Tov's Kabbalistic Critique of Jewish Philosophy in the Commentary on the Sefirot: Study and Text* (Ann Arbor, 1982).

Shimushei tehilim (Uses of the Psalms) (Sabbionetta, 1552; Kraków, 1648). English version in Gottfried Selig, *Use of the Psalms* (Boston, 1943).

Shimushei torah (Uses of the Torah). Introduction published as *Ma'ayan haḥokhmah* (see above).

Deals with the magical use of the letters of the Torah.

Shirot olat hashabat (Songs of the Sabbath Sacrifice). *Songs of the Sabbath Sacrifice: A Critical Edition*, ed. Carol Newsom (Harvard Semitic Studies, 27; Atlanta, Ga., 1985). *4Q Serek Shirot olat hashabat (The Qumran Angelic Liturgy)*, ed. and trans. C. Newsom (Cambridge, Mass., 1982) (Hebrew with English translation). Discoveries in the Judaean Desert, 11 has the final version of the text of the songs found in the fourth cave in Qumran. DJD 23 has the texts of the eleventh cave.

Qumran priestly-mystical literature on the angelic liturgy in the heavenly Temple arranged according to the priestly solar calendar of 364 days divided into fifty-two sabbatical weeks; second to first centuries BCE.

Shiur komah, in *Synopse zur Hekhalot-Literatur*, ed. Schäfer et al. Critical edition and English translation in Cohen, *The Shi'ur Qomah*.

Mystical theosophical doctrine relating to the image of the divine stature, ascribing to it names, measures, and bodily attributes of immense cosmic measures; first centuries CE; Heikhalot literature. On the text see Scholem, 'Shi'ur Qomah'; Cohen, *The Shi'ur Qomah*; Farber-Ginat, 'Studies in Shi'ur Komah'.

Shivḥei metatron (In Praise of Metatron), in *Synopse zur Hekhalot-Literatur*, ed. Schäfer et al., §§384–488. Partial English translation in Halperin, *Faces of the Chariot*; Elior, *Three Temples*, ch. 10.

Heikhalot mystical tradition centred around the angel of the countenance Metatron, previously known as Enoch son of Jared, who was taken to heaven.

SHNEUR ZALMAN OF LYADY, *Boneh yerushalayim* (Builder of Jerusalem), ed. Hayim Eliezer Hakohen Bihovski (Jerusalem, 1926).

—— *Tanya* (Slavuta, 1797; Kefar Habad, 1980). Includes *Likutei amarim* (Collections of Sayings); *Sha'ar hayiḥud veha'emunah* (Gate of Unity and Faith); *Igeret hakodesh* (Holy Epistle). English translation by Nissan Mindel, *Rabbi Schneur Zalman*, 2 vols. (Brooklyn, 1969–73); bi-lingual edition by Nissan Mindel, Zalman Posner, and Immanuel Schochet (London, 1973).

Habad, hasidic mysticism of the last third of the eighteenth century; the most influential book in the consolidation and dissemination of Habad hasidism.

—— *Torah or* (Light of the Torah) (Kapost, 1832; Vilna 1899; Brooklyn, 1978). On the book see Elior, *Paradoxical Ascent to God*.

Habad mystical theosophy; comprehensive, systematic, and profound discussion of the perception of divinity and the mystical divine worship; written in the eighteenth and nineteenth centuries.

—— *Torat ḥayim* (Torah of Life) (Kapost, 1826; Brooklyn, 1974).

A homiletic hasidic book by two Habad teachers, Shneur Zalman of Lyady and his son Dov Ber. It is usually ascribed to the son in hasidic bibliography but has important teachings of the father.

SOLOMON OF LUTSK, *Divrat shelomoh* (Speech of Solomon) (Zolkiew, 1848; repr. Jerusalem, 1955). On him see Schatz-Uffenheimer's introduction to Dov Ber of Mezherich, *Magid devarav leya'akov* (Jerusalem, 1976).

Hasidic thoughts and teachings of the Maggid of Mezhirech as introduced by his student, who was a central figure in printing kabbalistic and hasidic books in the last decades of the eighteenth century.

SOLOMON SHLOMEL BEN HAYIM OF DREZNITZ, *Shivḥei ha'ari* (In Praise of Isaac Luria) (Ostraha, 1794). Ed. Jacob Moshe Hillel (Jerusalem, 1991).

Lurianic hagiography of the seventeenth century, a text that had a profound effect on mystical circles throughout the Jewish world since its readers strove to imitate the mystical perceptions and practices of Luria. On him see *Toledot ha'ari*, ed. Benayahu.

Songs and Praises of the Shabateans [Shirot vetishbaḥot shel hashabeta'im], ed. Moshe Atiash, G. Scholem, and Y. Ben-Tsevi (Jerusalem, 1946).

Late seventeenth- and early eighteenth-century poetical-mystical literature of the Doenmeh.

Songs of the Sabbath Sacrifice, see *Shirot olat hashabat*

Synopse zur Hekhalot-Literatur, ed. Peter Schäfer, Margarete Schlüter, and Hans Georg von Mutius (Tübingen, 1981).

A synoptic collection of seven medieval manuscripts of the Heikhalot literature written or copied in Germany in the circles of the German Jewish Pietists of the twelfth and thirteenth centuries. The origins of the Heikhalot tradition are in the talmudic period; the texts are written and published in Hebrew and Aramaic; the introduction is in German. Portions of this literature are available in English translation in books by Scholem, *Jewish Gnosticism*; P. Alexander, 3 Enoch in *Old Testament Pseudepigrapha*, ed. Charlesworth, i. 223–315; Halperin, *Faces of the Chariot*; Schäfer, *Hidden and Manifest God*; Janowitz, *The Poetics of Ascent*; Swartz, *Mystical Prayer*; Elior, *The Three Temples*; Jacobs, *Jewish Mystical Testimonies*, 26–34.

TABUL, JOSEPH IBN, *Derush ḥeftsivah* (Sermon 'Delight is in Her'), in Masud Hadad Cohen, *Simḥat kohen* (A Priest's Joy) (Jerusalem, 1921).

TESTAMENT OF LEVI, in *Old Testament Pseudepigrapha*, ed. Charlesworth, i. 788–95.

A priestly tradition from the second century BCE about the history of Levi. The Aramaic text was found in Qumran among the Dead Sea Scrolls. The priestly-mystical tradition profoundly transforms the image of Levi, arguing that he was chosen by the angels to be the founder of the priesthood in the times of the patriarchs. On Levi in the Testament of Levi see Kugel, 'Levi's Elevation to the Priesthood'.

Toledot ha'ari (Life of Isaac Luria), ed. Meir Benayahu (Jerusalem, 1967).

Lurianic hagiography, sixteenth and seventeenth centuries. The text was first printed as *Kavanot uma'aseh nisim* (Constantinople, 1720).

Tsava'at harivash (The Testament of Israel Ba'al Shem Tov), collection of sayings by Israel Ba'al Shem Tov and the Maggid of Mezhirech, first printed in 1794. *Shivḥei habesht*, ed. B. Mintz (Jerusalem, 1969), 213–34. A modern annotated edition: *Tsava'at harivash*, ed. Jacob Immanuel Schochet (Brooklyn, NY, 1975). English translation by id., *Tzava'at Harivash* (Brooklyn, NY, 1998).

Hasidic writings from the later part of the eighteenth century, which include some of Israel Ba'al Shem Tov's teachings. The book had an immense effect on the consolidation of the new hasidic identity. It was burnt by the opponents of hasidism in Vilna. On the history of the book in the hasidic–mitnagdic controversy see Wilensky, *Hasidim and Mitnagdim*.

VIDAS, ELIJAH B. MOSES DE, *Reshit ḥokhmah* (Beginning of Wisdom) (Venice, 1579). Ed. K. Waldmann (Jerusalem, 1984).

Kabbalah and ethical literature, from the second part of the sixteenth century.

The book was 'adopted' by hasidic circles as a moral and mystical guide to daily conduct.

VITAL, HAYIM, *Ets ḥayim* (Tree of Life) (Korets, 1794; Warsaw, 1891; Jerusalem, 1910).

The main composition of Lurianic kabbalah in the sixteenth and seventeenth centuries. The book introduces a new perception of the divine world and human worship. The introduction to the book, written by Vital, is the most important testimony on the struggle of the kabbalah to gain a prominent spiritual position in the sixteenth century.

—— *Mavo she'arim* (Opening of the Gates) (Jerusalem, 1984).

Lurianic kabbalah of the sixteenth century, the first of eight volumes that include Lurianic kabbalah, called *Shemonah she'arim*.

—— *Sefer hagilgulim* (Book of Reincarnations) (Frankfurt, 1684; Jerusalem, 1987).

Lurianic kabbalah (sixteenth century) contributed to dissemination of the belief in reincarnation and the conclusions derived from it regarding ritual slaughter and levirate marriage.

—— *Sefer haḥezyonot* (Book of Visions). Ed. Aharon Ze'ev Aescoly and Naftali Ben-Menahem (Jerusalem, 1954). English translation in Faierstein, *Mystical Autobiographies*.

A mystical autobiography recording dreams and visions of Hayim Vital, a major kabbalist in the second half of the sixteenth century who lived in Safed and Damascus and edited and disseminated the first recensions of Lurianic kabbalah.

—— *Sha'ar hagilgulim* (Gate of Reincarnations) (Jerusalem, 1912, 1978, 1981). One of the 'Eight Gates'.

Sixteenth-century Lurianic kabbalah; mysticism; theory of the soul and doctrine of reincarnation of the souls.

—— *Shemonah she'arim* (Eight Gates) (Saloniki, 1852; Jerusalem, 1974; 1988).

A series of eight books ('Gates') written by Vital, containing a systematic presentation of Lurianic kabbalah divided by topic.

Wadi Daliyeh, II, and Qumran Miscellanea, pt. 2: *The Samaria Papyri from Wadi Daliyeh*, ed. D. M. Gropp, J VanderKam, and M. Brady (Discoveries in the Judaean Desert, 28: Oxford, 2001).

Wisdom of Ben Sira, ed. Moshe Tsevi Segal (Jerusalem, 1953).

Wisdom literature of the early second century BCE; parts of the book were found in Qumran among the Dead Sea Scrolls and in the Cairo Genizah. Important traditions concerning Enoch son of Jared, the founder of the mystical-priestly lore, and the high priest Simeon the Just (Shimon Hatsadik) of the priestly house of Zadok are included in the book.

WOLF, ZE'EV, of Zhitomir, *Or hame'ir* (Shining Light) (Korets, 1798; Jerusalem, 1968).

Eighteenth-century hasidism from the circle of the Maggid of Mezhirech. The book contains remarkable teachings on language and on the hasidic perception of the mystical connotation of the Shekhinah.

ZADOK HAKOHEN OF LUBLIN, *Tsidkat hatsadik* (Righteousness of the Righteous) (Lublin, 1902; Jerusalem, 1987). On the author see Brill, *Thinking God.*

Polish hasidism of the nineteenth century; he was a follower of the hasidic school of Izbica.

Zohar (*Sefer hazohar*, Book of Splendour), attributed to R. Shimon bar Yohai [real author: Moses de León], first published in Mantua and Cremona in 1558. Ed. Reuben Margaliot (Jerusalem, 1984). Partial English translation in Tishby (ed.), *Wisdom of the Zohar.* The first three portions are fully translated by Daniel Matt, *Zohar* (Pritzker Edition), 1–2 (Stanford, 2006).

A medieval kabbalistic composition written in the thirteenth century in Spain in Aramaic, but ascribed to R. Shimon bar Yohai, a sage who lived in the second century. The exceptional structure, language, and contents of the book made it one of the central sources of mystical inspiration for the following centuries. On the book see Scholem, *Major Trends*; Liebes, 'How the Zohar was Written'; Hellner-Eshed, *A River Issues Forth*; Giller, *The Enlightened.*

SECONDARY SOURCES

AESCOLY, AHARON ZE'EV, *Messianic Movements in Judaism* [Hatenuot hameshihiyot beyisra'el] (Jerusalem, 1987).

ALEXANDER, PHILIP S., 'The Historical Setting of the Hebrew Book of Enoch', *Journal of Jewish Studies*, 28 (1977), 156–80.

ALONI, NEHEMIA, 'The Date of *Sefer yetsirah*' [Zeman hiburo shel sefer yetsirah], *Temirin*, 2 (Jerusalem, 1982), 41–50.

ARBEL, VITA DAPHNA, *Beholders of Divine Secrets: Mysticism and Myth in the Hekhalot and Merkavah Literature* (Albany, NY, 2003).

ASAF, DAVID, 'Apostate or Saint: A Voyage in the Footsteps of the Son of Rabbi Shneur Zalman of Lyady' [Mumar o kadosh: masa be'ikevot mosheh beno shel rav shene'ur zalman miliadi], *Tsiyon*, 54 (2000), 453–515.

AUSTIN, JOHN L., *How to Do Things with Words*, ed. J. O. Urmson and M. Sbias (2nd edn., Cambridge, Mass., 1975).

AVIVI, YOSEF, 'R. Hayim Vital's Writings on Lurianic Kabbalah' [Kitvei r. hayim vital bekabalat ha'ari], *Moriyah*, 10 (1981), 71–91.

BALABAN, MAIER, *History of the Frankist Movement* [Letoledot hatenuah hafrankistit], 2 vols. (Tel Aviv, 1934–5).

BAT-MIRIAM, YOKHEVED, *From Afar: Songs* (Tel Aviv, 1985).

BENAYAHU, MEIR, 'In Praise of the Ari' [Shivḥei ha'ari], *Areshet*, 3 (1961), 144–65.

—— *Joseph, my Chosen: Studies on R. Joseph Caro* [Yosef beḥiri: meḥkarim betoledot maran rabi yosef karo] (Jerusalem, 1993).

BEN-SHELOMOH, YOSEF, 'On the Problem of the Uniqueness of Religion in Rudolf Otto's Philosophy' [Live'ayat yiḥudah shel hadat bafilosofiyah shel r. oto]', in S. Pines (ed.), *Memorial Book for Jacob Friedmann* [Sefer zikaron leya'akov fridman] (Jerusalem, 1974).

—— 'The Problem of Pantheism in the Mysticism of a Theistic Religion: R. Moses Cordovero and Meister Eckhart' [Be'ayat hapante'izem bamistikah shel dat te'istit: r. mosheh kordovero umaister ekhart], in id., *Revelation of Faith and Understanding* [Hitgalut emunah utevunah] (Ramat Gan, 1976), 71–86.

—— *The Theology of Moses Cordovero* [Torat ha'elohut shel r. mosheh kordovero] (Jerusalem, 1965).

BERGER, DAVID, *The Rebbe, the Messiah, and the Scandal of Orthodox Indifference* (London and Portland, Ore., 2001).

BETZ, HANS DIETER, *The Greek Magical Papyri in Translation, including the Demotic Spells* (2nd edn., Chicago, 1986).

BIALIK, HAYIM NAHMAN, *Collected Works of Hayim Nahman Bialik: Literary Matters* [Kol kitvei ḥayim naḥman bialik: divrei sifrut] (Tel Aviv, 1954).

—— 'Language Closing and Disclosing' [Gilui vekhisui balashon], in id., *Collected Works*, 22–31. Trans. Yael Lotan in *Ariel: A Quarterly of Arts and Letters in Israel*, 50 (1979), 255–61.

—— *Selected Poems*, trans. Ruth Nevo (Jerusalem, 1981).

—— 'The Young Man of Padua [= Moses Hayim Luzzatto]' [Habaḥur mipadova], in id., *Collected Works*, 158–63.

BILU, YORAM, *Without Bounds: The Life and Death of Rabbi Ya'aqov Wazana* (Detroit, 2000).

BÖTTRICH, CHRISTFRIED, *Weltweisheit, Menschheitsethik, Urkult: Studien zum slavischen Henochbuch* (Tübingen, 1992).

BRILL, ALAN, *Thinking God: The Mysticism of Rabbi Zadok of Lublin* (New York and Jersey City, NJ, 2002).

BUBER, MARTIN, *Ecstatic Confessions*, ed. Paul Mendes-Flohr, trans. Esther Cameron (San Francisco, 1985).

CARLEBACH, ELISHEVA, *The Pursuit of Heresy: Rabbi Moses Hagiz and the Sabbatian Controversies* (New York, 1990).

CHAJES, JEFFREY HOWARD, *Spirit Possession and the Construction of Early Modern Jewish Religiosity* (Ann Arbor, 2000).

COHEN, MARTIN (ed.), *The Shi'ur Qomah: Liturgy and Theurgy in Pre-Kabbalistic Jewish Mysticism* (Lanham, Md., 1983).

COHEN-ALLORO, DORIT, 'Magic and Sorcery in the Zohar' [Magiyah vekhishuf besefer hazohar] (Diss., Hebrew University of Jerusalem, 1989).

COLLINS, JOHN J., *The Apocalyptic Imagination: An Introduction to the Jewish Matrix of Christianity* (New York, 1984).

DAN, JOSEPH, *The Ancient Jewish Mysticism*, trans. Shmuel Himelstein (Tel Aviv, 1993).

—— *Jewish Mysticism*, 4 vols. (Northvale, NJ, 1998–9).

—— *Jewish Mysticism and Jewish Ethics* (Seattle, 1986).

—— *The Occult Theories of the Hasidei Ashkenaz* [Torat hasod shel ḥasidei ashkenaz] (Jerusalem, 1968).

—— *On Holiness: Religion, Ethics, and Mysticism in Judaism and Other Religions* [Al hakedushah: dat, musar, umistikah bayahadut uvedatot aḥerot] (Jerusalem, 1997).

—— 'The Religious Significance of *Sefer Yetsirah*' [Hamashma'ut hadatit shel sefer yetsirah], *Jerusalem Studies in Jewish Thought*, 11 (1993), 7–35.

—— 'The Story of Joseph della Reina' [Sipur yosef dela reina], in id., *The Medieval Jewish Story* (Jerusalem, 1975).

—— *The Unique Cherub Circle: A School of Mystics and Esoterics in Medieval Germany* (Tübingen, 1998).

—— (ed.), *The Early Kabbalah*, trans. Ronald C. Kiener (New York, 1986).

—— (ed.), *The Heart and the Fountain: An Anthology of Jewish Mystical Experience* (Oxford and New York, 2002).

—— and ESTER LIEBES (eds.), *The Library of Gershom Scholem on Jewish Mysticism: Catalogue*, 2 vols. (Jerusalem, 1999).

DINUR, BEN-ZION, *At the Turn of the Generations* [Bemifneh hadorot] (Jerusalem, 1955; 2nd edn. 1972). English translation in Hundert (ed.), *Essential Papers on Hasidism*.

DODDS, ERIC R., *The Greeks and the Irrational* (Berkeley, 1959).

DUBNOW, SIMON, *History of Hasidism* [Toledot haḥasidut] (3rd edn., Tel Aviv, 1967). Partial English translation in Hundert (ed.), *Essential Papers on Hasidism*.

ELIOR, RACHEL, 'Between *Yesh* and *Ayin*: The Doctrine of the Zadik in the Works of Rabbi Jacob Isaac, the Seer of Lublin', in Ada Rapoport-Albert and Steven J. Zipperstein (eds.), *Jewish History: Essays in Honour of Chimen Abramsky* (London, 1988), 393–455.

—— 'Breaking the Boundaries of Time and Space in Kabbalistic Apocalypticism', in Albert I. Baumgarten (ed.), *Apocalyptic Time* (Leiden, 2000), 187–97.

—— 'Changes in the Concept of God in Jewish Thought' [Temurot bemusag ha'el bamaḥashavah hayehudit], in Kerem (ed.), *Spectrum of Opinions*, ii (1992), 13–35.

—— 'Changes in Religious Thought of Polish Hasidism: Between Fear and Love and Depth and Hue' [Temurot bamahashavah hadatit behasidut polin: bein yirah ve'ahavah le'omek vegavan], *Tarbits*, 62 (1993), 381–432.

—— 'The Concept of God in Hekhalot Literature', trans. Dena Ordan in Joseph Dan (ed.), *Binah: Studies in Jewish Thought*, ii (New York, 1989), 97–129. English translation of 'Yihudah shel hatofa'ah hadatit besifrut haheikhalot: demut ha'el veharhavat gevulot hahasagah', *Jerusalem Studies in Jewish Thought*, 6/1–2 (1987), 13–64.

—— 'The Controversy over Habad's Legacy' [Hamahaloket al moreshet habad], *Tarbits*, 49 (1980), 166–86.

—— 'The Doctrine of Transmigration in *Galya Raza*', in Fine (ed.), *Essential Papers on Kabbalah*, 243–69.

—— 'Dov Ber Schneersohn's *Kuntres hahitpa'alut*', *Kiryat sefer*, 54 (1979).

—— 'From Earthly Temple to Heavenly Shrines: Prayer and Sacred Song in the Hekhalot Literature and its Relation to Temple Tradition', *Jewish Studies Quarterly*, 4 (1997), 393–455.

—— 'Jacob Frank's *Divrei ha'adon*' [Divrei ha'adon leya'akov frank], in Elior (ed.), *Dream and its Interpretation*, ii. 471–548.

—— 'The Jewish Calendar and Mystical Time' [Haluah hayehudi vehazeman hamisti], in *The Jewish Calendar* [Luah hashanah ha'ivri] (The Beit Hanasi Circle for Bible and Jewish Sources [Hug beit hanasi letanakh ulemekorot beit yisra'el], 5; Jerusalem, 1996), 22–42. For an English translation see Elior, *The Three Temples*.

—— 'Merkabah Mysticism', review of David Halperin, *The Faces of the Chariot*, in *NUMEN*, 37 (1990), 223–49.

—— 'Messianic Expectations and Spiritualization of Religious Life in the Sixteenth Century', *Revue des Études juives*, 145 (1986), 35–49; repr. in D. B. Ruderman (ed.), *Essential Papers on Jewish Culture in Renaissance and Baroque Italy* (New York, 1992), 283–98.

—— 'The Metaphorical Relationship between God and Man and the Continuity of Visionary Reality in Lurianic Kabbalah' [Hazikah hametaforit bein ha'el la'adam uretsifutah shel hamamashut hahezyonit bekabalat ha'ari'], in Elior and Liebes, *Lurianic Kabbalah*, 47–57.

—— *The Mystical Origins of Hasidism* (Oxford, 2006).

—— 'Mysticism, Magic and Angelology: The Perception of Angels in Hekhalot Literature', *Jewish Studies Quarterly*, 1 (1993–4), 5–53.

—— 'The Paradigms of *Yesh* and *Ayin* in Hasidic Thought', in Rapoport-Albert (ed.), *Hasidism Reappraised*, 168–79.

—— *The Paradoxical Ascent to God: The Kabbalistic Theosophy of Habad Hasidism*, trans. Jeffrey M. Green (Albany, NY, 1993) (English translation of *Torat ahdut hahafakhim: hate'osofiyah hamistit shel habad* (Jerusalem, 1992)).

ELIOR, RACHEL, 'R. Joseph Karo and R. Israel Ba'al Shem Tov: Mystical Metamorphosis, Kabbalistic Inspiration, and Spiritual Internalization' [Rabi yosef karo verabi yisra'el ba'al shem tov: metamorfozah mistit, hashra'ah kabalit vehafnamah ruḥanit'], *Tarbits*, 65 (1996), 671–709.

—— 'R. Nathan Adler and the Frankfurter Pietists: Pietistic Groups in Eastern and Central Europe during the Eighteenth Century', in K. E. Grözinger (ed.), *Jüdische Kultur in Frankfurt am Main: Von den Anfängen bis zur Gegenwart* (Wiesbaden, 1997), 135–77.

—— 'Reality in the Test of Fiction: Dreams in Mystical Thought. The Freedom of Disassociation and Combination' [Metsi'ut bemivḥan habidayon: haḥalom bamaḥashavah hamistit: ḥerut haperuk vehatseruf], in Kerem (ed.), *Spectrum of Opinions*, v. 63–79.

—— 'Schäfer's *Geniza-Fragmente zur Hekhalot Literature*', review article, *Jewish Quarterly Review*, 80 (1989), 142–5.

—— 'The Struggle for the Status of Kabbalah in the Sixteenth Century' [Hama'avak al ma'amadah shel hakabalah bame'ah ha-16], *Jerusalem Studies in Jewish Thought*, 1 (1981), 177–90. For an English translation see Elior, 'Messianic Expectations'.

—— *Theology in the Second Generation of the Habad Hasidic Movement* [Torat ha'elohut bador hasheni shel ḥasidut ḥabad] (Jerusalem, 1982).

—— *The Three Temples: On the Emergence of Jewish Mysticism*, trans. David Louvish (Oxford, 2004).

—— '"You Have Chosen Enoch from among Mankind": Enoch the "Righteous Scribe" and the Library of the "Priests, the Sons of Zadok"' ['Ḥanoch baḥarta mibenei adam': ḥanokh 'sofer hatsedek' vehasifriyah shel 'hakohanim benei tsadok'], in R. Elior and P. Schäfer (eds.), *Creation and Re-Creation in Jewish Thought: Festschrift in Honor of Joseph Dan on the Occasion of his Seventieth Birthday* (Tübingen, 2005), Hebrew section, 15–64.

—— (ed.), *The Dream and its Interpretation: The Shabatean Movement and its Aftermath—Messianism, Shabateanism, and Frankism* [Haḥalom veshivro: hatenuah hashabeta'it usheluḥoteiha—meshiḥiyut, shabeta'ut, ufrankism] (Jerusalem, 2001) = *Jerusalem Studies in Jewish Thought*, 16–17 (2001), 471–548.

—— and YEHUDA LIEBES (eds.), *Lurianic Kabbalah* [Kabalat ha'ari] (Jerusalem, 1992) = *Jerusalem Studies in Jewish Thought*, 10 (1992).

ERIKSON, ERIK, *Young Man Luther: A Study in Psychoanalysis and History* (London, 1959).

ETKES, IMMANUEL, *The Besht: Magician, Mystic and Leader*, trans. Saadia Sternberg (Waltham, Mass., 2005).

—— 'Magic and Masters of the Name in Ashkenazi Society at the Turn of the Seventeenth to Eighteenth Centuries' [Mekomam shel hamagiyah uva'alei hashem baḥevrah ha'ashkenazit bemifneh hame'ot ha-17–18], *Tsiyon*, 60 (1995), 69–104.

FAIERSTEIN, MORRIS, *All is in the Hands of Heaven: The Teachings of Rabbi Mordecai Joseph Leiner of Izbica* (New York and Hoboken, NJ, 1989).

FARBER-GINAT, A., 'Studies in Shi'ur Komah', in *Masuot: Studies in Kabbalah Literature and Jewish Thought in Memory of Ephraim Gottlieb* [Masuot: meḥkarim besifrut hakabalah uvemaḥashevet yisra'el mukdashim lezikhro shel efrayim gotlib] (Jerusalem, 1994), 361–94.

FINE, LAWRENCE, 'The Contemplative Practice of Yiḥudim in Lurianic Kabbalah', in Green (ed.), *Jewish Spirituality*, ii. 64–98.

—— *Physician of the Soul, Healer of the Cosmos: Isaac Luria and his Kabbalistic Fellowship* (Stanford, Calif., 2003).

—— (ed.), *Essential Papers on Kabbalah* (New York, 1995).

FOGEL, MOSHE, 'The Sabbatian Character of *Ḥemdat yamim*: A Re-examination', in Elior (ed.), *Dream and its Interpretation*, ii. 365–422.

GARB, YEHONATAN, *The Chosen Few Will Be Numbered in Flocks* [Yeḥidei segulah yiheyu le'adarim] (Jerusalem, 2005)

GEERTZ, CLIFFORD, *The Interpretation of Cultures* (New York, 1973).

GILLER, PINCHAS, *The Enlightened Will Shine: Symbolization and Theurgy in the Later Strata of the Zohar* (Albany, NY, 1993).

GINSBURG, ELLIOT K., *The Sabbath in the Classical Kabbalah* (Albany, NY, 1989).

GINZBURG, SIMEON, *R. Moses Hayim Luzzatto and his Contemporaries: An Anthology of Letters and Documents* [Rabi mosheh ḥayim lutsato uvenei doro: osef igerot ute'udot] (Tel Aviv, 1937). English trans. *The Life and Works of Moses Hayyim Luzzatto, Founder of Modern Hebrew Literature* (Westport, Conn., 1975).

GOLDISH, MATT, *The Sabbatean Prophets* (New York, 2002).

—— (ed.), *Spirit Possession in Judaism: Cases and Contexts from the Middle Ages to the Present* (Cambridge, Mass., 2004).

GOTTLIEB, EPHRAIM, *Studies in Kabbalah Literature* [Meḥkarim besifrut hakabalah] (Tel Aviv, 1976).

GREEN, ARTHUR, *Keter: The Crown of God in Early Jewish Mysticism* (Princeton, 1997).

—— *Tormented Master: A Life of Rabbi Nahman of Bratslav* (University, Ala., 1979).

—— 'Typologies of Leadership and the Hasidic Ẓaddiq', in *Jewish Spirituality*, ii. 127–56.

—— 'The Zadik as Axis Mundi in Later Judaism', *JAAR* 45 (1977), 327–47.

—— (ed.) *Jewish Spirituality*, 2 vols. (World Spirituality, 13–14; London, 1986–7).

GRIES, ZE'EV, *Book, Author, and Story in Early Hasidism: From Israel Ba'al Shem Tov to Menahem Mendel of Kotsk* [Sefer sofer vesipur bereshit haḥasidut: min habesht ve'ad menaḥem mendel mikotsk] (Tel Aviv, 1992).

GRÖZINGER, KARL E., 'The Names of God and the Celestial Powers: Their Function and Meaning in the Hekhalot Literature', *Jerusalem Studies in Jewish Thought*, 6/1–2 (1987), 53–70.

GRUENWALD, ITHAMAR, *Apocalyptic and Merkavah Mysticism* (Leiden, 1980).

—— *From Apocalypticism to Gnosticism: Studies in Apocalypticism, Merkavah Mysticism and Gnosticism* (Frankfurt am Main, 1988).

—— 'Magic and Myth: Research and Historical Reality' [Hamagiyah vehamitos: hamehkar vehametsiut hahistorit], in Haviva Pedaya (ed.), *Myth in Judaism* [Hamitos bayahadut] (Eshel be'er sheva, 4; Jerusalem and Beersheba, 1996), 15–28.

—— 'A Preliminary Critical Edition of Sefer Yezira', *Israel Oriental Studies*, 1 (1971), 132–77.

—— 'Writing, Epistles, and the Name of God: Magic, Spirituality, and Mysticism' [Haketav, hamikhtav, vehashem hameforash: magiyah, ruhaniyut, umistikah], in *Masuot: Studies in Kabbalistic Literature and Jewish Thought in Memory of Ephraim Gottlieb* [Masuot: mehkarim besifrut hakabalah uvemahashevet yisra'el mukdashim lezikhro shel efrayim gotlib] (Jerusalem, 1994), 75–98.

HALLAMISH, MOSHE, *An Introduction to the Kabbalah*, trans. Ruth Bar-Ilan and Ora Wiskind-Elper (Albany, NY, 1999).

HALPERIN, DAVID, *The Faces of the Chariot: Early Jewish Responses to Ezekiel's Vision* (Tübingen, 1988).

HARAN, MENAHEM, *The Biblical Collection* [Ha'asufah hamikra'it] (Jerusalem, 1996).

HELLNER-ESHED, MELILA, *A River Issues Forth from Eden: On the Language of Mystical Experience in the Zohar* [Venahar yotse me'eden: al safah hahavayah hamistit bazohar] (Tel Aviv, 2005).

HESCHEL, ABRAHAM JOSHUA, *Theology of Ancient Judaism* [Torah min hashamayim be'aspaklaryah shel hadorot], 3 vols. (London and New York, 1962–5; Jerusalem, 1990).

HILMAN, HAYIM MEIR, *My Master's House* [Beit rabi] (Berditchev, 1903).

HIMMELFARB, MARTHA, *Ascent to Heaven in Jewish and Christian Apocalypses* (New York and Oxford, 1993).

HUNDERT, GERSHON D. (ed.), *Essential Papers on Hasidism: Origins to the Present* (New York, 1991).

HUS, BOAZ, *On Golden Foundations: The Kabbalah of Simon ibn Lavi* [Al adnei paz: hakabalah shel r. shimon ibn lavi] (Jerusalem, 2000).

IDEL, MOSHE, *Absorbing Perfections: Kabbalah and Interpretation* (New Haven, 2002).

—— *Golem: Jewish Magical and Mystical Traditions on the Artificial Anthropoid* (Albany, NY, 1990).

—— *Hasidism: Between Ecstasy and Magic* (Albany, NY, 1995).

—— 'Hitbodedut as Concentration in Ecstatic Kabbalah', in Green (ed.), *Jewish Spirituality*, i. 405–38.

—— 'Inquiries into the Doctrine of *Sefer hameshiv*' [Iyunim beshitato shel sefer hameshiv], *Sefunot*, 17 (1983), 185–266.

—— *Kabbalah: New Perspectives* (New Haven, 1998).

—— *The Mystical Experience in Abraham Abulafia*, trans. Jonathan Chipman (Albany, NY, 1988).

—— 'The New is Forbidden by the Torah' [Ḥadash asur min hatorah], *Tsiyon*, 54, pt. 2 (1989), 223–41.

—— 'The Perception of the Torah in the Heikhalot Literature and its Evolution in the Kabbalah' [Tefisat hatorah besifrut haheikhalot vegilguleiha bakabalah], in *Jerusalem Studies in Jewish Thought*, 1 (1981–2), 23–84.

—— *Rabbi Menahem Recanati the Kabbalist* [Rabi menaḥem rekanati hamekubal] (Tel Aviv, 1998).

—— 'Seclusion as Concentration in Ecstatic Kabbalah' [Hitbodedut kerikuz bakabalah ha'ekstatit], *Daat*, 14 (1985), 35–82.

—— 'Solomon Molcho as a Magician' [Shelomoh molkho kemagikon], *Sefunot*, third book, 18 (1985), 193–219.

—— *Studies in Ecstatic Kabbalah* (Albany, NY, 1988).

INGE, WILLIAM RALPH, *Christian Mysticism* (1912; New York, 1956).

JACOBS, LOUIS, *Jewish Mystical Testimonies* (London, 1978).

—— *The Jewish Mystics* (Jerusalem, 1976).

—— *Seeker of Unity* (London, 1966).

JAMES, WILLIAM, *The Varieties of Religious Experience: A Study in Human Nature* (New York, 1929).

JANOWITZ, NAOMI, *The Poetics of Ascent: Theories of Language in a Rabbinic Ascension Text* (Albany, NY, 1989).

KAHANA, ABRAHAM, *Rabbi Israel Ba'al Shem Tov* [Rabi yisra'el ba'al shem tov] (Zhitomir, 1900).

—— (ed.), *Apocryphal Literature* [Sefarim ḥitsonim] (Tel Aviv, 1937).

KATZ, JACOB, *Halakhah and Kabbalah* [Halakhah vekabalah] (Jerusalem, 1984).

—— *Tradition and Crisis: Jewish Society at the End of the Middle Ages*, trans. Bernard D. Cooperman (New York, 1993).

KATZ, STEVEN T., 'Language, Epistemology, and Mysticism', in id. (ed.), *Mysticism and Philosophical Analysis* (Oxford, 1978).

KATZ, STEVEN T. (ed.), *Mysticism and Religious Traditions* (Oxford, 1983).

KEREM, DROR (ed.), *The Spectrum of Opinions and World-Views about Dreams in Jewish Culture* [Migvan de'ot vehashkafot al hahalom betarbut yisra'el], ii (Tel Aviv, 1992) and v (Tel Aviv, 1995).

KIMELMAN, REUVEN, *Lekha Dodi and Kabbalat Shabbat: Their Mystical Significance* [Lekha dodi vekabalat shabat: hamashma'ut hamistit] (Jerusalem, 2002).

KOPFER, EFRAYIM, 'The Visions of Asher ben Me'ir of Lemlein' [Hezyonotav shel asher ben me'ir hamekhuneh lemlin], *World Congress of Jewish Studies*, 8 (1976), 385–423.

KRAUSHAR, ALEXANDER, *Jacob Frank: The End to the Sabbataian Heresy*, ed. Herbert Levy (Lanham, Md., 2001).

KUGEL, JACOB, 'Levi's Elevation to the Priesthood in Second Temple Writings', *Harvard Theological Review*, 86 (1993), 1–64.

KUYT, ANNELIES, *The Descent to the Chariot: Towards a Description of the Terminology, Place, Function and Nature of* Yeridah *in Hekhalot Literature* (Tübingen, 1995).

LESSES, REBECCA MACY, *Ritual Practices to Gain Power: Angels, Incantations, and Revelation in Early Jewish Mysticism* (Harrisburg, Pa., 1998).

LIEBES, YEHUDA, *The Creation Doctrine of Sefer Yetsirah* [Torat hayetsirah shel sefer yetsirah] (Jerusalem and Tel Aviv, 2001).

—— ' "De Natura Dei": On the Development of Jewish Myth and Jewish Messianism', in id., *Studies in Jewish Myth and Jewish Messianism*, trans. Batya Stern (Albany, NY, 1993), 1–64.

—— 'How the Zohar was Written', in id., *Studies in the Zohar*, 85–138.

—— 'The Messiah of the Zohar: On R. Simeon bar Yohai as a Messianic Figure', in id., *Studies in the Zohar*, 1–84.

—— 'Myth versus Symbol in the Zohar and in Lurianic Kabbalah', in Fine (ed.), *Essential Papers on Kabbalah*, 212–42.

—— 'New Directions in Kabbalah Studies' [Kivunim hadashim beheker hakabalah], *Pe'amim*, 50 (1992), 150–70.

—— *The Secret of Shabatean Faith* [Sod ha'emunah hashabeta'it] (Jerusalem, 1995).

—— *The Sin of Elisha: The Four Who Entered Paradise and the Nature of Talmudic Mysticism* [Heto shel elisha: arba'ah shenikhnesu lapardes vetivah shel hamistikah hatalmudit] (Jerusalem, 1986; repr. 1990).

—— *Studies in the Zohar*, trans. Arnold Schwartz, Stephanie Nakache, and Penina Peli (Albany, NY, 1993).

—— ' "Two Young Roes of a Doe": The Secret Sermon of Isaac Luria before his Death', in Elior and Liebes (eds.), *Lurianic Kabbalah*, 113–70.

—— 'Zohar and Eros' [Zohar ve'eros], *Alpayim*, 9 (1994), 69–119.

LOEWENTHAL, NAFTALI, *Communicating the Infinite: The Emergence of the Habad School* (Chicago and London, 1990).

LOUTH, ANDREW, *Eros and Mysticism: Early Christian Interpretation of the Song of Songs* (London, 1992).

MAGID, SHAUL, *Hasidism on the Margin: Reconciliation, Antinomianism and Messianism in Izbica/Radzin Hasidism* (Madison, 2003).

—— (ed.), *God's Voice from the Void: Old and New Studies in Bratslav Hasidism* (Albany, NY, 2002).

MCGINN, BERNARD, *The Foundations of Mysticism* (New York, 1994).

MARK, ZEVI, *Mysticism and Madness in the Works of R. Nahman of Bratslav* [Mistikah veshigaon biyetsirat rabi naḥman mibratslav] (Tel Aviv, 2003).

MATT, DANIEL C., 'Ayin: The Concept of Nothingness in Jewish Mysticism', in R. K. C. Forman (ed.), *The Problem of Pure Consciousness: Mysticism and Philosophy* (New York and Oxford, 1990), 121–59.

MEIER, MENAHEM, 'Joseph of Hamadan: A Critical Edition of the *Sefer Ta'amey ha-Mitzvot* ("Book of Reasons of the Commandments"), attributed to Isaac ibn Farhi, sec. 1. Positive Commandments' [Yosef haba meshushan] (Ph.D. diss., Brandeis University, 1974).

MEROZ, RONIT, 'Redemption in the Doctrine of R. Isaac' [Ge'ulah betorat ha'ari] (Ph.D. diss., Jerusalem, 1988).

MONDSHINE, YEHOSHUA, *Kerem Habad: Study and Research in the Teachings of Habad, History of Hasidism and its Ways* [Kerem ḥabad: iyun umeḥkar bemishnat ḥabad, divrei yemei ḥasidut vedarkhei haḥasidim] (Kefar Habad, 1987).

MORRAY-JONES, C. R. A., 'Paradise Revisited (2 Cor. 12: 1–12): The Jewish Mystical Background of Paul's Apostolate, part 1: The Jewish Sources', *Harvard Theological Review*, 86/2 (1993), 177–217.

—— *A Transparent Illusion: The Dangerous Vision of Water in Hekhalot Mysticism. A Source-Critical and Tradition-Historical Inquiry* (Leiden, 2002).

NICKELSBURG, GEORGE W., '1 Enoch', in M. Stone (ed.), *Jewish Writings of the Second Temple Period* (Assen, 1984), 89–96.

—— *1 Enoch 1: A Commentary on the Book of 1 Enoch, Chapters 1–36; 81–108* (Minneapolis, 2001).

NIGAL, GEDALIA, 'Ahijah the Shilonite, the Teacher of R. Israel Ba'al Shem Tov' [Aḥiyah hashiloni, moro verabo shel r. yisra'el ba'al shem tov], *Sinai*, 71 (1972), 150–9.

ORENT, LEAH, 'Ethical and Mystical Elements in the Doctrine of R. Shneur Zalman of Lyady in Comparison with Ethical and Mystical Elements in Other Cultures' [Yesodot etiyim umistiyim betorato shel r. shene'ur zalman miliadi behashva'ah lazikah shebein yesodot etiyim umistiyim betarbuyot aḥerot] (Ph.D. diss., Hebrew University of Jerusalem, 2001).

ORLOV, ANDREI A., *The Enoch-Metatron Tradition* (Tübingen, 2005).

ORON, MICHAL, 'Dream, Vision, and Reality in Hayim Vital's *Sefer haḥezyonot*' [Ḥalom ḥazon umetsiut besefer haḥezyonot leḥayim vital], in Elior and Liebes (eds.), *Lurianic Kabbalah*, 299–310.

—— *Hapeliah vehakaneh: Their Kabbalistic Elements, Religious and Social Position, and Literary Design* [Hapeliah vehakaneh: yesodot hakabalah shebahem, emdatam hadatit vehaheveratit itsuvam hasifruti] (Jerusalem, 1980).

OTTO, RUDOLF, *The Idea of the Holy: An Enquiry into the Non-rational Factor in the Idea of the Divine and its Relation to the Rational*, trans. John W. Harvey (London, 1923; repr. 1972).

—— *Mysticism East and West: A Comparative Analysis of the Nature of Mysticism*, trans. Bertha L. Bracey and Richenda C. Payne (New York, 1932).

PEDAYA, HAVIVA, *Nahmanides, Exaltation: Cyclical Time and Sacred Text* [Haramban, hitalut: zeman maḥzori vetekst kadosh] (Tel Aviv, 2003).

—— *Name and Sanctuary in the Teaching of Rabbi Isaac the Blind* [Hashem vehamikdash bemishnat rabi yitsḥak sagi nahor] (Jerusalem, 2001).

The Penguin Book of Hebrew Verse, ed. and trans. T. Carmi (Harmondsworth, 1981).

RAPOPORT-ALBERT, ADA, 'God and the Zaddik as Two Focal Points of Hasidic Worship', *History of Religion*, 18 (1979), 296–325.

—— 'On the Position of Women in Shabateanism' [Al ma'amad hanashim bashabeta'ut], in Elior (ed.), *Dream and its Interpretation*, 143–327.

—— (ed.) *Hasidism Reappraised* (London, 1996).

ROSMAN, MOSHE, *The Founder of Hasidism: A Quest for the Historical Ba'al Shem Tov* (Berkeley, 1996).

RUBIN, TSEVIYAH, *Quotations from the Zohar in the Torah Commentary of Menahem Recanati* [Hamuvaot misefer hazohar baperush al hatorah lerabi menaḥem rekanati] (Jerusalem, 1992).

—— 'R. Moses Hayim Luzzatto and the Zohar' [Ramḥal vehazohar: ḥiburim uferushim] (Ph.D. thesis, Hebrew University of Jerusalem, 1997).

—— 'Sermon on Dragons by Rabbi Joseph Ibn Tabul' [Derush hataninim lerabi yosef ibn tabul] (MA thesis, Hebrew University of Jerusalem, 1985).

SCHÄFER, PETER, *Hekhalot-Studien* (Tübingen, 1988).

—— *The Hidden and Manifest God: Some Major Themes in Early Jewish Mysticism*, trans. Aubrey Pomerance (Albany, NY, 1992).

—— 'Jewish Magic Literature in Late Antiquity and Early Middle Ages', *Journal of Jewish Studies*, 41 (1990), 75–91.

SCHARFSTEIN, BEN-AMI, *The Mystic Experience* [Haḥavayah hamistit] (Tel Aviv, 1972).

SCHATZ-UFFENHEIMER, RIVKA, *Hasidism as Mysticism: Quietist Elements in Eighteenth Century Hasidic Thought*, trans. Jonathan Chipman (Princeton, 1993).

—— *The Messianic Idea after the Expulsion from Spain* [Hara'ayon hameshiḥi aḥarei gerush sefarad], ed. R. Elior (Jerusalem, 2005).

SCHECHTER, SOLOMON, 'Safed in the Sixteenth Century: A City of Legists and Mystics', in id., *Studies in Judaism* (Philadelphia, 1924), 202–85.

SCHIRMANN, H., *Hebrew Poetry in Spain and Provence* [Hashirah ha'ivrit bisefarad uve-provans] (Jerusalem, 1954).

SCHOLEM, GERSHOM, 'Barukhia Russo', in id., *The Messianic Idea*, 142–66.

—— *Bibliographia Kabbalistica* (Berlin, 1933).

—— 'The Deed of Association of Luria's Disciples' [Shetar hahitkasherut shel talmidei ha'ari], *Tsiyon*, 5 (1940), 133–60.

—— '*Devekut* or Communion with God' [Devekut o hitkasherut intimit im elohim], in *Explications and Implications*, 325–50. English version in *Review of Religion*, 14 (1950), 115–39.

—— 'The "Divine Mentor" of Rabbi Yosef Taitazak and the Revelations Attributed to Him' [Hamagid shel r. yosef taitazak vehagiluyim hameyuḥasim lo], *Sefunot*, 11 (1971) = *Sefer yavan*, 1 (1971), 67–112.

—— *The Dreams of R. Mordecai Ashkenazi, a Follower of Shabetai Tsevi* [Ḥalomotav shel hashabeta'i rabi mordekhai ashkenazi] (Jerusalem, 1938).

—— *Explications and Implications: Writings on Jewish Heritage and Renaissance* [Devarim bego], ed. A. Shapira, 2 vols. (Tel Aviv, 1976).

—— 'The Historical Image of Israel Ba'al Shem Tov' [Demuto hahistorit shel habesht], in *Explications and Implications*, 287–324.

—— 'A Homily on Redemption by Rabbi Shlomo Turiel' [Derush al hage'ulah lerabi shelomoh leveit turiel], *Sefunot*, 1 (1957), 62–79.

—— *Jewish Gnosticism, Merkabah Mysticism and Talmudic Tradition* (2nd edn., New York, 1965).

—— 'Kabbalah', *Encyclopedia Judaica*, 10 (Jerusalem, 1971), cols. 489–653 = G. Scholem, *Kabbalah* (Jerusalem, 1974).

—— *Kabbalah Manuscripts* [Kitvei hayad bekabalah] (Jerusalem, 1930), 83–9.

—— *The Kabbalah of Sefer hatemunah and of Abraham Abulafia* [Hakabalah shel sefer hatemunah veshel avraham abulafiyah], ed. Y. Ben-Shelomoh (Jerusalem, 1976).

—— *Major Trends in Jewish Mysticism*, trans. G. Lichtheim (New York, 1941; repr. 1954).

—— 'The Meaning of the Torah in Jewish Mysticism', in id., *On the Kabbalah*, 32–86.

SCHOLEM, GERSHOM, *The Messianic Idea in Judaism and Other Essays on Jewish Spirituality* (New York, 1971).

—— 'The Name of God and the Linguistic Theory of the Kabbalah', *Diogenes*, 79 (1972), 59–80; 80 (1973), 164–9.

—— *On the Kabbalah and its Symbolism*, trans. R. Manheim (New York, 1969).

—— *On the Mystical Shape of the Godhead: Basic Concepts in the Kabbalah*, trans. J. Neugroschel and J. Chipman (New York, 1991).

—— *Origins of the Kabbalah*, trans. Allan Arkush, ed. R. J. Zwi Werblowsky (Princeton, 1987).

—— 'Redemption through Sin', in id., *The Messianic Idea*, 78–141.

—— 'Religious Authority and Mysticism', in id., *On the Kabbalah*, 5–31.

—— 'Sabbatai Sevi', *Encyclopedia Judaica*, 14 (1971), cols. 1219–54.

—— *Sabbatai Sevi: The Mystical Messiah, 1626–1676*, trans. R. J. Zwi Werblowsky (Princeton, 1973).

—— 'Shekhinah: The Feminine Element in Divinity', in id. *On the Mystical Shape of the Godhead*, 140–96.

—— 'Shi'ur Qomah: The Mystical Shape of the Godhead', in id., *On the Mystical Shape of the Godhead*, 15–55.

—— *Studies in Shabateanism* [Meḥkarei shabeta'ut], ed. Y. Liebes (Tel Aviv, 1994).

—— 'Tradition and New Creation in the Ritual of the Kabbalists', in id., *On the Kabbalah*, 118–57.

—— and YISACHAR YOEL, *Hebrew Manuscripts of the National Library in Jerusalem, A: Kabbalah* [Kitvei hayad ha'ivriyim hanimtsa'im beveit hasefarim hale'umi biyerushalayim A: Kabalah] (Jerusalem, 1930).

SEGAL, ALAN, *Two Powers in Heaven: Early Rabbinic Reports about Christianity and Gnosticism* (Leiden, 1977).

STACE, WALTER T., *Mysticism and Philosophy* (London, 1960).

STEIN, DINA, *Maxim, Magic, Myth: A Folkloristic Perspective of Pirkei de Rabbi Eliezer* [Mimrah, magiyah, mitos: pirkei derabi eli'ezer le'or meḥkar hasifrut ha'amamit] (Jerusalem, 2005).

SUESSMANN, JACOB, 'Research on the History of Halakhah and the Judaean Desert Scrolls' [Ḥeker toledot hahalakhah umegilot midbar yehudah], *Tarbits*, 59 (1990), 11–76. (English summary in DJD 10, ed. E. Qimron and J. Strugnell (Oxford, 1994).)

SWARTZ, MICHAEL D., *Mystical Prayer in Ancient Judaism: An Analysis of Ma'aseh Merkavah* (Tübingen, 1992).

—— *Scholastic Magic: Ritual and Revelation in Early Jewish Mysticism* (Princeton, 1996).

TALMAGE, FRANK, 'Apples of Gold: The Inner Meaning of Sacred Texts in Medieval Judaism', in Green (ed.), *Jewish Spirituality*, i. 313–55.

TAMAR, DAVID, 'The Messianic Dreams and Visions of Rabbi Hayim Vital' [Ḥalomotav veḥezyonotav hameshiḥiyim shel r. ḥayim vital], *Shalem*, 4 (Jerusalem, 1984), 211–29.

—— *Studies in the History of the Jews in the Land of Israel and Italy* [Meḥkarim betoledot hayehudim be'erets yisra'el ve'italyah] (Jerusalem, 1973).

TAMBIAH, STANLEY J., 'A Performative Approach to Ritual', *Proceedings of the British Academy*, 65 (1979), 113–69.

TISHBY, ISAIAH, *Commentary on the Aggadot* (Jerusalem, 1945).

—— *The Doctrine of Evil and the Husk in Lurianic Kabbalah* [Torat hara vehakelipah bekabalat ha'ari] (Jerusalem, 1942; repr. 1984).

—— *Kabbalah Research and its Ramifications* [Ḥikrei kabalah usheluḥoteiha], 3 vols. (Jerusalem, 1982–93).

—— 'The Messianic Agitation in the Circle of Rabbi Moshe Hayim Luzzatto in the Light of a Messianic Ketuba and Poems' [Hatesisah hameshiḥit beḥugo shel rabi mosheh ḥayim lutsato le'oram shel ketubah veshirim meshiḥiyim], in *Kabbalah Research*, iii. 729–55.

—— 'The Messianic Idea and Messianic Trends in the Rise of Hasidism' [Hara'ayon hameshiḥi vehamegamot hameshiḥiyot betsemiḥat haḥasidut], *Tsiyon*, 32 (1967), 1–45.

—— 'On the Problems of the Book *Galya raza*' [Live'ayot sefer galya raza], *Tsiyon*, 48 (1983), 103–6.

—— *Paths of Faith and Heresy* [Netivei emunah uminut] (Ramat Gan, 1964).

—— 'Revolution in Kabbalah Research', review article on Moshe Idel, *Kabbalah: New Perspectives* [Hafikhah beḥeker hakabalah (al sifro shel mosheh idel: kabalah: perspektivot ḥadashot)], *Tsiyon*, 54 (1989), 209–22.

—— 'Symbol and Religion in Kabbalah' [Hasemel vehadat bakabalah], in id., *Paths of Faith and Heresy*.

—— (ed.), *The Wisdom of the Zohar: An Anthology of Texts*, trans. David Goldstein, 3 vols. (Oxford, 1989).

UNDERHILL, EVELYN, *Mysticism: A Study in the Nature and Development of Man's Spiritual Consciousness* (London, 1926; repr. New York, 1955).

—— *Practical Mysticism: A Little Book for Normal People* (New York, 1914).

URBACH, EPHRAIM E., *The Sages: Their Concepts and Beliefs*, trans. Israel Abrahams (Jerusalem, 1975).

—— 'The Traditions about Merkabah Mysticism in the Tannaitic Period', in E. E. Urbach, R. J. Zwi Werblowsky, and C. Wirszubski (eds.), *Studies in Mysticism and*

Religion Presented to Gershom G. Scholem on his Seventieth Birthday (Jerusalem, 1967), 1–28.

URBACH, EPHRAIM E., 'When did Prophecy Cease?' [Matai paskah hanevuah?], *Tarbits*, 17 (1946), 1–11.

URBAN, MARTINA, *Hermeneutics of Renewal: A Study of Hasidic Anthologies of Martin Buber* (Jerusalem, 2002).

VANDERKAM, JAMES, 'The Book of Enoch', in *Qumran Cave 4, XXVI: Cryptic Texts and Miscellanea, part 1*, ed. Stephen J. Pfann et al. (Discoveries in the Judaean Desert, 36; Oxford, 2000).

—— *Enoch, a Man for All Generations* (Columbia, SC, 1995).

—— *Enoch and the Growth of an Apocalyptic Tradition* (Washington, DC, 1984).

VERMAN, MARK, *The Books of Contemplation: Medieval Jewish Mystical Sources* (Albany, NY, 1992).

—— *The History and Varieties of Jewish Meditation* (Northvale, NJ, 1996).

VERMES, GEZA, *The Complete Dead Sea Scrolls in English* (London, 1997).

—— *The Dead Sea Scrolls in English*, 4th edn. (London, 1995).

WEBER, MAX, *On Charisma and Institution Building: Selected Papers*, ed. S. N. Eisenstadt (Chicago, 1968).

—— *Theory of Social and Economic Organization*, trans. A. M. Henderson and T. Parsons (Boston, Mass., 1963).

WEISS, JOSEPH, 'Mystical Hasidism and Hasidism of Faith: A Typological Analysis', in S. Magid (ed.), *God's Voice from the Void: Old and New Studies in Bratslav Hasidism* (Albany, NY, 2002), 277–85.

—— 'The Question in Rabbi Nahman of Bratslav's Doctrine' [Hakushiyah betorat rabi nahman mibratslav], in id., *Studies in Bratslav Hasidism* [Mehkarim behasidut bratslav] (Jerusalem, 1976), 109–49.

—— *Studies in East European Jewish Mysticism*, ed. David Goldstein (Oxford, 1985).

—— 'Via Passiva in Early Hasidim', in id., *Studies in Eastern European Jewish Mysticism*, 69–83.

WERBLOWSKY, RAFAEL JEHUDA ZWI, *Joseph Karo: Lawyer and Mystic* (Philadelphia, 1980).

WILENSKY, MORDECAI, *Hasidim and Mitnagdim* [Ḥasidim umitnagedim], 2 vols. (Jerusalem, 1970; expanded edn., Jerusalem, 1990).

WIRSCHOWSKY, HAYIM, *Between the Lines: Kabbalah, Christian Kabbalah, Shabbateanism* [Bein hashitin: kabalah, kabalah notserit, shabeta'ut], ed. M. Idel (Jerusalem, 1990).

—— 'The Shabatean Ideology of the Messiah's Conversion according to Nathan of Gaza' [Ha'ide'ologiyah hashabeta'it shel hamarat hamashi'aḥ lefi natan ha'azati], in id., *Between the Lines*, 121–51.

—— 'The Shabatean Theology of Nathan of Gaza' [Hate'ologiyah hashabeta'it shel natan ha'azati], in id., *Between the Lines*, 152–88.

WOLFSON, ELLIOT R., *Abraham Abulafia: Kabbalist and Prophet. Hermeneutics, Theosophy and Theurgy* (Los Angeles, 2000).

—— *Through a Speculum that Shines: Vision and Imagination in Medieval Jewish Mysticism* (Princeton, 1994).

WOODS, RICHARD (ed.), *Understanding Mysticism* (Garden City, NY, 1980).

YADIN, YIGAEL, *The Temple Scroll: The Hidden Law of the Dead Sea Sect* (London, 1985).

YOSHA, NISIM, 'The Philosophical Background of a Shabatean Theologian: Understanding the Theology of Abraham Miguel Cardozo' [Hareka hafilosofi lete'olog shabeta'i: kavim lehavanat torat ha'elohut shel avraham miguel cardozo'], in id. *Galut aḥar golah* [Exile after Diaspora] (Jerusalem, 1988), 541–72.

ZAEHNER, RICHARD, *Mysticism Sacred and Profane: An Inquiry into Some Varieties of Praeternatural Experience* (London, 1961).

ZAK, BERAKHAH, *In the Gates of Rabbi Moses Cordovero's Kabbalah* [Besha'arei hakabalah shel rabi mosheh kordovero] (Be'er Sheva and Jerusalem, 1995).

ZWELLING, JEREMY, 'Joseph of Hamadan's Sefer Tashak, a Critical Edition with Introduction' (Ph.D. diss., Brandeis University, 1975).

... ...

Index

A

Aaron 86, 127
Aaron, Rabbi 137
Abaye, grave of 117
Abraham 26, 38, 81
Abraham ben Isaac of Granada 26, 128
Abravanel, Isaac 139
Abulafia, Abraham 137
  on awakening 74
  excommunication 94
  followers 146
  mystical experience 62
  on text 44–5
  works 74, 77
abundance, divine 18, 44–5, 55
abyss 6, 30, 39, 82, 90
acacia tree 21, 124, 131
Acre, kabbalists 143, 151
Adam 38
adam kadmon mikol kedumim (primordial man)
  5, 8, 9, 132, 133, 148
adat hayaḥad (the holy congregation) 51
Adir bamarom (Mighty in Heaven) 27, 91, 151
Adler, Nathan 51, 53, 85, 95, 152–3
Adu'el 50
Age of Judgement 98
Age of Mercy 98
aggadah 13, 154
Agnon, S. Y. 17 n.
Ahijah the Shilonite 81, 90
Ahilai, Rabbi 127
Akhnai's oven 25
Akiva 138–9
  ascended to heaven 51, 83, 91
  on ascending to the chariot 67
  companion of Ishmael 138, 145
  crossing of boundaries 83
  death 69, 94, 138
  depiction of 86
  descended to the *merkavah* 50, 65, 83
  entered the *pardes* 50, 51, 65, 83, 86, 91, 138
  figure of 83
  Heikhalot literature 26, 38, 138
  on image of God 48
  influence 13, 51, 71, 81, 154
  mystical experience 9

  return with Oral Torah and Merkavah
    tradition 91, 139
  revelation to 91
  vision of heaven 7
  works 91
Alkabets, Solomon 6, 52, 99, 147, 151, 155
Almoli, Solomon 130, 155–6
Alsheikh, Moses 147
amulets 112, 114, 128
angel(s):
  concept of 92
  in heavenly temples 51, 127, 133
  names of 42, 91, 127
  praising God 125–6
  priests and 18
  redeeming 90, 131
  responding 90, 133
  revelations 24, 38
  revolt against God 82
  singing 126, 131, 139
  teachings 53
  visitations 66
  world of 18, 73, 84
  see also cherubs; *ofanim*
anshei hayaḥad (the people of the unification)
  92
  see also unification
apotheosis 79, 84, 86–7
Arafel 49, 87
Aramaic 60
Ari, the, *see* Luria, Isaac
Ark, Noah's 40, 77
Ark of the Covenant 21, 124
ark (word) 40, 104, 107
arousal, human and divine 55
Arpilei tohar (Clouds of Purity) 27
ascending:
  Akiva's ascent 91, 138–9
  to the chariot (*merkavah*) 7, 8, 9, 67, 81
  emanations 55
  Enoch's ascent 91
  to heaven 16, 17, 26, 51, 58, 61–2, 66, 68, 82,
    83, 87, 113, 116
  to the *heikhalot* 51, 55
  Ishmael's ascent 108
  ladder 20, 21, 42, 54, 68, 99, 109, 119

ascending (*cont.*):
  letters 4
  Moses' ascent 88, 91
  mystical ascent of the Besht 69–71, 89 n.
  to the *pardes* 86
  souls 71, 89
  to the throne of glory 90
  to the upper worlds 65, 71, 85, 112, 138
  to the world of emanation 81
Ashkenazi, Elisha 153
Ashkenazi, Mordecai 84, 85, 149
authority:
  charismatic religious 60, 73
  confrontation with 93–6
  divine 22, 90
  external sources 61
  heavenly voices as source of 90 n.
  mystical 24–5, 57, 73, 74
  mystical relationship with 102–3
  rabbinic 91, 96
  traditional 23–5, 93–4
Avodat hakodesh (Holy Worship) 84, 135
Avot derabi natan 138
Ayelet ahavim 155
ayin 39–40, 44, 50
Azikri, Ele'azar 53, 140–1
Azriel ben Solomon of Gerona 77, 79, 139,
  142

B
Ba'al Shem Tov (Besht) 145
  ascent of his soul 69–71, 89
  autobiographical descriptions 69–71, 85
  followers 53, 140, 145
  influence of 144, 152
  influences on 71, 138, 145
  on ladder of ascension 68
  on letters and words 40, 104, 107
  mental state 64–5 n.
  mystical experience 10, 62, 67
  persecution of 95
  revelation to 51
  teachings 72 n.
  on world and higher world 49, 93
  on worship 100
Bar Kokhba 69, 154
bar Yohai, Shimon (Rashbi) 154
  Ahijah association 138
  as holy light 89
  influence of 13, 52, 71, 90, 145
  Karo as incarnation of 63
  life 154

mystical communication with 81
  revelation to 50, 91
  Shavuot association 88
  visions 72
  Zohar 13, 26, 50, 91, 151, 154
Barcelona, Jewish–Christian debate 150
Barukhyah Russo 84, 89, 95, 139–40, 145
Bat-Miriam, Yokheved 37
Being:
  hidden meaning of 28
  infinity of the 30
Beit yosef 88, 147
Ben Azai 79–80
Ben porat yosef 145
Ben Sira 126, 142
Ben Zoma 94
Bereshit rabah 87, 129, 138
Berit halevi 155
Berit menuḥah 128
Bezalel 104, 109
Bialik, Hayim Nahman 11, 57
Binah (thought) 31
body 36
Boker le'avraham 137
Book of Contemplation 5, 21 n.
Book of Jubilees, *see* Jubilees
boundaries:
  blurring 37, 45, 57, 58, 63
  breaching 12, 22, 60, 61, 95, 98, 102, 114
  contemplation of 22
  crossing 16, 50, 55, 57, 78, 83, 94, 106
  dangers of breaching 114
  deconstruction of 8
  extending 21
  of language 17, 46
  obliterating 59
  of permitted and forbidden 100
  of reality 22, 46, 50, 58, 146
  of tradition 97, 146
  transcending 2, 15, 38, 50, 73, 74, 78, 89, 93
Bratslav, hasidism 101, 152
'breaking of the vessels' (*shevirat kelim*) 5, 18,
  98, 132
Byzantine period 83, 131, 135

C
calendar 82, 84, 91–2, 99, 141–2
Cardozo, Abraham Michael 27, 84, 137
Castile 52
chariot, heavenly, see *merkavah*
charisma 68, 73, 91
Charles V, Habsburg emperor 156, 157

cherub, unique (*hakeruv hameyuḥad*) 5, 9, 10, 50, 52
cherubs, cherubim:
  concept 4, 46, 87
  divine chariot of the 21 n., 80, 81, 90, 133
  fiery 58
  in Garden of Eden 80, 81
  gender 81
  ḥashmal and *ḥashmalah* 49, 50, 79, 87
  holy 20
  in Holy of Holies 80, 81
  mystic vision 81
  at Sinai 81
  singing 81
  voice of 62, 65
  wings of 59, 81, 125–6
children of light and children of darkness 51, 81, 98
Chmielnicki persecutions 153
Christianity, conversion to 95, 96, 145, 152, 153
circles and straightness (*igulim veyosher*) 5
cleaving (*devekut*) 45, 55, 77–8, 105
Clement VII, Pope 157
commandments:
  divine (*ta'amei hamitsvot*) 92, 148
  613: 36
concealment 39–40
Constantinople 143, 153, 155
  see also Istanbul
contemplation 5, 11, 22, 55, 123, 133
Cordovero, Moses 151
  followers 141, 143
  on groups of kabbalists 52
  influences on 147, 151, 155
  mystical experience 51
  revelation to 51
  on Torah 36
  works 27, 84, 100, 131, 151
countenance(s):
  angel of the 9, 78, 129, 130
  concept 5, 132
  partsufim 5, 46
  prince of the 10, 114, 136
creation:
  Creator and 19
  doctrine of 18
  language and 35–6, 106
  mysteries of 4, 35
  mystical history 136
  purpose of 124
  story 82
  Torah of 98

creatures, heavenly living (*ḥayot hakodesh*):
  Akiva on 7
  Ezekiel's vision 17, 59, 101
  in rabbinic thought 21
  running back and forth 4, 29, 39
  singing 43, 65
  standing by the throne 75
crown (*keter*) 5, 21 n., 113, 115

D
Da'at (knowledge) 31
Damascus 27, 55, 142
Daniel 88
David, King 138
David ben Judah Hehasid 99
de Vidas, Elijah ben Moses 44, 141
Dead Sea Scrolls 20 n., 21 n., 25, 82 n., 120
death:
  of kings (*mitat hamelakhim*) 5, 132
  overcoming 78
deconstruction (*peruk*) 41, 112, 117, 120–1
  yiḥud as 121
Degel maḥaneh efrayim 145
della Reina, Joseph 83–4, 95, 146
Delphi, oracle 118
demons, world of 78, 81
'depth' 98, 101
Derush ḥeftsivah 143, 147
descenders of the chariot (*yoredei merkavah*):
  achievements 10, 23
  Akiva 50, 83
  characteristics 84 n.
  congregation of the 51
  expression 90
  Heikhalot literature 136
  holy societies 51 n.
  Ishmael 83, 144
  Luria 73
  Metatron's role 149
  revelations to 68
  world of 99
descending to the chariot (*yeridah lamerkavah*):
  aim of mystics 17, 54, 114
  mystical concept 58
  by poetry 128
desire, consuming 55
devekut (adherence) 121
  see also cleaving
devotion 44, 64, 92
diagonal borders, twelve 123, 133
dichotomies 97
Dionysus 118

divestment of corporeality 55
divine:
  abundance 18, 44–5, 55
  authority 22, 90
  commandments (*ta'amei hamitsvot*) 92, 148
  and earthly 91–2
  and human 55, 133
  language 19, 66, 104–5
  speech (*dibur shekhinah*) 5
Divrat shelomoh (Speech of Solomon) 156
Divrei ha'adon (The Words of the Lord) 27, 85,
  93, 100, 146
Divrei halomot (Words of Dreams) 157
Doenmeh sect 139, 145, 154
Dov Ber, the Maggid of Mezhirech 140
  followers 102, 145, 146, 154, 156, 157
  life 140
  on principles of hasidism 100
  works 140
dreams 15, 42, 66, 155–6
dress 93, 127

E
earthly and divine 91–2
Ecclesiastes 38, 63
Eden, Garden of 70, 71, 80, 81, 138
Egypt 138, 142, 143
ehyeh asher ehyeh (I am who I am) 50
Eibeschutz, Jonathan 96
Eibeschutz, Wolf 96
Eichenstein, Rabbi Tsevi Hirsch, of Zhidachov
  144
ein sof (infinitude) 5, 50
Ein Sof (the hidden God) 144
Ele'azar, Rabbi, of Worms 127
Eliezer the Great 71, 141
Elijah:
  elevation of 127
  life span 138
  mystic's relationship with 81, 90
  revelation of (*gilui eliyahu*) 25, 58, 73, 89,
    143, 144
  visitation of 38, 66, 72
Elimah rabati 151
Elimelekh of Lyzhansk 140, 146
Elisha ben Avuyah (Aher) 83 and n., 94
elyonim vetahtonim 51
emanation:
  ascending and descending 55
  Ben Azai's revelation 79
  concept 90, 132
  doctrine of 18, 111

drawing down 44
  initiating 44
  letters and 44–5
  origins 48
  process 144
  receiving 44
  Torah of 98, 139
  world of 18, 81, 111
End of Days 98, 99, 100
Enoch, books:
  1 (Ethiopic) Enoch 25, 58, 62, 82, 116, 142,
    149
  2 (Slavonic) Enoch 26, 50, 82, 142
  3 Enoch, see *Sefer heikhalot*
Enoch son of Jared 141–2
  ascension to heaven 25–6, 58, 78, 91
  figure of 13, 82–3, 90, 136
  priestly tradition 91
  revelation to 91
  solar calendar 91
  taken by God 30 n.
  works 91
Enoch-Metatron 82–3, 86, 94, 108, 141, 149
Eshel avraham 149
Eshet ne'urim (Wife of Youth) 156
'essence' 39, 48
Ethiopia 156, 157
Ets hayim (Tree of Life) 55, 72, 84, 133, 143
evil:
  depth of 29
  domains of holy and 99
  forces of 6, 53, 55, 70, 78, 84
  origins of good and 20
  realm (*kelipot*) 90
  side (*sitra ahra*) 17
exaltation 45
excommunication:
  Abulafia 94
  Adler 95, 152
  Elisha ben Avuyah 94
  followers of Schneersohn 96
  Frank, Jacob 64
  hasidic authors 64
  Leiner 96
  Luzzatto (Ramhal) 53, 64, 95, 151
  mystics 66, 93–4, 96–7
  Nathan of Gaza 95
  Shabetai Tsevi 95, 154
  transgressions punishable by 93
exile:
  constraints of 5
  continuous 76, 132

end of 84
female figure 87
influence on mysticism 13, 16, 18
redemption and 20, 75, 77, 84, 87, 100, 133,
  135
Shekhinah 6, 52, 63–4, 88, 99
from Spain 6
Torah of 99
Exodus, book of 129
Exodus from Egypt 138
Ezekiel:
  exile 16
  prophecy 49, 87
  vision 13, 17, 21 n., 39, 49, 59, 79, 101, 110
  vision of divine chariot 16, 81, 86, 90, 125,
    126
Ezra ben Shelomoh of Gerona 49, 142

F
father 6, 90
female and male, *see* male and female
fire:
  black and white 33, 43
  holy 78–81
  immersing in the river of 77 n.
  punishment by 83, 94
Flood 77
Frank, Jacob 145–6
  conversion of 95
  followers 53
  influences on 140
  life 84, 85, 93, 145–6, 152
  mystical experience 51
  persecution 64, 95
  revelation to 51
  vision 100
  works 27, 85, 93, 100, 146
Frankfurt 53, 152
Frankism 93
freedom 47, 121

G
Galicia, hasidism 146
Galya raza (Revealed Secrets) 27, 62, 76, 84,
  95, 99–100, 130, 135
garment 18, 39–40, 85, 111, 121
gazing at the king's beauty (*tsefiyah bamelekh
  beyofyo*) 55, 77 n.
Genesis 28, 29, 30 n., 36, 141
Genesis Apocryphon 142
Genizah 128
geonim 68

Germany:
  messianism 146
  mystics 95, 139
  pietists 5, 127
Gerona, kabbalism 139, 150
Gershon of Kutow 69
Gikatilla, Joseph 26, 46, 104, 146–7
gilgul (transmigration of souls) 5, 148
Ginat egoz (Garden of Nuts) 146
God:
  concept of 18, 92
  creation of 84
  creation process 109
  faces of 48, 131, 132
  hidden (Ein Sof) 144
  hidden names of 46–7
  hidden will of 51
  image of 47–8, 50, 82, 85, 99, 110, 132
  incarnations of 140
  infinite power of 104
  name of 46, 50, 78, 111, 113–15, 126, 129
  perpetual presence 105
  relationship with Torah 122
  revolt of angels against 82
  Shekhinah and 92, 99
  speech of, direct 99
  stature of, see *shiur komah*
  Torah as speech of 39
golem 112
Gordon, Jakuthiel 38

H
Habad 140, 154–5
Haggadah 155
Hakeronikah 146
Hakohen, Rabbi Binyamin 42, 62
halakhah 13, 23, 147
Halevi, Judah 68, 110
halitsah, concept of 92
Hammai, Rabbi 5 n.
hashem hameforash (the Explicit Name, the
  ineffable Name) 50, 114, 115, 126
Hashmal 49, 87
hashmal and *hashmalah* 49, 50, 79, 87
hasidism:
  early writings 157
  groups 53
  Habad 137, 140
  leadership 93, 137, 140, 148, 152
  mystical tradition 64, 140
  principles of 100
  tsadik doctrine 146

Hasmonean:
  period 99
  priests 150
Hayat, Judah 137
Ḥayat hakaneh (The Creature of the Reeds) 27,
  84, 88, 91, 156–7
Ḥayei ha'olam haba (Life of the Next World)
  44, 137
Hayim of Amdor 140
ḥayot hakodesh, see creatures, heavenly living
Hebrew language 35, 60, 110, 115, 136
heikhal ken tsipor, see sanctuary of the bird's nest
heikhalot (heavenly sanctuaries, temples) 46, 51,
  55, 83–4, 92, 133
Heikhalot literature:
  authors 135–6
  conceptions in 21 n.
  description of meeting heavenly power 16
  description of the throne addressing God 75
  descriptions of ascending or descending to
    the chariot 7, 54
  descriptions of ascent to heavenly sanctuaries
    62, 66
  figure of Enoch-Metatron 86
  God's hidden image 110–11
  Holy Name 129
  hymns 75
  knowledge of names 128
  Nehuniah ben Hakanah 153
  prayer of sanctification 127
  texts 26, 28
  use of language 115, 131
Heikhalot rabati 68, 113, 114, 124, 128, 136,
  145, 153
Heikhalot tradition/period 59, 65, 67, 79, 92,
  141, 144
Heikhalot zutarti (The Small Treatise of the
  Heavenly Sanctuaries) 26, 48, 136, 138
Ḥemdat yamim (Beloved of Days) 27, 62
Hemdat Yamim group 53
hidden reality 3–5, 18, 30, 132
Hokhmah (wisdom) 31
Holy of Holies:
  Ark 21
  cherubim 80, 81
  connection with heavenly temples 81
  devir 129
  high priest entering 59, 80, 81, 86, 126,
    138
  mystic's hope to enter 17
Holy Jew, *see* Jacob Isaac of Przysucha
Holy Land 77

Holy Spirit 118
holy spirit (*ruaḥ hakodesh*) 143
Horowitz, Jacob Isaac (the Seer of Lublin) 146
  doctrine of 98, 100–2, 146
  'fall' 96
  followers 148, 150
  influences on 89, 140, 146
  mental state 65 n.
  mystical experience 62
  revelation to 91
  works 85
Horwitz, Aaron Halevi, of Starosielce 131, 137,
  140
House of God group 53
husk(s) 43, 76, 78, 81, 99

I
Ibn Aderet, Solomon 137
Ibn Tabul, Joseph 111, 143, 147
Igeret hakodesh 40, 69, 72, 85, 145
illumination:
  description of 89
  divine 22, 24, 52, 62, 97
  experience of 12
  moment of 80
  mystical conversion 67
  mystical interpretative 27
  from text 45
image of man 47–8
Imrei shefer (Good Words) 137
incest 93, 131, 135, 139–40
infinitude:
  concealing 40
  divine 37, 38, 39, 47
  divine text 33, 131
  ein sof 5, 50
  hidden divine 107
  of language 38
  term 90
  world of 111, 119
Isaac the Blind (Sagi Nahor) 10, 62, 144
Isaac ben Samuel of Acre 143
Ishmael ben Elisha 144–5
  ascended to heaven 16, 83
  death 69, 94, 144
  descended to the *merkavah* 83, 144
  entered the Holy of Holies 86
  entered the innermost sanctuary 50, 51
  entered the *pardes* 83
  figure of 13, 69, 83, 86, 144–5
  Heikhalot literature 26
  mentor of 67, 153

on Metatron 65, 78, 108
mystical conversion 67, 78–9
revelation to 115
use of Holy Name 129–30
Ishmail, Rabbi 7
Islam, conversion to 95, 139, 145, 153, 154
Israel, Land of:
  Heikhalot literature 135
  Jewish settlement 156, 157
  kabbalists 69, 137, 149, 155
  Karo's settlement in 88, 147, 155
  vision of 76–7, 132
Istanbul 130
  see also Constantinople
Italy:
  messianism 139
  Molcho's death 147
Iwanie 53

J
Jacob 13
Jacob Isaac, the Holy Jew of Przysucha 148
Jacob Joseph, Rabbi, of Polonnoye 68, 138, 145, 156
Jacob of Marvège 42
Jerusalem:
  destruction by Romans 16
  priests 150
  renewal of Jewish settlement 150
Jesus 89, 94
Jewish mystical thought:
  definitions 14
  hidden reality 3
  tradition 89–90
  understanding 19
Joffe, Rabbi Mordecai, of Vienna 38
Joseph of Hamadan 147–8
Josephus (Joseph ben Matityahu) 127
Jubilees, Book of 34, 62, 82, 142
Judaean desert 91
Judaism, conversion to 156, 157

K
kabalat shabat (welcoming the sabbath) 92
kabbalah:
  concepts 38–40
  groups 52–3
  kabbalists 135–6, 137, 139, 140–1, 142–3, 146–51, 153, 155–7
  Lurianic 6, 52, 55–6, 73
  mythical tradition 85
  reading of Torah 42, 44, 46

in Safed 5, 92
world of language and speech 108
Kabbalah of R. Meshulam the Zadokite 49
Kara, Avigdor, of Prague 26
Karo, Joseph 147
  ascent to heavenly schools 71–2
  on divine voice 89
  on Enoch 30 n.
  followers 52, 147, 151
  influence 89, 155
  influences on 148, 157
  life 147
  magid of 49, 63, 88, 89, 147
  mystical experience 10, 62, 64, 89, 157
  on mystical worship 99
  relationship with Moses 88
  revelation to 51, 60, 91, 147
  works 6, 27, 72 n., 84, 91, 99, 147
Kedushah 127
kelipah (husk) 99
  see also husk(s)
kelipot (evil realm) 90
Ketem paz (Pure Gold) 27
kidush hashem (sanctification of the holy name) 13
king:
  in his beauty 10, 17, 83
  death of kings (*mitat hamelakhim*) 5, 132
  gazing at the king's beauty (*tsefiyah bamelekh beyofyo*) 55, 77 n.
  messiah 38, 70
  sceptre 131
  symbol of holy male powers 99
kingdom 87, 90, 99
Kitsur misefer pitron halomot (The Interpretation of Dreams) 156
kohanei korev (the priests of *korev*) 51
Kook, Abraham Isaac Hakohen 27, 96
Korets 102, 157
Kotsk, Rabbi of 65 n.
  see also Morgenstern, Menahem Mendel
Kudsha berikh hu 133
Kuf-lamed-het pithei hokhmah (138 Gates of Wisdom) 151
Kuntres hahitbonenut (Tract on Contemplation) 140
Kuntres hahitpa'alut (Tract on Ecstasy) 140
kushya (a question) 101

L
ladder 13, 20, 21, 68, 99, 109
language:
  bi-directional 119

language (*cont.*):
  conventional 111–12
  creative power 157
  divine 19, 66, 104–5
  Hebrew, *see* Hebrew
  magical 111–12, 114–19, 129
  mystical 8–9, 17, 20, 31, 46, 106–12, 120–1,
    123–4, 131
  narrative 31
  peruk (linguistic deconstruction) 157
  ritual 111–12, 119
  secrets of 82
  theory of 136
  visionary 48
Lavi, Simeon 27
Leib, Rabbi, of Vilna 38
Leiner, Mordecai Joseph, of Izbica 89, 96, 98,
    101, 148, 150, 157
'Lekha dodi' 155
Lelo meitsarim (Beyond Boundaries) 85
Lemlein, Asher 95, 139
letters:
  circular lines of 55
  cleaving to the 55, 105
  creation by 106, 108, 109–10
  emanation and 44–5
  glowing 45, 108
  of holy language 119–20
  in kabbalistic tradition 44, 46, 77, 108, 147
  magical names 129
  mystical view of 35–6, 106–12
  of the name of God 112, 115
  number of 43
  numerical value 77, 106 n.
  secret meaning of 136
  sefirot and 105–6
  souls and 40, 104, 107, 108
  of the Torah 22–3
  tseruf (letter-combination theory) 157
  as vessels 40
Levi Isaac of Berditchev 140
life, eternal 93, 131, 146
Life of my Teacher Rabbi Nahman, The 85
light(s):
  bright 18
  children of 51, 81, 98
  dark 18
  darkening (*or hanehshakh*) 5, 9
  divine 28, 40, 122
  forces of 76
  hashmal 79
  heavenly 41–2, 45, 122
  hidden 121
  letters and 45
  mystical experiences 62, 63, 67
  opening for 40, 104, 107
  pure light of life 5
  sevenfold 28
  of the Shekhinah 67
  shining lights of the splendour 21 n.
  soul and 48
  spirit of 18
  splendorous (*tsah tsahot*) 5, 9
  splendorous brilliant (*tsah umetsuhtsah*) 5, 90
  that does not include thought (*or she'ein bo
    mahashavah*) 6, 81
  that includes thought (*or sheyesh bo
    mahashavah*) 6, 81
Likutei amarim (Collections of Sayings) 155
Likutei moharan (Collections of the Sayings of
    R. Nahman) 152
Lilith 99
livnat hasapir, see sapphire
Luria, Isaac (the Ari) 143–4
  art of unification 117
  death 95
  description of 72–3
  on divine emanation 48
  followers 52, 53, 54, 141, 142–3, 147
  influence 84, 93
  kabbalistic doctrine 55, 88–9, 91, 98, 100, 143
  life 143
  on love 54
  mystical experience 10, 62
  revelation to 51, 143
  soul ascending to heaven 71
Luzzatto, Moses Hayim (Ramhal) 151–2
  description of 85
  followers 53
  life 151
  magid of 38, 42, 53, 63, 89, 91, 151
  mystical experience 10, 62–4
  persecution of 53, 95, 151
  revelation to 42, 51, 62–4, 91, 100
  on Torah 37, 45
  works 27, 53, 88–9, 91, 151

M
Ma'arekhet elohut (System of Divinity) 131, 137
ma'aseh merkavah 56
Ma'aseh merkavah (Deed of the Chariot) 136, 145
Ma'aseh ta'atuim (Deed of Mischief) 85
Ma'ayan hahokhmah (Fountain of Wisdom) 128
madness 1, 32, 64–5, 94–6, 118, 152

magic 31, 116, 126, 128
magical language, *see* language
magid (angelic mentor):
  Ashkenazi's 149
  Karo's 49, 63, 88, 89, 147
  Luria's 73
  Luzzatto's 38, 42, 53, 63, 89, 91, 151
  role of 58, 59, 73, 90
  Taitazak's 148
Magid devarav leya'akov 140
Magid meisharim (Upright Sayings) 27, 60, 63,
  84, 91, 99, 133, 147
Maimonides 138
male and female 48–9, 87, 92–3, 99, 136, 131
man, primordial, see *adam kadmon*
Mann, Thomas 64
Manot halevi 155
Mantino, Jacob 157
Mantua 60, 95, 157
Mare'ot hatsove'ot (The Reflecting Mirrors) 99
Masmeryah 127
Master of the Zohar (group) 52
meditation, mystical 62–3, 70, 92, 97
Mefasher helmin (Interpreter of Dreams) 156
Megilat hahodayot (Thanksgiving Scroll) 150
Megilat hapesharim 150
Megilat setarim (Scroll of Secrets) 27, 85, 144
Mei hashilo'ah (Waters of Shiloah) 89, 96, 98,
  148, 150, 157
Me'irat einayim (Enlightenment of the Eyes) 143
melaveh malkah ('accompanying the queen') 92
Menaham Mendel of Kotsk, *see* Morgenstern
Menahem Recanati 42, 99, 148, 149
mercy, age of 43, 98, 132
merkavah (divine chariot throne):
  ascending to the 7, 8, 9, 67, 81
  beholders of the 81, 91, 92
  concept 75, 86
  descending in/to the 17, 50, 55, 58, 73, 83,
    114, 128
  expressions involving 90
  Ezekiel's vision 16, 81, 86, 90, 125, 126
  gazing on the 17, 51, 67, 90
  hymn of the 92, 124
  importance to Jewish mysticism 13
  part of 'other reality' 4
  parts of the upper 36
  prohibition against expounding 10, 11, 90
  study of 46, 80, 127
  voyagers (*yoredei merkavah*) 10, 11; *see also*
    descenders of the chariot
  world of the 18, 133, 139

Merkavah tradition 78, 79, 133
Meshulam the Zadokite 49
Mesilat yesharim (Path of the Upright) 151
messiah:
  coming of the 84, 85, 99, 100, 139
  concept 6, 13, 17, 87, 133
  heavenly residence of the 70, 90
  mystical encounters with 9, 38, 74
  mystics as messianic figures 84
  Shabateanism 153–4
metaphor, mystical 57, 123, 132
Metatron 149
  angel of the countenance 9, 78
  Enoch-Metatron 82–3, 86, 94, 108, 141, 149
  figure of 149
  Heikhalot literature 136
  names 115–16
  punishment of 83, 94
  transformation 30 n., 78, 79
  visitation of 38, 81
  words of 9, 90, 108
metempsychosis 131
  see also souls
metivta direkia (heavenly schools) 90
Mezhirech, Maggid of, *see* Dov Ber
Middle Ages:
  descriptions of hidden reality 4
  doctrines 99
  figures of mystics 50, 83
  kabbalah 52
  mystical activity 55, 87
  mystical terms 90
Midrash 79, 123
Miktsat ma'asei hatorah 150
Milei deshamaya (Celestial Worlds) 141
Minhat yehudah 137
Mishnah:
  figure of Ishmael 144–5
  importance to mystical tradition 13
  on names 126
  relationship with Shekhinah 60, 64
  teachers of 138, 154
Mishneh torah 138
Mishtak 65
mispar (number, the ten elements of being)
  21 n., 106, 108
Molcho, Solomon (Diego Perez) 156–7
  death 60, 64, 95, 147, 157
  identification with Daniel 88
  life 156–7
  mystical experience 51, 62, 84
  persecution 95

Molcho, Solomon (Diego Perez) (*cont.*):
　relationship with Taitazak 148
　revelation to 50, 91
　works 27, 84, 99
moreh hatsedek, see Teacher of Righteousness
Morgenstern, Menahem Mendel, of Kotsk 96,
　　148, 150
　see also Kotsk, Rabbi of
Moses:
　ascending the heights 50, 88
　figure of 13, 86, 87–8, 90, 154
　internalization of 63, 88, 89
　male aspect of divinity 87
　redeemer of the Shekhinah 63
　revelation to 20 n., 91
　Shavuot associations 88, 92
　Torah text 33–4
　vision of cherubim 49, 81
Moses Hagiz 151
Moses Hayim Ephraim of Sudylkov 71 n.
Moses de Léon 146, 151, 154
Moses ben Nahman, *see* Nahmanides
Moses ben Shneur Zalman 96
mother 6, 90
mystic(s):
　attributes 57–60
　image of the 50
　persecution of 93–7
　portraits of mystics 85–6
　relationship with religious establishment 93–4
　world-view 18
mystical:
　concepts 4–6, 18, 21, 55–6, 84–5, 90–1,
　　131–2
　experience 102–3
　freedom 121
　language, *see* language
　literature 8, 11, 28, 33, 82, 86–7, 102–3, 112,
　　123
　term 1
　visions 124
mysticism:
　analysis 14
　connections 12–13
　definitions 2–3
　goal 3, 8
　importance of 1

N
Nahman of Bratslav 65 n., 85, 96, 101, 152
Nahmanides (Moses ben Nahman, Ramban)
　　33, 43, 47, 111, 150

Name, The 111, 113–14
name(s):
　of angels 42, 91, 127
　dangers of 113
　explicit name of God 126
　hidden names of God 46
　holy 42, 46, 112–13, 126, 127
　knowledge of 128
　magical 129
　numerical value of biblical 77
　sacred 115
　Torah as code of 46–7, 122
　use of (*shimush beshemot*) 44, 55
Nathan of Gaza 53, 62, 84, 95, 100, 153, 154
Nathan Neta Hanover 153
Nehuniah ben Hakanah 26, 50, 67, 83, 153
Netiv mitsvoteikha (Path of your
　　Commandments) 144
nikbat tehom rabah (the abyss) 6, 90
Noah's Ark 40, 77
norms, sacred 23
numbers 29, 36, 76–7, 82, 105–6, 133

O
Odel, daughter of Ba'al Shem Tov 152
ofanim 20, 21 n.
opening (divine reflection) 40–1
Or ha'emet 140
Or hame'ir (Shining Light) 41, 44, 119, 157
Or hasekhel (Light of the Mind) 77, 137
Or ne'erav 151
Or torah 140
Or yakar (Glorious Light) 151
Otsar hage'onim (The Geonic Treasury) 66, 138
Otsar hayim (Life's Treasure, by Isaac ben
　　Samuel) 143
Otsar hayim (Treasure of Life, by Isaac Safrin of
　　Komarno) 144
Otto, Rudolf 65
Ottoman empire 148, 156

P
Padua 38, 151
pardes (divine inner sanctum, orchard):
　concept 13, 138
　entering the 8, 9, 10, 17, 50, 51, 55, 65, 67,
　　73, 80, 83, 91, 138
　part of 'other reality' 4
　study of 46
Pardes rimonim (Orchard of Pomegranates) 100,
　　131, 151
partsufim (countenances) 5, 46

Paul 61–2, 94, 118
perfection, human 28
persecution 16, 53, 64, 66, 93–7
Perush al hatorah (Commentary on the Torah) 149, 150
Perush ha'agadot (Commentary on the Aggadot of the Talmud) 77, 79, 139, 142, 149
peshat (text) 41
Pesher ḥavakuk 150
Pesikta derav kahana 138
Phaedrus 118
phenomena, ecstatic 66
Philo 126
pillar 70, 71, 74, 81
Pirkei derabi eli'ezer 141
Pitron ḥalomot (Solving Dreams) 156
Plato 12, 118
Plotinus 10–11
Poland:
    hasidism 146
    messianism 145–6
Portugal 156
prayer 54, 73, 92
priesthood:
    abandoned 75
    heavenly metamorphosis of 86 n., 87
    restoration 17
    role in mystical tradition 13, 127
    separatist 125
    symbols of 86
    usurping 99, 150
priests:
    angelic 11, 18, 75, 127
    Enoch's role 142, 149
    high priest 16, 59, 80–1, 86, 115, 126, 138, 144
    of *korev* 11, 18, 51, 92
    magical language 128
    Qumran 51, 125, 126, 136, 150
    Zadokite 86, 136, 150
Primo, Samuel 84, 153
primordial man, see *adam kadmon*
prophecy 8, 24, 66, 86
prophetic:
    language 4
    period 67
    trance 118
    vision 58, 68
Provence 52
Przysucha, hasidism 148
Psalms 79
Pseudo-Sa'adiah 113 n.

Q
Qumran:
    figure of Enoch 141–2
    holy congregation 51
    mystical writings 91, 141–2
    prayer of sanctification 127
    priests of 51, 125, 126, 136, 150
    'Songs of the Sabbath Sacrifice' 125
    Teacher of Righteousness 61, 86, 150

R
Ra'aya mehemna 88, 94–5, 98, 99
Ram, family of 77
Ramban, *see* Nahmanides
Ramhal, *see* Luzzatto
Rashbi, *see* bar Yohai, Shimon
Rashi 129
Raza demeheimanuta (The Secret of Faith) 27, 154
Raza gali 130
razei olam (mysteries of creation, secrets of the world) 4, 55
reality:
    boundaries 22, 46, 50
    hidden 3–5, 18, 30, 76, 104
    historical 133
    internal 65
    mystical 76
    new 124
    other 3–4, 7, 19, 30, 58, 69
    ritual 76
    sensory 15
    visionary 4–8
reconstruction (*tseruf, devekut*) 120–1
redemption:
    date of 100
    destruction and 132
    exile and 20, 75, 77, 84, 87, 100, 133, 135
    hopes for 89
    messianic expectations 85, 135
    passage to 133
    of the Shekhinah 6, 17, 52, 53, 55, 63, 84, 99, 100
    Shimon bar Yohai 154
    sign of 130
reincarnation:
    doctrine 92, 99, 100, 133, 135, 148
    end of 77
    Frank's views 145
    mystical tradition 17, 84, 97
Renaissance 50, 52
Reshit ḥokhmah (Beginning of Wisdom) 141

Resisei lailah (Night Dew) 157
restitution (*tikun olam*) 5, 55
Reuveni, David 156, 157
revelation:
    angelic 24, 38
    authority derived from 23, 24–5
    concepts drawn from 15
    content of 131
    divine language 19
    of Elijah (*gilui eliyahu*) 143, 144
    infinite divine 105
    to Luzzatto 100
    mystical 16
    nature of 20
    ongoing 24–5, 66–7, 98 n.
    reason for 130
    of the Shekhinah 25, 66, 99, 147
Roman empire 69, 138, 156, 157
Rosh Hashanah 111
Rovigo, Abraham 149
Russia, persecution of mystics 95

S

sacrifice of the soul (*mesirat nefesh*) 55
Safed:
    ceremonies 92
    holy groups 52
    kabbalists 5, 71, 73, 140, 141, 142–3, 147,
        151, 152, 155
    writings from 27, 55, 60
Safrin, Isaac Judah Jehiel, of Komarno (Rabbi
    Isaac Eizik of Komarno) 27, 51, 62, 85,
    144
Sagi Nahor, *see* Isaac the Blind
Saint-Exupéry, Antoine de 1
Salonika:
    group of Joseph Taitazak 52
    Shabatean movement 139, 145
sanctuaries, heavenly, see *heikhalot*
sanctuary of the bird's nest (*heikhal ken tsipor*)
    90
Sandalfon 22
sapphire (*sapir*):
    brightness of (*livnat hasapir*) 4, 108
    connection with vision of the divine 105–6
    letters and 105–6
    sefirot and 21 n., 106
    word 28 n.
Satan 95, 99
scepticism 101, 102
Schneersohn, Dov Ber 131, 137
Schneersohn, Menahem Mendel 96

Scholem, Gershom 75
secrets:
    hidden awesome 44
    revelation of 130–1, 154
    of the world (*razei olam*) 4, 55
Seer of Lublin, *see* Horowitz
sefar (number) 28, 105, 106
sefer (book) 28, 105, 106
Sefer berit menuhah (The Book of the Covenant
    of Rest) 26
Sefer gerushin (The Book of Banishments) 27,
    84, 151
Sefer ha'ahlamah . . . inyan pitron halomot
    (Concerning the Interpretation of Dreams)
    155–6
Sefer habahir (The Book of Elucidation) 4, 26,
    62, 83, 94, 99, 123, 126, 133, 153
Sefer haheikhalot, see *Sefer heikhalot*
Sefer hahezyonot (The Book of Visions) 27, 84,
    117, 143
Sefer hakaneh (The Book of Wonder) 26, 153
Sefer hakaneh vehapeli'ah (The Book of Reed
    and Wonder) 26
Sefer hamalakh hameshiv (The Answering
    Angel) 27, 62, 84, 95, 99, 136
Sefer hamalkhut (Book of Monarchy) 147–8
Sefer hamefo'ar (The Glorious Book) 99, 156
Sefer ha'ot (Book of the Letter) 137
Sefer hapeliah (The Book of Wonder) 26
Sefer harazim (The Book of Mysteries) 26, 28,
    128, 131
Sefer haredim (Book of the Devout) 140
Sefer hatemunah (The Book of the Image) 26,
    43, 98, 99, 111, 136, 153
Sefer hayat hakaneh 99
Sefer hayihud 47
Sefer hazohar, see Zohar
Sefer heikhalot (Book of Heavenly Sanctuaries,
    3 Enoch) 78, 83, 107, 136, 142, 149
Sefer yetsirah (The Book of Creation):
    allusions to 126
    authorship 10, 26
    commentaries on 74, 139, 143, 156
    concepts 4, 21 n., 106, 123
    date 4
    on letters 105, 106, 109, 113 n.
    opening text 28–9
    study of 74
sefirah (counting) 106
sefirot (spheres):
    concept 18
    description of ten 48

division of 139
doctrine 92, 99
letters and 105–6
manifested dimensions of the deity 144
realm of the 17
study of the 46
ten 21 n.
ten *sefirot* of infinite nothingness 4, 9, 10, 23, 28–9, 42, 50, 132, 133
unification of the 52, 55
world of the 41, 84
see also spheres
Sender, Alexander 144
Septuagint 138
Sermon on Redemption, A 84
seven:
cosmic cycles (*shemitot*) 5, 90
cycle of fallow years (*shemitah*) 136
firmaments (*shivah reki'im*) 4
spheres 136
supernal sanctuaries (*shivah heikhalot elyonim*) 4
temples 132
throne chariots (*sheva merkavot*) 4
wondrous sanctuaries (*shivah devirei pele*) 4
words of wonder 132
Sha'ar hagilgulim (Gate of Reincarnations) 84
Sha'ar hasho'el (Gate of the Enquirer) 139
Sha'ar hayihud veha'emunah (Gate of Unity and Faith) 155
Sha'ar ruah hakodesh (Gate of the Holy Spirit) 84
Sha'arei orah (Gates of Light) 26, 46, 104, 147
Sha'arei tsedek (Gates of Justice) 147
Shabatean:
groups 53, 139
hunter 151
legal modifications 93
literature 6, 100
movement 139–40, 146, 152
mysticism 137
Shabetai Tsevi 153–4
conversion 64, 154
definition of boundaries 100
on equality for women 60 n.
figure of 84
followers 53, 137, 139–40, 145
imprisonment 64, 95
influence 89
life 153–4
manic depressive 95
mystical experience 51, 62

revelation to 51, 91
works 27, 154
'shade' 98, 101
shalhavot shel esh mitpazerot umitkabetsot (fiery flames scattered and reassembled) 4
Shavuot 88, 90, 92
She'elot uteshuvot min hashamayim (Responsa from Heaven) 42
Shekhinah:
concept 5, 13, 64, 99
description in Zohar 49
doctrine of the 157
exiled 6, 88
God and the 38, 50, 87, 133
letters and the 111
light of the 62, 67
redemption of the 6, 17, 53, 55, 63, 84, 99, 100
resurrection 93
revelation of the 25, 66, 99, 147
speech of the 89 n.
status 92
voice of the 58, 60, 64, 81, 90
words of the 9, 46, 72, 73, 74, 124
shell(s) (*kelipah*) 6, 18
shemitot (eternal sevenfold cycles, fallow years) 46
Shemonah she'arim (Eight Gates) 143
Shemtov of Faro 47
shetei haruhot (two spirits) 50
shevirah (Breaking of Vessels) 98
Shimon ben Azai 94
Shimon bar Yohai (Rashbi), *see* bar Yohai
Shimushei torah (Uses of the Torah) 128, 129
shirot olat hashabat, see Songs of the Sabbath Sacrifice
shiur komah (stature of God) 4, 13, 46, 50, 99, 110–11, 138
Shiur komah (R. Akiva) 26, 128, 131, 136
Shivhei ha'ari 71, 143
Shivhei habesht 128, 145
Shivhei metatron (In Praise of Metatron) 26, 136, 149
Shneur Zalman of Lyady 154–5
followers 137, 140
Habad movement 154–5
imprisonment 95, 155
on letters 109, 119
son of, converts to Christianity 96
works 119, 131, 155
on worlds 49, 93
Shoresh yishai 155

Shulḥan arukh 88, 147
Shulḥan arukh harav 155
Sidur tefilah shel harav (The Rabbi's Prayer Book) 155
Simha Bunem of Przysucha 148, 150
Simḥat kohen 147
Sinai 20 n., 67, 70–1, 79, 80, 81, 88
sipur (the story of the creation of the world) 105
Sipurei ma'asiyot (Hasidic Tales) 152
sitra aḥra 6
sitra dikedushah 6
Sitrei torah (Secrets of the Torah) 137
slaughter, ritual 92, 152
Socrates 118
Sodei razaya 127
Sofer, Moses 152
Solomon of Lutsk 102, 156
Song of Songs 142, 147, 155
Songs of the Sabbath Sacrifice (*shirot olat hashabat*) 26, 51, 54, 92, 125, 127, 128
souls:
    human soul (*neshamah*) 64
    letters and 40, 104, 107, 108
    living and dead 70, 81
    revealed and hidden 81
    revelations of 53, 61
    of the righteous 123
    sacrifice of the (*mesirat nefesh*) 55
    salvation of 130
    sefirot and 84
    Torah and *sefirot* and 35, 109
    transformed 81
    transmigration of (*gilgul neshamah*) 5, 72, 81, 131, 135
    tree of (*ilan haneshamot*) 21 n., 90, 99, 131, 133
    in the upper worlds 117
Spain:
    exile from 6, 139, 147, 148, 155
    group of the Master of the Zohar 52
    kabbalists 142, 143
sparks (*nitsotsot*) 6, 17–18, 46, 55, 76, 145
'speaking in tongues' 118
speech:
    divine (*dibur shekhinah*) 5, 35, 37, 39, 90, 144
    God's direct 99
    human 35, 106
    inner 61
    language and 107, 108
    letters and 108, 110
    magical 116
    meaningless 117, 118–19

    of the Shekhinah 90
    unfolding of divine being 104
    world of (*olam hadibur*) 4, 64, 89, 90, 111, 157
spheres:
    concept 29
    divine 31 n.
    doctrine of the 147
    heavenly 17
    hidden 18
    in hidden reality 106
    infinitude and 90
    luminous 10, 17, 46
    sefirot 18, 31 n., 46, 50, 105
    sevenfold division 136
    singing 126
    study of 46
    tree of the 4
    world of 99
Sternhartz, Nathan, of Nemirov 153
suckling (*yenikah*) 6, 90
Sukat Shalom, group of 53
symbols 124
Synopse zur Hekhalot-Literatur 104

T
ta'amei hamitsvot (mystical connotation of the commandments) 148
Ta'amei hamitsvot (Reasons of the Commandments, by Joseph of Hamadan) 147
Ta'amei hamitsvot (Reasons of the Commandments, by Menahem Recanati) 149
'tabernacle of testimony' 101–2
Taitazak, Joseph 52, 148, 155
Talmud 62, 72, 126, 139, 157
    Babylonian 147
    Jerusalem 80, 147
Tanya 155
Teacher of Righteousness (*moreh hatsedek*) 51, 61, 86, 92, 94, 99, 150
tefillin 93
Temple:
    calendar 99
    destruction 4, 69, 75, 83, 86, 93, 135, 157
    divine service 92
    eternal sacred fire 79
    First 93, 126
    heavenly 86, 125–6, 133
    Holy of Holies, *see* Holy of Holies
    inner sanctuary 144

loss of 132
mystical transformation 83, 86 n.
pathways between earthly and upper temples 87
place in mysticism 13
priests 126, 127; *see also* priests
Second 24, 86, 92, 93, 135, 157
Yom Kippur 80, 87
temples, seven 132
Ten Commandments 91
'Terumah', commentary on 147
tevah (ark, word) 40, 107, 110
text:
   literal biblical 40–1, 45–6
   revealed 34, 41
   revealed and concealed 43, 45–6
   sacred 44–5
Thanksgiving Scroll 150
Tiferet 50
tikun (rectificatory prayer) 92
tikun (Restitution of the Broken Vessels) 98
tikun ḥatsot (midnight vigil) 92
tikun leil shavuot (vigil of Shavuot) 92
tikun tefilot 155
time, cycles of 98
Tishah Be'av fast 93
tohu 39
Toledot ha'ari 71, 143
Toledot ya'akov yosef 138
Tomer devorah (The Palm Tree of Deborah) 151
Torah:
   annihilation of the 140
   black fire upon white fire 43
   code of holy names 46–7, 122
   concepts 18
   covering and uncovering 122
   of Creation 98
   delight of the Holy One in the 56
   divine speech 39
   of Emanation 98, 139–40
   of exile 99
   existence in heaven and earth 35
   faces 35
   female aspect 87
   image of God 36
   kabbalistic study 44–5
   language 35–6
   letters of the 23, 109
   meaning of the 24, 121
   observance of commandments of 36–7
   Oral 49, 91
   origin 33–5

prince of the 44
of redemption 99
secrets of the 47, 55, 73, 84
sefer as 105
Shekhinah and 87, 92
six first principles 34–7
stripping it from its wrapping 41
study of the 37, 38, 92
words as 43, 45
Written 49
yoke of the 123
torah de'atsilut (Torah of Divine Emanation) 139, 145
Torah or (Light of Torah) 93, 155
torat kavanot (doctrine of intentions) 144
Tosefta *Ḥagigah* 138
tradition:
   aggadic 131
   ancient Jewish 4, 10, 49, 126
   ascent to heaven 87
   biblical 126, 131
   esoteric 44, 51, 53–4, 56
   hasidic mystical 64
   Heikhalot 65, 67, 79, 92, 113, 141, 144
   kabbalistic 44, 52, 85, 92, 119
   magical 114, 116–17
   Merkavah 78, 79, 80, 91, 133
   mystical 20, 25, 28, 34–8, 39–40, 46–7, 50, 56, 66, 84, 88, 93, 94, 97, 105–7, 109, 111
   normative Jewish 23, 24–5, 28
   priestly 80, 87, 91, 126
   relationship with mysticism 23 n.
   ritual 132
   sacred 21
   visionary 125
   written 3, 8, 12, 63, 124
   written mystical 85
   zoharic 91, 130
tranquillity 101
transformation, mystical, in historical perspective 49–56
transmigration, *see* souls
Tree of Knowledge, doctrine of the 18, 98
Tree of Life, doctrine of the 18, 98
tree of souls/spirits (*ilan haneshamot*) 4, 21 n., 90, 99, 131, 133
tree of the spheres (*ilan hasefirot*) 4
Tripoli 137
truth, universal transcendental 12 n.
tsadik 89, 101, 117, 146
tsadik hador (righteous man of the generation) 152

tsaḥtsaḥot (luminous spheres) 5, 46
Tsava'at harivash 93, 104
tsimtsum (contraction) 5
Turiel, Solomon ben Shimon 84, 99, 156
Turkey 60, 147, 155

U
unification:
  concept 44, 92
  deconstruction (*yiḥud*) 121
  generation in heavenly world 54
  magical language 116–18, 121, 129
  meaningless 114
  redemption through 133
  renewal through 124
  of the *sefirot* 52, 55
union (*yiḥud*) 55
unique cherub 5, 9, 10, 50, 52
Unity, wondrousness of His 21 n.

V
Valéry, Paul 118
vessel(s):
  breaking of the 5, 18, 98, 132
  concept 18
  letters as 40
  mystics as 60, 101
  sefirot 48
Vienna, book burning 98
violin singing by itself 89 n.
Virgin Mary 89
vision:
  complete 15
  fragments of 15
  heavenly 66
  language of 8
  masculine and feminine elements 87
  messianic 88, 99, 100
  mystical language 124
  in mysticism 1–3, 8, 31–2, 53, 57, 71
  no limits 11
  'other reality' 7–8
  renewed 5
  revelation 124, 131
visionary reality 4–8
Vital, Hayim 142–3
  on Luria 54, 72
  mystical experience 50, 62
  relationship with Luria 73, 117, 142–3, 147
  revelation to 51
  on unification 117, 118
  works 27, 52, 55, 84, 143

voice, divine 46, 52, 60, 64, 67, 88–9, 98
Volhynia, hasidism 140

W
Wazana, Jacob 85, 146
Weber, Max 73
wheels 21 n., 125, 126
wisdom, thirty-two paths of (*lamed bet netivot peliot ḥokhmah*) 4, 28, 105, 132–3
words:
  arks 40, 104, 107
  deconstructed 119
  exposing real divine essence 40
  formulation of spiritual reality 31
  letters and 16, 36, 37, 39, 107, 111, 119
  magic 112
  magical language 118
  meaningless 111, 115, 117
  sacred 85
  seven words of wonder 132
  of Torah 43, 45
workers of the field 91
world:
  hidden and revealed 104, 132
  imaginary inner 31–2
  real external 31–2
  restitution of the (*tikun olam*) 5
World of Disruption 98
World of Reformation 98
worship in fear 98
worship in love 98

Y
Yavneh, academy 157
'Yedid nefesh' (Friend of my Soul) 141
yesh 39–40, 44
Yeshuot meshiḥo 139
yeteh veyavo (coming all the time) 106
Yeven metsulah 153
yibum, concept of 92
yiḥud, see unification
Yohanan ben Zakai 11, 157
Yom Kippur:
  cherubim 81
  heavenly temples 81, 87
  high priest entering Holy of Holies 59, 80, 126, 138
  liturgy 69, 111, 144
yoredei merkavah, see descenders of the chariot

Z
Zadok Hakohen 86, 150, 157

Ze'ev Wolf of Zhitomir 41, 119, 140
Zipporah 88
Zohar (The Book of Splendour):
  authorship 10, 26, 50, 52 n., 62, 88, 91, 146,
    151, 154
  doctrines 99, 133, 135
  on hidden reality 4
  influence 13, 130, 147
  language of the 48
  on letters 45
  new 38, 53, 100
  on 'pillar known to kabbalists' 74
  popularity of 92
  on priest entering Holy of Holies 59
  related works 91
  on secret literary group 52
  on Shekhinah 49
  study of 53
  on Torah 34
Zohar ḥai (Living Zohar) 144
Zot liyehudah (This Is for Judah) 137
Zot zikaron (This to Remember) 85, 89

Printed and bound by CPI Group (UK) Ltd, Croydon, CR0 4YY

13/04/2025

14656576-0002